Gaelic-English
English-Gaelic
DICTIONARY

D0528375

Gaelic-English
English-Gaelic
DICTIONARY

GEDDES & GROSSET

Published 2004 by Geddes & Grosset,
David Dale House, New Lanark, ML11 9DJ

Gaelic–English dictionary compiled by Dougal Buchanan,
English–Gaelic dictionary compiled by RLS Ltd

Pronunciation system devised by
and © Michael Bauer, 2004

Introduction by Michael Bauer

Copyright © 1998, 2004 Geddes & Grosset

First printed 1998
Reprinted 2000
Revised 2004

ISBN 1 84205 324 8

Printed and bound in Poland, OZGraf S.A.

Contents

Abbreviations

abbrev	abbreviation	*m/f*	a noun, the gender of which may change according to what it names, its case (often the genitive) or its dialect
adj	adjective		
adv	adverb		
anat	anatomy		
arith	arithmetic		
art	article	*milit*	military term
aux	auxiliary	*mus*	music
coll	colloquial term	*n*	noun
comput	computing	*neg*	negative
conj	conjunction	*npl*	plural noun
corres	correspondence	*occas*	occasionally
derog	derogatory	*orthog*	orthography
esp	especially	*part*	particle
excl	exclamation	*pers*	personal
f	noun (feminine)	*phys*	physical
fam	familiar	*pl*	plural
fig	figurative use	*poet*	poetical term
fin	financial	*poss*	possessive
fml	formal	*pp*	present or past participle
govt	government	*pref*	prefix
gram	grammar	*prep*	preposition
imper	imperative	*pron*	pronoun
interj	interjection	*refl*	reflexive
interr	interrogative	*rel*	relative
law	law term	*relig*	religion
ling	linguistics	*sing*	singular
lit	literature, literary	*usu*	usually
m	noun (masculine)	*v*	verb
math	mathematics	*vulg*	vulgar
med	medical		

Introduction

As a pocket dictionary of Gaelic, this publication is a convenient reference for anyone interested in Gaelic. It covers a broad range of terms and phrases for a wide variety of possible applications in both traditional and modern settings.

Gaelic has many sounds foreign to English and its orthography, though highly efficient and regular, is not immediately accessible to the newcomer. This makes the new Pronunciation Guide used in this dictionary particularly useful as a source of information.

There are various places which offer a variety of Gaelic language and cultural courses, both short term or immersion. For courses and more information on either you are best advised to contact either the Gaelic College in Skye (Sabhal Mòr Ostaig, Teanga IV44 8RQ www.smo.uhi.ac.uk) or Stow College in Glasgow (Stow College, 43 Shamrock St., Glasgow G4 9LD www.stow.ac.uk).

But whatever your aims this dictionary offers an intriguing starting point into one of Europe's most fascinating languages.

1   Using this Dictionary

You must bear in mind that Gaelic is an inflecting language and has a process commonly referred to as lenition whereby the first sound of a word is affected by preceding words or particles. People relatively unfamiliar with the language should bear the following points in mind when using this dictionary:

- Lenition manifests itself in the spelling as an <h> inserted after the first consonant of a word. When searching for a word you will find it under its (unlenited) root form by mentally removing the <h>. In the phrase *mo mhàthair* for example, *mhàthair* will be found under *màthair*.
- After certain particles, <h-> is prefixed to a following word. You will find it under its root form without the <h-> (see the following entry for an example).
- Cases often manifest themselves by changing the sound of a final consonant which is shown in the spelling by inserting an <i> before

the last consonant. Words also can add a final -e. Again, terms are listed in their root forms, so in the phrases *dath mo leabhair* and *balla na h-eaglaise*, *leabhair* and *eaglaise* will be found under *leabhar* and *eaglais* respectively.

Some of the less obvious changes are:

a	→	oi
a	→	ui
a	→	i
ea	→	ei & i
eò	→	iùi
eu	→	èi & eòi
io	→	i
ìo	→	i
o	→	ui
ò	→	ùi.

2 Spelling System and Pronunciation

Written Gaelic undoubtedly looks daunting at first sight with its profusion of vowels, h's and seemingly silent letters. But it is a very efficient tool for spelling the many sounds of Gaelic and much more regular and easy to learn to read than English. Here are just two very important points to help you on your way:

Like many other languages, Gaelic uses two letter combinations to represent certain sounds. Think of English sip and **sh**ip or far and fear. The same thing happens in Gaelic in a very regular fashion. The most obvious is the insertion of H after a consonant. This is to show that the consonant has been "softened" or "lenited". Thus **m**, pronounced [m] becomes **mh**, pronounced as [v] and so on. Lenition is extremely common in Gaelic and you will come across it all the time.

In most cases, Gaelic has at least two variants of the same consonant. There are two C's, two D's, three L's and so on. In order to spell that without having to use a profusion of symbols, the medieval Gaelic scribes came up with an ingenious way of indicating the pronunciation of a consonant through its environment. This is akin to what happens to G in English *gone* and *gin* for example – only much more regular. A consonant which is flanked by A O or U vowels may be thought of as "normal" (more commonly referred to as "broad" or **leathann** in Gaelic. However, if it is flanked by E and I vowels their pronunciation changes and it becomes "slender" or **caol**. So in many cases these slenderising vowels are not "pronounced" but have the important function of indicating the consonant quality.

One good set of examples are the words *càrn* (meaning a heap) and *ceàrn* (meaning a corner). The only difference in the pronunciation of these two words is in the first C: *càrn* (because it is followed by a broad vowel) is [kārn] and *ceàrn* (because the C is followed by a slender vowel) is [k'ārn] – but there is no E vowel to be heard as such. That is what most of those silent letters are there for.

Below is a guide to the pronunciation used in this dictionary. The first column contains the symbol used, the second an explanation of the sound or how it is made and the third contains the IPA symbol for the sound in question to help those who are familiar with that system.

[a]	an [a] sound with a clear quality like in Scots or Northern English last: **cas** [kas]	a
[ ]	same as [a] only long: **bà** [bā]	a:
[b]	as P in combinations like **sp**it: **cab** [kab]	ɓ
[ch]	as in Scots lo**ch**, or German Ba**ch**. This sound is made by holding your tongue in a K position and squeezing air through a small gap between your tongue and the roof of your mouth: **ach** [ach]	x
[ch']	as in German i**ch**. This sound is like [ch] only a lot more forward at your hard palate: **eich** [ech']	ç
[d]	as T in combinations like **st**ick but with the tip of your tongue touching the base of your teeth: **ad** [ad]	ḓ
[d']	similar to J in **j**ungle, but voiceless. This means that if you put your hand on your adam's apple you feel no vibration while making this sound. It is like the difference between **p**ad (no voicing) and **b**ad (voicing) in English: **diùid** [d' d']	ḓ
[e]	a clear [e] sound like the first vowel in English m**ai**d or Scots they came: **eich** [ech']	e
[ ]	like [e] only long: **ceum** [k m]	e:
[ɛ]	as in English m**e**t: **bean** [bɛn]	ɛ
[ɛ̄]	like [ɛ] only long: **mè** [mɛ̄]	ɛ:

11

[ə]	a "neutral vowel" as in English an: casan [kasən]	ə
[f]	as in English: af [af]	f
[g]	as K in combinations like skunk: gad [gad]	g̊
[g']	like [g] only a lot more forward at your hard palate: ged [g'ed]	g̊ʲ
[gh]	to make this sound, start by saying GA. Now say it again, but this time allow some air to flow between your tongue and where your tongue touches the roof of your mouth throughout the GA. Now drop the vowel. It is the right sound when you can hold the [gh] without the vowel for more than 5 seconds: ghad [ghad]	ɣ
[gh']	like [gh] only a lot more forward at your hard palate approximating a Y sound: dhi [gh'i]	j
[h]	as in English: shon [hon]	h
[ʰ]	a not fully pronounced [h] sound which occurs before P, T, C in the middle or at the end of words in Gaelic but is never written in the spelling (before slender consonants this is pronounced further forward in the mouth): mac [maʰk]	ʰ/ç
[i]	as in English see, but a lot shorter: thig [hig']	i
[]	as in English see: chì [ch']	iː
[ɪ]	as in English bid: àlainn [āLɪN']	ɪ
[k]	as in English: cas [kas]	k
[k']	like [k] only a lot more forward at your hard palate: mic [miʰk']	kʲ
[L]	a "dark L". This sound is made by touching the base of your teeth with the tip of your tongue while lowering the back of your tongue (imagine having a large a piece of candy at the back of your mouth) and then making an L sound: lag [Lag]	ɫ
[L']	a "palatal L". This sound is made by squeezing the back of your tongue against the roof of your mouth and then making an L sound. It occurs in Italian meglio or Spanish caballo: leag [L'eg]	ʎ

12

[l]	as in English: baile [balɪ]	l
[m]	as in English: **m**ac [maʰk]	m
[N]	a "dark N". This sound is made by touching the base of your teeth with the tip of your tongue while lowering the back of your tongue (imagine having a large a piece of candy at the back of your mouth) and then making an N sound: a**nn** [auN]	ṉ
[N']	a "palatal N". This sound is made by squeezing the back of your tongue against the roof of your mouth and then making an N sound. It occurs in Italian sig**n**ora or Spanish cañón: **n**ì [N']	ɲ
[n]	as in English: ca**n**a [kanə]	n
[ng]	similar English ri**ng**: lo**ng** [Lɔung]	ŋg
[o]	a clear [o] sound like in Scottish English s**o**. It occurs in French agn**eau** and German **O**hr: b**o**g [bog]	o
[ ]	like [o] only long: b**ò** [b]	o:
[o]	a so called "unrouded" [o]. This sound is made by putting your mouth into an [o] position and then spreading your lips <u>without</u> moving your tongue (imagine that you are grinning widely while saying [o]): g**o**id [god']	ɤ
[ ]	same as [o] only long: **adh**bran [ɤbran]	ɤ:
[ɔ]	as in English malt, but a lot shorter: s**o**na [sɔnə]	ɔ
[ɔ̃]	as in English malt: **ò**g [ɔ̃g]	ɔ:
[p]	as in English: **p**ana [panə]	p
[R]	as in Russian erno. This sound is made by producing a rolled R as in Scottish English ba**rr**el or Spanish pe**rr**o while lowering the back of your tongue (imagine having a large a piece of candy at the back of your mouth): bà**rr** [b R]	ʀ
[r]	a "tapped R" as in Spanish pe**r**o. This sound is made by rapidly tapping the bony ridge behind your teeth with the tip of your tongue once: ca**r**an [karan]	ɾ

13

[r']	as [r] but with the tip of your tongue touching the base of your teeth: **mìr** [m r']	rʲ
[s]	as in English but with slightly less lip rounding: **san** [sən]	s
[š]	as in English **sh**ip, but with slightly spread lips: **seo** [šɔ]	ʃ
[t]	as in English T but with the tip of your tongue touching the base of your teeth: **tana** [tanə]	t̪
[t']	similar to English **ch**ick, but with slightly spread lips: **teas** [t'es]	t̪ʲ
[u]	as in English y**ou**, but a lot shorter: **uga** [ugə]	u
[ ]	as in English y**ou**: **cù** [k]	u:
[u]	a so called "unrounded" [u]. This sound is made by putting your mouth into an [u] position and then spreading your lips <u>without</u> moving your tongue (imagine that you are grinning widely while saying [u]). It occurs in Japanese ts**u**ru: **ui**seag [ušag]	ɯ
[ ]	as [u] only long: **aom** [m]	ɯ:
[v]	as in English **v**eal: **bho** [vo]	v
[y]	as in English **y**ear. This sound is never written in the spelling but occurs after certain slender B P F M sounds: **beò** [bjɔ]	j
[.]	an audible "breaking" of a long vowel into two syllables. These sounds are is best thought of as two separate vowels coming together, somewhat similar to combinations like r**aw o**il in English: o**gha** [o.ə]	.

3 Stress

In Gaelic, stress generally falls onto the first syllable of a word. In those instances where this is not the case the stressed syllable has been marked in italic print in the phonetic transcription. This mostly happens with certain adverbs and compound nouns e.g. ***an-seo*** [ənšɔ]

4   Initial Vowels

In Gaelic, words that begin with a vowel have what is called "soft onset" which means that it is not preceded by a glottal stop (as in the Cockney pronunciation of butter as *bu'er*). Instead they are preceeded by a glide, a bit like a very faint y sound. In some instances this is very audible (for example in word beginning with *eò-* or *iu-*), but generally very weak.

5   More on Softening (Lenition)

It can be very confusing when you are trying to look up a word because softening changes the first sound of a word. Since it is so common in Gaelic, here is a list of how softening changes the spelling and the pronunciation of a sound. Remember that the broadness/slenderness of a consonant depends on the vowels around it. So the spelling inserts H after the consonant and there are two possible pronunciations (broad vs slender).

Spelling	Pronunciation Broad Consonants	Spelling	Pronunciation Slender Consonants
b > bh	[b] > [v]	b > bh	[bj] > [vj]
c > ch	[k] > [ch]	c > ch	[k'] > [ch']
d > dh	[d] > [gh]	d > dh	[d'] > [gh']
f > fh	[f] > silent	f > fh	[f] > silent
g > gh	[g] > [gh]	g > gh	[g'] > [gh']
l > l	[L] > [L]	l > l	[L'] > [l]
m > mh	[m] > [v]	m > mh	[m] > [vj]
n > n	[N] > [n]	n > n	[N'] > [n]
p > ph	[p] > [f]	p > ph	[pj] > [fj]
r > r	[R] > [r]	r > r	[R] > [r]
s > sh	[s] > [h]	s > sh	[š] > [hj]
t > th	[t] > [h]	t > th	[t'] > [hj]

Although softening may seem a rather strange concept at first, it is very common in many languages, even English. It often occurs when a consonant gets stuck between two vowels and "softens" to a weaker consonant or disappears – hence the term Leniton. Think of the German word **Mutter** and the English **mother**, where the T in the middle has weakened to a TH.

There is one difference with Gaelic and the other Celtic languages. Historically this softening does not only happen in the middle of words, but also at the beginning. The reason this is not always obvious today is because in many cases the vowel that caused softening in the first place has been lost. For example, **an fhois** is lenited because thousands of years ago **an** used to be **sinda** – which ended in a vowel and therefore softened the F in **fois**. So it all makes sense in a way.

Gaelic–English Dictionary

A

a [ə] *prep* to. • *rel pron* that. • *poss pron* his/her.

a'[1] [ə] *art* the; of the.

a'[2] *see* **ag.** [ə]

ab [ab] *m* abbot.

abachadh [abəchəgh] *m* ripening.

abaich [abıch'] *adj* mature, ripe. • *v* mature, ripen.

abaichead [abıch'əd] *m* maturity, ripeness.

abaid [abıd'] *f* abbey.

abair [abır'] *v* say.

abair amadan! [abır' amadan] *excl* what a fool!

abairt [abıršd'] *f* phrase, expression.

àbhacas [āvəʰkəs] *m* mirth, ridicule.

àbhachd [āvəchg] *f* humour.

àbhachdach [āvəchgəch] *adj* amusing.

abhag [afag] *f* terrier.

abhainn [avıN'] *f* river.

àbhaist [āvıšd'] *f* custom, habit.

àbhaisteach [āvıšd'əch] *adj* usual.

a-bhàn [əvān] *adv* down.

a-bhon-dè [əvōN'd'ē] *adv* day before yesterday.

a-bhon-raoir [əvōNRoir'] *adv* night before last.

a-bhon-uiridh [əvōNur'ı] *adv* year before last.

a-bhos [əvōs] *adv* over here, hither.

ablach [abLəch] *m* carcase.

abstol [absdəL] *m* apostle.

aca [aʰkə] *prep pron* at them. • *poss pron* their.

acadamh [aʰkədəv] *m* academy.

acaid [aʰkıd'] *f* stabbing pain.

acainn [aʰkıN'] *f* apparatus; tools.

acainneach [aʰkıN'əch] *adj* equipped.

acair [aʰkır'] *f* anchor.

acaire [aʰkır'ə] *f* acre.

acarsaid [aʰkırsəd'] *f* harbour, mooring.

ach [ach] *conj* but.

achadh [achəgh] *m* field.

ach a-mhàin [ach avān] *prep* except, apart from.

a-chaoidh [əchoiy] *adv* always, for ever.

achd [achg] *f* (*politics*) act.

a-chèana [əch'ēnə] *adv* already.

a chèile [ə ch'ēlı] *pron* each other.

a chiall! [ə ch'iaL] *excl* good heavens!

a chionn [əch'ūN] *prep* because of.

a chionn is gu [əch'ūN sgə] *conj* because.

achlais [achLıš] *f* armpit.

achlasan [achLasan] *m* armful.

achmhasan [achvəsən] *m* reprimand.

a-chum [əchūm] *prep* for.

a-chum is gu [əchūm sgə] *conj* in order that.

a' cnàmh na cìre [ə krāv nə k'īr'ı] chewing the cud; mulling things over.

acraich [aʰkrıch'] *v* anchor, moor.

acras [aʰkrəs] *m* hunger.

acrasach [aʰkrəsəch] *adj* hungry.

actair [agdɛr'] *m* actor.

a' cur [ə kur] *part* snowing.

ad [ad] *f* hat.

adag [adag] *f* haddock.

adha [a.ə] *m* liver.

a dh'aindheoin [əghaN'ən] *prep* in spite of.

a dh'aithghearr [əghach'aR] *adv* soon.

adhaltraiche [o.əLtrıch'ə] *m* adulterer.

adhaltranas [o.əLtrənəs] *m* adultery.

a dh'aon ghnothach [əghūnə ghro.əch] *adv* expressly, deliberately.

a dh'aon rùn [əghūnə Rūn] *adv* expressly, deliberately.

adhar [a.ər] *m* air, sky.

adharc [o.ərk] *f* horn.

adharcach [o.ərkəch] *adj* horned.

a dh'easbhaidh [əgh'ɛsvı] *adv* lacking, needed.

a dh'fhad [əghad] *adv* long, in length.

a dh'ionnsaigh [əgh'ūNsıch] *prep* to, towards; against.

a dhìth [əgh'ī] *adv* lacking, required; in short supply.

adhartach [o.əršdəch] *adj* progressive.

adhartas [o.əršdəs] *m* progress.

adhbhar [ōvər] *m* cause, reason.

adhbhar-gàire [ōvərgār'ı] *m* laughing stock.

adhbrann [ōbrəN] *f* ankle.

a dheòin no a dh'aindeoin [əgh'ŌN' nə əghaN'ən] *adv* willy-nilly.

a dh' fhad [əghad] *adv* long, in length.

aoradh [ūrəgh] *m* worship.

a' dol bàs [ə dɔL bās] *part* dying out.

Afraga [afrəgə] *m* Africa.

Afraganach [afrəgənəch] *m/adj* African.

ag, a' [əg] [ə] *part introducing pres part.*

agad [agəd] *prep pron* at you (*sing*). • *poss pron* your (*sing*).

agaibh [agıv] *prep pron* at you (*pl*). • *poss pron* your (*pl*).

againn [agıN'] *prep pron* at us. • *poss pron* our.

agallamh [agəLəv] *m* interview; conversation.

agam [agəm] *prep pron* at me. • *poss pron* my.

ag eudach rithe [əg ēdəch r'i.ə] jealous about her.

àgh [ōgh] *m* joy; good fortune.

agh [ogh] *f* heifer.

aghaidh [ō.ıy] *f* face; nerve, cheek.

aghaidh-choimheach [ō.ıcho.ıch'] *f* mask.

aghann [oghəN] *f* frying pan.

a ghaoil! [ə ghūl] *excl* love! dear!

àghmhor [ōghvər] *adj* pleasant; joyful.

a ghràidh! [ə ghrāy] *excl* dear! love!

agus [agəs] *conj* and.

a h-uile càil [ə hulı kāl] everything.

a h-uile duine [ə hulı duN'ə] everyone, everybody.

a h-uile sian [ə hulı šıən] *f* everything.

aibidil [abɪd'ɪl] f alphabet.

aibidealach [abɪd'əLəch] adj alphabetical.

aice [ɛʰk'ɪ] prep pron at her. • poss pron her.

àicheadh [āch'əgh] m denial.

àicheadh [āch'əgh] v deny.

aideachadh [ad'əchəgh] m confession.

aidich [ad'ɪch'] v confess, own up.

aifrionn [afr'əN] m Mass.

aig [ɛg'] prep at; in the possession of.

aig a' cheann thall [ɛg' ə ch'auN hauL] adv in the end, eventually.

aig àmannan [ɛg' auməNən] adv at times.

aig an taigh [ɛg' ən toy] adv at home.

aig baile [ɛg' balɪ] adv at home.

aige [ɛg'ɪ] prep pron at him. • poss pron his.

àigeach [āig'əch] m stallion.

aighearach [agh'ərəch] adj cheerful, merry.

aighearachd [agh'ərəchg] f cheerfulness.

aigne [eg'nɪ] f spirit; mind.

aig Sealbh tha brath! [ɛg' šaLav ha bra] excl Heaven knows!

ailbhinn [alɪvɪN'] f flint.

àile [ālɪ] m air, atmosphere.

àileach [āləch] adj airy.

aileag [alag] f (with art) **an aileag** [ə Nalag] hiccups.

àill [āL'] f desire, will.

àilleag [āL'ag] f jewel.

àillidh [āL'ɪ] adj shining; beautiful.

aillse [aL'šɪ] f cancer.

aillseag [aL'šag] f caterpillar.

ailtire [alt'ɪr'ə] m architect.

ailtireachd [alt'ɪr'əchg] f architecture.

Aimeireaga [amer'əgə] f America.

Aimeireaganach [amer'əgənəch] m/adj American.

aimhreit [air'ɪt'] f disorder, trouble.

aimhreiteach [air'ɪt'əch] adj quarrelsome.

aimsir [ɛmɛšɪr'] f weather.

aimsireil [ɛmɛšɪr'ɛl] adj temporal; climatic.

ain- [aN'] prefix un-.

aindheoin [aN'ən] f reluctance.

aindheonach [aN'ənəch] adj reluctant.

aineach [aN'əch] adj (gram) imperative.

aineolach air [aN'əLəch ɛr'] adj unfamiliar with.

aineolas [aN'əLəs] m ignorance.

aingeal [aing'aL] m angel.

ainm [ɛnɛm] m name.

ainmeachadh [ɛnɛməchəgh] m naming; mentioning.

ainmear [ɛnɛmɛr] m noun.

ainmeil [ɛnɛmɛl] adj famous.

ainmhidh [ɛnɛvɪ] m animal.

ainmich [ɛnɛmɪch'] v name; mention.

ainmneach [ɛnɛmN'əch] adj (gram) nominative.

ainneamh [aN'ɪv] adj scarce, rare.

ainneart [aN'əršd] m violence.

aintighearn [aN't'ɪ.ərn] m tyrant, oppressor.

air [ɛr'] prep on; about. • prep pron on him, on it (m).

air adhart [ɛr' o.əršd] adv forwards, onwards.

air a dheagh dhòigh [ɛr'ə gh'o ghōy] on good form; chuffed.

air aghaidh [ɛr' ō.ɪy] *adv* forward(s).

air ais [ɛr' ɛš] *adv* back; ago.

air allaban [ɛr' aLəban] *adv* wandering.

air an dùthaich [ɛr' ən dū.ɪch'] *adv* in the country.

air an spot [ɛr' ən sboʰt] *adv* on the spot.

air a phronnadh [ɛr' ə froNəgh] *adv* drunk.

air ball [ɛr' bauL] *adv* immediately.

air banais [ɛr' banɪš] *adv* at a wedding.

air beulaibh [ɛr' biaLɪv] *prep* in front of.

air bhàinidh [ɛr' vāN'ɪ] *adv* mad with rage.

air bhog [ɛr' vog] *adv* afloat.

air bhoile [ɛr' volɪ] *adv* furious, raging.

air bith [ɛr' bih] *adv* any at all.

air bòrd [ɛr' bōrd] *adv* aboard, on board.

air chall [ɛr' chauL] *adv* lost.

airchealladh [ɛr'ch'əLəgh] *m* sacrilege.

air chois [ɛr' choš] *adv* up and about.

air choreigin [ɛr' chəreg'ɪn] *adj* some or other.

air chor is gu [ɛr' chor sgə] *conj* so that.

air chrith [ɛr' ch'r'ih] *adv* shaking, shivering.

air chuthach [ɛr' chu.əch] *adv* mad; furious.

air chothrom a [ɛr' chorəm] *conj* able to, fit to.

air corra-bìod [ɛr' kɔRəbīd] *adv* on tiptoe.

air cùl [ɛr' kūL] *prep* behind.

air cùlaibh [ɛr' kūLɪv] *prep* behind.

air cumha is gu [ɛr' ku.ə sgə] *conj* on condition that.

àird [ārd'] *f* point, promontory.

air dàir [ɛr' dār'] *adv* on heat, rutting.

àirde [ārd'ɪ] *f* height; (*mus*) pitch.

aire [ar'ɪ] *f* attention.

air deireadh [ɛr' d'era'əgh] *adv* last.

air dheireadh [ɛr' gh'er'əgh] *adv* lagging behind.

air dhòigh is gu [ɛr' ghōy sgə] *conj* so that; in order that.

air dòigh [ɛr' dōy] *adv* in good order.

air do shocair! [ɛr' də hɔʰkɛr'] *excl* steady on! go easy!

air dreach [ɛr' drech] *adv* looking like.

air eagal gu [ɛr' egal gə] *conj* lest; for fear that.

àireamh [ār'əv] *f* number.

àireamhair [ār'əvɛr'] *m* calculator.

àireamh fòn [ār'əv fōn] *f* phone number.

air èiginn [ɛr' ēg'iN'] *adv* hardly, barely; with difficulty.

air fad [ɛr' fad] *adv* entirely, completely; all.

air falbh [ɛr' falav] *adv* away, gone.

air feadh [ɛr' fyogh] *prep* throughout, all over.

air fleòdradh [ɛr' flōdrəgh] *adv* floating.

air flod [ɛr' flɔd] *adv* floating, afloat.

airgead [ɛr'ɛg'əd] *m* money; silver.

airgeadach [ɛr'ɛg'ədəch] *adj* well-off, monied.

airgead-pòcaid [ɛr'ɛg'əd pōʰkɪd'] *m* pocket-money.

airgead pronn [ɛr'ɛg'əd prouN] *m* small change.

airgead ullamh [ɛr'ɛg'əd uLəv] *m* ready money, cash.

air iasad [ɛr' iəsəd] *adv* on loan.

airidh [ar'ı] *adj* worthy, deserving.

àiridh [ār'ı] *f* shieling.

air iomrall [ɛr' imərəL] *adv* wandering; astray, erring.

air iteig [ɛr' iʰt'ɛg'] *adv* flying, on the wing.

air leth [ɛr' L'eh] *adv* apart; exceptional.

air leth-mhisg [ɛr' L'evišg'] *adv* tipsy.

air leth-shùil [ɛr' L'ehūl] *adv* one-eyed.

air mo aigne [ɛr' meg'nı] *adv* on my mind.

air mo aire [ɛr' mar'ı] *adv* on my mind.

air mhisg [ɛr' višg'] *adv* drunk.

air mhodh eile [ɛr' vɔgh elı] *adv* otherwise, alternatively.

air mo chùram [ɛr' mə chūrəm] *adv* on my mind; under my responsibility.

air mo sgàth [ɛr' mə sgā] *adv* for my sake.

àirneis [ārN'ıš] *f* furniture.

àirneis-chogaidh [ārN'ıščɔgı] *m* munitions.

air neo [ɛR N'ɔ] *conj* or else, otherwise.

air sgàth [ɛr' sgā] *prep* on account of, because.

air sgàth is gu [ɛr' sgā sgə] *conj* because.

airson [ɛRsɔn] *prep* for; in favour of. • *conj* in order to.

airson a rèic [ɛRsɔn ə rēʰk'] *adv* sale, for.

air snàmh [ɛr' sNāv] *adj* inundated, flooded.

air stailc [ɛr' sdalk'] *adv* on strike.

air thoiseach air [ɛr' hɔšəch ɛr'] *prep* ahead of.

airtnealach [aršN'əLəch] *adj* sad, weary.

air thuaiream [ɛr' huər'əm] *adv* at random.

air uairean [ɛr' uər'ən] *adv* at times.

air uaireann [ɛr' uər'əN] *adv* occasionally.

air urras [ɛr' uRəs] *adv* on bail.

aiseag [ašəg] *f* ferry.

aiseal [ašaL] *f* axle.

aisean [ašan] *m* rib.

aiseirigh [ašer'ı] *f* resurrection; resurgence.

Aisia [ēšə] *f* (*with art*) **an Aisia** [ə N'ēšə] Asia.

Aisianach [ēšənəch] *m/adj* Asian.

aisling [ašling'] *f* dream; vision.

aiste¹ [ašt'ı] *f* essay.

aiste² [ašt'ı] *prep pron* out of her, out of it (*f*).

àite [āʰt'ı] *m* place.

àiteach [āʰt'əch] *m* cultivation.

àiteachas [āʰt'əchəs] *m* agriculture.

àite-coise [āʰt'ıkɔšı] *m* pedestrian crossing.

aiteal [aʰt'aL] *m* glimpse.

aiteamh [aʰt'əv] *m* thaw.

àite-còmhnaidh [āʰt'ıkōnı] *m* dwelling place.

àite-fuirich [āʰt'ıfur'ıch'] *m* dwelling place.

àiteigin [āʰt'eg'ın] *m* some place or other.

àite-suidhe [āʰt'ısui.ı] *m* seat, sitting place.

aithghearr [ach'aR] *adj* short; quick; abrupt.

aithghearrachd [ach'aRəchg] *f* short cut. • *adv* **an aithghearrachd** [ən ach'aRəchg] swiftly, sharpish.

aithne [aN'ı] *f* acquaintance.

aithnich [aN'ıch'] *v* know, recognise.

aithreachail [ar'əchal] *adj* repentant.

aithreachas [ar'əchəs] *m* repentance.

aithris [ar'ıš] *v* recite. • *m* report.

àitich [āʰt'ıch'] *v* cultivate.

aitreabh [aʰt'r'əv] *m* building; dwelling.

àl [āL] *m* litter, young.

àlainn [āLıN'] *adj* lovely; fine.

a laoigh! [ə Loy] *excl* my love! my dear!

Alba [aLabə] *f* Scotland.

Albais [aLabıš] *f* Scots language.

Albannach [aLabəNəch] *m/adj* Scotsman, Scot; Scottish.

alcol [aLkəL] *m* alcohol.

allaban [aLəban] *m* wandering.

allaidh [aLı] *adj* wild.

allt [auLt] *m* stream, burn.

alt [aLt] *m* joint; method; (*gram*) article.

altachadh [aLtəchəgh] *m* (*prayer*) grace.

altair [aLtır'] *f* altar.

altraim [aLtrəm] *v* foster; nurse.

am[1] *poss* [əm] *poss pron* their.

am[2] [əm] *art* the.

àm [aum] *m* time. • *adv* **aig amannan** [ɛg' aməNən] at times. • **an t-àm a dh'fhalbh** [ən taum ə ghaLav] the past.

a-mach [əmach] *adv* out (*motion*).

a-mach air a' bhus [əmach ɛr' ə vus] *adv* overflowing.

a-mach à seo! [əmach a šo] *excl* get out!

amadan [amadan] *m* (male) fool, silly man.

amaideach [amad'əch] *adj* foolish, silly.

amaideas [amad'əs] *m* foolishness.

a-màireach [əmār'əch] *adv* tomorrow.

amais [amıš] *v* aim; hit upon.

amaiseach [amıšəch] *adj* accurate.

amalach [aməLəch] *adj* complicated.

amar [amər] *m* basin; pool.

amar-ionnlaid [aməriüNLıd'] *m* wash basin.

amar-snàmh [amərsNāv] *m* swimming pool.

am bitheantas [əm bihəntəs] *adv* usually, normally.

am bliadhna [əm bliənə] *adv* this year.

am broinn [əm broiN'] *prep* inside, within.

am bròn [əm brōn] *adv* in mourning.

am feasd [əm fesd] *adv* ever; for ever.

amh [af] *adj* raw; unripe.

amhaich [avıch'] *f* neck; throat.

a-mhàin [əvāN'] *adv* only.

àmhainn [āvıN'] *f* oven.

amharas [avərəs] *m* suspicion.

amharasach [avərəsəch] *adj* suspicious, distrustful.

amharc [au.ərk] *m* sight.

am measg [əm mesg] *prep* among.

a-muigh [əmuy] *adv* outside (*location*).

an¹ [ən] *art* the; of the.

an² [ən] *poss pron* their.

an³ [ən] *prep* in.

an-abaich [anabɪch'] *adj* unripe; premature.

anabarrach [anabaRəch] *adj/adv* extreme(ly).

an aghaidh [ən ō.iy] *prep* against.

anail [anal] *f* breath.

an ainm an àigh! [ən ɛnɛm ə Nāy] *excl* in Heaven's name!

anainn [anɪN'] *f* eaves.

an àite [ən āʰt'ɪ] *prep* instead of.

a-nall [əNāL] *adv* over here, hither (*motion*).

anam [anam] *m* soul.

ana-mhiann [ana viəN] *m* lust.

an àrd [ən ārd] *adv* up (*motion*).

anart [anəršt] *m* linen.

anart bàis [anəršd bāš] *m* shroud.

an-asgaidh [ənasgɪ] *adv* free of charge.

an ath bhliadhna [ən ah vliaNə] *adv* next year.

an ath dhoras [ən ah ghorəs] *m* next door.

an ath oidhche [ən ah oi.ch'ɪ] *adv* tomorrow night.

an ceann [ən k'auN] *prep* (*of time*) in, after.

an ceann a chèile [ən k'auN əch'ēlɪ] *adv* one after the other, in succession.

an ceartuair [ən k'aršdər'] *adv* just now, presently.

an clàr a aodainn [ən kLār ūdiN'] *adv* full in the face.

an coimeas ri [ən kɔməs r'i] *prep* compared to.

an coinneimh [ən koN'ɪv] *prep* towards.

an cois [ən kɔš] *adv* near; accompanying.

an comhair [ən ko.ɪr'] *prep* in the direction of.

an comhair a chinn [ən ko.ɪr' ə ch'iN'] *adv* head first.

an comhair a thoisich [ən ko.ɪr' ə hɔšɪch'] *adv* frontwards.

an-còmhnaidh [ənkōnɪ] *adv* always, constantly.

an crochadh [ən krɔchəgh] *adv* hanging.

an crochadh air [ən krɔchəgh ɛr'] *prep* depending on.

an cumantas [ən kuməndəs] *adv* commonly, normally.

an dà chuid [ən dā chud'] *pron* both.

an dà latha [ən dā La.a] *m* changed days.

an dàn [ən dān] *adv* destined, ordained.

an dara cuid a no b [ən darə kud' eɪ no bī] either a or b.

an-dè [ənd'ē] *adv* yesterday.

an dèideadh [ən d'ēd'əgh] toothache.

an dèidh [ənd'ē] *prep* after.

an dèidh sin? [ənd'ē šin] *adv* so?

an-diugh [ənd'u] *adv* today.

an dòlas! [ən dōLəs] *excl* woe is me!

an-dràsta [əndrāsdə] *adv* just now.

an-dràsta fhèin [əndrāsdə hēn] *adv* this instant.

an droch-shùil [ən drɔch hūl] *f* the evil eye.

an ear [əN'ɛr] *adv* eastern.

an-earar [əN'ɛrər] *adv* day after tomorrow.

an eisimeil [ən ešɪmɛl] *adv* dependent (on).

anfhann [anauN] *adj* infirm.

an-fhoiseil [anǝšɛl] *adj* restless, uneasy.

an impis [ǝn īmpɪš] *conj* about to.

an-ìochdmhor [an iǝchgvǝr] *adj* merciless, pitiless.

an iomadh-chomhairle [ǝn iumǝghcho.ɪrlǝ] in a quandary.

an ire mhath [ǝn īr'ɪ va] *adv* quite, fairly; just about.

an làthair [ǝn Lā.ɪr'] *adv* present.

a-nìos [ǝniǝs] *adv* up (*up from below towards speaker*).

a-nise [ǝnišɪ] *adv* now.

an là roimhe [ǝn La.a Rɔi.ɪ] *adv* the other day.

an lùib [ǝn Luib] *prep* involved in/ with.

anmoch [anamɔch] *adj* late.

ann[1] [auN] *adv* there.

ann[2] [auN] *prep pron* in him; in it (*m*).

annad [aNǝd] *prep pron* in you (*sing*).

annaibh [aNɪv] *prep pron* in you (*pl*).

annainn [aNɪN'] *prep pron* in us.

annam [aNǝm] *prep pron* in me.

ann an [auN ǝn] *prep* in.

ann an cabhag [auN ǝn kafag] *adv* in a hurry.

ann an dà-rìreabh [auN ǝn darīr'ǝv] *adv* serious, in earnest.

ann an droch staid [auN ǝn drɔch sdad'] *adv* in a bad way.

annas [aNǝs] *m* rarity; novelty.

annasach [aNǝsǝch] *adj* novel; odd.

anns a' bhad [auNs ǝ vad] *adv* immediately.

anns a' chiad dol-a-mach [auNs ǝ ch'iad dǝLǝmach] in the first instance.

anns an [auNs ǝn] *prep* in the.

anns an dealachadh [auNs ǝn d'ɛLǝchǝgh] *adv* on parting.

annta [auNtǝ] *prep pron* in them.

a-nochd [ǝNɔchg] *adv* tonight.

an-raoir [ǝRūr'] *adv* last night.

an sàs [ǝn sās] *adv* captured; involved.

an-seo [ǝnšɔ] *adv* here (*location*).

an-sheo [anǝ hyɔ] *adv* here (*location*).

an-shin [anǝ hin] *adv* there (*location*).

an-shiud [anǝ hid] *adv* there, yonder (*location*).

anshocrach [anahɔʰkrǝch] *adj* uneasy.

an-sin [ǝnšin] *adv* there (*location*).

an-siud [ǝnšid] *adv* there, yonder (*location*).

an taca ri [ǝn taʰkǝ r'i] *prep* compared to, alongside.

an taic ri [ǝn taiʰk' r'i] *prep* leaning on/against; in comparison with.

an taobh a-muigh [ǝn tūv ǝmuy] *m* outside (*location*).

an taobh an ear [ǝn tūv ǝN'ɛr] *m* east.

an taobh an iar [ǝn tūv ǝN'iǝr] *m* the west.

an taobh a-staigh [ǝn tūv ǝsdoy] *m* inside.

an taobh sear [ǝn tūv šɛr] *m* the east.

an taobh siar [ǝn tūv šiǝr] *m* the west.

an t-Eilean Sgitheanach [ǝn t'elansgī.ǝnǝch] *m* (the Isle of) Skye.

an tòir air [ən tōr' ɛr'] *prep* in pursuit of; looking for.

an toiseach [ən tɔšəch] *adv* at first.

an uair a [ə Nuər'ə] *conj* when.

an uairsin [ə Nuər'šin] *adv* then, next.

a-nuas [ənuəs] *adv* down (*down from above towards speaker*).

an-uiridh [ənur'ı] *adv* last year.

a-null [əNūL] *adv* thither; over (*motion*).

a-null thairis [əNūL har'ıš] *adv* abroad, overseas (*motion*).

an urra ri [ən uRə r'i] *prep* responsible for; in charge of.

aocoltach [ūkɔLtəch] *adj* dissimilar.

aodach [ūdəch] *m* cloth; clothes.

aodach-leapa [ūdəch L'ɛʰpə] *m* bedclothes.

aodach oidhche [ūdəch oi.ch'ı] *m* nightclothes.

aodann [ūdəN] *m* face; hillface.

aodionach [ūd'anəch] *adj* leaky.

aoibhneach [oivN'əch] *adj* glad.

aoigh [ui] *m* guest; resident.

aoigheachd [ui.chg] *f* hospitality.

aoigheil [ui.ɛl] *adj* generous; hospitable.

aoir [ūr'] *f* satire.

aois [ūš] *f* age.

aol [ūL] *m* lime.

aon [ūn] *adj* one.

aonach [ūnəch] *m* moor, moorland.

aonad [ūnəd] *m* unit.

aona deug [ūnə d'iag] *adj* eleventh.

aonadh [ūnəgh] *m* union.

aonadh-cèaird [ūnəgh k'ārd'] *m* trade union.

aonaich [ūnıch'] *v* unite, combine.

aonaran [ūnəran] *m* hermit; loner.

aonaranach [ūnəranəch] *adj* lonely; desolate.

aon chuid a no b [ūn chud' ei nə bī] either a or b.

aon deug [ūn d'iag] *n* eleven.

aon fhillte [ūn iL't'ı] *adj* uncomplicated.

aon inntinneach [ūn iN'd'ıN'əch] *adj* unanimous.

aonta [ūndə] *m* agreement.

aontaich [ūndıch'] *v* agree.

aosta [ūsdə] *adj* old, aged.

aotrom [ūtrəm] *adj* light; trivial.

aotromaich [ūtrəmıch'] *v* lighten; alleviate.

aotroman [ūtrəman] *m* bladder.

aparan [aʰparan] *m* apron.

ar (n-) [ar] *poss pron* our.

àr [ār] *m* slaughter.

àra [ārə] *f* kidney.

àrach [ārəch] *m* rearing, upbringing.

àrachas [ārəchəs] *m* insurance.

àradh [ārəgh] *m* ladder.

àraich [ārıch'] *v* raise, bring up.

àraid [ārıd'] *adj* particular; peculiar.

àraidh [ārı] *adj* particular; exceptional.

ar-a-mach [arəmach] *m* rebellion, rising.

aran [aran] *m* bread.

ar-aon [ərūn] *adv* both.

arbhar [ara.ər] *m* corn.

àrc [ārk] *f* cork.

Arcach [arkəch] *adj/n* Orcadian.

Arcaibh [arkıv] *m* Orkney.

àrdachadh [ārdəchəgh] *m* promotion; rise.

àrdaich [ārdıch'] *v* raise; increase.

àrdan [ārdan] *m* pride, arrogance.

àrdanach [ārdanəch] *adj* proud, arrogant.

àrd-doras [ārd dɔrəs] *m* lintel.

àrd-easbaig [ārd esbɪg'] *m* archbishop.

àrd-ìre [ārd īr'ɪ] *adj* (*education, etc*) higher, high-level.

àrd mo chlaiginn [ārd mə chLag'ɪN'] *adv* at the top of my voice.

àrd-ollamh [ārdɔLəv] *m* professor.

àrdsgoil [ārdsgɔl] *f* secondary school.

àrd-ùrlar [ārdūrLər] *m* stage, platform.

àrd-urram [ārduRəm] *m* honour, distinction; reverence.

a-rèir [ərēr'] *prep* according to.

a-rèir choltais [ərēr' chɔLtɪš] *adv* seemingly, apparently.

a-rèist [ərēšd'] *adv* in that case.

argamaid [argəmɪd'] *f* argument.

a-riamh [əriəv] *adv* ever.

a-rithist [əri.ɪšd'] *adv* again.

ar leam [ar ləm] *v* I consider.

arm [aram] *m* army.

armachd [araməchg] *f* armour.

armaich [aramɪch'] *v* arm.

arm-lann [aramLəN] *f* armoury.

arsa [arsə] *v* say, says, said.

àrsaidh [ārsɪ] *adj* ancient.

àrsaidheachd [ārsɪ.əchg] *f* archaeology.

àrsair [ārsɛr'] *m* archaeologist.

às [as] *prep* out of, from. • *prep pron* out of him, out of it (*m*).

às a' cheud [as ə ch'iad] *adv* percent.

às a' chumantas [as ə chuməntəs] *adv* out of the ordinary.

asad [asəd] *prep pron* out of you (*sing*).

asaibh [asɪv] *prep pron* out of you (*pl*).

asaid anabaich [asɪd' anabɪch'] *f* miscarriage.

asainn [asɪN'] *prep pron* out of us.

asal [asaL] *f* ass; donkey.

asam [asəm] *prep pron* out of me.

às an amharc [as ən au.ərk] *adv* out of sight.

às an làthair [as ən Lā.ɪr'] *adv* out of sight.

às aonais [as ūnɪš] *prep* without.

as bith cò [əs bi kō] *prep* whoever.

as bith cuine [əs bi kuN'ɪ] *adv* whenever.

as bith dè [əs bi d'ē] *prep* whatever.

às d' aonais [as tūnɪš] without you.

às eugmhais [as ēgɪš] *prep* without.

à sealladh [a šaLəgh] *adv* out of sight.

asgaidh [asgɪ] *f* present, gift.

a shìorraidh! [ə hiəRɪ] *excl* for Heaven's sake!

às leth [as L'e] *prep* on behalf of.

às mo chiall [as mə ch'iaL] *adv* out of my mind.

às mo rian [as mə riən] *adv* out of my mind.

asta [asdə] *prep pron* out of them.

a-staigh [əsdogh'] *adv* in, inside (*location*).

astar [asdər] *m* distance; speed.

a-steach [əsd'ach] *adv* in, inside (*motion*).

a-steach do [əsd'ach də] *prep* into.

as t-fhoghar [əs tovər] *adv* in Autumn.

Astràilia [asdrālia] *f* Australia.

Astràilianach [asdrālianəch] *m*/*adj* Australian.

as ùr [as ūr] *adv* afresh; anew.

at [aʰt] *v* swell, puff up. • *m* swelling.

ataireachd [aʰtər'əchg] *f* (*of sea*) swell, surge.

ath [ah] *adj* next.

àth¹ [āh] *f* kiln.

àth² [āh] *m* ford.

ath- [ah] *prefix* re-.

athair [ahɪr'] *m* father; progenitor.

athair-cèile [ahɪr'kēlɪ] *m* father-in-law.

athaireil [ahɪr'ɛl] *adj* fatherly.

athaiseach [ahɪšəch] *adj* dilatory.

ath-aithris [a har'ɪš] *v* repeat.

a thaobh [ə hūv] *prep* concerning.

atharrachadh [ahRəchəgh] *m* change, alteration.

atharraich [ahəRɪch'] *v* change, alter.

atharrais [ahəRɪš] *v* imitate, mimic.

ath-bheòthachadh [ah vyɔ̄.əchəgh] *m* renaissance.

ath-bheòthaich [ah vyɔ̄.ɪch'] *v* revive.

ath-chruthaich [ah chruhɪch'] *v* recreate.

ath-dhìol [ah gh'iəL] *v* repay.

ath-leasachadh [ah lesəchəgh] *m* redevelopment; (*with art*) **an t-Ath-leasachadh** [ən tah lesəchəgh] the Reformation.

ath-leasaich [ah lesɪch'] *v* redevelop.

ath-nuadhachadh [ah nuəchəgh] *m* renewal.

ath-nuadhaich [ah nuə.ɪch'] *v* renew.

athraichean [ar'ich'ən] *mpl* forefathers.

ath-sgrìobh [ah sgrīv] *v* rewrite.

ath-sgrùdadh [ah sgrūdəgh] *m* revision.

a thuilleadh air [ə huiL'əgh] *prep* in addition to.

B

b' àbhaist dhomh [bāvɪšd' ghə] *v* I used to.

bac [baʰk] *v* prevent; obstruct.

bacach [baʰkach] *adj* lame. • *m* lame person.

bacadh [baʰkəgh] *m* prevention; obstacle.

bacan [baʰkan] *m* hobble.

bachall [bachəL] *m* crozier.

bachlach [bachLəch] *adj* curly.

bachlag [bachLag] *f* curl, ringlet.

bachlaich [bachLich'] *v* curl.

bad [bad] *m* place; clump.

badan [badan] *m* thicket.

baga [bagə] *m* bag; hand-bag.

bagaid [bagɪd'] *f* bunch; cluster.

bagair [bagɪr'] *v* threaten.

bagairt [bagɪršd'] *f* threat.

bàgh [bāgh] *m* bay, cove.

bagradh [bagrəgh] *m* threat.

bàidh [bāy] *f* affection; favour.

bàidheil [bāyɛl] *adj* kindly.

baidhsagal [baisəgəL] *m* bicycle.

baile [balɪ] *m* township, village. • *adv* **aig baile** [ɛg' balɪ] at home.

bailead [baləd] *m* ballad.

baile beag [balɪ beg] *m* village, small town.

baile mòr [balɪ mōr] *m* town, city.

baile-margaid [balɪmaragɪd'] *m* market town.

baile-puirt [balɪpuršd'] *m* sea port.

bàillidh [bāL'ı] *m* bailiff; baillie.

b' àill leam? [baL'əm] *adv* pardon?

bàine [bāN'ı] *adj* whiter, whitest.

bàinead [bāN'əd] *f* whiteness.

bainne [baN'ı] *m* milk.

bainne lom [baN'ı Ləum] *m* skimmed milk.

bàirdse [bārd'šı] *f* barge.

bàirlinn [bārlıN'] *f* (*law*) summons.

bàirneach [bārN'əch] *f* barnacle, limpet.

baist [bašd'] *v* baptise, christen.

Baisteach [bašd'əch] *adj/m* Baptist.

baisteadh [bašd'əgh] *m* baptism.

bàl [bāL] *m* (*dance*) ball.

balach [baLəch] *m* boy, lad.

balachan [baLəchan] *m* wee boy.

balbh [baLav] *adj* dumb; speechless.

balbhan [baLavan] *m* dumb person.

balg [baLag] *m* abdomen; blister.

balgair [baLagɛr'] *m* fox; rogue.

balgam [baLagəm] *m* sip; swig.

balgan [baLagan] *m* mushroom; toadstool.

balgan-buachair [baLagambuəchır'] *m* edible mushroom.

ball [bauL] *m* organ; member.

balla [baLə] *m* wall.

bàlla [bāLə] *m* ball.

ball-acainn [bauLaʰkıN'] *m* tool.

ballach [baLəch] *adj* speckled, spotted.

ball-airm [bauLer'em] *m* weapon.

ball-àirneis [bauLārnıš] *m* piece of furniture.

ballan [baLan] *m* tub.

ball-aodaich [bauLūdıch'] *m* garment.

ball-basgaid [bauLbasgıd'] *m* basketball.

ball-bodhaig [bauLbo.ıg'] *m* bodily organ.

ball-coise [bauLkɔšı] *m* football.

ball-dòbhrain [bauLdōrɛN'] *m* (*on skin*) mole.

ball-maise [bauLmašı] *m* ornament.

ball pàrlamaid, BP [bauLpārLəmıd'] *m* member of Parliament, MP.

ballrachd [bauLrəchg] *f* membership.

ball-seirce [bauLšer'k'ı] *m* beauty spot.

ball-stèidhe [bauLšt'ē.ı] *m* baseball.

bàn [bān] *adj* blonde; white; blank; fallow.

bana bhuidseach [bana vud'šəch] *f* witch.

bana charaid [bana charıd'] *f* female friend or relative; (*corres*) **A Bhana-charaid** [ə vana charıd'] Dear Madam.

bana chliamhainn [bana ch'liəvɛN'] *f* daughter-in-law.

ban adhaltraiche [ban ōəLtrıch'ə] *f* adulteress.

bànag [bānag] *f* sea trout.

bana ghaisgeach [bana ghašg'əch] *f* heroine.

banail [banal] *adj* womanly, feminine.

banais [banıš] *f* wedding.

Ban Albannach [ban aLabəNəch] *f* Scotswoman.

banaltram [banaLtrəm] *f* nurse.

bana mhaighistir-sgoile [bana vaišd'ır' sgɔlı] *f* school-mistress.

bana phrionnsa [bana friuNsə] *f* princess.

banarach [banarəch] *f* milkmaid, dairymaid.

banca [bankə] *m* bank.

bancair [bankɛr'] m banker.

bancaireachd [bankɪr'əchg] f banking.

bàn-dhearg [bāngh'ɛrag] adj light red.

ban dia [ban d'ia] f goddess.

ban diùc [ban d'ūʰk] f duchess.

bàn-ghorm [bānghərəm] adj pale blue.

ban ìompaire [ban īmpər'ə] f empress.

ban leòmhann [ban L'ɔ̄.əN] f lioness.

bann [bauN] m strip; bandage.

banntach [bauNdəch] m hinge.

banntrach [bauNdrəch] f widow(er).

ban ogha [ban o.ə] f grand-daughter.

bànrigh [bānri] f queen.

ban rùnaire [ban rūnər'ə] f (female) secretary.

baoghalta [bō.əLtə] adj stupid.

baoghaltachd [bō.əLtəchg] f stupidity.

baoit [bōʰt'] f (fishing) fly, bait.

baoiteag [bōʰt'ag] f (fishing) fly, bait.

baoth [bōh] adj foolish, simple.

bàr [bār] m (hotel, etc) bar.

barail [baral] f opinion.

baraille [barɪL'ɪ] m barrel.

bàrd [bāRd] m poet, bard.

bàrdachd [bāRdəchg] f poetry.

bàrr [bāR] m top; cream; crop.

Barrach [baRəch] m/adj Barra person, from Barra.

barrachd [baRəchg] f surplus; more. • prep **barrachd air** [baRəchg ɛr'] more than. • adv **a bharrachd** extra, in addition, **a bharrachd air sin** [ə vaRəchg ɛr' šin] moreover.

barragach [baRagəch] adj creamy.

Barraigh [baRay] m Barra.

barrall [baRəL] m shoelace.

barrantas [baRantəs] m pledge, guarantee.

bàrr na teangaidh [bāR nə t'ɛngɪ] m tip of the tongue.

bas [bas] f palm.

bàs [bās] m death.

bàsaich [bāsɪch'] v die.

bas-bhualadh [bas vuəLəgh] m applause.

basgaid [basgɪd'] f basket.

bàsmhor [bāsvər] adj mortal; deadly.

bàsmhorachd [bāsvərəchg] f mortality.

bata [baʰtə] m stick.

bàta [bāʰtə] m boat.

bata-coiseachd [baʰtəkošəchg] m walking stick.

bàta-aisig [bāʰtašɪg'] m ferry.

bàta-ràmh [bāʰtəRāv] m rowing boat.

bàta-sàbhalaidh [bāʰtəsāvəLɪ] m lifeboat.

bàta-siùil [bāʰtəšūl] m sailing boat.

bàta-smùide [bāʰtəsmūd'ɪ] m steamer.

bàta-teasairginn [bāʰtət'ɛsɪr'g'ɪN'] m lifeboat.

bàth [bā] v drown; muffle.

bàthach [bāhəch] f byre, cow-shed.

bathais [bahɪš] f forehead; impudence.

bathar [bahər] m goods, merchandise.

bàthte [bāʰt'ɪ] adj drowned.

bàta-iasgaich [bāʰtiəsgɪch'] fishing boat.

beach [byach] m bee; wasp.

beachd [byachg] *m* idea; opinion.

beachdail [byachgal] *adj* abstract.

beachd-smaoinich,
[byachgsmūnich'] *v* meditate.

beachlann [byachLəN] *m* beehive.

beag [beg] little by little.

beagan [began] *adv* a bit, slightly.
• *m* a little; few.

beag-nàrach [beg nārəch] *adj*
shameless.

bealach [byaLəch] *m* pass, col; detour.

bealaidh [byaLı] *m* broom.

Bealltainn [byauLtıN'] *f* May Day,
Beltane.

bean[1] [bɛn] *f* wife.

bean[2] [bɛn] *v* touch, meddle with.

bean- [bɛn] *prefix* woman-, female.

bean an taighe [bɛnəntɛhı] **bean-
taighe** [bɛntɛhı] *f* housewife;
landlady.

bean-bainnse [bɛnbaiN'šı] *f* bride.

bean-eiridinn [bɛner'ıd'ıN'] *f* nurse.

bean-ghlùine [bɛnghLūN'ı] *f* midwife.

beannachadh [byaNəchəgh] *m* beatification; greeting.

beannachd [byaNəchg] *f* blessing;
regards.

beannachd leibh! [byaNəchg loiv]
excl goodbye!

beannaich [byaNıch'] *v* bless.

beannaich do [byaNıch' dɔ] *v* greet.

beannaichte [byaNıch't'ə] *adj*
blessed.

bean phòsda [bɛn fɔsdə] *f* married
woman, Mrs.

bean ri [bɛn r'i] *v* brush against.

bean-shìthe [bɛnhī.ı] *f* fairy woman.

bean-taighe *see* **bean an taighe**.
[bɛn tɛhı]

bean-teagaisg [bɛn t'ɛgıšg'] *f* (female) teacher.

bean uasal [bɛnuəsəL] *f* noblewoman; (*fml*) **a Bhean uasal!** [ə
vɛnuəsəl] *excl* Madam! (*corres,
fml*) Dear Madam.

beàrn [byārn] *f* gap; notch.

beàrnan-bride [byārnanbr'īd'ı] *f*
dandelion.

Beàrnarach [byārnərəch] *m* Berneray person.

Beàrnaraigh [byārnəray] *f* Berneray.

beàrr [byāR] *v* shave; shear.

bearradair [byaRədɛr'] *m* barber.

beart [byaRšd] *f* machine.

beartach [byaRšdəch] *adj* rich,
wealthy.

beartas [byaRšdəs] *m* riches,
wealth.

beart-fhighe [byaRšdi.ı] *f* loom.

beatha [bɛhə] *f* life.

beathach [bɛhəch] *m* animal.

beathach-mara [bɛhəchmarə] *m*
sea-creature.

beathaich [bɛhıch'] *v* feed; maintain.

beatha-eachdraidh [bɛhɛchdrı] *f*
biography.

beic [behk'] *f* curtsey.

Beilg [belig'] *f* (*with art*) **a' Bheilg** [ə
velig'] Belgium.

Beilgeach [belig'əch] *m/adj* Belgian.

being [being'] *f* bench.

beinn [beiN'] *f* ben, mountain.

Beinn Nibheis [beiN'ivıš] *f* Ben Nevis.

beinn-teine [beiN't'enı] *f* volcano.

beir [ber'] *v irreg* bear; give birth
to.

beir air [bɛr' ɛr'] *v* seize; overtake.
beir air làimh air [bɛr' ɛr' lãiv ɛr'] *v* shake hands with.
beirm [ber'im] *f* yeast.
beò [byɔ] *adj* alive, living.
beò-ghlacadh [byɔ ghLaʰkəgh] *m* obsession.
beòshlaint [byɔLand'] *f* livelihood.
beothaich [byɔ.ıch'] *v* revive; liven up.
beothail [byɔ.al] *adj* lively, active.
beothalachd [byɔ.əLəchg] *f* vivacity.
beuc [biaʰk] *m* roar, bellow. • *v* roar, bellow.
beud [bēd] *m* harm, loss.
beul [biaL] *m* mouth.
beul a bhith [biaL ə vi] *adv* about to be.
beul-aithris [biaLahr'ıš] *f* oral tradition.
beulchar [biaLchər] *adj* plausible, smooth-talking.
beul ìochdair [biaL īachgɛr'] *m* lower lip.
beul-oideachas [biaLod'əchəs] *f* lore.
beul ri [biaL r'i] *prep* nearly.
beul uachdair [biaL uachgɛr'] *m* upper lip.
beum [bēm] *m* stroke; blow.
beum-grèine [bēmgrēnı] *m* sunstroke.
Beurla [byōRLə] *f* (*often with art*) **a' Bheurla** [ə vyōRLə] English.
beusach [bēsəch] *adj* modest; well-behaved.
beus-eòlas [bēsyōLəs] *m* ethics.
bha [vã] *past tense of v* **bith**
bhàrr [vāR] ~ [far] *prep* off, down from.

bha spòrs agam [va sbɔrs agəm] *v* I enjoyed myself/had fun.
Bhèineas [vēnəs] *f* Venus.
bheir [ver'] *future tense of v* **thoir**
bho *see* **o**.
bhòt [vɔʰt] *v* vote.
bhuaibh *see* **uaibh**
bhuainn *see* **uainn**
bhuaipe *see* **uaipe**
bhuaithe *see* **uaithe**
bhuam *see* **uam**
bhuapa *see* **uapa**
bhuat *see* **uat**
bhur *see* **ur**
biadh [biəgh] *m* food; meal.
biadhlann [biəLəN] *m* refectory, canteen.
bian [bian] *m* fur, hide.
biast [biəsd] *f* beast.
biastail [biəsdal] *adj* bestial.
biath [biəh] *v* feed; fodder.
bìd[1] [bīd'] *v* bite.
bìd[2] [bīd'] *m* chirp.
bìdeag [bīd'ag] *f* fragment, crumb.
bidse [bid'šı] *f* bitch. • *excl* **a bhidse!** [ə vid'šı] sod it!
bile[1] [bilı] *f* lip, rim.
bile[2] [bilı] *m* (*politics*) bill.
bileag [bilag] *f* petal; (*commerce*) bill.
binid [binıd'] *f* rennet.
binn[1] [bīN'] *adj* sweet.
binn[2] [bīN'] *f* judgement; sentence.
binnean [biN'an] *m* peak.
binneas [biN'əs] *m* sweetness.
bìoball [bībəL] *m* bible.
bìoballach [bībəLəch] *adj* biblical.
biodach [bidəch] *adj* tiny; trifling.
biodag [bidag] *f* dirk, dagger.
bìog [biəg] *f* chirp. • *v* cheep, chirp.

biolar [byɔLər] *f* cress.

biona [binə] *f* bin.

biona-stùir [binə sdūr'] *f* dustbin.

bior [bir] *m* point; prickle.

biorach [birəch] *adj* sharp, pointed.

bioran [biran] *m* a pointed stick.

biorra-crùidein [biRəkrūd'ɛN'] *m* kingfisher.

bior-ròstaidh [biRōsdɪ] *m* (*cooking*) spit.

biotais [bihtɪš] *m* beet.

bìrlinn [bīrlɪN'] *f* galley, birlinn.

bith[1] [bih] *f* existence, being. • *v* be.

bith[2] [bīh] *f* tar, pitch.

bith- [bi] *prefix* ever-.

bith bheò [bih vyō] *adj* ever-living, immortal.

bith bhuan [bih vuən] *adj* eternal, everlasting.

bitheanta [bihəndə] *adj* frequent, common.

bitheantas [bihəndəs] *m* frequency.

bith-eòlas [bih yōLəs] *m* biology.

bithis [bi.ɪš] *f* screw.

bithiseach [bi.ɪšəch] *adj* spiral.

blais [bLaš] *v* taste.

blàr [bLār] *m* plain; battle(field).

blas [bLas] *m* flavour; accent.

blasad [bLasəd] *m* taste.

blasad bidh [bLasəd bī] *m* bite to eat.

blasaich [bLasɪch'] *v* flavour.

blasmhor [bLasvər] *adj* full of flavour.

blasta [bLasdə] *adj* tasty.

blàth[1] [bLā] *m* bloom, blossom.

blàth[2] [bLā] *adj* warm; affectionate.

blàthaich [bLā.ɪch'] *v* warm.

blàth-chridheach [bLā ch'r'ī.əch] *adj* warm-hearted.

blàths [bLās] *m* warmth.

bleideag [bled'ag] *f* flake.

bleith [bleh] *v* grind, pulverise.

bleoghainn [blɔ.ɪN'] *v* milk.

bliadhna [bliənə] *f* year.

bliadhnach [bliənəch] *adj* yearling.

bliadhnail [bliənal] *adj* annual, yearly.

bliadhna-leum [bliənəlēm] *f* leap year.

bliadhna ùr [bliənə ūr] *f* new year.

blian [blian] *v* sunbathe.

bloigh [bLɔy] *f* half.

bloighd [bLɔid] *f* fragment, splinter.

bloinigean-gàraidh [bLɔN'ɪg'angārɪ] *m* spinach.

blonag [bLɔnag] *f* lard.

bò [bō] *f* cow.

bò-bhainne [bōvaN'ɪ] *f* milk cow.

bobhla [bouLə] *m* bowl.

boc [bɔ^hk] *m* billy goat; roebuck.

bòc [bɔ^hk] *v* swell, bloat.

bòcan [bɔ^hkan] *m* apparition; bogyman.

boc-earba [bɔkɛrabə] *m* roe-buck.

bochd [bɔchg] *adj* poor; unfortunate; poorly.

bochdainn [bɔchgɪN'] *f* poverty; misfortune.

bogsa [bɔgsə] *m* box.

bogsa ciùil [bɔgsə k'ūl] *m* accordion.

bogsa fòn [bɔgsə fōn] *m* phonebox.

bocsair [bɔ^hksɛr'] *m* boxer.

bogsa litrichean [bogsə Lih't'r'ɪch'ən] *m* letterbox.

bod [bɔd] *m* penis.

Bòd [bōd] *m* Bute.

bodach [bɔdəch] *m* old man, old guy.

Bodach na Nollaig [bɔdəch nə NɔLɛgʲ] *m* Santa Claus.

bodach-ròcais [bɔdəchRɔ̄ʰkɪš] *m* scarecrow.

bodach-sneachda [bɔdəchšN'ɛchgə] *m* snowman.

bodhaig [bo.ɪgʲ] *f* body.

bodhair [bo.ɪrʲ] *v* deafen.

bodhar [bo.ər] *adj* deaf. • *m* deaf person.

bòdhran [bō.ran] *m* bodhran.

bodraig [bɔdrɪgʲ] *v* bother, trouble.

bog[1] [bog] *adj* soft; tender. • *v* soak, steep.

bog[2] [bog] *v* bob, dip.

bogadaich [bogədɪch'] *f* bouncing, bobbing.

bogaich [bogɪch'] *v* soften.

bog fliuch [bog fluch] *adj* soaking wet.

bogha [bo.ə] *m* bow; curve.

bogha-frois [bo.əfrɔš] *m* rainbow.

boglach [bogLəch] *f* bog.

bòid [bōdʲ] *f* oath; swearing.

Bòideach [bōdʲəch] *m/adj* from Bute.

bòidhchead [bōich'əd] *f* beauty.

bòidheach [bōi.əch] *adj* pretty, beautiful.

boile [bɔlɪ] *f* madness; frenzy.

boillsg [bɔLʲšgʲ] *m* flash; gleam. • *v* flash; glitter, shine.

boillsgeach [bɔLšgʲəch] *adj* gleaming; glittering.

boinne [bɔN'ɪ] *f* drop.

boinneag [bɔN'ag] *f* droplet.

boireann [bɔrʲəN] *adj* female, feminine.

boireannach [bɔrʲəNəch] *m* woman, female.

boireannaich [bɔrʲəNɪch'] *mpl* womenfolk.

boireannta [bɔrʲəNdə] *adj* effeminate.

boiseag [bošag] *f* slap; palmful.

boladh [bɔLəgh] *m* smell.

bò-laoigh [bōLuy] *f* in-calf cow.

bolgan [bɔLɔgan] *m* bulb.

boltrach [bɔLtrəch] *m* smell; perfume.

boma [bɔmə] *m* bomb.

bonaid [bɔnɪdʲ] *f* bonnet, cap.

bonaid bhiorach [bɔnɪdʲ virəch] *f* Glengarry (bonnet).

bonn [bouN] *m* base; coin.

bonnach [bɔNəch] *m* bannock; scone.

bonnach uighe [bɔNəch ui.ɪ] *m* omelette.

bonn airgid [bouN ɛrʲɛgʲɪdʲ] *m* coin; silver medal.

bonn còmhraidh [bouN kōrɪ] *m* chat.

bonn cuimhne [bouN kuiN'ɪ] *m* medal.

bonn-dubh [bouNdu] *m* heel.

borb [bɔrɔb] *adj* wild, barbarous.

borbair [bɔrɔbɛrʲ] *m* barber.

bòrd [bɔ̄rd] *m* board; table.

bòrd-ceadachaidh [bɔ̄rdk'edəchɪ] *m* licensing board.

bòrd-dàmais [bɔ̄rdāmɪš] *m* draught board.

bòrd-dubh [bɔ̄rdu] *m* blackboard.

bòrd-geal [bɔ̄rdgʲaL] *m* whiteboard.

bòrd-iarnaigidh [bɔ̄rdiərnɪgʲɪ] *m* ironing board.

bòrd-sgrìobhaidh [bɔ̄rdsgrīvɪ] *m* desk.

bòrd slàinte [bɔ̄rdsLāN'dʲɪ] *m* health board.

bòstail [bōsdal] *adj* boastful.

botal [bɔʰtəL] *m* bottle.

botal teth [bɔʰtəL t'e] *m* hotwater bottle.

bòtann [bɔ̄ʰtəN] *m* boot, wellie.

bothan [bɔhan] *m* cottage; shebeen.

bothan àiridh [bɔhan ār'ɪ] *m* sheiling bothy.

bracaist [braʰkɪšd'] *f* breakfast.

brach [brach] *v* ferment; *(boil, etc)* gather.

brachadh [brachəgh] *m* fermentation; pus.

bradan [bradan] *m* salmon.

brag [brag] *m* bang.

bragail [bragal] *adj* boastful.

braich [braich'] *f* malt.

braid [brad'] *f* theft, thieving.

bràigh[1] [brāy] *m* upper part; upland.

bràigh[2] [brāy] *m* captive; hostage.

bràighdeanas [brāid'ənəs] *m* captivity.

braidhm [broim] *m* fart.

braisead [brašəd] *f* impetuosity.

bràiste [brāsd'ɪ] *f* brooch.

bràmair [brāmɪr] *m* girlfriend.

branndaidh [brauNdɪ] *f* brandy.

braoisg [brūšg'] *f* grin; grimace.

braoisgeil [brūšg'ɛl] *adj* grinning.

braon [brūn] *v* drizzle. • *m* drop;.

bras [bras] *adj* hasty; bold.

brat [braʰt] *m* cover; mat; cloak.

bratach [braʰtəch] *f* banner, flag.

brath[1] [brah] *v* betray; inform on.

brath[2] [brah] *m* knowledge; advantage.

bràth [brāch] *m* judgement; **gu bràth tuilleadh** [gə brāch tuL'əgh] *adv (with neg v)* never again.

brathadair [brahədɛr'] *m* betrayer.

brathadh [brahəgh] *m* betrayal.

bràthair [brāhɪr'] *m* brother.

bràthair-athar [brāhɪr'ahar] *m* uncle.

bràthair-cèile [brāhɪr'k'ēlɪ] *m* brother-in-law.

bràthair-màthar [brāhɪr'māhar] *m* uncle.

brat-leapa [braʰtL'ɛʰpə] *m* bedcover, coverlet.

brat-ùrlair [braʰtūrLɪr'] *m* carpet.

breab [br'eb] *v* kick. • *m* kick.

breabadair [br'ebədɛr'] *m* weaver; daddy-long-legs.

breac[1] [br'ɛʰk] *adj* speckled, variegated.

breac[2] [br'ɛʰk] *m* trout.

breacadh-seunain [br'ɛʰkəghšianɛN'] *m* freckles.

breacag [br'ɛʰkag] *f* bannock.

breacan [br'ɛʰkan] *m* plaid, tartan cloth.

breacanach [br'ɛʰkanəch] *adj* tartan.

breac bhallach [br'ɛʰk vaLəch] *adj* freckled.

breac-òtraich [br'ɛʰkɔ̄ʰtrɪch] *f (with art)* **a' bhreac-òtraich** [ə vr'ɛʰkɔ̄ʰtrɪch'] chicken pox.

buinneach [buN'əch] *f (with art)* **a' bhuinneach** [ə vuN'əch] diarrhoea.

brèagha [br'ia.ə] *adj* fine, lovely.

Breatannach [br'eʰtəNəch] *m/adj* Briton; British.

breice [br'eʰk'ɪ] *f* brick.

breicire [br'eʰk'ɪr'ə] *m* bricklayer.

brèid [br'ēd'] *m* kerchief; patch.

brèid shoithichean [br'ēd' ho.ɪch'ən] *m* dishcloth.

brèige [br'ēg'ɪ] *adj* deceitful; artificial.

breisleach [br'ešləch] *m* confusion; delirium.

breislich [br'ešlıch'] v talk irrationally.

breith[1] [br'e] f birth.

breith[2] [br'e] f decision; sentence.

breith anabaich [br'e anabıch'] f abortion.

breithnich [br'enıch'] v judge; assess.

breug [br'iag] f lie.

breugach [br'iagach] adj lying.

breugaire [br'iagər'ə] m liar.

breug-riochd [br'iag riəchg] m disguise.

breun [br'ēn] adj putrid, corrupt.

briathar [br'iəhər] m term.

briathran [br'iəhrən] mpl statements, words.

briathran teicneolach [br'iəhrən teʰk'N'ɔLəch] mpl technical terms.

brib [br'īb] v bribe. • f bribe.

brìgh [br'ī] f meaning; essence; energy.

brìghmhor [br'īvər] adj pithy; energetic.

briogais [br'igıš] f trousers, breeches.

briosgaid [br'isgıd'] f biscuit.

bris [br'iš] v break, smash.

briseadh [br'išəgh] m break, fracture.

briseadh-cridhe [br'išəghkrī.ı] m heartbreak.

briseadh-dùil [br'išəghdūl] m disappointment.

briseadh-latha [br'išəghLa.a] m daybreak.

brisg [br'išg'] adj crisp; brittle.

briste [br'išd'ı] adj broken, smashed.

britheamh [br'ihəv] m judge.

broc [broʰk] m badger.

brochan [brochan] m porridge.

brod [brɔd] v drive on; encourage. • m goad, prod.

bròg [brɔg] f shoe, boot.

broilleach [brɔL'əch] m bosom, chest.

broinn [brɔiN'] f interior.

bròn [brɔn] m sadness, sorrow.

brònach [brɔnəch] adj sad, sorrowful.

brosnachadh [brɔsnəchəgh] m encouragement.

brosnachail [brɔsnəchal] adj encouraging.

brosnaich [brɔsnıch'] v encourage; arouse.

brot [brɔʰt] m soup, broth.

broth [brɔh] m rash.

brù [brū] f womb; belly; bulge.

bruach [bruəch] f (river, etc) bank.

bruadair [bruədır'] v dream.

bruadar [bruədər] m dream.

brùchd [brūchg] v burst out; belch. • m belch.

brù-dhearg [brūgh'ɛrag] m robin.

bruich [brich'] v cook; boil. • adj cooked; boiled.

bruicheil [brich'ɛl] adj sultry.

brùid [brūd'] m brute; beast.

brùidealachd [brūd'əLəchg] f brutality.

brùideil [brūd'ēl] adj brutal.

bruidhinn [bri.ıN'] v talk, speak. • f talk, talking.

bruidhinn ri [bri.ıN' r'i] v talk to.

bruidhneach [briN'əch] adj talkative, chatty.

bruis [bruš] f brush.

bruis-aodaich [bruš ūdıch'] f clothes brush.

bruis-fhiaclan [bruš iəʰkLən] *f* toothbrush.

bruisig [brušıg'] *v* brush.

brùite [brūʰt'ı] *adj* bruised; oppressed.

brùth [brūh] *v* bruise; shove.

bruthach [bru.əch] *m* bank, slope.

bruthainneach [bru.ıN'əch] *adj* sultry.

bu, b' [bə] *v* was, were; would be.

buachaille [buəchəL'ı] *m* cowherd.

buachailleachd [buəchəL'əchg] *f* cattle herding.

buachaillich [buəchəLıch'] *v* herd cattle.

buachar [buəchər] *m* cowdung.

buadh [buəgh] *f* quality, virtue.

buadhair [buəghɛr'] *m* adjective.

buadhmhor [buəvər] *adj* effective; successful.

buaic [buəʰk'] *f* wick.

buaidh [buəy] *f* victory; success; influence.

buail [buəl] *v* hit.

buail a-steach [buəl əšd'ach] *v* call in, drop in.

buail bas [buəl bas] *v* applaud.

buaile [buəlı] *f* sheepfold.

buailteach [buəlt'əch] *adj* liable, apt to.

buain [buəN'] *f* reaping, harvest(ing).

buair [buər'] *v* upset; tempt.

buaireadh [buər'əgh] *m* temptation.

buaireas [buər'əs] *m* anxiety; confusion.

buaireasach [buər'əsəch] *adj* troublesome.

bualadh [buəLəgh] *m* blow.

buan [buən] *adj* lasting, durable.

buannachd [buəNəchg] *f* profit, advantage.

buannaich [buəNıch'] *v* win.

buar [buər] *m* herd.

bucaid [buʰkıd'] *f* bucket.

bucas [buʰkəs] *m* box.

bu chiatach orm [bə ch'iəʰtəch ərom] *v* I should.

bu chòir dhomh [bə chōr' ghə] *v* I ought, I should.

bugair [bugır'] *m* bugar.

buideal [bud'aL] *m* bottle.

buidhe [bui.ı] *adj* yellow; lucky.

buidheach [bui.əch] *adj* thankful, grateful.

buidheachas [bui.əchəs] *m* gratitude.

buidheagan [bui.agan] *f* yolk.

buidheann [bui.əN] *m* group; firm.

buidheann-cluich [bui.əNkLuch'] *m* playgroup.

buidheann-obrach [bui.əNəbrəch] *m* working party.

buidheann-òigridh [bui.əNōig'r'ı] *m* youth club/group.

buidheann-strì [bui.əNsdr'ī] *m* pressure group.

buidhe-ruadh [bui.ı ruəgh] *adj* auburn.

buidhinn [bui.ıN'] *v* win.

buidhre [buir'ı] *f* deafness.

buidseach [bud'šəch] *m* wizard.

bùidsear [būd'šɛr] *m* butcher.

buige [buig'ı] *f* softness; moistness.

buil [bul] *f* consequence; conclusion.

buileach [buləch] *adv* completely, quite.

buileann [buləN] *f* loaf.

builgean [bulig'an] *f* bubble.

builgeanach [bulig'anəch] *adj* bubbly.

builich air [bulıch' ɛr'] *v* bestow upon.

buill a' chuirp [buL' ə chuir'p] *mpl* parts of the body.

buille [buL'ɪ] *f* blow; emphasis; (*mus*) beat.

buille cridhe [buL'ɪ krī.ɪ] *f* heartbeat.

buill-ghineamhain [buL'*gh'in*əvɛN'] *mpl* genitals.

buin do [buN' də] *v* belong to; be related to.

buinnig [buN'ɪg'] *v* win.

buin ri [buN' r'ɪ] *v* interfere with.

buinteanas [buN'd'ənəs] *m* links, relationship.

buirbe [bur'ibɪ] *f* barbarity, wildness.

bumailear [bumalɛr] *m* oaf; no-user.

bun [bun] *m* base, bottom, foot.

bunait [bunat'] *f* foundation, fundamentals.

bunaiteach [bunat'əch] *adj* stable; fundamental(ist).

bunasach [bunəsəch] *adj* radical.

bun-dealain [bun d'alɛN'] *m* power point.

bun-os-cionn [bunɔsk'ūN] *adv* upside down.

bun-sgoil [bunsgɔl] *f* primary school.

buntàta [buntãʰtə] *m* potato(es).

buntàta pronn [buntãʰtə prouN] *m* mashed potato(es).

bùrach [būrəch] *m* mess, guddle.

bùrn [būrn] *m* water (*Lewis dialect*).

burraidh [buRɪ] *m* fool, blockhead.

bus[1] [bəs] *m* bus.

bus[2] [bus] *m* mouth; grimace, pout.

bùth [bū] *f* shop.

bùth-chungaidh [bū chungɪ] *f* pharmacist's.

bùth-èisg [bū ēšg'] *f* fish shop.

C

cab [kab] *f* gob.

cabach [kabəch] *adj* talkative.

cabadaich [kabədɪch'] *f* chatter.

cabaireachd [kabɪr'achg] *f* chatter.

càball [kābəL] *m* cable.

cabar [kabər] *m* rafter, pole; caber.

cabar droma [kabər drɔmə] *m* ridge pole.

cabar fèidh [kabər fēy] *m* deer's antlers.

cabhag [kafag] *f* haste.

cabhagach [kafagəch] *adj* hurried, hasty.

cabhlach [kauLəch] *m* fleet.

cabhsair [kausɛr'] *m* pavement, causeway.

cabstair [kabsdɛr'] *m* horse's bit.

cac [kaʰk] *v* defecate. • *m* excrement.

càch [kāch] *pron* other people, the others.

càch a chèile [kāch ə ch'ēlɪ] *pron* each other.

cadal [kadəL] *m* sleep.

cadalach [kadəLəch] *adj* sleepy.

cafaidh [kafɪ] *f* café.

cagailt [kagɪlt'] *f* hearth, fireside.

cagainn [kagɪN'] *v* chew.

cagair [kagɪr'] *v* whisper.

cagar [kagər] *m* whisper; secret.

caibe [kaibɪ] *m* spade; mattock.

caibeal [kaibəL] *m* chapel.

caibideal [kabɪd'ɛl] *m* chapter.

caibideal a h-aon [kabɪd'ɛl əhūn] chapter one.

caidil [kad'ɪl] v sleep.

caidil gu math! [kad'ɪl gə ma] excl sleep well!

càil[1] [kāl] f desire; appetite.

càil[2] [kāl] m thing.

cailc [kalk'] f chalk.

caileag [kalag] f girl, lassie.

caill [kaiL'] v lose; miss.

caill do rian [kaiL' də rian] v go out of your mind.

cailleach [kaL'əch] f old woman; wifie; hag.

cailleach dhubh [kaL'əch ghu] f nun.

cailleach-oidhche [kaL'əchoi.ch'ɪ] f owl.

caill mùn [kaiL' mūn] v wet oneself.

caillte [kaiL'tɪ] adj lost.

caillteach [kaiL't'əch] adj ruinous.

càil sam bith [kāl səm bi] m anything at all.

càin[1] [kāN'] v scold.

càin[2] [kāN'] f duty, levy.

cainb [kanib] f hemp.

caineal [kanaL] m cinnamon.

cainnt [kaiN'd'] f speech, language.

caiptean [kabd'ɛn] m captain, skipper.

càir [kār'] v repair.

càirdeach do [kārd'əch də] related to.

càirdean [kārd'ən] mpl friends; relations.

càirdeas [kārd'əs] m friendship; kinship.

càirdeas fola [kārd'əs foLə] m blood relationship.

càirdeil [kārd'ɛl] adj friendly.

càirdineal [kārd'ɪnaL] m cardinal.

càireas [kār'əs] m (in mouth) gum(s).

cairgein [karig'ɛN'] m carrageen.

cairt[1] [karšt'] v tan (leather); muck out.

cairt[2] [karšt'] f card; chart.

cairt[3] [karšt'] f cart.

cairt-bhòrd [karšd'vōrd] m cardboard.

cairt-chluiche [karšd'chLuch'ɪ] f playing card.

cairteal [karšd'aL] m quarter.

cairteal na h-uarach [karšd'aL nə huərəch] m quarter hour.

cairt-iùil [karšd'iūl] f navigation chart.

cairt-Nollaig [karšd'noLɛg'] f Xmas card.

cairt-phuist [karšd'fušt'] f postcard.

càise [kāšɪ] m cheese.

caise [kašɪ] f abruptness; impetuosity.

caisg [kašg'] v abate; prevent.

Càisg [kāšg'] f (with art) **a' Chàisg** [ə chāšg'] Easter.

caismeachd [kašməchg] f alarm; march.

caisteal [kašdaL] m castle.

càite? [kāt'ɪ] interrog adv where?

caith [kah] v wear; spend; consume; waste.

caitheamh [kahəv] m (with art) **a' chaitheamh** [ə chahəv] tuberculosis.

caithte [kaʰt'ɪ] adj worn-out; consumed.

caithteach [kaʰt'əch] adj wasteful.

Caitligeach [kaʰtlɪgəch] m/adj Catholic.

càl [kāL] m cabbage, kale.

cala [kaLə] m harbour.

càl-colaig [kāL kɔLɛg'] *m* cauliflower.

calg [kaLag] *m* prickle.

calg-dhìreach [kaLagg*h*'ïr'əch] *adv* completely.

calg-dhìreach an aghaidh [kaLagg*h*'ïr'əch ən ō.ï] *adv* dead against.

call [kauL] *m* loss; waste.

calla [kaLə] *adj* tame, domesticated.

callaich [kaLɪch'] *v* tame, domesticate.

callaid [kaLɪd'] *f* fence; hedge.

calltainn [kauLtɪN'] *m* hazel.

calma [kaLamə] *adj* stout; sturdy.

calman [kaLaman] *m* dove, pigeon.

calpa[1] [kaLapə] *m* (*leg*) calf.

calpa[2] [kaLpə] *m* (*fin*) capital.

cam [kaum] *adj* bent, curved.

camachasach [kama chasəch] *adj* bow-legged.

camag [kamag] *f* curl, ringlet; bracket.

camagach [kamagəch] *adj* curled, curly.

caman [kaman] *m* shinty stick.

camanachd [kamanəch*g*] *f* shinty.

camara [kamara] *m* camera.

camas [kaməs] *m* bay.

càmhal [kā.əL] *m* camel.

camhanaich [kavanɪch'] *f* dawn, twilight.

campa [kampə] *m* camp.

campaich [kampɪch'] *v* camp.

can [kan] *v* say.

cana [kanə] *m* tin, can.

canabhas [kanavəs] *m* canvas.

canach [kanəch] *m* bog cotton.

can air [kan ɛr'] *v* say for.

cànan [kānan] *m* language, tongue.

cànanach [kānanəch] *adj* linguistic.

canastair [kanəsdɛr'] *m* tin, can, canister.

Canadach [kanadəch] *m/adj* Canadian.

can ri [kan r'i] *v* call.

caochail [kūchal] *v* change, alter; die.

caochladh [kūchLəgh] *m* change, alteration.

caochlaideach [kūchLɪd'əch] *adj* changeable, fickle.

caog [kūg] *v* blink; wink.

caogad [kūgad] *m* fifty.

caoidh [kūy] *v* lament, weep; mourn.

caol [kūL] *adj* narrow; thin. • *m* strait, kyle.

caolan [kūLan] *m* gut, intestine.

caol an droma [kūL ən drɔmə] *m* small of the back.

caol an dùirn [kūL ən dūrN'] *m* wrist.

caolas [kūLəs] *m* strait, kyle(s).

Caolas Bòideach [kūLəs bōd'əch] *m* Kyles of Bute.

caol na coise [kūL nə kɔšɪ] *m* ankle.

caol-shràid [kūLrād'] *f* vennel, alley.

caon [kūn] *adj* wily.

caomh [kūv] *adj* dear, beloved.

caomhain [kūvɛN'] *v* save, economise.

caora [kūrə] *f* sheep, ewe.

caorann [kūrəN] *f* rowan.

car[1] [kar] *m* turn; stroll; trick. • *as adv* a bit, somewhat.

car[2] [kar] *prep* during, for.

càr [kār] *f* car.

carabhaidh [karavɪ] *m* boyfriend.

carach [karəch] *adj* wily; unreliable.

carachd [karəch*g*] *f* wrestling.

caractar [karaktər] *m* (*play, etc*) character.

càradh [kārəgh] *m* repair; state, condition.

caraich [karıch'] *v* move.

càraich [kārıch'] *v* repair.

caraiche [karıch'ə] *m* wrestler.

caraid[1] [karıd'] *m* friend, relative; (*corres*) **A Charaid** [ə charıd'] Dear Sir; **A Chàirdean** [ə chārd'ən] Dear Sirs.

càraid[2] [kārıd'] *f* pair; twins.

càraid phòsda [kārıd' fōsdə] *f* married couple.

car a' mhuiltein [kar ə vult'ɛN'] *m* somersault.

caran [karan] *adv* a bit, slightly.

carbad [karabəd] *m* vehicle; carriage; craft.

carbad-eiridinn [karabədər'ıd'ıN'] *m* ambulance.

cargu [kargu] *m* cargo.

càrn [kārn] *v* pile up; accumulate. • *m* heap; cairn; hill.

càrnaid [kārnıd] *f* carnation.

càrnan [kārnan] *m* cockroach.

càrn-cuimhne [kārnkuiN'ı] *m* monument.

càrr [kārn] *f* dandruff.

carragh [kaRəgh] *m* rock; stone pillar.

carraig [kaRɛg'] *f* rock.

carson? [karsən] *interrog adv* why?

carson a chiall? [kəRsən ə ch'iaL] *excl* why on earth?

cartadh [karšdəgh] *m* mucking out.

carthannas [karhəNəs] *m* kindness; charity.

cas[1] [kas] *f* foot; leg; handle.

cas[2] [kas] *adj* steep; impetuous;.

càs [kās] *m* difficulty, predicament.

casad [kasəd] *m* cough.

casadaich [kasədıch'] *v* cough.

casa-gobhlach air [kasagoLəch ɛr'] *prep* astride.

casaid [kasıd'] *f* complaint; accusation.

cas-chrom [kaschrəum] *f* footplough.

casgadh [kasgəgh] *m* prevention.

casgair [kasgɛr'] *v* slay, massacre.

casgairt [kasgıršd'] *f* slaughter, butchery.

casgan [kasgan] *m* brake.

casg-gineamhainn [kasginəvıN'] *m* contraception; contraceptive.

cas-lom [kasLəum] *adj* barefoot, barelegged.

cas-ruisgte [kasrūšg't'ı] *adj* barefoot, barelegged.

cas toisich [kas tošıch'] *f* foreleg.

cat [kaht] *m* cat.

cat fiadhaich [kaht fiə.ıch'] *m* wildcat.

cath [kah] *m* battle; warfare.

càth [kāh] *f* chaff.

cathadh [kahəgh] *m* snowdrift.

cathag [kahag] *f* jackdaw.

cathair [kahır'] *f* chair; city.

cathair-chuibhle [kahır'chuilı] *f* wheelchair.

cathair-eaglais [kahır'ɛgLıš] *f* cathedral.

cath-bhuidheann [kahvui.əN] *f* batallion.

cead [k'ed] *m* permission; permit, licence.

ceadach [k'edəch] *adj* tolerant.

ceadachail [k'edəchal] *adj* permissive.

ceadaich [k'edıch'] *v* permit, allow.

ceadaichte [k'edıch't'ı] *adj* allowed.

cairt-shiubhail [karšt'hiu.al] *m* passport.

cead dràibhidh [k'ed drāivɪ] *m* driving licence.

cead telebhisein [k'ed televĭšεN'] *m* television licence.

ceàird [k'ārd'] *f* trade, craft.

cealg [k'aLag] *f* deceit; hypocrisy.

cealgach [k'aLagəch] *adj* deceitful; hypocritical.

cealgair [k'aLagεr'] *m* deceiver, cheat; hypocrite.

cealla [k'aLə] *f* (*biol*) cell.

ceanalta [k'anəLtə] *adj* pretty, comely.

ceangail [k'ε.al] *v* tie; join.

ceangal [k'ε.əL] *m* connection; bond.

ceann [k'auN] *m* head; end.

ceannach [k'aNəch], **ceannachd** [k'aNəchg] *m* purchase, buying, shopping.

ceannaich [k'aNɪch'] *v* buy.

ceannaich air dhàil [k'aNɪch' εr' ghāl] *v* buy on credit.

ceannaiche [k'aNɪch'ə] *m* purchaser; merchant.

ceannard [k'aNərd] *m* leader; chief.

ceann-cinnidh [k'auN k'iN'ɪ] *m* clan chief.

ceann daoraich [k'auN dūrɪch'] *m* hangover.

ceann-feadhna [k'auN fyoghnə] *m* clan chief.

ceann goirt [k'auN gɔršd'] *m* sore head, headache.

ceann-làidir [k'auN Lād'ɪr'] *adj* headstrong.

ceann-pholan [k'auN fɔLan] *m* tadpole.

ceann-rùisgte [k'auN Rūšg't'ɪ] *adj* bareheaded.

ceannsaich [k'auNsɪch'] *v* conquer; control; tame.

ceannsal [k'auNsəL] *m* authority.

ceannsalach [k'auNsəLəch] *adj* authoritative.

ceann-simid [k'auN šimɪd'] *m* tadpole.

ceann-suidhe [k'auN sui.ɪ] *m* president.

ceann-uidhe [k'auN ui.ɪ] *m* destination.

ceap¹ [k'εʰp] *m* block; lump.

ceap² [k'εʰp] *m* cap.

ceapach [k'εʰpəch] *m* (garden) plot, bed.

ceapaire [k'εʰpər'ə] *m* sandwich.

cearb [k'εrab] *f* rag; defect.

cearbach [k'εrabəch] *adj* clumsy; ragged.

cearc [k'εrk] *f* hen.

cearcall [k'εrkəL] *m* circle, ring.

cèard [k'ērd] *m* tinker, smith.

cèardach [k'ērdəch] *f* smithy.

cèard-airgid [k'ērd εr'εg'id'] *m* silversmith.

cèard-umha [k'ērd u.ə] *m* coppersmith.

cèàrn [k'ārn] *m* corner; district.

cèàrnach [k'ārnəch] *adj* square.

cèàrnag [k'ārnag] *f* square.

cèàrr [k'āR] *adj* wrong; left.

cèàrraiche [k'āRɪch'ə] *m* gambler.

ceart [k'aršt] *adj* correct; just; same.

ceartachadh [k'aršdəchəgh] *m* correction; marking.

ceartaich [k'aršdɪch'] *v* correct; put right.

ceartas [k'aršdəs] *m* justice.

ceart gu leòr [k'aršd gə L'ɔ̄r] *adv* right enough; okay!

ceart-mheadhan [k'aršd vian] *m* dead centre.

ceart-uilinn [k'aršd uliN'] *f* right angle.

ceasnachadh [k'esnəchəgh] *m* questioning; questionnaire.

ceasnaich [k'esnɪch'] *v* question; interrogate.

ceathach [k'ehəch] *m* fog; vapour.

ceathrad [k'erəd] *m* forty.

ceathramh [k'erəv] *adj* fourth. • *m* quarter.

ceathrar [k'erər] *m* foursome.

cèic [k'ɛ̄hk'] *f* cake.

cèidse [k'ɛ̄d'ši] *f* cage.

ceil (air) [k'el ɛr'] *v* hide, conceal (from).

cèile [k'ēlɪ] *m* spouse; counterpart.

cèilidh [k'ēlɪ] *m* visit; ceilidh.

ceileir [k'elɪr'] *v* sing sweetly, warble.

ceilp [k'elp] *f* kelp.

Ceilteach [k'elt'əch] *m/adj* Celt; Celtic.

ceimig [k'emɪg'] *f* chemical substance.

ceimigeachd [k'emɪgəchg] *f* chemistry.

ceimigear [k'emɪgɛr] *m* chemist.

cèin [k'ēn] *adj* foreign; faraway.

cèir [k'ēr'] *f* wax.

cèir-chluaise [k'ēr'chLuəši] *f* ear wax.

cèis [k'ēš] *f* frame; envelope.

cèiseag [k'ēšag] *f* cassette.

ceist [k'ešd'] *f* question; problem; point.

ceisteachan [k'ešd'əchən] *m* questionnaire.

ceistear [k'ešd'ɛr] *m* questioner; question master.

Cèitean [k'ēʰt'an] *m* (*with art*) **an Cèitean** [ən k'ēʰt'an] May.

ceithir [k'ehɪr'] *m/adj* four.

ceò [k'ɔ̄] *m* mist; haze; smoke.

ceòl [k'ɔ̄L] *m* music.

ceòladair [k'ɔ̄Lədər'] *m* musician.

ceòl beag [k'ɔ̄Lbeg] *m* light music for the pipes.

ceòlmhor [k'ɔ̄Lvər] *adj* musical; melodious.

ceòl mòr [k'ɔ̄Lmōr] *m* classical pipe music, pibroch.

ceòthach [k'ɔ̄hach] *adj* misty.

ceud [k'iəd] *m* hundred.

ceudameatair [k'iədəmɛtɛr'] *m* centimetre.

ceudamh [k'iədəv] *adj* hundredth.

ceud mìle fàilte! [k'iəd mīlɪ fālt'ɪ] *excl* a hundred thousand welcomes!

ceudna [k'iadnə] *adj* same.

ceud taing! [k'iəd taing'] *excl* many thanks! thanks a lot!

ceum [k'ēm] *m* step; pace; degree.

ceum air cheum [k'ēm ɛr' ch'ēm] *adv* step by step.

ceumnachadh [k'ēmnəchəgh] *m* graduation.

ceumnaich [k'ēmnɪch'] *v* graduate.

ceumnaiche [k'ēmnɪch'ə] *m* graduate.

ceus[1] [k'ēs] *v* crucify.

ceus[2] [k'ēs] *m* suitcase.

ceusadh [k'ēsəgh] *m* crucifixion.

cha, chan [cha] [chan] *part negating the clause or sentence*.

cha bheir mi hò-rò-gheallaidh air . . . [cha vɛr' mi hō rō gh'aLɪ ɛr'] I don't give a toss for . . .

cha b' urrainn dhomh gun . . . [cha buRıN' ghə gən] I couldn't help.

chaidh [chay] *past tense of v* **rach**.

chaidh agam air [chay agəm ɛr'] *v* I managed it.

cha mhòr [cha vōr] *adv* nearly.

cha mhòr nach [cha vōr nach] *conj* almost.

chan *see* **cha.** [chan]

chan fhada thuige! [chan ad huig'ı] it won't be long!

chan iongnadh e! [chaN' iənəch ɛ] no wonder!

cha leig thu leas . . . [cha L'eg' u les] *v* you don't need to.

chì [ch'ī] *future tense of v* **faic**.

cho [cho] *adv* so, as.

cho luath is . . . [cho Luəs] *conj* as soon as . . .

cho math sin [cho ma šin] *adv* that good, as good as that.

chuala [chuəLə] *past tense of v* **cluinn**.

chuca *see* **thuca.**

chugad *see* **thugad.**

chugaibh *see* **thugaibh.**

chugainn *see* **thugainn.**

chugam *see* **thugam.**

chuice *see* **thuice.**

chuige *see* **thuige.**

chun [chun] *prep* to, towards, up to.

chun an-seo [chun ə šə] *adv* up to now, so far.

chunnaic [chuNık'] *past tense of v* **faic**.

ciad [k'iad] *adj (with art)* **a' chiad** [ə ch'iad] the first.

ciad-fhuasgladh [k'iaduəsgləgh] *m* first aid.

ciall [k'iaL] *f* sense(s); meaning.

ciallach [k'iaLəch] *adj* sensible.

ciallaich [k'iaLıch'] *v* mean.

ciamar? [k'imər] *interrog adv* how?

cia mheud? [k'e viad] *interrog adv* how many? how much?

cian [k'ian] *adj* distant; long. • *m* distance; remoteness.

cianail [k'ianal] *adj* sad.

cianalach [k'ianaləch] *adj* homesick.

cianalas [k'ianaLəs] *m* sadness.

ciar [k'iər] *adj* dark; swarthy; dun.

ciatach [k'iətəch] *adj* pleasant; attractive.

cidhe [k'i.ı] *m* quay.

cidsin [k'id'šın] *m* kitchen.

cileagram [k'iləgram] *m* kilogram.

cilemeatair [k'iləmɛʰtɛr'] *m* kilometre.

cill [k'īL'] *f* cell; church; kirkyard.

cineal [k'inaL] *m* race; species.

cinn [k'īN'] *v* grow; multiply.

cinneadail [k'iN'ədal] *adj* clannish.

cinneadh [k'iN'əgh] *m* clan; people; surname.

cinneas [k'iN'əs] *m* growth.

cinne-daonna [k'iN'ı dūNə] *m (with art)* **an cinne-daonna** [ən k'iN'ı dūNə] mankind.

cinnt [k'īN'd'] *f* certainty.

cinnteach [k'īN'd'əch] *adj* certain; confident.

ciobair [k'ībɛr'] *m* shepherd.

cìoch [k'īəch] *f* breast.

cìochag [k'īəchag] *f* valve.

ciomach [k'iməch] *m* prisoner; detainee.

cion [k'in] *m* lack; desire.

cionta [k'ində] *m* guilt; guilty action.

ciontach [k'indəch] *adj* guilty. • *m* guilty person; offender.

ciontaich [k'indɪch'] v commit an offence.

ciora [k'irə] f pet sheep.

ciorram [k'iRəm] m disability, handicap.

ciorramach [k'iRəməch] adj disabled, handicapped. • m disabled person; (pl with art) **na ciorramaich** [nə k'iRəmɪch'] the disabled.

ciotach [k'iʰtəch] adj left-handed.

cipean [k'iʰpan] m stake; tether post.

cìr [k'īr'] v comb. • f comb; cud.

cìrean [k'īr'an] m (of hen, etc) comb, crest.

cìr-mheala [k'īr'vyaLə] f honeycomb.

cìs [k'īš] f tax; taxation.

cìs-chusbainn [k'īšchusbɪN'] f customs duty.

cìs-chinn [k'īšch'īN'] f poll tax.

cìs-oighreachd [k'īšoir'əchg] f inheritance tax.

ciste [k'išt'ɪ] f (furniture) chest.

ciste-chàir [k'išt'ɪchār'] f car boot.

ciste-laighe [k'išt'ɪLai.ɪ] f coffin.

ciste-urrais [k'išt'uRɪš] f trust fund.

ciùb [k'ūb] m cube.

ciùbach [k'ūbəch] adj cubic.

ciùbhran [k'ūran] m drizzle, shower.

ciudha [k'u.ə] f queue.

ciùin [k'ūN'] adj gentle; quiet; calm.

ciùineas [k'ūN'əs] m calm, calmness.

ciùinich [k'ūN'ɪch'] v quieten, calm down.

ciùraig [k'ūrɪg'] v (bacon, etc) cure.

ciùrr [k'ūR] v hurt; torture.

ciùrrte [k'ūRt'ɪ] adj hurt, injured.

clabar-snàimh [kLabər sNāiv] m flipper.

cill-mhanach [k'īL'vanəch] m cloister.

clach [kLach] v stone. • f stone; (fam) testicle.

clachach [kLachəch] adj stony.

clachair [kLachɛr'] m (stone-)mason.

clachan [kLachan] m village; kirktown; kirkyard.

clach-bhalg [kLachvaLag] f (toy, etc) rattle.

clach-chuimhneachan [kLachchuiN'əchan] f memorial, monument.

clach-ghràin [kLachghrāN'] f granite.

clach-mheallain [kLachvyaLɛN'] f hailstone.

clach na sùla [kLach nə sūLə] f eyeball.

clach uasal [kLach uəsəL] f precious stone.

cladach [kLadəch] m shore, beach.

cladh [kLogh] m kirkyard, cemetery.

cladhaich [kLo.ɪch'] v dig.

cladhaire [kLo.ər'ə] m coward.

cladhaireach [kLo.ər'əch] adj cowardly.

clag [kLag] m bell.

clagarsaich [kLagərsɪch'] f clinking; rattling.

clag-rabhaidh [kLagRavɪ] m alarm bell.

claidheamh [kLai.əv] m sword.

claidheamhair [kLai.əvɛr'] m swordsman.

claidheamh caol [kLai.əv kūL] m rapier.

claigeann [kLag'əN] m skull.

clàimhean [kLāivan] *m* latch.

clais [kLaš] *f* ditch; furrow.

claisneachd [kLašnəchg] *f* hearing.

clamhan [kLavan] *m* buzzard.

clann [kLauN] *f* children; clan.

clann-nighean [kLauN'i.an] *f* (*collective*) girls.

claoidh [kLuy] *v* exhaust; vex.

claoidhte [kLuit'ı] *adj* exhausted.

claon [kLūn] *v* incline; go astray; pervert. • *adj* awry; oblique; perverse.

claonadh [kLūnəgh] *m* slant, slope; squint; perversion.

clàr [kLār] *m* board; table; record.

clàraich [kLārıch'] *v* record.

clàr-amais [kLāramıš] *m* index.

clàr-aodainn [kLārūdıN'] *m* brow, forehead.

clàr-dùthcha [kLārdūchə] *m* map.

clàr-fhiacail [kLāriəhkıl] *f* incisor.

clàr-gnothaich [kLārgrɔ.ich'] *m* agenda.

clàr-innsidh [kLārīšı] *m* table of contents.

clàr-oideachais [kLārod'əchıš] *m* curriculum.

clàrsach [kLārsəch] *f* harp; Celtic harp, clarsach.

clàrsair [kLārsɛr'] *m* harper.

clàr-tìde [kLārt'īd'ı] *m* timetable.

clas [kLas] *m* class.

clasaigeach [kLasıgəch] *adj* classical.

cleachd [klachg] *v* use; accustom.

cleachdadh [klachgəgh] *m* habit; practice.

cleachte ri [klachtı r'i] *adj* accustomed to, used to.

cleas [kles] *m* feat; trick.

cleasachd [klesəchg] *f* conjuring; juggling.

cleasaiche [klesıchə] *m* actor; comic; conjurer.

cleas-chluich [kleschLuich'] *f* comic film/play.

clèir [klēr'] *f* clergy; Presbytery.

clèireach [klēr'əch] *m* clergyman; clerk. • *m/adj* Presbyterian.

clèireachail [klēr'əchal] *adj* clerical.

cleòc [klɔʰk] *m* cloak.

clì [klī] *adj* left.

cliabh [kliav] *m* pannier; creel; (*anat*) chest.

cliamhainn [kliə.ıN'] *m* son-in-law.

cliath [kliah] *v* (*agric*) harrow. • *f* grate, bars; harrow.

cliathach [kliahəch] *f* side, flank.

cliath-theine [kliahenı] *f* fire grate.

cliath-uinneig [kliauN'ɛg'] *f* window bars.

cliomaid [klīmıd'] *f* climate.

clis [kliš] *adj* nimble.

cliseachd [klišəchg] *f* nimbleness, agility.

clisg [klišg'] *v* start, jump; startle.

clisgeach [klišg'əch] *adj* jumpy, on edge; timid.

clisgeadh [klišg'əgh] *f* start, fright.

clisgear [klišg'ɛr] *m* exclamation.

clisg-phuing [klišg'fuing'] *f* exclamation mark.

cliù [klū] *m* fame; reputation.

cliùiteach [klūʰt'əch] *adj* famous, celebrated.

cliùthaich [klū.ich'] *v* praise.

clò¹ [kLɔ̄] *m* cloth; tweed.

clò² [kLɔ̄] *m* print; printing press.

clòbha [kLɔ̄və] *f* clove.

clobha [kLɔu.ə] *m* tongs.

clòbhar [kLɔ̄bər] *m* clover.

clobhsa [kLousə] *m* (*in tenement, etc*) close.

clò-bhuail [kLɔ̄vuəl] v print.

clò-bhuailte [kLɔ̄vuəlt'ɪ] adj printed.

clò-bhualadair [kLɔ̄vuəLədɛr'] m printer(s).

clò-bhualadh [kLɔ̄vuəLəgh] m printing; publication.

clò-chadal [kLɔ̄chadaL] m doze, dozing.

clochar [kLɔchər] f convent.

clogaid [kLɔgɪd'] f helmet.

clòimh [kLɔ̄y] f wool.

clòimhteachan [kLɔ̄it'əchan] m eiderdown.

Clò Mòr na Hearadh [kLɔ̄mōr nə hɛrəgh] m Harris Tweed.

closach [kLɔsəch] f carcase.

clòsaid [kLɔ̄sɪd'] f closet.

clò-sgrìobh [kLɔ̄sgrīv] v type.

clò-sgrìobhadair [kLɔ̄sgrīvədɛr'] m typewriter.

clò-sgrìobhadh [kLɔ̄sgrīvəgh] m typing; typescript.

clò-sgrìobhaiche [kLɔ̄sgrīvɪch'ə] m typist.

cluain [kLuaN'] f meadow, pasture.

cluaineas [kLuaN'əs] m retirement.

cluaran [kLuəran] m thistle.

cluas [kLuəs] f ear; handle.

cluasag [kLuəsag] f pillow.

cluas-fhàinne [kLuəsāN'ɪ] f earring.

club [kLub] m club.

clùd [kLūd] m rag; cloth.

cluich [kLuch] m play; game. • v play.

cluich-bùird [kLuch'būrd'] m board game.

cluicheadair [kluch'ədɛr'] m player; actor.

cluinn [kLuiN'] v hear.

cnag [krag] v crunch; bang, knock. • f bang, knock.

cnag-aodaich [kragūdɪch'] f clothes peg.

cnag-dealain [kragd'ɛLɛN'] f electric plug.

cnag na cùise [krag nə kūšɪ] f the crux of the matter.

cnàimh [krāiv] m bone.

cnàimh an droma [krāiv ən drɔmə] m the spine, the backbone.

cnàimheach [krāivəch] m skeleton.

cnàimhseag [krāivšag] f acne; blackhead.

cnàimh-slinnein [krāivšliN'ɛN'] f shoulder-blade.

cnàimh-uga [krāivugə] m collarbone.

cnàmh [krāv] v chew; digest.

cnàmhach [krāvəch] adj bony.

cnàmh a' chìr [krāv ə ch'īr'] v chew the cud.

cnap [kraʰp] m block; lump, knob.

cnapach [kraʰpəch] adj lumpy, nobbly.

cnap-starra [kraʰp sdaRə] m stumbling block.

cnatan [kraʰtan] m (often with art) cold, **tha an cnatan orm** [ha ən kraʰtan ɔrəm]I have a cold; **an cnatan mòr** [ən kraʰtan mōr] m influenza.

cnead [kr'ed] m groan.

cnèadaich [kr'iadɪch'] v caress; stroke.

cneutag [kr'iaʰtag] f small ball, puck.

cnò [krɔ̄] f nut.

cnoc [krɔʰk] m hill.

cnocach [krɔʰkəch] adj hilly.

cnocan [krɔʰkan] m hillock.

cnò-challtainn [krɔ̄chauLtɪN'] m hazelnut.

cnò-Fhrangach [krɔ̄rangəch] *m* walnut.

cnò-thalmhainn [krɔ̄haLavɪN'] *m* peanut.

cnuas [kruəs] *v* chew; ponder.

cnuimh-thalmhainn [kruivhaLavɪN'] *f* earthworm.

co- [kɔ] *prefix* co-.

cò? [kɔ̄] *interrog pron* who? which?

cò aca [kɔ̄ aʰkə] *conj* whether.

co-aimsireil [kɔ.ɛmɛšɪrɛl] *adj* contemporary.

cò air bith? [kɔ̄ ɛr' bi] *interrog pron* whoever?

co-dhalta [kɔghaLtə] *m* foster brother/sister

cò am fear? [kɔ̄ əm fɛr] which one?

co-aoiseach [kɔ.ūšəch] *m/adj* contemporary.

co-aontaich [kɔ.ūntɪch'] *v* agree.

cò às? [kɔ̄ as] *adv* where from?

cobhair [kɔ.ɪr'] *f* help; relief.

cobhair orm! [kɔ.ɪr' ɔrəm] *excl* help! help me!

cobhar [kɔ.ər] *m* foam.

co-bhuail [kɔvuəl] *v* collide.

còc [kɔ̄hk] *m* (*fuel*) coke.

còcaire [kɔ̄ʰkər'ə] *m* cook, chef.

còcaireachd [kɔ̄ʰkər'əchg] *f* cookery.

cochall [kɔchəL] *m* husk; hood.

co-cheangail [kɔch'e.al] *v* tie together; connect.

co-cheangailte [kɔch'e.alt'ɪ] *adj* linked together.

co-chomann [kɔchoməN] *m* commune; co-operative.

co-chòrd [kɔ chɔ̄rd] *v* agree mutually.

co-chothrom [kɔ choRəm] *m* balance, equilibrium.

co-chruinnich [kɔ chruiN'ɪch'] *v* assemble.

co-chruinneachadh[kɔchruiN'əchəgh] *m* assembly; collection.

còco [kɔ̄ʰkə] *m* cocoa.

co-dhèanta [kɔ gh'iantə] *adj* put together.

co-dhiù [kogh'ū] *conj* whether.

co-dhiù [kogh'ū] *adv* anyway; at least.

co-dhlùthaich [kɔ ghLū.ɪch'] *v* condense.

co-dhùin [kɔdhūN'] *v* conclude; end.

co-dhùnadh [kɔghūnəgh] *m* conclusion; end.

co-èigneachadh [kɔ.ēg'r'əchəgh] *m* compulsion.

co-èignich [kɔ.ēg'r'ɪch'] *v* compel.

cofaidh [kɔfi] *m* coffee.

co-fharpais [kɔ.arpɪš] *f* competition.

co-fharpaiseach [kɔ.arpɪšəch] *m* competitor.

co-fhlaitheas [kɔ.Laihəs] *m* commonwealth.

co-fhreagair [kɔ.regɪr'] *v* match; correspond.

co-fhulangach [kɔ.uLəngəch] *adj* sympathetic.

co-fhulangas [kɔ.uLəngəs] *m* sympathy.

cofhurtachd [kɔ.uršdəchg] *f* consolation; comfort.

cofhurtaich [kɔ.uršdɪch'] *v* comfort, console.

cofhurtail [kɔ.uršdal] *adj* comfortable.

cò fon ghrèin . . . ? [kɔ̄ fɔn ghrēn] who on earth . . . ?

cogadh [kɔgəgh] *m* war; warfare.

cogais [kɔgɪš] f conscience.

co-ghin [kɔgh'in] v mate, copulate.

co-ghineadh [kɔgh'inəgh] m mating, copulation.

co-ghnìomhair [kɔghriəvɛr'] m adverb.

coibhneas [koiN'əs] m kindness, kindliness.

coibhneil [koiN'ɛl] adj kind, kindly.

coidse [kɔd'ši] f coach.

còig [kõg'] m/adj five.

còigeamh [kõg'əv] adj fifth.

còignear [kõg'N'ɛr] m fivesome.

coigreach [koig'r'əch] m foreigner; stranger.

coileach [koL'əch] m (fowl) cock.

coileach-gaoithe [koL'əchgui.ı] m weathercock.

coilean [kɔlən] v accomplish; complete.

coileanta [kɔləndə] adj completed; perfect.

coilear [kɔlɛr] m collar.

coille [koL'ı] f wood.

coilleag [koL'ag] f cockle.

coillear [koL'ɛr] m forestry worker; woodcutter.

coille mhòr [koL'ı võr] f forest.

coimeas [koiməs] f comparison; like(s) of. • v compare, liken.

coimeasach [koiməsəch] adj comparable.

coimh- [kə] prefix co-.

coimheach [koi.əch] adj foreign; unfamiliar. • m foreigner; stranger.

coimhead [koi.əd] v watch; look.

coimhead air [koi.əd ɛr'] v look at.

coimhead ri [koi.əd r'i] v expect.

coimhearsnach [kɔi.əršnəch] m neighbour.

coimhearsnachd [kɔi.əršnəchg] f neighbourhood.

coimheatailt [kɔvɛtalt'] f alloy.

coimhlion [kɔlən] v accomplish; complete.

coimisean [kɔmišan] m commission.

coimpiutair [kɔmpyuʰtɛr'] m computer.

coineanach [kɔN'anəch] m rabbit.

còinneach [kõN'əch] f moss.

coinneal [koN'aL] f candle.

coinneamh [koN'əv] f meeting.

coinnich [koN'ıch'] v congregate.

coinnich ri [koN'ıch'] v meet.

coinnleir [koiN'L'ɛr'] m candlestick.

co-ionnan [kɔ.iuNan] adj identical, the same.

còir [kõr'] f obligation; right; justice. • adj decent; worthy; kindly.

coirbte [koribt'ı] adj corrupt.

coirce [kɔrk'ı] m oats.

coire[1] [kɔr'ı] f wrong; blame.

coire[2] [kɔr'ı] m kettle; cauldron; corrie.

coireach [kɔr'əch] adj guilty; responsible. • m guilty person; offender.

coirich [kɔr'ıch'] v blame.

còir-shlighe [kõr'li.ı] f right of way.

coiseachd [kɔšəchg] f walking.

coisich [kɔšich'] v walk.

coisiche [kɔšichə] m walker, pedestrian.

coisinn [kɔšiN'] v win; earn.

còisir [kõšir'] f choir.

coisrig [kɔšr'ıg'] v consecrate; devote.

coitcheann [kɔʰt'əN] adj common; communal; general, universal.

coithional [kɔhɛnaL] adj congregation.

coitich [kɔʰt'ıch'] v urge.

co-labhairt [kɔLavı'ršt'] f confer-
ence.

cola-breith [kɔLa br'eh] m birthday.

cola-deug [kɔLa d'ag] m fortnight.

colaiste [kɔLəšd'ı] f college.

colann [kɔLəN] f body.

colbh [kɔLɔv] m column.

Colla [kɔLə] m Coll.

Collach [kɔLəch] m/adj from Coll.

collaidh [kɔLı] adj sensual, carnal.

coltach [kɔLtəch] adj likely.

coltach ri [kɔLtəch r'i] prep like.

coltaich ri [kɔLtəch r'i] v compare
to.

coltas [kɔLəs] m appearance.

com [kɔum] m bosom, chest area.

coma [komə] adj indifferent; un-
concerned.

coma co-dhiubh [komə kogh'ū] adj
quite indifferent.

comain [komɛN'] f obligation.

coma leat! [komə laʰt] excl never
mind! don't worry!

comanachadh [komanəchəgh] m
Communion.

comanaich [komanıch'] v take
Communion.

comanaiche [komanıch'ı] m com-
municant.

comann [komaN] m association;
club, society.

comann eachdraidh [komaN ɛchdrı]
m history society.

comar [komər] f confluence.

comas [komas] m ability; faculty.

comasach [komasəch] adj able.

comasach air [komasəch ɛr'] capable of.

comas inntinn [komas īN'tıN'] m
mental ability.

comataidh [komətı] f committee.

combaist [kɔumbıšd'] f compass.

comh- [kɔ] prefix co-.

comhachag [ko.əchag] f barn-owl.

comhair [ko.ır'] f direction.

comhairle [ko.ərlı] f advice; council.

comhairleach [ko.ərləch] m adviser.

comhairlich [ko.ərlıch'] v advise.

comhairliche [ko.ərlıch'ə] m councillor.

comharrachadh [kɔhəRəchəgh] m
marking, correction.

comharradh [kɔhəRəgh] m mark;
sign; symbol.

comharradh-ceiste
[kɔhəRəghk'ešd'ı] m question
mark.

comharradh-rathaid
[kɔhəRəghRa.ıd'] m road sign.

comharradh-stiùiridh
[kɔhəRəghsd'ūr'ı] m landmark.

comharraich [kɔhəRıch'] v mark,
correct.

comhart [kɔ.əršd] m (of dog) bark.

comhartaich [kɔ.əršdıch'] v (of dog)
bark.

còmhdach [kōdəch] m cover, covering.

còmhdaich [kōdıch'] v cover.

còmhdaichte [kōdıch't'ə] adj covered.

còmhdhail [kō.al] f congress, con-
ference.

co-mheasgaich [kɔvisgıch'] v inter-
mix, mix; amalgate; mingle.

cò mheud? [kō viad] interrog adv
how much? how many?

còmhla¹ [kōlə] adv together.

còmhla² [kōlə] m/f door.

còmhlan [kōLan] m band; company.

còmhlan-ciùil [kōLank'ūl] *m* (*mus*) band, group.

còmhla ri [kōLə r'i] *prep* with, along with.

còmhnaich [kōnıch'] *v* live, dwell.

còmhnaidh [kōnı] *f* dwelling.

còmhnard [kōnard] *adj* level; smooth. • *m* plain; level ground.

còmhradh [kōradh] *m* conversation, talk.

còmhradh beag [kōragh beg] *m* chat.

còmhrag [kōrag] *f* combat; conflict.

còmhrag dithis [kōrag d'i.ıš] *f* duel.

còmhraiteach [kōrat'əch] *adj* talkative, chatty.

còmhstri [kōsdri] *f* strife; competition.

com-pàirtich [kompāršdıch'] *v* take part.

companach [kompanəch] *m* companion; pal.

companaidh [kompanı] *f* firm, company.

companas [kompanəs] *m* companionship.

comraich [komrıch'] *f* sanctuary.

còn [kōn] *m* cone.

conaire [konər'ə] *f* rosary.

conaltrach [konaltrəch] *adj* social; sociable.

conaltradh [konaltrəgh] *m* conversation; company.

conasg [konəsg] *m* gorse, whins.

constabal [konsdəbaL] *m* constable.

connadh [koNəgh] *m* fuel.

connlach [kouNLəch] *f* straw.

connrag [kouNrag] *f* consonant.

connsachail [kouNsəchal] *adj* quarrelsome; argumentative.

connsaich [kouNsıch] *v* argue, quarrel.

connspaid [kouNsbıd] *f* dispute, controversy; wrangling.

connspaideach [kouNsbıd'əch] *adj* disputatious; controversial.

conntraigh [kouNtray] *f* neap tide.

consal [konsaL] *m* consul.

consan [konsan] *m* consonant.

co-obrachadh [ko.obrəchəgh] *m* co-operation; co-operative.

co-obraich [ko.obrıch'] *v* co-operate.

co-ogha [ko.o.ə] *m* cousin.

co-oibriche [ko.obr'ıch'ə] *m* fellow worker.

cop [koʰp] *m* foam, froth.

copach [koʰpəch] *adj* frothy, foaming.

copag [koʰpag] *f* dock, docken.

cupan [kuʰpan] *m* cup.

copar [koʰpər] *m* copper.

co-phòitear [kofōʰt'ɛr] *m* drinking companion.

cor [kor] *m* state, condition.

còraichean daonna [kōrıch'ən dūNə] *fpl* human rights.

corcair [korkɛr'] *adj* purple.

corcais [korkıš] *f* cork.

còrd[1] [kōrd] *v* agree.

còrd[2] [kōrd] *m* cord.

còrdadh [kōrdəgh] *m* agreement, understanding.

còrd ri [kōrd r'i] *v* please.

còrn [kōrn] *m* drinking horn; corn.

Còrn [kōrn] *f* (*with art*) a' Chòrn [ə chōrn] Cornwall.

Còrnach [kōrnəch] *m/adj* Cornishman; Cornish.

corp [korp] *m* body; corpse.

corpailear [korpalɛr] *m* corporal.

corp-làidir [kɔrpLād'ır'] *adj* able-bodied.

corporra [kɔrpəRə] *adj* bodily, corporal.

còrr [kɔ̄R] *adj (number)* odd. • *m (with art)* **an còrr** [ən kɔ̄R] the rest, everything else; anything else.

corra [kɔRə] *adj* odd, occasional.

corrag [kɔRag] *f* finger.

corra-ghritheach [kɔRəghri.əch] *f* heron.

corran [kɔRan] *m* sickle.

còrr is [kɔ̄R is] *prep* more than.

còs [kɔ̄s] *m* hollow.

còsach [kɔ̄səch] *adj* hollow.

co-shamhlachd [kɔhauLəchg] *f* parable.

cosg [kɔsg] *v* cost; spend; waste. • *m* cost; waste.

cosgail [kɔsgal] *adj* costly.

cosgais [kɔsgıš] *f* cost.

cosgaisean siubhail [kɔsgıšən šu.al] *fpl* travel costs.

co-sheirm [kɔherim] *f* harmony.

co-shinte [kɔhīnt'ı] *adj* parallel.

cosnadh [kɔsnəgh] *m* earning; employment; work.

costa [kɔsdə] *m* coast.

còta [kɔ̄ʰtə] *m* coat.

còta-bàn [kɔ̄ʰtəbān] *m* petticoat.

còta-leapa [kɔ̄ʰtəL'ɛʰpə] *m* dressing gown, housecoat.

còta-mòr [kɔ̄ʰtəmōr] *m* overcoat.

cotan [kɔʰtan] *m* cotton.

cothrom [kɔRəm] *adj (number)* even. • *m* chance, opportunity; balance.

cothromach [kɔRəməch] *adj* fair; decent.

cothromaich [kɔRəmıch'] *v* weigh; balance.

cothrom na Fèinne [kɔRəm nə fēN'ı] *m* fair chance.

co-thuit [kɔhuʰt'] *v* coincide.

co-thuiteamas [kɔhuʰt'əməs] *m* coincidence.

càbhach [krāvəch] *adj* devout, pious.

cràdh [krāgh] *m* pain; anguish.

craiceann [kraʰk'əN] *m* skin.

càidh [krāy] *v* pain; torment.

cràidhteach [krāit'əch] *adj* grievous, painful.

càin [krāN'] *f* sow.

crann [krauN] *m* mast; plough; crane; bolt; *(with art)* **an Crann** [ən krauN] the Saltire, St Andrew's Cross; **an Crann-Ceusaidh** [ən krauNk'ēsı] Christ's Cross.

crannag [kraNag] *f* pulpit; milk churn; crannog.

crannchur [krauNchər] *m* drawing lots; fate.

crann-fiona [krauNfiənə] *m* vine.

crann-sgaoilidh [krauNsgūlı] *m* transmitter; TV mast.

crann-sneachda [krauNsN'ɛchgə] *m* snowplough.

crann-tarsainn [krauNtarsıN'] *m* crossbar.

craobh [krūv] *f* tree.

craol [krūL], *less common* **craobh-sgaoil** [krūvsgūl] *v* diffuse; broadcast.

craoladh [krūLəgh] *m* broadcasting.

craos [krūs] *m* maw; gluttony.

craosach [krūsəch] *adj* gluttonous.

craosaire [krūsər'ə] *m* glutton.

crasg [krasg] *f* crutch (for walking).

crosgan [krɔsgan] *m* starfish.

crath [krah] *v* shake, tremble; brandish.

creach [kr'ɛch] *v* plunder; ruin. • *f* ruination; plunder.

creachann [kr'ɛchən] *m* scallop.

crèadh [kr'ɛ̄] *f* clay.

crèadhadair [kr'ɛ̄.ədɛr'] *m* potter.

crèadhadaireachd [kr'ɛ̄.ədɛr'əchg] *f* pottery.

creag [kr'eg] *f* crag; hill.

creagach [kr'egəch] *adj* craggy.

creamh [kr'ɛv] *m* leek.

creapan [kr'ɛʰpan] *m* stool.

creathail [kr'ɛhal] *f* cradle.

creid [kr'ed'] *v* believe; think, consider.

creideamh [kr'ed'əv] *m* belief; trust; religion.

creideas [kr'ed'əs] *m* trust.

crèim [kr'ɛ̄m] *v* nibble.

crèis [kr'ɛ̄š] *f* grease.

crèiseach [kr'ɛ̄šəch] *adj* greasy.

creithleag [kr'ɛlag] *f* cleg, horsefly.

creud [kr'ɛ̄d] *f* creed.

creutair [kr'ɛ̄ʰtɛr'] *m* creature.

creutair bochd [kr'ɛ̄ʰtɛr' bəchg] *m* poor soul.

criathar [kr'iəhər] *m* sieve, riddle.

criathraich [kr'iəhrɪch'] *v* sieve, riddle.

crìdhe [kr'ī.ɪ] *m* heart; courage.

crìdhealas [kr'ī.əLəs] *m* heartiness; conviviality.

crìdheil [kr'ī.ɛl] *adj* hearty; jovial.

crìoch [kr'iəch] *f* end; boundary.

Crìochan [kr'iəchən] *fpl (with art)* **na Crìochan** [nə kr'iəchən] the Borders.

crìochnach [kr'iəchnəch] *adj* finite.

crìochnaich [kr'iəchnɪch'] *v* finish.

crìochnaichte [kr'iəchnɪch't'e] *adj* finished.

criomag [kr'imag] *f* bit; crumb; (*pl* **criomagan** [kr'imagən] bits and pieces, odds and ends.

crìon [kr'iən] *v* wither; dry up. • *adj* tiny; petty; withered.

crìoplach [kr'iʰpLəch] *m* cripple.

crios [kr'is] *m* belt.

Crìosdachd [kr'iəsdəchg] *f* Christendom.

Crìosdaidh [kr'iəsdɪ] *m* Christian.

Crìosdaidheachd [kr'iəsdɪ.əchg] Christianity.

Crìosdail [kr'iəsdal] *adj* Christian.

Crìosdalachd [kr'iəsdaləchg] Christian-ness.

criostal [kr'isdaL] *m* crystal.

crith [kr'i] *v* tremble, shiver. • trembling, shivering.

critheanach [kr'ihənəch] *adj* shaky; scary.

crith-thalmhainn [kr'ihaLavɪN'] earthquake.

crò [krɔ̄] *m* cattle pen, fold.

croch [krɔch] *v* hang.

crochadair [krɔchədɛr'] *m* hangman; hanger.

crochadh [krɔchəgh] *m* hanging.

crochte [krɔcht'ɪ] *adj* hung; hanged.

crodh [kro] *m* cattle, livestock.

crodh-bainne [krobaN'ɪ] *m* dairy cows.

crodh-dàra [krodārə] *m* breeding cattle.

crò-dhearg [krɔ̄gh'ɛrag] *adj* crimson.

cròg [krɔ̄g] *f* paw; fist.

cròic [krɔ̄iʰk'] *f* antler.

croich [krɔich'] *f* gallows. • *excl* **na croiche!** [nə kroich'ɪ] damned X! bloody X!

crois [krɔš] *f* cross; crucifix.

crois rathaid [krɔš] f crossroads.

croit[1] [krɔiʰt'] f croft.

croit[2] [krɔʰt'] f (on back) hump.

croitear [krɔʰt'ɛr] m crofter.

croitse [krɔʰt'ši] f (for walking) crutch.

crom [krɔum] v bend, incline; descend, climb down. • adj bent, crooked; curved.

cromag [krɔmag] f hook; comma; cromag, crook.

cromagan turrach [krɔmagən tuRach] fpl inverted commas.

crom air [krɔum ɛr'] v set to.

cromchasach [krɔumchasəch] adj bandy-legged.

cron [krɔn] m harm; fault.

cronaich [krɔnɩch'] v chide, scold.

cronail [krɔnal] adj harmful, hurtful.

crònan [krɔ̄nan] m humming; murmuring; buzzing; (stags) belling.

crò snàthaid [krɔ̄ sNāhɩd'] m eye of needle.

crosta [krɔsdə] adj cross; naughty.

crotach [krɔʰtach] adj humpbacked.

crotal [krɔ̄ʰtaL] m lichen.

cruach [kruach] v heap, stack. • f heap; rick.

cruachann [kruachəN] f hip.

cruadal [kruadaL] m hardship; hardihood.

cruadalach [kruadaLəch] adj difficult; hardy.

cruadhaich [kruəi.ɩch'] v harden; solidify.

cruaidh [kruəy] f steel. • adj hard; harsh; hardy.

cruaidh-chàs [kruəichās] m emergency; tight corner.

cruaidh-chrìdheach [kruaich'r'ī.əch] adj hard-hearted.

cruan [kruən] m enamel.

cruas [kruəs] m hardness; harshness; toughness.

crùb [krūb] v crouch; cringe; crawl.

crùbach [krūbəch] adj lame. • m lame person.

crùbag [krūbag] f crab.

crùban [krūban] m crouch, squat.

crùdh [krū] v (horse) shoe.

crudha [kru.ə] m horseshoe.

cruinn [kruiN'] adj round; accurate; assembled.

cruinne [kruiN'ɩ] f sphere, globe; (with art) **a' chruinne** [ə chruiN'ɩ] the earth, the globe.

cruinneachadh [kruiN'əchəgh] m gathering, assembly; collection.

cruinne-cè [kruiN'ɩk'ē] f (with art) **a' chruinne-cè** [ə chruiN'ɩk'ē] the world.

cruinn-eòlas [kruiN' yōLəs] m geography.

cruinnich [kruiN'ɩch'] v gather, assemble; (fruit, etc) pick.

cruinn-leum [kruiN'lēm] m standing jump.

crùisgean [krūšg'an] m oil lamp, cruisie.

cruit-chòrda [kruʰt'chōrdə] f harpsichord.

cruitheachd [krui.əchg] f creation; (with art) **a' Chruitheachd** [ə chrui.əchg] the world; the universe, Creation.

cruithear [krui.ɛr] m creator; (with art) **an Cruithear** [ən krui.ɛr] God, the Creator.

Cruithneach [kruiN'əch] m/adj Pict; Pictish.

cruithneachd [kruiN'əchg] *f* wheat.

crùn [krūn] *v* crown. • *m* crown.

crùnadh [krūnəgh] *m* crowning, coronation.

cruth [kruh] *m* shape; figure; appearance.

cruthaich [kruhıch'] *v* create.

cù [kū] *m* dog.

cuach [kuəch] *f* bowl, quaich.

cuagach [kuəgəch] *adj* bent; limping.

cuaille [kuəL'ı] *m* club, cudgel.

cuairt [kuəršt'] *f* circuit; stroll; trip.

cuan [kuan] *m* sea, ocean; **an Cuan Sgìth** [ən kuan sgī] the Little Minch; **an Cuan Siar** [ən kuan šiar] the Atlantic Ocean.

cuaraidh [kuarı] *m* quarry.

cuaran [kuəran] *m* sandal.

cuartaich [kuərštıch'] *v* surround; enclose.

cùbaid [kūbıd'] *f* pulpit.

cubhaidh [kuvı] *adj* fitting.

cùbhraidh [kūrı] *adj* sweet, fragrant.

cucair [kuʰkɛr'] *f* cooker.

cù-chaorach [kūchūrəch] *m* sheepdog.

cùdainn [kūdıN'] *f* large tub.

cudrom [kudrəm] *m* weight; importance; stress.

cudromach [kudrəməch] *adj* weighty, important.

cugallach [kugəLəch] *adj* unsteady; dodgy; unreliable.

cuibhle [kuilı] *f* wheel.

cuibhle-stiùiridh [kuilısd'ūr'ı] *f* steering wheel.

cuibhreach [kuirəch] *m* chain.

cuibhreann [kuirəN] *m* portion; allowance.

cuibhreann-ciorraim [kuirəNk'īRəm] *m* disability allowance.

cuibhrich [kuir'ıch] *v* chain.

cuibhrig [kuir'ıg'] *f* quilt, coverlet.

cuid [kud'] *f* share; part. • *pron* some.

cuid-aodaich [kud'ūdıch'] *f* clothes, clothing.

cuideachadh [kud'əchəgh] *m* help.

cuideachail [kud'əchal] *adj* helpful.

cuideachd[1] [kud'əchg] *f* company; companions.

cuideachd[2] [kud'əchg] *adv* too, also.

cuideachdail [kud'əchgal] *adj* sociable, fond of company.

cuideigin [kud'eg'ın] *f* someone, somebody.

cuide ri [kud'ı r'i] *prep* with, along with.

cuidhteag [kuiʰt'ag] *f* whiting.

cuidhteas [kuiʰt'əs] *m* receipt; riddance.

cuidich [kud'ıch'] *v* help, assist.

cuid oidhche [kud' oi.ch'ı] *f* night's lodging.

cùil [kūl] *f* corner, nook.

cuilbheart [kulivɛršt] *f* trick; stratagem.

cuilc [kulk] *f* reed; cane.

cùil-chumhang [kūlchu.əng] *f* tight corner, fix.

cuilc Innseanach [kulk īšəNəch] *f* bamboo.

cuileag [kulag] *f* fly, house-fly.

cuilean [kulan] *m* puppy; cub.

cuimhne [kuiN'ı] *f* memory; remembrance.

cuimhneachan [kuiN'əchan] *m* memorial; memorandum.

cuimhneachan-cogaidh [kuiN'əchankɒgı] *m* war memorial.

cuimhnich [kuiN'ıch'] *v* remember.

cuimir [kuimır'] *adj* succinct; neat; shapely.

Cuimreach [kumr'əch] *m/adj* Welshman; Welsh.

Cuimrigh [kumr'ı] *f* (*with art*) **a' Chuimrigh** [ə chumr'ı] Wales.

cuimsich [kuimšich'] *v* aim.

cuine? [kuN'ı] *interrog adv* when?

cuing [kuing'] *f* yoke; (*with art*) **a' chuing** [ə chuing'] *f* asthma.

cuinneag [kuiN'ag] *f* bucket; milking pail.

cuinnean [kuiN'an] *m* nostril.

cuip [kuiʰp] *v* whip. • *f* whip.

cuir [kur'] *v* put; send; (*seed, etc*) sow, plant.

cuir a dh'iarraidh [kur' əghiəRı] *v* send for.

cuir air [kur' ɛr'] *v* light, turn/switch on; put on, don.

cuir air an spàrr [kur' ɛr' ən spāR] *v* save; stow away.

cuir air an teine [kur' ɛr' ən t'enı] *v* light the fire.

cuir air ath latha [kur' ɛr' ən ah La.a] *v* defer, put off.

cuir air bhonn [kur' ɛr' vouN] *v* found, set up.

cuir air chois [kur' ɛr' choš] *v* found, set up.

cuir air dòigh [kur' ɛr' dōy] *v* organise; put right.

cuir air earalas [kur' ɛr' ɛraLəs] *v* forewarn, alert.

cuir air flod [kur' ɛr' fləd] *v* float; launch.

cuir air leth [kur' ɛr' L'eh] *v* put aside; save.

cuir air meidh [kur' ɛr' mey] *v* balance.

cuir air mheomhair [kur' ɛr' vyə.ır'] *v* commit to memory.

cuir air snàmh [kur' ɛr' sNāv] *v* inundate, flood.

cuir aithne air [kur' aN'ı ɛr'] *v* get to know.

cuir a-mach [kur' ə mach] *v* bring up, vomit.

cuir am bogadh [kur' əm bogagh] *v* steep.

cuir am breislich [kur' əm brešlıch'] *v* confuse, mix up.

cuir am fad [kur' əm fad] *v* lengthen, make longer.

cuir an cèill [kur' ən k'ēL'] *v* express, put into words.

cuir an clò [kur' ən kLō] *v* print; publish.

cuir an cràdh [kur' ən krāgh] *v* torture.

cuir an eanchainn à [kur' əN' ɛnachıN' a] *v* brain.

cuir an geall gu [kur' ən g'yauL gə] *v* bet that.

cuir an òrdugh [kur' ən ōrdu] *v* put in order.

cuir an sàs [kur' ən sās] *v* capture; arrest.

cuir an suarachas [kur' ən suərəchəs] *v* belittle, disparage.

cuir an tairgse [kur' ən tɛrig'ši] *v* make available.

cuir an teagamh [kur' ən t'ɛgəv] *v* cast doubt upon.

cuir às an teine [kur' as ən t'enı] *v* put the fire out.

cuir às do [kur' as də] *v* abolish; kill.

cuir às mo leth ... [kur' as mə le] *v* accuse me of. ...

cuir bacadh air [kur' baʰkəgh ɛr'] *v* obstruct; prevent.

cuir bun-os-cionn [kur' bunəsk'ūN] v upend, overturn.

cuir bus air [kur' bus ɛr'] v grimace, pout.

cuir cabhag air [kur' kafag ɛr'] v rush, hurry.

cuir car de [kur' kar d'e] v move.

cuir ceart [kur' k'aršd] v correct, put right.

cuir cèilidh air [kur' k'ēlɪ ɛr'] v go to see, visit.

cuir cleas air [kur' kles ɛr'] v play a trick/joke on.

cuir clisgeadh air [kur' klišg'əgh ɛr'] v startle.

cuir coire air [kur' kor'ɪ ɛr'] v blame, lay blame on.

cuir cruinn [kur' kruiN'] v toss coin.

cuir crìoch air [kur' krīch' ɛr'] v complete, finish.

cuir dàil air [kur' dāl ɛr'] v delay.

cuir dath air [kur' dah ɛr'] v colour.

cuir dheth [kur' gh'eh] v turn/switch off; doff, take off; talk away, jabber on.

cuir do thaic orm/rium [kur' də haihk' ərəm/r'ium] v lean on me; depend on me.

cuir dragh air [kur' drogh ɛr'] v worry; bother, trouble.

cuireadh [kur'əgh] m invitation.

cuir eagal air [kur' egal ɛr'] v frighten.

cuir earbsa ann an [kur' ɛrabsə auN ən] v put trust in, rely on.

cuir eòlas air [kur' yōLəs ɛr'] v get to know.

cuir fàilte air [kur' fālt'ɪ ɛr'] v welcome.

cuir fios do [kur' fis də] v let know, inform.

cuir fodha [kur' fo.ə] v sink, scuttle.

cuir fon choill [kur' fən choL'] v outlaw.

cuir geall [kur' gyauL] v place a bet.

cuir gruaim air [kur' gruaim] v frown, scowl.

cuir gu feum [kur' gə fēm] v use, utilise.

cuir impidh air [kur' īmpɪ ɛr'] v persuade, urge.

cuir iongantas air [kur' iəndəs ɛr'] v amaze, astound.

cuir luach air [kur' Luach ɛr'] v value; evaluate.

cuirm [kurim] f feast, banquet.

cuir ma sgaoil [kur' mə sgūl] v set free.

cuirm-bhainnse [kurimvaiN'šɪ] f wedding reception.

cuirm-chnuic [kurimchruk'] f picnic.

cuirmeach [kuriməch] adj festive.

cuir meal do naidheachd air [kur' myaL də nɛ.əchg ɛr'] v congratulate.

cuir mo chùl ri [kur' mə chūL r'i] v turn my back on.

cuir mùig air [kur' mūig' ɛr'] v frown, scowl.

cuir oillt air [kur' oiL't' ɛr'] v terrify; horrify.

cuir rian air [kur' Rian ɛr'] v put in order, organise.

cuir romham [kur' Rɔ.əm] v make up my mind, resolve (to).

cuir smùid [kur' smūd'] v smoke, emit smoke.

cuir seachad [kur' šachəd] v pass, spend.

cuir sneachd [kur' šN'ɛchg] v snow.

cuir stad air [kur' sdad ɛr'] v put a stop/end to.

cùirt [kūršd'] f court.

cùirtean [kūršd'an] m curtain.

cùirteil [kūršd'ɛl] adj courteous; courtly.

cuir thairis [kur' har'ıš] v overflow.

cuir thar a chèile [kur' har əch'ēlı] v set at loggerheads.

cuir timcheall [kur' t'imich'əL] v send/pass round.

cùirt-lagha [kūršt'Loghə] f law court.

cuir urram air [kur' uRəm ɛr'] v honour.

cùis [kūš] f matter, business; (pl) **cùisean** [kūšən] things, matters.

cùis-bheachd [kūšvyachg] f abstraction, abstract idea.

cùisear [kūšɛr] m (gram) subject.

cùis-ghràin [kūšghrāN'] f abomination.

cùis-lagha [kūšLoghə] f lawsuit.

cuisle [kušlı] f vein; pipe.

cuislean [kušlən] m flute.

cuisle-chinn [kušlıch'iN'] f aorta.

cuisle-chiùil [kušlıch'ūl] f flute.

cuisle-mhòr [kušlıvōr] f artery.

cùl [kūL] m nape; hair of head; back.

cùlaibh [kūLıv] m back part. • adv **cùlaibh air beulaibh** [kūLıv ɛr' biaLıv] back to front; vice versa.

culaidh [kuLı] f garment; suit of clothes; habit, object.

culaidh-choimheach [kuLıchɔi.əch] f fancy dress.

culaidh-fharmaid [kuLıaramıd'] f object of envy.

cularan [kuLəran] m cucumber.

cùl-chàin [kūLchāN'] v slander.

cùl-chàineadh [kūLchāN'əgh] m slander, backbiting.

cullach [kuLəch] m boar.

cùl-mhùtaire [kūLvūʰtər'ə] m smuggler.

cùl-mhùtaireachd [kūLvūʰtər'əchg] f smuggling.

cùl na h-amhaich [kūL nə havıch'] f the back of the neck.

cùl na làimhe [kūL nə Lāivı] m the back of the hand.

cultar [kuLtər] m culture.

cum [kum] v shape, form.

cùm [kūm] v keep.

cumadh [kuməgh] m shape, form.

cùm air [kūm ɛr'] v continue, go on. • excl **cùm ort!** [kūm ɔršt] keep at it! on you go!

cùm air ais [kūm ɛr' ɛš] v hold back, delay.

cùm a-mach [kūm əmach] v assert, claim.

cuman [kuman] m bucket; milking pail.

cumanta [kumandə] adj common, ordinary.

cumantas [kumandəs] m usualness, normality.

cùm às an làthair [kūm as ən Lāhır'] v keep away; keep out of sight.

cùm caismeachd ri [kūm kašməchg r'i] v keep time to.

cùm faire [kūm far'ı] v keep watch/ guard.

cumha¹ [ku.ə] f lament, elegy.

cumha² [ku.ə] m stipulation, condition.

cumhach [ku.əch] adj conditional.

cumhachd [ku.əchg] m power; might; (electric) power.

cumhachdach [ku.əchgəch] adj powerful; mighty.

cumhachd tuinne [ku.əchg tuiN'ı] m wave power.

cumhang [ku.əng] *adj* narrow.

cùmhnant [kūnənd] *m* covenant; contract.

cùm ris! [kūm r'iš] *excl* stick at it! keep it up!

cùm smachd air [kūm smachg ɛr'] *v* keep control of.

cùm suas [kūm suəs] *v* maintain, support.

cùm sùil air [kūm sūl ɛr'] *v* keep an eye on.

cùm taic ri [kūm taiʰk' r'i] *v* support.

cùm taobh ri [kūm tūv r'i] *v* side with, favour.

cunbhalach [kunuvaLəch] *adj* even, regular; steady.

cungaidh [kungɪ] *f* materials; ingredients.

cungaidh-leighis [kungɪ le.ɪš] *f* medicine, drug.

cunnart [kuNəršd] *m* danger, risk.

cunnartach [kuNəršdəch] *adj* dangerous, risky.

cùnnradh [kūNrəgh] *m* contract; deal.

cùnnt [kūNd] *v* count.

cùnntas [kūNdəs] *m* counting; (*finance*) account; narration; score.

cùnntasachd [kūNdəsəchg] *f* accountancy.

cùnntasair [kūNdəsɛr'] *m* accountant.

cuntair [kundɪr'] *m* (*shop, etc*) counter.

cupa [kuʰpə] *m* cup.

cuplachadh [kuʰpLəchəgh] *m* copulation, mating.

cuplaich [kuʰpLɪch'] *v* couple, copulate.

cùpon [kūpɔn] *m* coupon, voucher.

cur [kur] *m* placing; sending.

currach [kuRəch] *f* coracle.

canù [kanū] *f* canoe.

curaidh [kurɪ] *m* hero.

cùram [kūrəm] *m* care; responsibility.

cùramach [kūrəməch] *adj* careful; prone to worry.

cur na mara [kur nə marə] *m* seasickness.

curran [kuRan] *m* carrot.

curracag [kuRəʰkag] *f* lapwing.

cùrsa [kūrsə] *m* course.

cur-seachad [kuršachəd] *m* hobby, pastime.

cùrtair [kuršdɪr'] *m* curtain.

cus [kus] *m* excess, too much.

cusbainn [kusbɪN'] *f* (*tax*) customs.

cusp [kusp] *f* chilblain.

cuspair [kuspɛr'] *m* subject, topic; (*gram*) object.

cut [kuʰt] *v* gut.

cutair [kuʰtɛr'] *m* fish-gutter.

cuthach [ku.əch] *m* madness; rage.

cuthag [ku.ag] *f* cuckoo.

D

dà [dā] *n/adj* two.

dachaigh [dachɪ] *f* home.

dà chànanach [dā chānanəch] *adj* bilingual.

dad [dad] *f* thing, anything.

dadaidh [dadɪ] *m* dad, daddy.

dadam [dadəm] *m* atom; tiny piece.

dà dheug [dā riag] *adj* twelve.

dad ort! [dad ɔršt] *excl* never mind! don't worry!

dag [dag] *m* pistol.

dail [dal] *f* meadow; dale.

dàil [dāl] *f* delay.

dàimh [dāiv] *f* relationship, ties.

dàimheach [dāivəch] *adj* relative.

daingeann [daing'əN] *adj* firm, solid.

daingneach [daing'anəch] *f* fort; stronghold.

daingnich [daing'anɪch'] *v* fortify; consolidate; confirm.

dàir [dār'] *m* rutting, heat.

dall [dauL] *v* blind. • *adj* blind. • *m* blind man.

dàmais [dāmɪš] *f* draughts.

damh [dav] *m* stag.

dàmhair [dāvɪr'] *f* rutting; (*with art*) **an Dàmhair** [ən dāvɪr'] October.

damhan-allaidh [davanaLɪ] *m* spider.

dàn[1] [dān] *m* fate, destiny.

dàn[2] [dān] *m* poem; song.

dàna [dānə] *adj* daring; impudent; arrogant.

dànachd [dānəchg] *f* poetry, verse.

danns [dauNs] *v* dance.

dannsa [dauNsə] *m* dance.

dannsadh [dauNsəgh] *m* dancing.

dannsair [dauNsɛr'] *m* dancer.

dàn spioradail [dān spirədal] *m* hymn.

daoimean [dūman] *m* diamond.

daoine [dūN'ɪ] *mpl* people; kinsfolk.

daoine mòra [dūN'ɪ mōrə] *mpl* big shots, bigwigs.

daoine-sìth [dūN'ɪšī] *mpl* fairyfolk.

daolag [dūLag] *f* beetle.

daolag-bhreac [dūLagvrɛhk] *f* ladybird.

daonna [dūNə] *adj* human.

daonnan [dūNan] *adv* always, constantly.

daor [dūr] *adj* dear, expensive.

daorach [dūrəch] *f* drunkenness; spree.

daorachail [dūrəchal] *adj* intoxicating.

daorsa [darsə] *f* captivity.

darach [darəch] *m* oak.

dàrna deug [dārnə d'iag] *adj* twelfth.

dàrna [dārnə] *adj* second.

dà-sheaghach [dā hoghəch] *adj* ambiguous.

dàta [dāʰtə] *m* data.

dath [da] *v* colour; dye. • *m* colour; dye.

dath-bhacadh [da vaʰkəgh] *m* colour bar.

dath-dhall [da ghauL] *adj* colour-blind.

dathte [daht'ɪ] *adj* coloured; dyed.

dà uair [dā uər'] *adv* twice.

de [d'e] *prep* of; from; made of.

dè [d'ē] *pron* what, what?

doirbh [doriv] *adj* hard, difficult.

deachd [d'achg] *v* dictate.

deachdadh [d'achgəgh] *m* dictation.

deachdaire [d'achgər'ə] *m* dictator.

deagh [d'ō] *adj* good. • *adv* well.

deagh bheusan [d'ō vēsən] *f* morals.

deagh chrìdheach [d'ō ch'ī.əch] *adj* good-hearted.

deagh thoil [d'ō hɔl] *f* good will.

dealachadh [d'ɛLəchəgh] *m* parting.

dealachadh-pòsaidh [d'ɛLəchəghpōsı] *m* divorce.

dealaich [d'ɛLıch] *v* part; separate; (*elec*) insulate.

dealan [d'ɛLan] *m* electricity.

dealanach [d'ɛLanəch] *m* lightning.

dealanaich [d'ɛLanıch] *v* electrify.

dealanair [d'ɛLanɛr'] *m* electrician.

dealan-dè [d'ɛLan ə'dē] *m* butterfly.

dealasach [d'ɛLəsəch] *adj* eager, zealous.

dealbh [d'ɛLav] *m* picture; painting; shape. • *v* picture; design; construct.

dealbh-chluich [d'ɛLavchLuch'] *m* play.

dealbh-chumadh [d'ɛLavchuməgh] *m* diagram.

dealbh-èibhinn [d'ɛLavēvıN'] *m* cartoon.

dealg [d'ɛLag] *f* prickle, thorn; pin.

deàlrach [d'āLrəch] *adj* shining, shiny.

deàlraich [d'āLrıch'] *v* shine, flash, glitter.

dealt [d'ɛLt] *m* dew.

dè am fonn? [d'ēm fɔuN] (*fam*) how are you?

deamhais [d'e.ıš] *m* shears.

deamhan [d'ɛ.an] *m* demon.

dèan [d'ian] *v* do; make.

dèan a' chùis [d'ian ə chūš] *v* suffice, do the job/trick.

dèan a' chùis air [d'ian ə chūš ɛr'] *v* manage; defeat.

dèanadach [d'ianədach] *adj* industrious, active.

dèan aoradh [d'ian ūrəgh] *v* worship.

dèan altachadh [d'ian aLtəchəgh] *v* say grace.

dèan an gnothach [d'ian ən gro.əch] *v* be just the job, do the trick.

dèan bàidh do [d'ian bāy dɔ] *v* do a favour for.

dèan beic [d'ian behk'] *v* curtsey.

dèan braoisg [d'ian brūšg'] *v* grin; grimace.

dèan breug [d'ian briag] *v* lie, tell a lie.

dèan bruadar [d'ian bruədər] *v* dream.

dèan cabhag [d'ian kafag] *v* hurry, make haste.

dèan cadal [d'ian kadəL] *v* sleep.

dèan casad [d'ian kasəd] *v* cough.

dèan casaid air [d'ian kasıd' ɛr'] *v* accuse; make a complaint against.

dèan cnead [d'ian kred] *v* groan.

dèan coimeas eadar [d'ian kɔıməs edər] *v* compare.

dèan còmhradh [d'ian kōrəgh] *v* talk, converse.

dèan cron air [d'ian krɔn ɛr'] *v* harm, injure.

dèan crùban [d'ian krūban] *v* crouch, squat.

dè an dòigh? [d'ē ən dōy] *(fam)* how're you doing?.

dèan dragh [d'ian drogh] *v* worry oneself.

dèan dragh do [d'ian drogh də] *v* cause worry to.

dèan dùrdail [d'ian dūrdal] *v* coo.

dèan faire [d'ian far'ı] *v* be on guard.

dèan faite-gàire [d'ian faʰt'ıgār'ı] *v* smile.

dèan fanaid air [d'ian fanıd' ɛr'] *v* mock, ridicule.

dèan fead [d'ian fed] *v* whistle.

dèan feum [d'ian fēm] *v* come in handy.

dèan feum do [d'ian fēm də] *v* do good to; be useful to.

dèan foill air [d'ian foiL' ɛr'] *v* cheat.

dèan gàirdeachas [d'ian gārd'əchəs] *v* rejoice.

dèan gàire [d'ian gār'ı] *v* laugh.

dèan gràgail [d'ian grāgal] *v* caw, croak.

dèan imrich [d'ian imir'ıch'] *v* move house.

dèan iolach [d'ian iLəch] *v* shout.

dèan iomradh air [d'ian imərəgh ɛr'] *v* mention.

dèan malairt [d'ian maLəršt'] *v* trade, do business.

dèan mèirle [d'ian mērlı] *v* steal.

dèan miodal (do) [d'ian midal də] *v* flatter, fawn (on).

dèan mo dhìcheall [d'ian mə gh'īch'əL] *v* do my utmost.

dèan mùn [d'ian mūn] *v* urinate.

deanntag [d'auNdag] *f* nettle.

dèan oilbheum (do) [d'ian ɔlvēm də] *v* give offence (to).

dè rud? [d'ē rud] *(fam)* what?

dèan sèisd air [d'ian šēšd' ɛr'] *v* besiege.

dèan sgairt [d'ian sgaršd'] *v* yell.

dèan sodal do [d'ian sɔdal də] *v* fawn on, butter up.

dèan sreothart [d'ian sdrɔhəršd] *v* sneeze.

dèan stad [d'ian sdad] *v* stop, call a halt.

dèan sùgradh [d'ian sūgrəgh] *v* make merry, sport.

dèan suidhe! [d'ian sui.ı] *excl* sit down! take a seat!

dèan sùil bheag ri [d'ian sūl veg r'i] *v* wink at.

dèan suiridhe ri [d'ian sur'ı.ə r'i] *v* court.

dèan tàir air [d'ian tār' ɛr'] *v* despise, disparage.

dèan tarcais air [d'ian tarkıš ɛr'] *v* despise.

dèan ulfhart [d'ian uLəršt] *v* howl.

dèan ùrnaigh ri [d'ian ūrnı] *v* pray to.

dearbh [d'ɛrav] *adj* same. • *v* prove; test.

dearbhadh [d'ɛravəgh] *m* proof; test, trial.

dearc [d'ɛrk] *f* berry.

dearcag [d'ɛrkag] *f* little berry.

dearg [d'ɛrag] *adj* red; *(fam)* utter, complete.

deargann [d'ɛragəN] *f* flea.

deargaich [d'ɛragıch'] *v* redden.

dearmad [d'ɛraməd] *m* neglect, negligence; omission.

dearmadach [d'ɛramədəch] *adj* negligent; neglectful.

dearmaid [d'ɛramıd'] v omit, neglect (to do something).

deàrrsaich [d'āRsıch'] v shine.

deas [d'es] f south. • adj south; right(-hand); ready; finished; active.

deasachadh [d'esəchəgh] m preparation; editing.

deasaich [d'esıch'] v prepare; edit.

deasaich biadh [d'esıch' bıəgh] v cook.

deasaichear [d'esıch'ɛr] m editor.

deasbad [d'esbəd] m discussion, debate.

deasg [d'esg] m desk.

deas-ghnàth [d'es ghrā] m ceremony.

dè a tha a dhìth air? [d'ē ha ə gh'ī ɛr'] what does he require?

dè tha dol? [d'ē ha dɔL] excl (fam) what's doing?

dè tha thu ris? [d'ē ha u r'iš] excl what are you up to?

de chois [d'e chɔš] adv on foot.

dè do bheachd? [d'ē də vyachg] what do you think?

dè do chor? [d'ē də chōr] excl (fam) how're you doing?

dè fon ghrèin? [d'ē fɔn ghr'ēn] excl what on earth?

deich [d'ech'] n/adj ten.

deichead [d'ech'əd] m decade.

deicheamh [d'ech'əv] adj tenth.

deichnear [d'eich'nɛr] m ten (people).

dèideadh [d'ēd'ədh] m (with art) an dèideadh [ən d'ēd'əgh] toothache.

dèideag [d'ēd'ag] f pebble; toy.

dèidheil air [d'ē.ɛl ɛr'] adj fond of, keen on.

deigh [dey] f ice.

dèile [d'ēlı] f board, plank.

dèilig ri [d'ēlıg' r'i] v deal with, handle.

deimhinne [d'evıN'ə] adj sure, certain.

dèine [d'ēnı] f eagerness; fervour.

dèirc [d'ɛrk'] f charity, alms.

dèirceach [d'ɛrk'əch] m beggar. • adj charitable.

deireadh [d'erədh] m end.

deireannach [d'erəNəch] adj last, final.

deisciobal [d'ešg'əbaL] m disciple.

deise [d'ešı] f suit (of clothes).

deiseil [d'ešɛl] adj ready; finished; clockwise; sunwise; handy.

dè na tha e? [dē nə ha ɛ] how much is it?

deò [d'ɔ] f (with art) an deò [ən d'ɔ] the breath of life.

deoch [d'ɔch] f drink; booze.

deoch-làidir [d'ɔchLād'ır'] f alcohol; alcoholic drink.

deoch an dorais [d'ɔch ən dɔrıš] f parting drink.

deoch-slàinte [d'ɔchsLāN'd'ı] f (drink) toast.

deoghail [d'ɔ.al] v suck; absorb.

deòin [d'ɔN'] f consent; willingness.

deònach [d'ɔNəch] adj willing.

deònach air [d'ɔNəch ɛr'] prepared to.

dè a tha a' dol? [d'ē ha ə dɔL] what's going on?

deuchainn [d'iachıN'] f examination, test; trying time.

deuchainn-lann [d'iachıNLəN] m laboratory.

deudach [d'ēdəch] adj dental.

deug [diag] suffix -teen.

deugaire [diagər'ə] m teenager.

deur [d'iar] m tear, teardrop.

dh'[gh], dha [gha] (*for* do) *prep* to (before vowels and *fh*).

dhà [ghā] *prep pron* to him; for him; to it; for it (*m*).

dhachaigh [ghachɪ] *adv* home(wards).

dhaibh [ghaiv] *prep pron* to them; for them.

dheth[1] [gh'eh] *adv* off.

dheth[2] [gh'eh] *prep pron* of him; off him; of it; off it (*m*).

dhì [gh'ī] *prep pron* of her; off her; of it; off it (*f*).

dhibh [gh'iv] *prep pron* of you; off you (*pl*).

dhinn [gh'iN'] *prep pron* of us; off us.

dhiom [gh'iəm] *prep pron* of me; off me.

dhiot [gh'iəʰt] *prep pron* of you; off you (*sing*).

dhith [gh'ih] *prep pron* to her; for her; to it; for it (*f*).

dhiubh [gh'u] *prep pron* of them; off them.

dhomh [ghə] *prep pron* to me; for me.

dhuibh [ghuiv] *prep pron* to you; for you (*pl*).

dhuine! dhuine! [ghuN'ɪ ghuN'ɪ] *excl* oh dear! oh dear!

dhuinn [ghuiN'] *prep pron* to us; for us.

dhut [ghuʰt] *prep pron* to you; for you (*sing*).

dia [diə] *m* god.

diabhal [d'iəvəL] *m* devil.

diabhlaidh [d'iəvLɪ] *adj* devilish, fiendish.

diadhachd [d'iəghəchg] *f* godhead; godliness; theology.

diadhaidh [d'iəghɪ] *adj* pious, godly.

dìollaid [d'iəLɪd'] *f* saddle.

dian [d'iən] *adj* eager; fierce; intense.

dian-ruith [d'iənruih] *f* headlong rush.

DiarDaoin [d'iəršdūN'] *m* Thursday.

dias [d'iəs] *f* ear of corn.

dibhearsan [d'ivɛršan] *m* fun; entertainment.

dìblidh [d'ïblɪ] *adj* abject.

dìcheall [d'ïch'əL] *m* diligence, application.

dìcheallach [d'ïch'əLəch] *adj* diligent; hardworking.

dì-cheannaich [d'ïch'aNɪch'] *v* behead.

DiCiadain [d'ɪk'iədɛN'] *m* Wednesday.

DiDòmhnaich [d'ɪdōnɪch'] *m* Sunday.

dìg [d'īg'] *f* ditch.

DihAoine [d'ɪhūN'ɪ] *m* Friday.

dìle [d'īlɪ] *f* heavy rain; flood.

dìleab [d'īləb] *f* legacy.

dìleas [d'īləs] *adj* faithful, trusty.

dìle bhàthte [d'īlɪ vāʰt'ɪ] *f* downpour.

DiLuain [d'ɪLuəN'] *m* Monday.

DiMàirt [d'ɪmāršt'] *m* Tuesday.

dìmeas [d'īmɛs] *m* disrespect; contempt.

dinn [d'īN'] *v* stuff, cram.

dinnear [d'īN'ɛr] *f* dinner.

dìobair [d'ïbɪr'] *v* desert, abandon.

dìobhair [d'ïvɪr'] *v* vomit, sick up.

dìochuimhne [d'iəchənɪ] *f* forgetfulness; oblivion.

dìochuimhneach [d'iəchənəch] *adj* forgetful.

dìochuimhnich [d'iəchənɪch'] *v* forget.

diofar [d'ifər] *f* difference; importance.

diofarach [d'ifərəch] *adj* different.

diogail [d'igal] *v* tickle.

diogalach [d'igaLəch] *adj* ticklish.

dìoghail [d'ĩ.al] *v* repay; take revenge.

dìoghaltas [d'ĩ.aLtəs] *m* revenge.

dealas [d'aLəs] *m* zeal; enthusiasm.

dìolain [d'iəLɛN'] *adj* bastard, illegitimate.

diomb [d'umb] *m* indignation; displeasure.

diombach [d'umbəch] *adj* out of sorts; indignant.

dìombuan [d'iəmbuən] *adj* transient, fleeting.

dìomhain [d'iəvɛN'] *adj* vain; idle.

dìomhair [d'iəvɛr'] *adj* secret.

dìomhanas [d'iəvənəs] *m* vanity, futility.

dìon [d'iən] *v* protect, shelter. • *m* protection, shelter.

dìonach [d'iənəch] *adj* sheltering; safe; wind and watertight.

dìorrasach [d'iəRəsəch] *adj* keen; tenacious.

dìosail [d'iəsal] *m* diesel.

dìosgail [d'iəsgal] *f* creaking; crunching.

dìosgan [d'iəsgan] *m* grating; squeaking.

diosgo [disgɔ] *m* disco.

dìreach [d'ĩr'əch] *adj* straight; upright; just.

dìreach! [d'ir'əch] *excl* quite!, just so!, exactly!

dìreadh [d'ĩr'əgh] *m* ascent; climbing.

dìrich[1] [d'ĩr'ich'] *v* straighten.

dìrich[2] [d'ĩr'ich'] *v* climb.

DiSathairne [d'ısahərnı] *m* Saturday.

dìsne [d'ĩšnı] *m* dice.

dìt [d'ĩht'] *v* condemn, sentence.

dìteadh [d'ĩht'əgh] *m* condemnation; sentence.

dìth [d'ĩ] *m* lack, want.

dìthean [d'ĩhan] *m* flower.

dithis [d'i.ıš] *f* two, twosome, pair.

dìthreabh [d'ĩrəv] *f* desert, wilderness.

diùc [d'ũhk] *m* duke.

diùid [d'ũd'] *adj* shy, timid.

diùlt [d'ũLt] *v* refuse; disown.

diù nan . . . [d'ũ nən/nəN/nəN'] the worst of . . .

Diùra [d'ũrə] *f* Jura.

Diùrach [d'ũrəch] *m/adj* from Jura.

dleasdanas [dlesdənəs] *m* duty.

dlighe [dli.ı] *f* right, due.

dligheach [dli.əch] *adj* rightful, legitimate.

dlùth [dLũ] *adj* near; dense.

dlùthaich [dLũ.ich'] *v* draw near, approach.

dlùths [dLũs] *m* density.

do[1], **d'** [də] [d] *poss pron* your (*sing*).

do[2], **a** [də] [ə] *prep* to; into; for.

do- [də] *prefix* un-, in-, im-.

dòbhran [dõran] *m* otter.

dòchas [dõchəs] *m* hope.

do-dhèanta [dəgh'iantə] *adj* impossible.

dòigh [dõy] *m* way, manner; condition.

dòigh-beatha [dõi bɛhə] *m* lifestyle, way of life.

dòighean [dõi.ən] *mpl* customs; manners.

dòigheil [dõi.ɛl] *adj* proper; in good order.

doille [dɔL'ɪ] f blindness.

doilleir [doL'ər'] adj dark; gloomy.

doilleirich [doL'ər'ɪch'] v darken; obscure.

doimhne [doiN'ɪ] f (with art) **an doimhne** [ən doiN'ɪ] the deep.

doimhneachd [doiN'əchg] f depth.

doimhnich [doiN'ɪch'] v deepen.

doinnean [doiN'an] f storm, tempest.

doirbh [dor'iv] adj hard, difficult.

doire [dor'ɪ] f grove, thicket, copse.

dòirt [dōršd'] v pour; shed; flow.

do-labhairt [doLavəršd'] adj unspeakable.

dolar [doLər] m dollar.

dol-a-mach [doLəmach] m behaviour, conduct.

dòlas [dōLəs] m grief.

dol-às [doL as] m way out, escape.

dol fodha na grèine [doL fɔ.ə nə grēnɪ] m sunset.

dòmhail [dō.al] adj crowded; dense.

domhainn [dɔ.ɪN'] adj deep; profound.

domhan [dɔ.an] m (with art) **an Domhan** [ən dɔ.an] the Universe.

dona [dɔnə] adj bad; naughty.

donas [dɔnəs] m badness, evil; (with art) **an Donas** [ən dɔnəs] the Devil.

donn [douN] adj brown; brown-haired.

donnal [dɔNəL] m howl.

donnalaich [dɔNəLɪch'] f howling.

doras [dɔrəs] m door.

dorcha [dɔrəchə] adj dark.

dorchadas [dɔrəchədəs] m darkness.

dòrlach [dōrLəch] m fistful, handful.

dòrn [dōrn] m fist.

dòrtadh-fala [dōršdəghfaLə] m bloodshed.

dos [dɔs] m bagpipe drone.

dotair [dɔʰtɛr'] m doctor.

doth [dɔh] v singe, scorch.

drabasdach [drabəsdəch] adj obscene.

dràbhail [drābhal] adj grotty.

drabhair [dra.ɛr'] m drawer.

dràc [drāʰk] m drake.

dragh [drogh] m trouble, bother; worry.

draghail [droghal] adj worrying; annoying.

dràibh [drāiv] v (car, etc) drive.

dràibhear [drāivɛr] m driver.

drama [dramə] m dram.

dràma [drāmə] m drama.

dranndan [drauNdan] m snarl(ing), growl(ing).

draoidh [druy] m druid; magician.

draoidheachd [drui.əchg] f wizardry, magic.

draoidheil [drui.ɛl] adj magic, magical.

draosda [drūsdə] adj smutty, lewd.

draosdachd [drūsdəchg] f smut, lewdness.

drathais [dra.ɪš] fpl underpants; pants, knickers.

dreach [dr'ɛch] m appearance, aspect; complexion.

dreallag [dr'ɛLag] f (child's) swing.

drèana [dr'ēnə] f drain, drainage ditch.

dreasa [dr'ɛsə] f dress.

dreasair [dr'ɛsɛr'] m dresser.

dreathan-donn [dr'ɛhandouN] m wren.

dreuchd [dr'iachg] f occupation, profession.

dreuchdail [dr'iachgal] *adj* professional.

driamlach [dr'iəmLəch] *f* fishing line.

drile [dr'ilɪ] *f* drill, auger.

drioftair [dr'iftɛr'] *m* (*fishing*) drifter.

drip [dr'iʰp] *f* bustle, state of being busy.

dripeil [dr'iʰpɛl] *adj* busy.

dris [dr'iš] *f* bramble; brier.

drithleann [dr'iləN] *m* sparkle, flash.

driùchd [dr'iūchg] *f* dew.

dròbh [drōv] *m* cattle drove.

dròbhair [drōvɛr'] *m* cattle-drover.

droch [droch] *adj* bad.

drochaid [drochɪd'] *f* bridge.

droch bheart [droch vyaršd] *f* vice; evil deed.

droch bheus [droch vēs] *f* bad manners.

droch chainnt [droch chaiN'd'] *f* bad language, swearing.

droch chòrdadh [droch chōrdəgh] *m* disagreement, bad terms.

droch ionnsaigh [droch iūN'sɪ] *f* physical assault.

droch isean [droch išan] *m* brat, naughty child.

droch nàdarrach [droch nādəRəch] *adj* ill-natured, ill-tempered.

droga [drogə] *f* drug; *pl* **drogaichean** [drogɪch'ən] (*illegal, etc*) drugs.

drùdhag [drū.ag] *f* drop; sip.

druid [drid'] *f* starling.

drùidh [drūy] *v* soak, penetrate (to skin).

drùidh air [drūy] *v* affect, make an impression on.

druim [druim] *m* back; ridge.

drùis [drūš] *f* lust, lechery.

drùiseach [drūšəch] *adj* lustful, lecherous.

druma [drumə] *f* drum.

duais [duəš] *f* wages; reward; award.

dual[1] [duəL] *m* character; birthright.

dual[2] [duəL] *m* curl, lock; plait.

dualaich [duəLɪch'] *v* curl; twist, plait.

dualchainnt [duəLchaiN'd'] *f* dialect.

dualchas [duəLchəs] *m* hereditary character.

dualtach [duəLtəch] *adj* inherent, natural; **dualtach a bhith** [duəLtəch ə vi] inclined to be.

duan [duan] *m* poem, song.

duanag [duanag] *f* song, ditty.

dùbailte [dūbəlt'ɪ] *adj* double; dual.

dubh [duh] *v* blacken. • *m* black; ink. • *adj* black; dark-haired.

dubhach [du.əch] *adj* gloomy; in a bad mood.

dubhadh [du.əgh] *m* eclipse.

dubhag [du.ag] *f* kidney.

dubhaigeann [du.aig'əN] *m* abyss, the deep.

dubhan [du.an] *m* hook.

dubhar [du.ər] *m* shade.

dubh às [duh as] *v* erase; blot out.

dubh-dhonn [dughouN] *adj* dark brown.

dubh-ghorm [dughorom] *adj* dark blue.

Dùbhlachd [dūLəchg] *f* (*with art*) **an Dùbhlachd** [ən dūLəchg] December.

dùbhlan [dūLan] *m* challenge.

dubh-nòta [du nōʰtə] *m* (*mus*) crotchet.

dùblaich [dūbLıch'] *v* double.
dùdag [dūdag] *f* bugle.
dubh-thràth [durã] *m* dusk.
dùil[1] [dūl] *f* hope; expectation.
dùil[2] [dūl] *f* created being; element.
duileasg [duləsg] *m* dulse.
duilgheadas [dulgh'ədəs] *m* difficulty; problem.
duilgheadasan sòisealta [dulgh'ədəsən sōsəLtə] *mpl* social problems.
duilich [dulıch'] *adj* hard, difficult; unfortunate. • *excl* **tha mi duilich!** [ha mi dulıch'] I'm sorry!
duilleach [duL'əch] *m* foliage.
duilleachan [duL'əchan] *m* leaflet.
duilleag [duL'ag] *f* leaf; page, sheet.
dùin [dūN'] *v* shut, close.
duine [duN'ı] *m* man; person; human being; husband. • *pron* someone; **duine sam bith** [duN'ı səm bi] anyone at all.
duinealas [duN'əLəs] *m* manliness; decisiveness.
duine cloinne [duN'ıkloN'ı] *m* child.
duineil [duN'ɛl] *adj* manly; decisive; mannish.
duine lag-chùiseach [duN'ı Lag chūšəch] *m* stick-in-the-mud.
duine-uasal [duN'uəsəL] *m* gentleman; nobleman.

dùinte [dūN'd'ı] *adj* closed, shut; introvert.
dùisg [dūšg'] *v* wake, awaken.
Duitseach [du^ht'šəch] *m/adj* Dutch person; Dutch.
dùn [dūn] *m* hill fort, fortress; conical hill.
dùnan [dūnan] *m* small hill; dung heap.
dùr [dūr] *adj* stubborn; dour.
dùrachd [dūrəchg] *f* seriousness; sincerity; greeting.
dùrachdach [dūrəchgəch] *adj* serious, earnest.
dùraig [dūrıg'] *v* dare.
durcan [durkan] *m* pine cone, fir cone.
dùrdail [dūrdal] *f* cooing.
dùsal [dūsəL] *m* slumber, snooze.
dusan [dusan] *m* dozen.
dùsgadh [dūsgəgh] *m* awakening.
duslach [dusLach] *m* dust.
dustach [dusdəch] *adj* dusty.
dustair [dusdɛr'] *m* duster.
dùthaich [dū.ıch'] *f* country; homeland; countryside.
dùthchas [dūchəs] *m* cultural inheritance.
dùthchasach [dūchəsəch] *adj* native, indigenous.

E

e [ɛ] *pron* he; him; it (*m*).
eabar [ɛbər] *m* mud, mire.
Eabhra [ɛvrə] *f* Hebrew (language).
Eabhrach [ɛvrəch] *m/adj* Hebrew.
eacarsaich [ɛ^hkərsıch'] *f* exercise.
each [ɛch] *m* horse.

each-aibhne [ɛchaivN'ı] *m* hippopotamus.
eachdraiche [ɛchdrıch'ə] *m* historian.
eachdraidh [ɛchdrı] *f* history.
eachdraidheil [ɛchdrı.ɛl] *adj* historical.

each-oibre [εchoibr'ı] *m* workhorse.

each-uisge [εchušg'ı] *m* waterhorse, kelpie.

eaconamachd [εkɔnəməchg] *f* economics.

eaconamaidh [εkɔnəmı] *m* economy.

eaconamair [εkɔnəmır'] *m* economist.

Eadailt [edalt'] *f (with art)* **an Eadailt** [ə N'edalt'] Italy.

Eadailteach [edalt'əch] *m/adj* Italian.

eadar [edər] *prep* between; among; both.

eadaraibh [edərıv] *prep pron* between you; among you.

eadarainn [edərıN'] *prep pron* between us; among us.

eadar dà bharail [edər dā varal] *adv* undecided; between two stools.

eadar-dhealachadh [edərgh'aLəchəgh] *m* difference; distinction.

eadar-dhealaich [edərgh'aLıch'] *v* differentiate; distinguish.

eadar-dhealaichte [edərgh'aLıcht'ə] *adj* different; distinct, separate.

eadar-nàiseanta [edərnāšəndə] *adj* international.

eadar-sholas [edərhɔLəs] *m* twilight.

eadar-theangachadh [edərhεngəchəgh] *m* translation.

eadar-theangaich [edərhεngıch'] *v* translate.

eadhon [eghən] *adv* even.

eadradh [edrəgh] *m* milking.

eag [eg] *f* nick, notch.

eagal [egaL] *m* fear, fright; **eagal mo bheatha** [egaL mə vεhə] the fright of my life.

eagalach [egaLəch] *adj* prone to fear; terrible, dreadful. • *adv* terribly, dreadfully.

eaglais [egLıš] *f* church; *(with art)* **an Eaglais Shaor** [ə N'egLıš hūr] the Free Church; **Eaglais na h-Alba** [egLıš nə haLabə] the Church of Scotland.

eala [εLə] *f* swan.

èalaidh [iaLı] *v* creep; sneak away.

ealain [εLεN'] *f* art; **Comhairle Ealain na h-Alba** [kɔ.ərlı εLεN' nə haLabə] the Scottish Arts Council.

ealanta [εLandə] *adj* artistic.

ealantair [εLaNdεr'] *m* artist.

eallach [εLach] *m* load, burden.

ealta [εLtə] *f (birds)* flock.

ealtainn [εLtıN'] *f* razor.

eanchainn [εnachıN'] *f* brain.

eanraich [εnarıch'] *f* soup, broth.

ear [εr] *f* east.

ear air [εr εr'] *prep* east of.

earalachadh [εraLəchəgh] *m* exhortation.

earalaich [εraLıch'] *v* exhort; caution.

Earranta, Earr. [εRəntə] *adj (company)* Limited, Ltd.

earb[1] [εrab] *v* trust.

earb[2] [εrab] *f* roe-deer.

earb à [εrab a] *v* trust in.

earball [εrabəL] *m* tail.

earbsa [εrabsə] *f* trust; confidence; reliance.

earbsach [εrabsəch] *adj* trusting; trustworthy.

eàrlas [iarləs] *m (financial)* deposit.

earrach [εRəch] *m* spring; **as t-earrach** [əs t'εrəch] in spring.

earrann [εRəN] *f* part, section; piece.

eas [es] *m* waterfall.

eas- [es] prefix in-, dis-, un-.

coileach-fiodha [kɔləchfyoghə] m pheasant.

easaonta [esũntə] f disagreement; dissent.

easbaig [esbɪg'] m bishop.

Easbaigeach [esbɪg'əch] m/adj Episcopalian. • adj episcopal.

easbhaidh [esvi] f lack, want, need.

easbhaidheach [esvi.əch] adj needy; needful, lacking.

eascaraid [eskarɪd'] m foe.

èasgaidh [iasgɪ] adj active; willing; **èasgaidh a dhèanamh** [iasgɪ ə gh'ianəv] willing/keen to do it.

easgann [esgəN] f eel.

eas-ùmhail [esũ.al] adj disobedient, insubordinate.

eas-urramach [esuRəməch] adj dishonourable.

eathar [ɛhər] m rowing boat.

eatorra [ɛhtərə] prep pron between them; among them.

èibhinn [ẽviN'] adj funny, amusing.

èibhleag [ẽvlag] f ember.

èideadh [ẽd'əgh] m dress, garb; uniform.

eidheann [e.əN] f ivy.

èifeachdach [ẽfəchgəch] adj effective; efficient.

eigh [ey] f ice.

eugh [ẽv] v shout, call. • f shout, cry.

eighe [e.ə] f (tool) file.

-eigin su [eg'ɪn] ffix some-.

èiginn [ẽg'ɪN'] f difficulty; trouble; need; violence.

Eilbheis [elevɪš] f (with art) an Eilbheis [ə N'elevɪš] Switzerland.

Eilbheiseach n/ [elevɪšəch] adj Swiss.

èildear [ẽld'ɛr] m church elder.

eile [elɪ] adj other; another.

eilean [elan] m island.

eileanach [elanəch] m islander.

Eilean a' Cheò [elanəch'ɔ̃] m (nickname) Skye.

Eilean Ì [elanĩ] m Iona.

Eilean Luing [elanLuɪng'] m Luing.

Eilean Ruma [elanrumə] m (the Isle of) Rum.

eilid [elɪd'] f hind.

eilthireach [elɪrəch] m foreigner; exile.

einnsean [ẽN'šan] m engine.

einnsean-smàlaidh [ẽN'šansmāLɪ] m fire engine.

Èipheit [ẽfɪt'] f (with art) an Eipheit [ə N'ẽfɪt'] Egypt.

Èipheiteach [ẽfɪt'əch] m/adj Egyptian.

eireachdail [erachgal] adj elegant; handsome.

eireag [erag] f pullet.

Èireannach [ẽr'əNəch] m/adj Irishman; Irish.

Èirinn [ẽr'ɪN'] f Ireland.

èirich [ẽr'ɪch] v rise, get up; rebel.

èirich do [ẽr'ɪch' də] v happen to, befall, become of.

eiridinn [er'ɪd'ɪN'] m nursing.

eiridnich [er'ɪd'nɪch'] v nurse, tend.

èirig [ẽr'ɪg'] f ransom.

èirigh na grèine [ẽr'ɪ nə grẽnɪ] f sunrise.

eirmseach [er'ɪmšəch] adj witty.

èist (ri) [ẽšd' r'i] v listen (to).

eisimealachd [ešɪmɛLəchg] f dependence.

eisimeileach [ešɪmɛLəch] adj dependent.

eisimpleir [ešɪmplər'] m example.

eist! [ẽšd'] excl hush! be quiet!

eitean [eʰt'an] m kernel; core.

eòlach [yɔL'ch] *adj* knowledgeable; acquainted.

eòlach air [yɔLəch] *adv* familiar with.

eòlaiche [yɔLɪch'ə] *m* expert.

eòlas¹ [yɔLəs] *m* knowledge; acquaintance.

eòlas² [yɔːLəs] *m* science.

eòlas-leighis [yɔLəs L'e.ɪš] *m* (*science of*) medicine.

eòrna [yɔrnə] *m* barley.

Eòrpa [yɔrpə] *f* Europe; (*with art*) **an Roinn Eòrpa** [ən RəiN'ɔrpə *m* Europe.

Eòrpach [yɔrpəch] *m/adj* European.

esan [ɛsən] *pron* (*emphatic form of* **e**) he; him.

eu- [ē] *prefix* un-, dis-, -less.

euchd [ēchg] *m* feat; achievement.

eucoir [ēkɔr'] *f* crime.

eucoireach [ēkɔr'əch] *m* criminal.

eu-coltach [ēkɔLtəch] *adj* dissimilar; unlikely.

eud [ēd] *m* jealousy; zeal.

eudach [ēdəch] *adj* jealous; zealous.

eudail [ēdal] *f* treasure; **mo eudail!** [mēdal] my dear!

eu-dòchas [edɔchəs] *m* hopelessness.

eun [ian] *m* bird, fowl.

eunan-àir [iananār'] *m* bird of prey.

eun-eòlas [ianyɔLəs] *m* ornithology.

eun-mara [ianmarə] *m* seabird.

eun-uisge [ianušg'ɪ] *m* waterfowl.

euslaint [ēsland'] *f* illness, ill-health.

euslainteach [ēsland'əch] *adj* ill, unhealthy. • *m* invalid; patient.

F

fàbhar [fāvər] *m* favour.

fabhra [faurə] *m* eyelid.

facal [faʰkəl] *m* word; saying.

fa chomhair [fa chou.ɪr'] *prep* opposite; in front of.

faclach [faʰkLəch] *adj* wordy, verbose.

faclair [faʰkLɛr'] *m* dictionary.

faclaireachd [faʰkLɛr'əchg] *f* lexicology; lexicography.

fad [fad] *m* length; the whole, all the.

fada [fadə] *adj* long; tall. • *adv* far, much.

fada air falbh [fad ɛr' faLav] *adv* faraway, distant.

fadachd [fadachg] *f* longing; nostalgia; impatience; boredom.

fadalach [fadaLəch] *adj* late; tedious; long drawn out.

fada nas fheàrr [fadə nə šāR] much/far better.

fad an latha [fad ən La.ə] *adv* all day, the whole day.

fada 'nur comain [fadə nər komɛN'] much obliged to you.

fad às [fad as] *adj* remote, distant; (*person*) withdrawn.

fàd mònach [fād mɔnəch] *m* a single peat.

fad na h-oidhche [fad nə hoi.ch'ɪ] *adv* all night.

fad na h-ùine [fad nə hūN'ɪ] *adv* all the time, constantly.

fad-shaoghalach [fadhū.əLəch] *adv* long-lived.

fad-shaoghalachd [fadhū.əLəchg] *f* longevity.

fàg [fāg] *v* leave; abandon.

faic [fɛʰk'] *v* see.

faiceall [fɛʰk'əL] *f* care, caution.

faiceallach [fɛʰk'əLəch] *adj* careful, cautious.

faiche [faich'ı] *f* meadow, grass park.

faicsinneach [fɛʰk'šıN'əch] *adj* visible; conspicuous.

faide [fad'ı] *f* length.

fàidh [fāy] *m* prophet, seer.

fàidheadaireachd [fāi.ədɛr'əchg] *f* prophecy.

faigh [faich'] *v* get, obtain; find.

faigh air ... [faich' ɛr'] *v* get to ..., manage to ...

faigh air adhart [faich' ɛr' o.əršd] *v* get on, progress.

faigh a-mach [faich' əmach] *v* find out, discover.

faigh bàs [faich' bās] *v* die, get killed.

faigh cron do [faich' krɔn də] *v* blame.

faigh cuidhteas de [faich' kuiʰt'əs d'e] *v* get rid/shot of.

faigh do sheise [faich' də hešı] *v* meet your match.

faighean [fai.an] *m* vagina.

faigh faire air [faich' far'ı ɛr'] *v* spot, catch sight of.

faigh lorg air [faich' Lɔrəg ɛr'] *v* track down, locate.

faigh muin [faich' muN'] *v* have sex, copulate.

faighneach [faiN'əch] *adj* inquisitive, enquiring.

faighnich [faiN'ıch'] *v* ask, enquire.

faigh seachad air [faich' šachəd ɛr'] *v* get over.

faigh seòl air [faich' šɔL ɛr'] *v* contrive to, manege to.

failc [falk'] *v* bathe.

faileas [falas] *m* shadow; reflection.

faileasach [falasəch] *adj* shadowy.

faillean [faL'an] *m* eardrum.

fàillig [fāL'ıg'] *v* fail.

fàillinn [fāL'ıN'] *f* failing, fault; blemish; failure.

falman [faLaman] *m* kneecap.

fail-mhuc [falvuʰk] *f* pigsty.

fàilte [fālt'ı] *f* welcome. • *excl* **fàilte oirbh!** [fālt' ɔr'iv] welcome to you! you're welcome!

fàilteach [fālt'əch] *adj* welcoming; hospitable.

fàilteachail [fālt'əchal] *adj* welcoming; hospitable.

fàiltich [fālt'ıch'] *v* welcome.

fang [fang] *f* sheepfold, fank.

fàinne [fāN'ı] *f* (*finger*) ring.

fàinne-phòsaidh [fāN'ıfōsı] *f* wedding ring.

fàinne-sholais [fāN'ıhɔLıš] *f* halo.

faire [far'ı] *f* guard; watch.

fàire [fār'ı] *f* horizon, skyline.

faireachdainn [farəchgıN'] *f* sensation; emotion, feeling.

fàireag [fār'ag] *f* gland.

fairich [far'ıch'] *v* feel; smell.

fairtlich air [faršd'lıch' ɛr'] *v* get the better of, defeat; baffle.

faisg [fašg'] *adj* near, close.

fàisg [fāšg'] *v* squeeze; wring.

faisge [fašg'ı] *f* nearness, closeness.

fàisneachd [fāšN'əchg] *f* prophecy.

faite-gàire [faʰt'ıgār'ı] *f* smile.

faitheam [fɛhəm] *m* hem.

faitich [faʰt'ıch'] *v* smile.

fàl [fāL] *m* hedge; verge.

falach [faLəch] *m* hiding, concealment.

falachd [faLəchg] *f* feud.

falach-fead [faLəch fed] *m* hide-and-seek.

falaich [faLɪch'] *v* hide.

falaichte [faLɪch't'ɪ] *adj* hidden, concealed.

falamh [faLəv] *adj* empty.

falamhachd [faLəvəchg] *f* emptiness; void.

falbh [faLav] *v* leave, go away.

falbh a dh'iarraidh [faLav ə gh'iəRɪ] *v* go to fetch/get.

falbh air dèirc [faLav ɛr' d'ērk'] *v* beg.

fa leth [fa leh] *adv* separate; apart.

fallainn [faLɪN'] *adj* sound, healthy; wholesome; able-bodied.

fallas [faLəs] *m* sweat; **tha fallas orm** [ha faLəs ərəm] I'm sweating.

fallasach [faLəsəch] *adj* sweaty.

fallsa [fauLsə] *adj* false, deceitful.

falmadair [faLamədər'] *m* helm.

falmhachd *see* **falamhachd**. [faLəvəchg]

falmhaich [faLəvɪch'] *v* empty.

falt [faLt] *m* (*of head*) hair.

famh [fav] *f* (*animal*) mole.

fàmhair [fāvɪr'] *m* giant.

fan [fan] *v* wait; stay.

fanaid [fanɪd'] *f* mockery, ridicule.

fan aig [fan ɛg'] *v* lodge with.

fan air [fan ɛr'] *v* wait for.

fànas [fānəs] *m* space; void.

fainear dhomh [faN'ɛr ghə] *adv* on my mind, in my thoughts.

fann [fauN] *adj* weak, faint.

fannaich [faNɪch'] *v* weaken.

fanntaig [fauNdɪg'] *v* faint, swoon.

faobhar [fūvər] *m* (*of blade*) edge.

faobharaich [fūvərɪch'] *v* sharpen.

faochadh [fūchəgh] *m* relief, respite.

faochag [fūchag] *f* whelk, winkle.

faod [fūd] *v* can, may, might.

faoighe [fui.ɪ] *f* begging, cadging.

faoileag [fūlag] *f* seagull.

faoilidh [fūlɪ] *adj* hospitable; generous; frank.

Faoilteach [fūlt'əch] *m* (*with art*) **am Faoilteach** [əm fūlt'əch] January.

faoin [fūN'] *adj* silly, foolish; empty-headed; futile.

faoineas [fūN'əs] *m* silliness, vacuity; futility.

faoinsgeul [fūN'sg'iaL] *m* myth, legend.

faoisid [fūšɪd'] *f* confession.

faoisidich [fūšɪd'ɪch'] *v* confess.

faothachadh [fū.əchəgh] *m* same as **faochadh**.

faothaich [fū.ɪch'] *v* relieve, alleviate.

far [far] *prep* from, down from.

far a [farə] *conj* where.

faradh [farəgh] *m* (*rail, etc*) fare.

fàradh [fārəgh] *m* ladder.

far-ainm [farɛnɛm] *m* nickname.

faram [faram] *m* loud noise.

faramach [faraməch] *adj* loud, noisy.

farchluais [farachLuəš] *f* eavesdropping.

fàrdach [fārdəch] *f* house; dwelling, lodging.

farmad [faraməd] *m* envy.

farpais [farpɪš] *m* competition.

farpaiseach [farpɪšəch] *m* competitor.

farranaich [faRanɪch'] *v* tease.

farsaing [farsɪng'] *adj* wide, broad.

farsaingeachd [farsɪngʹəchg] *f* width, breadth; area.

farspag [farspag] *f* black-backed gull.

fàs[1] [fās] *v* grow; become.

fàs[2] [fās] *adj* waste, uncultivated; barren.

fàsach [fāsəch] *m* desert, wilderness; deserted place.

fàsaich [fāsɪchʹ] *v* empty; depopulate.

fàsail [fāsail] *adj* desolate.

fasan [fasan] *m* fashion.

fasanta [fasantə] *adj* fashionable.

fasgach [fasgəch] *adj* sheltered; sheltering.

fasgadh [fasgəgh] *m* shelter, protection.

fasgain [fasgɛNʹ] *v* winnow.

fa sgaoil [fa sgūl] *adv* free, at liberty.

fastaich [fasdɪch] *v* hire, employ.

fastaidhear [fasdɪ.ɛr] *m* employer.

fàth [fāh] *m* cause; reason; opportunity.

fathann [fahəN] *m* rumour.

feabhas [fyɔ.əs] *m* improvement; excellence.

feachd [fɛchg] *f* army.

fead [fed] *v* whistle. • *f* (*noise*) whistle.

feadag [fedag] *f* (*instrument*) whistle; plover.

feadaireachd [fedɪrʹəchg] *f* whistling; playing a whistle.

feadan [fedan] *m* chanter; pipe, tube, spout.

feadhainn [fyɔ.ɪNʹ] *f* some; (*with art*) **an fheadhainn** [ə Nʹɔ.ɪNʹ] those, the ones.

feagal [fegal] *m* fear, fright (*dialectal form*).

feàirrde [fyāRdʹɪ] *adj* better.

fealladh [fyaLəgh] *m* foul; foul play.

fealla-dhà [fyaLə ghā] *f* joke, jest.

feall-falach [fyauLfaLach] *m* ambush.

feallsanach [fyauLsanəch] *m* philosopher.

feallsanachd [fyauLsanəchg] *f* philosophy.

feamainn [fɛmɪNʹ] *f* seaweed. • *v* manure (*usu with seaweed*).

feannag [fyaNag] *f* crow; ridge; lazybed.

feannag ghlas [fyaNag ghLas] *f* hooded crow.

feansa [fɛnsə] *f* fence.

fear [fɛr] *m* man; one.

fearail [fɛral] *adj* manly.

fearalachd [fɛraLəchg] *f* manliness.

fear-allabain [fearaLəbɛNʹ] *m* wanderer.

fearann [fɛrəN] *m* ground, land.

fear-bainnse [fɛrbaiNʹšɪ] *m* bridegroom.

fear-brèige [fɛrbrēgʹɪ] *m* puppet.

fear-cinnidh [fɛrkʹiNʹi] *m* clansman, fellow clansman.

fearg [fɛrag] *f* anger.

feargach [fɛragəch] *adj* angry.

feàrna [fyārnə] *f* alder.

feàrr [fyāR] *adj* better; best.

fear seach fear [fɛr šach fɛr] in turn; one by one.

feart [fyaršt] *f* attention, heed; quality, characteristic.

feasgar [fesgər] *m* afternoon; evening. • *adv* in the afternoon/ evening, p.m.

fèath [fia] *m* (*weather*) calm.

fèichear [fēchʹɛr] *m* debtor.

fèileadh beag [fēləgh beg] *m* kilt.

fèill [fēL'] *f* feast, festival, fair; sale, market.

Fèill Brìde [fēL'*brīd*'ı] *f* (*with art*) **an Fhèill Brìde** [aN' ēL'*brīd*'ı] Candlemas.

fèin[1] [fēn], **fhèin** [hēn] *refl pron* self; own.

fèin[2] [fēn] *m* (*with art*) **am fèin** [əm fēn] the ego, the self.

fèin-eachdraidh [fēnɛchdrı] *f* autobiography.

fèinealachd [fēnəLəchg] *f* selfishness.

fèineil [fēnɛl] *adj* selfish.

fèin-mholadh [fēnvɔLəgh] *m* conceit.

fèin-riaghladh [fēnriəLəgh] *m* self-government.

fèin-spèis [fēnsbēš] *f* conceit, self-regard.

fèis [fēš] *f* festival.

fèist [fēšd'] *f* feast, banquet.

feith [feh] *v* wait; stay.

fèith[1] [fē] *f* muscle; sinew; vein.

fèith[2] [fē] *f* bog, marsh.

feòil [fyōl] *f* meat; flesh.

feòladair [fyōLədər'] *m* butcher.

feòil-muice [fyōl*mui*ʰk'ı] *f* pork.

feòrag [fyōrag] *f* squirrel.

feòraich [fyōrıch'] *v* ask, enquire.

feuch [fiach] *v* try, attempt; try out, test.

feuch deuchainn [fiach d'iachıN'] *v* sit an exam.

feum [fēm] *v* must, have to; need. • *m* need; use, usefulness, good.

feumach [fēməch] *adj* needy, in need.

feumail [fēmal] *adj* useful, handy; necessary.

feur [fiar] *m* grass; hay.

feurach [fiarəch] *adj* grassy.

feuraich [fiarıch'] *v* graze.

feusag [fiasag] *f* beard.

feusgan [fiasgan] *m* mussel.

fhad 's a [adsə] *conj* while, as long as.

fhathast [ha.asd] *adv* yet; still.

fhèin[1] [hēn] *refl pron same as* **fèin**[1].

fhèin[2] [hēn] *adv* even.

fhuair [huər'] *past tense of v* **faigh**

fiabhras [fiəvrəs] *m* fever.

fiacail [fiəʰkal] *f* tooth; *pl* **fiaclan fuadain** [fiəʰklən fuədɛN'] false teeth, dentures.

fiach[1] [fiəch] *adj* worth, worthwhile; of value.

fiach[2] [fiəch] *m* value, worth; debt.

fiach[3] see **feuch**. [fiach]

fiach! [fiach] *excl* lo! behold!

fiachail [fiachal] *adj* worthy, respectable; valuable.

fiaclach [fiəʰkLəch] *adj* toothed, toothy; dental.

fiaclaire [fiəʰkLər'ə] *m* dentist.

fiaclan fuadain see **fiacail**.

fiadh [fiagh] *m* deer.

fiadhaich [fia.ıch'] *adj* wild; angry, furious.

fial [fiəL] *adj* generous; hospitable; tolerant.

fiamh [fiə] *adj* hue, tint; complexion; expression; fear.

fiamh-ghàire [fiəghār'ı] *m* smile.

fianais [fiənıš] *f* evidence, testimony.

fianaiseach [fiənıšəch] *m* witness.

fiar [fiər] *adj* bent; slanting; squinting; cunning.

fiar [fiər] *v* bend, curve; slant; squint.

fiaradh [fiərəgh] *m* slant; squint.

fiar-shùileach [fiərhūləch] *adj* squint-eyed.

fichead [fich'əd] *m* twenty, a score.

ficheadamh [fich'ədəv] *adj* twentieth.

fideag [fid'ag] *f* (*instrument*) whistle.

fidheall [fi.əL] *f* fiddle, violin.

fidhlear [fīlɛr] *m* fiddler, violinist.

fidir [fid'ir'] *v* appreciate, comprehend.

fige [fīg'ı] *f* fig.

figear [fig'ɛr] *m* (*numerical*) figure.

figh [fī] *v* weave; knit.

fighe [fi.ı] *f* weaving; knitting.

figheachan [fi.əchan] *m* pigtail, pony-tail.

figheadair [fi.ədər'] *m* weaver; knitter.

fighte [fīt'ı] *adj* woven; knitted.

fileanta [filandə] *adj* eloquent, articulate; fluent.

fileantach [filandəch] *m* native speaker; fluent speaker.

filidh [filı] *m* poet.

fill [fīL'] *v* fold; pleat; plait.

filleadh [fiL'əgh] *m* fold; pleat; plait.

fillte [fīL't'ı] *adj* folded; pleated; plaited.

film [filim] *m* film.

fine [finı] *f* clan; tribe.

fiodh [fyogh] *m* wood, timber.

fiolan-gòbhlach [fyuLangōLəch] *m* earwig.

fion [fiən] *m* wine.

fionan [fiənan] *m* vine.

fion-dearc [fiənd'ɛrk] *f* grape.

fion-geur [fiən giar] *m* vinegar.

fionn¹ [fyūN] *v* flay.

fionn² [fyūN] *adj* white.

fionnach [fyuNəch] *adj* hairy; rough, shaggy.

fionnadh [fyuNgh] *m* (*animal*) hair.

fionnaireachd [fyuNır'əchg] *f* coolness.

fionnan-feòir [fyuNanfyōr'] *m* grasshopper.

fionnar [fyuNər] *adj* cool, fresh; cold, off-hand.

fionnaraich [fyuNərıch'] *v* cool; refrigerate.

fionnsgeul [fyūNsgiaL] *m* legend.

fìor¹ [fiər] *adj* real; genuine.

fìor² [fiər] *adv* very.

fìor-uisge [fiərušg'ı] *m* pure water.

fios [fis] *m* knowledge; information; word, message, news.

fiosaiche [fisıch'ə] *m* prophet, seer; fortune teller.

fiosrach [fisrəch] *adj* well-informed.

fiosrachadh [fisrəchəgh] *m* information.

Fir Chlis [fir' ch'liš] *mpl* (*with art*) **na Fir Chlis** [nə fir' chl'iš] the Northern Lights, Aurora Borealis.

fireann [fir'əN] *adj* masculine, male.

fireannach [fir'əNəch] *m* man; male.

fireannach [fir'əNəch] *adj* truthful.

fireanta [fir'əndə] *adj* same as **fireann**.

fìrinn [fīr'ıN'] *f* truth.

fitheach [fi.əch] *m* raven.

fiù [fyū] *m* worth, value. • *adj* worth.

fiùdalach [fyūdaLəch] *adj* feudal.

fiù 's [fyūs] *adv* even.

flanainn [fLanıN'] *f* flannel.

flath [flah] *m* king, prince; ruler.

fleadh [flɛgh] *m* feast, banquet.

fleasgach [flesgəch] *m* youth, stripling; bachelor.

fleisg [fleš'g'] *f (elec)* flex.

fleòdradh [flɔ̄drəgh] *m* floating; buoyancy.

fliuch [fluch] *v* wet. • *adj* wet.

flùr[1] [fLūr] *m* flower.

flùr[2] [flūr] *m* flour.

flùranach [flūranəch] *adj* flowery.

fo [fɔ] *prep* under, beneath, below; affected by.

fo-aodach [fɔ ūdəch] *m* underwear.

fo bhlàth [fɔ vLā] *adv* in bloom.

fo bhròn [fɔ vrɔ̄n] *adv* sad, sorrowful.

fo chasaid [fɔ chasɪd'] *adv* accused.

fo chomain [fɔ chomɛN'] *adv* obliged.

fo chùram [fɔ chūrəm] *adv* anxious; preoccupied.

fòd [fɔd] *f (single)* peat; sod; clod of earth.

fodar [fɔdər] *m* fodder.

fodha [fɔ.ə] *prep pron* under him, under it (*m*).

fodhad [fɔ.əd] *prep pron* under you (*sing*).

fodhaibh [fɔ.ɪv] *prep pron* under you (*pl*).

fodhainn [fɔ.ɪN'] *prep pron* under us.

fodham [fɔ.əm] *prep pron* under me.

fo-dhearg [fɔgh'ɛrag] *adj* infra-red.

fo dhìmeas [fɔ gh'īmes] *adv* despised.

fodhpa [fɔʰpə] *prep pron* under them.

fo eagal [fɔ egaL] *adv* afraid.

fo fhiachaibh [fɔ iachɪv] *adv* obliged, under an obligation.

fògair [fɔ̄gɪr'] *v* banish, exile; drive out.

foghain [fɔ.ɛN'] *v* suffice, do, be enough. • *excl* **fòghnaidh sin!** [fɔ̄nɪ šin] that will do!

foghar [fɔ.ər] *m* autumn; harvest.

fo gheasaibh [fɔ gh'esɪv] *adv* spellbound, enchanted.

foghlaim [fɔ̄Lɪm] *v* educate.

foghlaimte [fɔ̄Lɪmt'ɪ] *adj* educated, learned.

foghlam [fɔ̄Ləm] *m* education; scholarship.

fòghnadh [fɔ̄nəgh] *m* sufficiency.

fòthannan [fɔ̄həNan] *m* thistle.

fo ghruaim [fɔ ghruəɪm] *adv* gloomy; grumpy, in ill-humour.

fògrach [fɔ̄grəch] *m* exile; fugitive; refugee.

fògradh [fɔ̄grəgh] *m* exile, banishment.

fòid *see* **fòd**. [fɔ̄d']

foidhpe [foɪʰpɪ] *prep pron* under her, under it (*f*).

foighidinn [foid'ɪN'] *f* patience.

foighdinneach [foid'ɪN'əch] *adj* patient.

foileag [fɔlag] *f* pancake.

foill [foɪL'] *f* deceit; fraud, deception; cheating.

foilleil [foɪL'ɛl] *adj* deceitful; fraudulent.

foillsich [foɪL'šich] *v* publish.

foillsichear [foɪL'šich'ɛr] *m* publisher.

fo imcheist [fɔ imich'ešd'] *adv* anxious; perplexed.

fo iomagain [fɔ imagɛN'] *adv* anxious, troubled.

fo iongnadh [fɔ iūnəgh] *adv* amazed; abashed.

foinne [foiN'ı] *m* wart.

foirfe [furfı] *adj* perfect; full-grown.

foirfeach [furfəch] *m* (church) elder.

foirmeil [forimɛl] *adj* formal.

fòirneart [fɔrN'ɛršd] *m* violence, force; oppression.

fois [foš] *f* rest, ease, leisure; peace.

fo-lèine [fɔ lēnı] *f* vest.

follais [foLıš] *f* evidentness, obviousness; clarity; openness.

follaiseach [foLıšəch] *adj* evident, clear; public.

fo-mhothachail [fɔ vɔ.əchal] *adj* subconscious.

fo mhulad [fɔ vulad] *adv* sad.

fòn [fɔn] *v* telephone. • *f* telephone.

fònaig [fɔnıg'] *v* telephone.

fo nàire [fɔ nār'ı] *adv* ashamed.

fonn [fouN] *m* tune; mood, state of mind.

fonnmhor [fouNvər] *adj* tuneful, melodious.

for [for] *m* attention; notice; concern.

fo-rathad [fɔ ra.ad] *m* underpass.

forc [fork] *f* fork.

forladh [fɔrLəgh] *m* (army, etc) leave.

forsair [forsɛr'] *m* forester, forestry worker.

fortan [fɔršdan] *m* fortune; luck. • *excl* **fortan leat!** [fɔršdan laʰt] good luck!

for-thalla [forhaLə] *m* foyer.

fosgail [fosgal] *v* open.

fosgailte [fosgalt'ı] *adj* open, opened; frank.

fosgladh [fosgLəgh] *m* opening, gap; opportunity.

fo smachd [fɔ smachg] *adj* under subjection.

fo smalan [fɔ smaLan] *adv* gloomy, melancholy.

fo-thiotalan [fɔhiʰt'ə Lən] *mpl* subtitles.

fo uallach [fɔ uəLəch] *adv* under stress.

fradharc see **radharc**

Fraingis [frang'ıš] *m* (with art) **an Fhraingis** [ən Rang'ıš] French (language).

Frangach [frangəch] *m/adj* Frenchman; French.

fraoch [frūch] *m* heather, heath, ling.

fraoidhneas [frūN'əs] *m* fringe.

fras [fras] *v* rain lightly, shower. • *f* shower; seed.

frasair [frasɛr'] *m* (bathroom) shower.

freagair [fr'egır'] *v* answer, reply; suit.

freagairt [fr'egıršd'] *f* answer, reply.

freagarrach [fr'egəRəch] *adj* suitable.

frèam [fr'ɛm] *m* frame, framework.

freasdail [fr'esdal] *v* serve, wait on.

freiceadan [fr'eʰk'ədan] *m* watch; guard; (with art) **am Freiceadan Dubh** [əm fr'eʰk'ədan du] the Black Watch.

freiceadan-oirthire [fr'eʰk'ədanər'ir'ə] *m* coastguard.

freumh [fr'ēv] *m* root.

frìde [fr'īd'ı] *f* corpuscle; insect.

frìoghan [fr'ighan] *m* bristle.

frionasach [fr'inasəch] *adj* worried; upset; vexing, niggling.

frìth [fr'īh] *f* moorland; deer forest.

frith-ainm [fr'ihɛnɛm] *m* nickname.

frithealadh [fr'ihəLəgh] *m* attendance, service.

frithearra [fr'ihəRə] *adj* touchy; peevish.

fritheil [fr'ihɛl] *v* serve, wait on.

frith-rathad [fr'ira.ad] *m* footpath; track.

froca [frɔʰkə] *m* frock.

fuachd [fuəchg] *f* cold, coldness; (*with art*) **am fuachd** [əm fuəchg] a/the cold.

fuadach [fuədəch] *m* banishment; driving away; *pl* (*with art*) **na Fuadaichean** [nə fuədıch'ən] (*hist*) the Highland Clearances.

fuadachadh [fuədəchəgh] *m same as* **fuadach**.

fuadaich [fuədıch'] *v* banish; drive away.

fuadain [fuədɛN'] *adj* artificial, false.

fuadan [fuədan] *m* wandering; exile.

fuaigh [fuəy] *v* sew; stitch; seam.

fuaigheal [fuəgh'al] *m* sewing; stitching; seaming.

fuaigheil [fuəgh'ɛl] *v* sew; stitch.

fuaighte [fuəıt'ı] *adj* sewn; stitched.

fuaim [fuəım] *f* noise; sound.

fuaimneach [fuəımnəch] *adj* noisy.

fuaimneachadh [fuəımnəchəgh] *m* pronunciation.

fuaimnich [fuəımnıch'] *v* pronounce.

fuaimreag [fuəımrag] *f* vowel.

fuaim-thonn [fuəımhɔuN] *m* sound wave.

fual [fuəL] *m* urine.

fuar [fuər] *adj* cold.

fuaradair [fuərədər'] *m* refrigerator, fridge.

fuaraich [fuərıch'] *v* cool, chill.

fuaraidh [fuərı] *adj* (*lit and fig*) cool, chilly.

fuaran [fuəran] *m* spring, well.

fuasgail [fuəsgal] *v* release; untie; disentangle; solve.

fuasgladh [fuəsgLəgh] *m* solution; absolution.

fuath [fuəh] *f* hatred, loathing.

fuathach [fuəhəch] *adj* hateful, detestable.

fuathaich [fuəhıch'] *v* hate, loathe, detest.

fùdar [fūdər] *m* powder.

fùdaraich [fūdərıch'] *v* powder.

fuidheall [fui.əL] *m* relic; remainder.

fuighleach [fuiləch] *m* rubbish, refuse.

fuil [ful] *f* blood.

fuiling [fulıng'] *v* suffer; bear, put up with.

fuil-mìos [fulmiəs] *f* menstruation, period.

fuilteach [fult'əch] *adj* bloody, gory.

fuiltean [fult'an] *m* (*single*) hair.

fuin [fuN'] *v* bake; knead.

fuineadair [fuN'ədər'] *m* baker.

fuirich [fur'ıch'] *v* stay; live, dwell; wait; **fuirich aig X** [fur'ıch' ɛg'] lodge with X. • *excl* **fuirich ort!** [fur'ıch' ɔršt] hang on! wait a minute! **fuirich orm ...** [fur'ıch' ɔrəm] let me see now ...

fùirneis [fūrN'ɛš] *f* furnace.

fulang [fuləng] *m* suffering; endurance, hardiness.

fulangach [fuləngəch] *adj* hardy; long-suffering; passive.

fulmair [fuLumɛr'] *m* fulmar.

urachail [furachal] *adj* watchful; observant; **furachail air** [furachal ɛr'] on the watch for.

uran [furan] *m* welcome, hospitality.

urasda [furəsdə] *adj* easy.

furm [furum] *m* form, bench.

furtachd [furšdəchg] *f* relief; consolation, solace.

furtaich [furšdɪch'] *v* console, comfort.

G

gabh [gav] ~ [go] *v* take; capture; perform.

gabhadh [gāvəgh] *m* danger, peril.

gabh a' ghrian [gav ə ghrian] *v* sunbathe.

gàbhaidh [gāvɪ] *adj* dangerous, perilous.

gabhail [gahal] *f* lease; course; reception, welcome.

gabh air [gav ɛr'] *v* make for.

gabh air do shocair [gav ɛr' do hɔʰkɪr'] *v* take things easily.

gabh air mhàl [gav ɛr' vāL] *v* rent.

gabhaltach [gavaLtəch] *adj* infectious.

gabhaltas [gavaLtəs] *m* tenancy; rented holding.

gabh an cùram [gav ən kūrəm] be converted, become devout.

gabh beachd [gav byachg] *v* form an opinion.

gabh brath air [gav brah ɛr'] *v* take advantage of.

gabh cead (de) [gav ked d'e] *v* take one's leave (of).

gabh cuairt [gav kuəršt'] *v* take a stroll; take a trip.

gabh do anail! [gav tanal] take a rest/breather!

gabh eagal [gav egal] *v* become afraid, take fright.

gabh fois [gav foš] *v* take a rest/break.

gabh gnothach ri [gav gro.əch r'i] *v* interfere with/in; get involved in.

gabh grèim air [gav grēm ɛr'] *v* take hold of, seize.

gabh iongantas [gav iūntəs] *v* be amazed.

gabh mo leisgeul! [gav mɔ lešg'ial] *excl* excuse me!

gabh mo thaobh [gav mɔ hūv] *v* take my side.

gabh nàire [gav nār'ɪ] *v* be/feel ashamed.

gabh os làimh [gav os Lāiv] *v* undertake, take on.

gabh pàirt [gav pāršt'] *v* participate.

gabh ri [gav r'i] *v* accept.

gabh seilbh air [gav šɛliv ɛr'] *v* take possession of.

gabh smùid [gav smūd'] *v (fam)* get drunk.

gabh socair [gav sɔʰkɪr'] *v* take one's ease.

gabh suim [gav suim] *v* care.

gabh truas de [gav truəs d'e] *v* take pity on.

gabh ùidh ann an [gav ūy auN ən] *v* take an interest in.

gach [gach] *adj* each, every.

gach aon [gach ūn] *adj* every single.

gach uile [gach ulı] *adj* each and every.

gad [gad] *m* supple stick, switch.

gadaiche [gadıch'ə] *m* thief.

gagach [gagach] *adj* stammering, stuttering.

Gàidheal [gē.aL] *m* Gael; Highlander; Gaelic speaker.

Gàidhealach [gē.əLəch] *adj* Highland.

Gàidhealtachd [gē.əLtəchg] *f* (*with art*) **a' Ghàidhealtachd** [gē.əLtəchg] the Highlands.

Gàidhlig [gālıg'] *f* (*also with art*) **Gàidhlig/a' Ghàidhlig** [ə ghālıg'] Gaelic (language).

gail [gal] *v* weep, cry.

gailbheach [galvəch] *adj* stormy.

gaileiridh [galər'ı] *m* art gallery.

gailleann [gaL'əN] *f* storm, tempest.

gainmheach [gɛnavəch] *f* sand.

gainne [gaN'ı] *f* scarcity.

gainnead [gaN'əd] *m* scarcity.

gàir [gār'] *v* laugh.

gàir [gār'] *m* cry; outcry.

gairbhe [gar'ıvı] *f* roughness; wildness.

gairbhead [gar'ıvəd] *m* roughness; wildness.

gàirdeachas [gārd'əchəs] *m* joy; rejoicing.

gàirdean [gārd'an] *m* arm.

gàireachdainn [gār'əchgıN'] *f* laughing, laughter.

gairleag [garlag] *m* garlic.

gairm [gor'im] *v* cry; call; crow. • *f* cry; call; cock-crow.

gairm-chogaidh [gor'imchəgı] *f* war-cry.

gairmeach [gor'iməch] *adj* (*gram*) vocative.

gàirnealair [gārN'aLɛr'] *m* gardener.

gàirnealaireachd [gārN'aLər'əchg] *f* gardening.

gaiseadh a' bhuntàta [gašəgh ə vuntā^htə] *m* potato blight.

gaisge [gašg'ı] *f* bravery, heroism.

gaisgeach [gašg'əch] *m* hero, champion.

gaisgeil [gašgɛl] *adj* brave, heroic.

gal [gaL] *m* crying, weeping.

galan [gaLan] *m* gallon.

galar [gaLar] *m* disease.

Gall [gauL] *m* Lowlander; non-Gael.

galla [gaLə] *f* bitch.

gallan [gaLan] *m* standing stone.

Gallda [gauLdə] *adj* Lowland.

Galldachd [gauLdəchg] *f* (*with art*) **a' Ghalldachd** [ə ghauLdəchg] the Lowlands.

gàmag [gāmag] *f* octave.

gamhainn [gavıN'] *m* stirk.

gamhlas [gauLəs] *m* malice, ill-will.

gamhlasach [gauLəsəch] *adj* malevolent, spiteful.

gann [gauN] *adj* scarce, scant, rare.

gaoid [gūd'] *f* blemish, defect.

gaoir [gūr'] *f* (*of anguish*) cry.

gaoisid [gūšıd'] *f* animal hair, horsehair.

gaol [gūL] *m* love. • *excl* **a ghaoil!** [ə ghūl'] darling! (my) love!

gaolach [gūLəch] *adj* loving; beloved.

gaoth [gū] *f* wind; (*with art*) **a' ghaoth** [ə ghū] wind, flatulence.

gaothach [gū.əch] *adj* windy; flatulent.

gàradh see **gàrradh** [gārəgh]

garbh [garav] *adj* rough; harsh; coarse. • *adv* (*fam*) very, terribly.

garg [garag] *adj* fierce; unruly.

gàrradh [gāRəgh] *m* wall, stone wall; garden.

gartan [garšdan] *m* garter.

gas [gas] *f* stalk; shoot. • *m* gas.

gasda [gasdə] *adj* handsome; splendid; (*fam*) great.

gath [ga] *m* barb; sting; spear; beam.

gath-grèine [gagrēnı] *f* sunbeam.

ge [ge] *conj* though.

gèadh [giagh] *m* goose.

geal [gyaL] *adj* white. • *m* white part of anything.

gealach [gyaLəch] *f* moon.

gealach an abachaidh [gyaLəch ən abachı] *f* harvest moon.

gealagan [gyaLagan] *m* egg white.

gealaich [gyaLıch'] *v* whiten.

gealbhonn [gyaLvouN] *m* sparrow.

geall [gyauL] *v* promise, pledge. • *m* bet, wager; promise.

gealladh [gyaLəgh] *m* promise.

gealladh-pòsaidh [gyaLəghpōsı] *m* engagement, betrothal.

gealltanach [gyauLtənəch] *adj* promising.

gealtach [gyauLtəch] *adj* cowardly; fearful.

gealtaire [gyauLtər'ə] *m* coward.

geama [gɛmə] *m* game, match.

geamair [gɛmɛr'] *m* gamekeeper.

geamhradh [gyaurəgh] *m* winter.

gean [g'ɛn] *m* mood, frame of mind.

geanmnachd [g'ɛnamnəchg] *f* chastity.

geanmnaidh [g'ɛnamnı] *adj* chaste.

geansaidh [g'ɛnsı] *m* jersey, jumper.

gèar [g'iar] *f* (*engine*) gear.

gearain [g'ɛrɛN'] *v* complain, grumble.

gearan [g'ɛran] *m* complaining; complaint.

gearanach [g'ɛranəch] *adj* complaining, querulous.

gearastan [g'ɛrasdən] *m* garrison; (*with art*) **An Gearastan** [ən g'ɛrasdən] Fort William.

Gearmailt [g'ɛramalt'] *f* (*with art*) **a' Ghearmailt** [ə gh'ɛramalt'] Germany.

Gearmailteach [g'ɛramalt'əch] *m/adj* German.

Gearmailteis [g'ɛramalt'ıš] *f* (*with art*) **a' Ghearmailtis** [əgh'ɛramalt'ıš] German (language).

geàrr[1] [g'āR] *v* cut; castrate. • *adj* short.

geàrr[2] [g'āR] *f* hare.

gearradh [g'aRəgh] *m* cut; *pl* **gearraidhean** [g'aRı.ən] (*financial*) cuts.

Gearran [g'aRan] *m* (*with art*) **an Gearran** [ən g'aRan] February.

gearran [g'aRan] *m* gelding; pony, garron.

geàrr-shealladh [g'āRhyaLəgh] *m* short-sightedness.

geas [g'es] *f* enchantment, spell.

geata [gɛʰtə] *m* gate.

ge b'e cò [ge bɛ kō] *pron* whoever.

ged a [gedə] *conj* though, although.

gèile [gēlı] *m* gale.

gèill [gēL'] *v* yield, surrender.

geimheal [g'evaL] *m* fetter, shackle.

geimhlich [g'evlıch'] *v* fetter, shackle.

geinn [g'ēN'] *m* chunk; wedge.

geir [g'er'] *f* suet; fat.

gèire [gēr'ı] *f* sharpness; bitterness.

geòcach [g'ɔʰkəch] *adj* greedy, gluttonous.

geòcaire [g'ɔʰkər'ə] *m* glutton.

geòcaireachd [g'ɔʰkər'əchg] *f* greed, gluttony.

geodha [g'ɔ.ə] *m* cove, narrow bay.

geòla [g'ɔLə] *f* yawl, small boat.

geòlas [g'ɔLəs] *m* geology.

ge-tà [getā] *adv* though.

geug [g'iag] *f* branch.

geum [g'ēm] *m* bellow; bellowing; lowing. • *v* bellow; low.

geur [g'iar] *adj* sharp; bitter; sarcastic.

geuraich [g'iarıch'] *v* sharpen.

geur-chùiseach [g'iar chūšəch] *adj* smart, shrewd.

gheibh [gh'ev] *future tense of v* **faigh**.

giall [g'iəL] *f* jaw.

Giblean [g'iblan] *m* (*with art*) **an Giblean** [ən g'iblan] April.

Giblinn see **Giblean**.

gidheadh [g'i.əgh] *adv* nevertheless.

gilb [g'ilib] *f* chisel.

gile [g'ilı] *f* whiteness.

gilead [g'iləd] *m* whiteness.

gille [g'iLı] *m* boy, lad; young man.

gille-brìghde [g'iLıbrīd'ı] *m* oystercatcher.

gin[1] [g'in] *v* beget; conceive; breed.

gin[2] [g'in] *pron* any; (*with neg v*) none.

gineal [g'inal] *m* progeny; race.

ginealach [g'inaLəch] *m* generation.

gineamhainn [g'inəvıN'] *m* conception; breeding.

ginideach [g'inid'əch] *adj* (*gram*) genitive.

giodar [g'idər] *m* sewage.

giodhar [g'i.ər] *m* (*engine*) gear.

giomach [g'iməch] *m* lobster.

gioma-goc [g'imə gɔʰk] *m* piggyback.

gionach [g'inəch] *adj* keen, ambitious; greedy.

gionaiche [g'inıch'ə] *f* greed: ambition.

giorrachadh [g'iRəchəgh] *m* shortening; curtailment; abbreviation.

giorrad [g'iRəd] *m* shortness.

giorraich [g'iRıch'] *v* shorten; abbreviate; curtail.

giosg [g'iəsg] *v* gnash.

giùlain [g'ūLəN'] *v* carry.

giùlan [g'ūLan] *m* carrying; carriage; behaviour.

giùran [g'ūran] *m* (*of fish*) gill.

giuthas [g'u.əs] *m* (*wood and tree*) pine, fir tree.

glac[1] [gLaʰk] *f* small valley; hollow; palm of hand.

glac[2] [gLaʰk] *v* catch, trap; grasp; apprehend.

glacte [gLaʰkt'ı] *adj* captured, trapped.

glagadaich [gLagədıch'] *f* clattering; rattling.

glaine [gLanı] *f* cleanliness.

glainne [gLaN'ı] *f* glass.

glainneachan [gLaN'əchən] *fpl* glasses, spectacles.

glais [gLaš] *v* lock.

glaiste [gLašd'ı] *adj* locked.

glam [gLam] *v* gobble, devour.

glan [gLan] *v* clean, cleanse. • *adj* clean; (*fam*) fine, grand.

glaodh[1] [gLūgh] *v* call, shout, yell. • *m* call, shout, yell.

glaodh[2] [gLū] *v* glue. • *m* glue.

glaodhan [gLū.an] *m* paste; pulp.

glas[1] [gLas] *f* lock.

glas[2] [gLas] *adj* grey; green.

glas-làmh [gLasLāv] *f* handcuff.

glasraich [gLasrɪch'] *f* vegetable(s), greens.

glè [glē] *adv* very.

gleac [glɛʰk] *v* struggle; wrestle. • *m* struggle; wrestling.

gleacadair [glɛʰkədər'] *m* wrestler.

gleadhar [glɛ.ər] *m* uproar.

gleadhraich [glɛrɪch'] *f* clamour, din.

gleann [glɛuN] *m* glen, valley.

glèidh [glē] *v* keep; save; conserve.

glèidhteachas [glēt'əchəs] *m* conservation.

Glèidhteachas Nàdair [glēt'əchəs Nādɪr'] *m* Nature Conservancy.

glè mhath [glē va] *adv/adj* very good; very well.

gleoc [glɔʰk] *m* clock.

gleus [glēs] *v* get ready; put in trim; adjust; (*mus*) tune. • *m* condition, trim; mood; (*mus*) tuning.

gleusda [glēsdə] *adj* ready; handy; in good trim; in good humour; (*mus*) tuned.

glic [gliʰk'] *adj* wise; clever; sensible.

gliog [glig] *m* (*sound*) drip, dripping.

gliongartaich [glingəršdɪch'] *m* clinking, jingling.

gloc [gLɔʰk] *v* cackle.

glocail [gLɔʰkal] *f* cackle, cackling.

gloinne [gLɔN'ɪ] *f* glass.

gloinneachan [gLɔN'əchən] *fpl* glasses, spectacles.

glòir [gLōr'] *m* glory; fame.

glòirich [gLōr'ɪch'] *v* glorify.

glòir-mhiann [gLōr'vian] *m* ambition.

glòrmhor [gLōrvər] *adj* glorious.

gluais [gLuəš] *v* move; touch, affect.

gluasad [gLuəsəd] *m* movement; gait; emotional arousal.

gluasadach [gLuəsədəch] *adj* capable of moving.

glug [gLug] *m* gurgling; gulping.

glugan [gLugan] *m* gurgling.

glug caoinidh [gLug kūN'ɪ] *m* sob.

glumag [gLumag] *f* pool (*in burn, etc*); puddle.

glùn [gLūn] *m* knee.

gnàth, gnàthas [grā] [grā.əs] *m* custom; habit.

gnàthach [grāhəch] *adj* customary, normal.

gnàthaich [grāhɪch'] *v* use; accustom; behave towards, treat.

gnè [gr'ɛ̄] *f* kind; species; gender.

gnìomh [gr'iəv] *m* act, action.

gnìomhach [gr'iəvəch] *adj* active; enterprising; hardworking.

gnìomhachas [gr'iəvəchəs] *m* industry; business; industriousness.

gnìomhaiche [gr'iəvɪch'ə] *m* executive.

gnìomhair [gr'iəvɛr'] *m* verb.

gnog [grog] *v* knock; nod.

gnothach [grɔ.əch] *m* business; matter, affair; errand.

gnù [grū] *adj* surly, sullen.

gnùis [grūš] *f* face; complexion; expression.

gob [gob] *m* beak, bill; (*fam*) gob; point.

gobach [gobəch] *adj* prattling, chattering.

gobaireachd [gobɪr'əchg] *f* prattle, prattling.

gobha [go.ə] *m* blacksmith.

gobhal [go.al] *m* fork; (*anat*) crotch.

gobhal-gleusaidh [go.al*glēsɪ*] *m* tuning fork.

gobhar [go.ər] *f* goat.

gobhlach [gōLəch] *adj* forked.

gobhlag[1] [gōlag] *f* pitch-fork, hay-fork.

gobhlag[2] [gōLag] *f* earwig.

gobhlan-gaoithe [gōLangū.ɪ] *m* swallow.

goc [gᴐʰk] *m* tap; stopcock.

gogail [gogal] *f* cackling; clucking.

goid [god'] *v* steal, thieve. • *f* stealing, thieving.

goil [gol] *v* boil; seethe.

goile [golɪ] *f* stomach.

goileach [goləch] *adj* boiling.

goileam [goləm] *m* prattle, tittle-tattle.

goireas [gor'əs] *m* resource, facility; (*pl*) **goireasan** [gor'əsən] public conveniences.

goireasach [gor'əsəch] *adj* handy, convenient.

goireasan see **goireas**.

goirid [gor'ɪd'] *adj* short; brief.

goirt [gᴐršd'] *adj* painful, sore; sour; bitter; severe.

goirtich [gᴐršd'ɪch'] *v* hurt.

goistidh [gošd'ɪ] *m* godfather; sponsor; gossip.

gòrach [gōrəch] *adj* stupid; foolish, daft.

gòraiche [gōrɪch'ə] *f* stupidity; foolishness.

gorm [gᴐrəm] *adj* blue; green.

gort [gᴐršd] *f* famine; starvation.

gràbhail [grāval] *v* engrave.

grad [grad] *adj* sudden; alert; agile.

gràdh [grā] *m* love. • *excl* **a ghràidh!** [ə ghrāy] love! dear!

gràdhach [grā.əch] *adj* loving, affectionate.

gràf [grāf] *m* graph.

gràg [grāg] *m* croak, caw.

gràgail [grāgal] *f* croaking, cawing.

gràin [grāN'] *f* hatred; loathing, disgust; **tha gràin agam air** [ha grāN' agəm ɛr'] I hate him/it.

gràineag [grāN'ag] *f* hedgehog.

gràineil [grāN'ɛl] *adj* hateful, abominable, loathsome.

gràinne [grāN'ɪ] *f* (*single*) grain (*of corn*).

gràinnean [grāN'an] *m* grain (*of sugar, etc*).

gràisg [grāšg'] *f* (*derog*) crowd; mob.

gràisgeil [grāšgɛl] *adj* uncouth, yobbish.

grama [gramə] *m* gram(me).

gramail [gramal] *adj* persistent.

gràmar [grāmər] *m* grammar.

gràmarach [grāmərəch] *adj* grammatical.

gràn [grān] *m* cereal; (*coll*) grain.

granaidh [granɪ] *f* granny.

grannda [grauNdə] *adj* ugly.

gràpa [grāʰpə] *m* (*agricultural*) fork.

gràs [grās] *m* grace; graciousness.

gràsmhor [grāsvər] *adj* gracious.

greadhnach [gr'ɛnəch] *adj* gorgeous; magnificent.

greallach [gr'aLəch] *f* entrails, innards.

greannach [gr'aNəch] *adj* ill-tempered.

greannmhor [gr'auNvər] *adj* cheerful, joyful.

greas [gr'es] *v* hurry, urge on. • *excl* **greas ort!** [gr'es ɔršd] hurry up!

grèata [gr'ɛʰtə] *m* grate; grating.

greideal [gr'ed'al] *f* griddle.

Grèig [gr'ēg'] *f* (*with art*) **a' Ghrèig** [ə ghr'ēg'] Greece.

greigh [gr'ey] *f* herd; flock; (*of horses*) stud.

greigheach [gr'ei.əch] *adj* gregarious.

grèim [gr'ēm] *m* grip, grasp, hold; (*med*) stitch.

grèim bidh [gr'ēm bī] *m* bite to eat.

grèim-cluaise [gr'ēmkLuəšı] *m* earache.

greimeil [gr'emɛl] *adj* resolute.

greimich ri/air [gr'emıch' r'i/ɛr'] *v* seize, grasp.

greimire [gr'emɪr'ə] *m* (*table*) fork.

greis [gr'eš] *f* while, time.

grèis [gr'ēš] *f* needlework, embroidery (*i.e. the activity, see* **obair-ghrèise** [obır'ghr'ēšı]).

greiseag [gr'ešag] *f* short while.

Greugach [gr'ēgəch] *m/adj* Greek person; Greek.

Greugais [gr'ēgıš] *f* (*with art*) **a' Ghreugais** [ə ghr'ēgıš] Greek (language).

greusaiche [gr'iasıch'ə] *m* shoemaker, cobbler.

grian [gr'ian] *f* sun.

grinn [gr'īN'] *adj* elegant, fine; neat; accurate.

grinneal [gr'iN'aL] *m* gravel; (*of sea, etc*) bottom.

grinneas [gr'iN'əs] *m* elegance; fineness; neatness.

grìogag [gr'īgag] *f* bead.

Grioglachan [gr'igLachan] *m* (*with* *art*) **an Grioglachan** [ən gr'igLachan] the Pleiades.

Griomasach [gr'iməsəch] *m/adj* Grimsay person, from Grimsay.

Griomasaigh [gr'iməsı] *m* Grimsay.

grìos [gr'ias] *m* (*cookery*) grill.

grìosaich [gr'iasıch'] *v* (*food*) grill.

griùlach [gr'ūLəch] *f* (*with art*) **a' ghriùlach** [ə ghr'ūLəch] measles.

grod [grɔd] *v* rot, putrefy. • *adj* rotten, rotted, putrid.

grodach [grɔdəch] *adj* grotty.

grodach-coimhead [grɔdəch kɔi.əd] *adj* (*fam*) grotty-looking.

grodadh [grɔdəgh] *m* rot, putrefaction.

gròiseid [grɔ̄šɛd'] *f* gooseberry.

gròsair [grɔ̄sɛr'] *m* grocer.

gruag [gruag] *f* (head of) hair.

gruagach [gruagəch] *f* maid, girl, young woman.

gruagaire [gruagər'ə] *m* hairdresser.

gruag-bhrèige [gruagvr'ēg'ı] *f* wig.

gruaidh [gruəy] *f* cheek.

gruaim [gruəim] *f* gloom, melancholy; scowl; sulkiness; grumpiness.

gruamach [gruəməch] *adj* gloomy; morose; sulking; grumpy.

grùdair [grūdɛr'] *m* brewer.

grùdaireachd [grūdɛr'əchg] *f* brewing.

grùid [grūd'] *f* lees, dregs, grounds; sediment.

grunn [grūN] *m* crowd; many, lots of.

grunnd [grūNd] *m* base; sea-bed.

grùnsgal [grūnsgəL] *m* growl, growling.

gruth [gruh] *m* curd(s); crowdie.

grùthan [grūhan] *m* (*usu animal*) liver.

gu[1] [gə] *prefix introducing an adverb.*

gu[2] see **gus**.

guailleachan [guaL'əchan] *m* shawl.

gual [guəL] *m* coal.

gualan [guəLan] *m* carbon.

gualann [guəLəN] *f* shoulder. *f* shoulder.

gual-fiodha [guəLfyoghə] *m* charcoal.

guanach [gruənəch] *adj* giddy, scatter-brained; coquettish.

guanag [guənag] *f* scatter-brained girl; coquettish girl.

gu bochd [gə bɔchg] *adv* poorly.

gu bràth [gə brāch] *adv* ever; for ever.

gu bràth tuilleadh [gə brāch tuL'əgh] *adv* (*with neg v*) nevermore.

gu buileach [gə buləch] *adv* entirely.

gucag [guʰkag] *f* (*botany*) bud; bubble.

gucag-uighe [guʰkagui.ɪ] *f* egg-cup.

gu 'chùl [gə chūL] *adv* through and through.

gu dè? [gud'ē] *pron* (*for emphasis*) what?, whatever?.

gu dearbh [gə d'ɛrav] *adv* indeed; definitely.

gu dearbh fhèin [gə d'ɛrav hēn] *adv* extremely.

gu diofair [gə d'ifər] *adv* of importance.

gu dubh dona [gə du dɔnə] *adv* absolutely terribly.

guga [gugə] *m* young gannet, young solan goose.

gu grad [gə grad] *adv* suddenly; shortly.

gu h-aon sgeulach [gə hūn sg'iaLəch] *adv* unanimously.

gu h-àraid [gə hār'ɪd'], **gu h-àraidh** [gə hār'ɪ] *adv* especially, particularly.

gu h-iomlan [gə hiəmLan] *adv* fully, absolutely.

guidh [guy] *v* beg, beseech; pray.

guidhe [gui.ɪ] *f* plea, entreaty; prayer.

guilbneach [gulibnəch] *m* curlew.

guin [guN'] *v* sting. • *m* sting.

guineach [guN'əch] *adj* sharp; acerbic; wounding.

guir [gur'] *v* hatch.

guirean [gur'an] *m* pimple, spot.

gu lèir [gə L'ēr'] *adv* entire, entirely.

gu leòr [gə L'ōr] *adv* enough, plenty.

. . . gu leth [gə L'e] *adv* . . . and a half.

gum see **gun**.

gu mì-fhortanach [gə mī ɔršdanəch] *adv* unfortunately.

gu minig [gə minig'] *adv* often.

gun[1] [gum] [gun] *conj* that.

gun[2] [gən] *prep* without.

gùn [gūn] *m* gown.

gun bhuannachd [gən vuəNəchg] *adv* fruitless.

gun chadal [gən chadaL] *adv* sleepless.

gun chaomhnadh [gən chūvnəgh] *adv* unsparingly.

gun chiall [gən ch'iaL] *adv* senseless; meaningless.

gun chùnntas [gən chūNdəs] *adv* countless, innumerable.

gun dòchas [gən dōchəs] *adv* hopeless.

gun fheum [gəN' ēm] *adv* useless.

gun fhios do X [gəN' is də] without X's knowledge.

gun fhios nach [gəN' is nach] *conj* lest, in case.

gun fhiù [gəN' ū] *adv* worthless.

gun ghluasad [gən ghLuəsəd] *adv* still, motionless.

gun luach [gən Luəch] *adj* worthless.

gun mheang [gən vɛng] *adj* flawless.

gunna [guNə] *m* gun.

gunnair [guNɛr'] *m* gunner.

gun nàire [gən Nār'ı] *adv* shameless.

gun obair [gən obır'] *adv* unemployed.

gùn-oidhche [gūnoich'ı] *m* nightgown.

gun sgillinn ruadh [gən sg'iLıN' ruəgh] *adv* (stony) broke.

gun smior [gən smir] *adj* spineless, wet.

gun teagamh [gən t'ɛgəv] *adv* doubtless, without a doubt.

gun tomhas [gən to.əs] *adj* incalculable, immeasurable.

gun uiread is [gən ur'əd ıs] *adv* without so much as.

gurraban [guRəban] *m* crouch, crouching position.

gu ruige [gu Rig'ı] *prep* up to, as far as; until.

gu ruige an-seo [gu Rig'ı ənšə] *adv* this far; so far, up to now.

gus, gu [gus] [gu] *conj* to, in order to. • *prep* to, towards, up to; until.

gu bhith . . . [gu vi] about to (be) . . .; **gu bhith a' falbh** [gu vi ə faLav] about to leave.

gu sealladh orm! [gu šaLəgh ərəm] *excl* my goodness!

gu sealladh sealbh oirnn! [gu šaLəgh šɛLav ərN'] *excl* Heaven preserve us!

gu sìorraidh [gu šiəRı] *adv* for ever.

gu sìorraidh bràth [gu šiəRı brāch] *adv* for ever and ever.

gu sònraichte [gu sōnrıch't'ə] *adv* especially, particularly.

guth [guh] *m* voice; news, word; mention; **gun guth air X** [gən ghuh ɛr'] not to mention X.

gu tur [gu tur] *adv* completely, totally, entirely.

H

halò [halō] *excl* hello/hullo.

heactair [hɛktɛr'] *m* hectare.

Hearach [hɛrach] *m/adj* Harris person, from Harris.

Hearadh [hɛrəgh] *f* (*with art*) **na Hearadh** [nə hɛrəgh] Harris.

heileacoptair [hɛləkəʰptɛr'] *m* helicopter.

hidrigin [hidrıg'ın] *m* hydrogen.

Hiort [hiršd] *f* St Kilda.

Hiortach [hiršdəch] *m/adj* St Kildan.

hò-rò gheallaidh [hō rō gh'aLı] *m* party, knees-up, hoolie.

I

i [ī] *pron* she, her, it (*f*).

iad [iəd] *pron* they, them.

iadsan [iədsən] *pron* (*emphatic*) they, them.

iall [iəL] *f* thong; dog's leash; strap; strop.

iall bròige [iəL brōg'ı] *f* shoe-lace.

ialtag [iəLtag] *f* (*creature*) bat.

iar [iər] *f* west.

iar-[1] [iər] *prefix* under-, deputy-; **iar-stiùiriche** [iər sd'ūr'ıch'ə] *m* deputy director.

iar-[2] [iər] *prefix* post-; **iar-cheumaiche** [iər ch'ēmnıch'ə] *m* postgraduate.

iar air [iər ɛr'] *prep* west of.

iarann [iərəN] *m* iron.

iargalta [iərgəLtə] *adj* churlish, surly.

iarla [iərLə] *m* earl.

iarmad [iərməd] *m* remnant.

iarmailt [iərmalt'] *f* (*with art*) **an iarmailt** [ə N'iərmalt'] the firmament, the heavens.

iarnaich [iərnıch'] *v* iron.

iar-ogha [iər o.ə] *m* great-grandchild.

iarr [iəR] *v* want; ask for; invite.

iarrtas [iəRtəs] *m* request; demand; (*job, etc*) application.

iasad [iəsəd] *m* borrowing; loan.

iasg [iasg] *m* fish.

iasgach [iasgəch] *m* (*deep-sea, etc*) fishing; angling.

iasgaich [iasgıch'] *v* fish.

iasgair [iasgɛr'] *m* fisherman; angler.

iadh [iəgh] *v* surround; enclose.

idir [id'ır'] *adv usu with neg* (not) at all.

ifhrinn [ir'ıN'] *f* hell.

ifhrinneach [ir'ıN'əch] *adj* hellish, infernal.

Ìle [īlı] *f* Islay.

Ìleach [īləch] *m/adj* Islay person, from Islay.

ìm [īm] *m* butter.

imcheist [imich'ešd'] *f* anxiety, perplexity, dilemma. • *adv* **ann an imcheist** [auN ən imich'ešd'] in a dilemma, perplexed.

imcheisteach [imich'ešd'əch] *adj* worried; worrying.

imich [imich'] *v* depart, go.

imleag [imilag] *f* navel.

imlich [imilıch'] *v* lick, lap. • *f* lick; licking.

ìmpidh [īmpı] *m* persuasion, urging.

ìmpidheach [īmpı.əch] *adj* persuasive.

ìmpireil [īmpır'ɛl] *adj* imperial.

ìmpireileas [īmpır'ɛləs] *f* imperialism.

imrich [imir'ıch'] *v* move house. • *f* moving house, flitting.

inbhe [inivı] *f* rank; level; adulthood.

inbheach [inivəch] *adj* adult. • *m* adult, grown-up.

inbheil [inivɛl] *adj* high-ranking.

inbhir [iN'ır'] *m* confluence; (*of watercourse*) mouth.

inc [ink] *m* ink.

ìne [īN'ɪ] f toenail, fingernail; claw, talon.

inneal [iN'aL] m machine; implement.

innealach [iN'aLəch] adj mechanical.

inneal-ciùil [iN'aLk'ūl] m musical instrument.

inneal-clàir [iN'aLkLār'] m record-player.

inneal-nighe [iN'aLN'i.ɪ] m washing machine.

inneal-smàlaidh [iN'aLsmāLɪ] m fire extinguisher.

innean [iN'an] m anvil.

innear [iN'ɛr] f dung, manure.

innidh [iN'ɪ] f bowels; intestines.

innis[1] [īš] v tell, inform; (story, etc) recount.

innis[2] [iniš] f island; haugh, inch.

innis breug [īš br'iag] v lie, tell a lie.

Innis Tìle [iN'ɪš t'īlɪ] m Iceland.

innleachd [īN'L'əchg] f device; inventiveness; intelligence; artfulness; stratagem.

innleachdach [īN'L'əchgəch] adj inventive; resourceful; intelligent; cunning.

innleadair [īN'L'ədər'] m engineer, mechanic.

innleadair-dealain [īN'L'ədərd'ɛLɛN'] m electrical engineer.

innleadaireachd [īN'L'ər'əchg] f engineering.

innleadair-thogalach [īN'L'əhogaLəch] m civil engineer.

innlich [īN'L'ɪch'] v invent, devise; plot.

Innseachan [īšəchən] mpl (with art) **na h-Innseachan** [nə hīšəchən] India; the Indies.

Innseanach [īšənəch] m/adj Indian.

innte [īN'd'ɪ] prep pron in her, in it (f).

inntinn [īN'd'iN'] f mind, intellect.

inntinneach [īN'd'ɪN'əch] adj interesting; mental, intellectual.

inntrig [īN'd'r'ɪg'] v (building, etc) enter.

ìobair [iəbɪr'] v (relig) sacrifice, offer up.

ìobairt [iəbɪršd'] f (relig) sacrifice, offering.

ìoc [iəhk] v pay. • m payment.

ìochd [iəchg] f compassion, mercy.

ìochdar [iəchgər] m bottom, base.

ìochdarach [iəchgərəch] adj lower; inferior, subordinate.

ìochdaran [iəchgəran] m inferior, subordinate; subject.

ìochdaranachd [iəchgəranəchg] f inferiority.

ìochdmhor [iəchgvər] adj compassionate, merciful.

ìocshlaint [iəhkLaN'd'] f medicine, remedy.

ìodhal [iəghəL] m idol.

ìodhlann [iəLəN] f stack-yard.

ìolach [iLəch] f shout.

ìolaire [iLər'ə] f eagle.

ìolaire bhuidhe [iLər'ə vui.ɪ] f golden eagle.

ìolra [iLrə] m/adj (gram) plural.

ioma- [imə] prefix multi-.

iomadach [imədəch] adj many (a).

iomadach uair [imədəch uər'] adv often, many a time.

iomadh [iməgh] adj adv many (a).

ioma-fhillte [imīL't'ɪ] adj complex, complicated; manifold.

iomagain [imagɛN'] f anxiety, worry.

iomagaineach [imagɛN'əch] adj anxious; worrying.

iomain [iumɛN'] *v* drive on (*esp livestock*); propel; play shinty. • *f* shinty.

iomair [iumɪr'] *v* (*boat*) row.

iomair an aon ràmh [iumɪr' ən ūn rāv] co-operate, pull together.

iomall [iuməL] *m* edge, periphery; limit; rim.

iomall a' bhaile [iuməL ə valɪ] *m* suburbs.

iomallach [iuməLəch] *adj* remote, isolated; marginal.

iomchaidh [iməch'ɪ] *adj* suitable; decent, proper.

iomchair [imchər'] *v* carry, transport.

iomhaigh [iəvay] *f* image; likeness; idol.

iomlaid [iumLɪd'] *f* exchange, barter; (*money*) change.

iomlan [iumLan] *adj* complete, full, absolute.

iomnaidh [iumnɪ] *f* solicitude.

iompachadh [iumpəchəgh] *m* conversion.

iompachan [iumpəchan] *m* convert, neophyte.

iompaich [iumpɪch'] *v* persuade; (*relig*) convert.

iompaire [īmpɪr'ə] *m* emperor.

iompaireachd [īmpɪr'əchg] *f* empire.

iomradh [imrəgh] *m* mention; report.

iomraiteach [imraʰt'əch] *adj* celebrated; notorious.

iomrall [imrəL] *m* mistake; going astray.

iomrallach [imrəLəch] *adj* mistaken, erroneous.

iomramh [imrəv] *m* rowing.

ion- [in] *prefix indicating* able to, worthy of.

ionad [inəd] *m* place, spot; centre.

ionadail [inədəl] *adj* local.

ionad-cosnaidh [inədkɔsnɪ] *m* job centre.

ionad-latha [inədLa.a] *m* day centre.

ionad-margaid[inədmarag'ɪd'], **ionad-margaidh** [inədmarag'ɪ] *m* marketplace.

ionad-obrach [inədobrəch] *m* job centre.

ionad-slàinte [inədsLāN'd'ɪ] *m* health centre.

ionad-stiùiridh [inədšd'ūr'ɪ] *m* management centre.

ionaltraich [inəLtrich'] *v* graze.

ionaltradh [inəLtrəgh] *m* grazing, pasture.

ionann [inəN] *adj* alike, identical.

ion-dhèanta [ingh'iantə] *adj* feasible, possible.

iongantach [iəndəch] *adj* strange; surprising; marvellous.

iongantas [iəndəs] *m* surprise, amazement; phenomenon, amazing thing.

iongna *see* **ìne**

iongnadh [iənəgh] *m* amazement.

ion-ithe [in ich'ɪ] *adj* eatable, edible.

ionmhainn [inɪvɪN'] *adj* dear, beloved.

ionmhas [inɪvəs] *m* treasure; finance.

ionmhasair [inɪvəsɛr'] *m* treasurer.

ionmholta [invoLtə] *adj* praiseworthy.

ionnan *see* **ionann**

ionndrainn [iuNdrɪN'] *v* miss, long for.

ionnlad [iuNLəd] *m* washing, ablutions.

ionnlaid [iuNLɪd'] *v* wash, bathe.

ionnsachadh [iuNsəchəgh] *m* learning.

ionnsaich [iuNsɪch'] *v* learn, study.

ionnsaichte [iuNsɪch't'ɪ] *adj* educated; trained.

ionnsaigh [iuNsɪ] *f* attack, assault; attempt.

ionnstramaid [iuNsdrəmɪd'] *f* instrument.

ionracas [inrə^hkəs] *m* honesty; justice; righteousness.

ionraic [inrɪ^hk'] *adj* honest; just; righteous.

iorgail [irgɪl] *f* tumult.

iorgaileach [irgɪləch] *adj* tumultuous.

ioronas [iərənəs] *m* irony.

ioronta [iərəndə] *adj* ironic.

Iosa [iəsə] *m* Jesus.

iosal *see* **ìseal**

Ioslamach [isLəməch] *adj* Islamic.

iotmhor [iə^htvər] *adj* (*land, etc*) parched; very thirsty.

ìre [īr'ɪ] *f* degree, level; stage.

ìriseal [ir'ɪšəL] *adj* low, lowly; humble.

ìrisleachd [ir'ɪšLəchg] *f* humility; lowliness.

ìrislich [ir'ɪšlɪch'] *v* humble; humiliate.

iris [ir'ɪš] *f* magazine, periodical.

is[1] [is] *v* am, is, are.

is[2] [ɪs] (*for* **agus**) *conj* and.

is beag orm X [is beg ɔrəm] *v* I don't like X.

isbean [isban] *m* sausage.

is toil leam X [stɔləm] *v* I like X.

is caomh leam X [skūləm] *v* I like X (Lewis dialect).

is ciar leam X [sk'iər ləm] *v* I take a dim view of X.

is cubhaidh dhomh [skuvɪ ghɔ] *v* it befits me.

is dòcha! [sdōchə] maybe!

is dòcha gun [sdōchə gun] *conj* perhaps.

is duilich leam [sdulɪch' ləm] *v* I find it hard to.

is duilich sin! [sdulɪch' šin] *excl* that's a shame!

ise [iši] *pron* (*emphatic*) she, her.

ìseal [īšəl], **ìosal** [iəsəL] *adj* low; lowly; humble; (*voice, etc*) quiet.

isean [išan] *m* chick; baby animal.

islich [īšlɪch'] *v* become lower; demote.

isneach [išnəch] *f* rifle.

Iosrael [isra.ɛl] *f* Israel.

Iosraelach [isra.ɛləch] *m/adj* Israeli, Israelite.

ist! [išd'] *excl* hush! be quiet!

ite [i^ht'ɪ] *f* feather; plumage; fin.

iteach [i^ht'əch] *adj* feathered.

iteachan [i^ht'əchan] *m* bobbin, spool.

iteag [i^ht'ag] *f* small feather; flying, flight.

iteagach [i^ht'agəch] *adj* feathered.

itealaich [i^ht'aLɪch'] *v* fly.

itealan [i^ht'aLan] *m* aeroplane, aircraft.

itealag [i^ht'aLag] *f* kite.

ith [ich'] *v* eat.

iubhar [iu.ər] *m* yew.

iuchair [iuchɪr'] *f* key; **iuchair-ghnìomha** [iuchɪr'ghr'iəvə] *f* (*IT*) function key.

Iuchar [iuchər] *m* (*with art*) **an t-Iuchar** [ən t'iuchər] July.

Iùdhach [iū.əch] *m/adj* Jew; Jewish.

iùil-tharraing [iūlhaRɪng'] *f* magnetism.

iùil-tharraingeach [iūlhaRɪng'əch] *adj* magnetic.

L

là *see* **latha** *except for holidays*

labhair [Lavɪr'] *v* speak, talk.

labhairt [Lavɪršd'] *f* speech, speaking.

lach [Lach] *f* (*bird*) duck.

lachdann [LachgəN] *adj* dun, tawny; khaki; swarthy.

ladar [Ladər] *m* ladle, scoop.

ladarna [Ladərnə] *adj* bold; shameless.

ladhar [Lo.ər] *m* hoof.

lag[1] [Lag] *adj* weak, feeble.

lag[2] [Lag] *m* hollow; pit.

lagaich [Lagɪch'] *v* weaken.

lag-chùiseach [Lag chūšəch] *adj* unenterprising.

lagh [logh] *m* law.

laghach [Lo.əch] *adj* nice; kind.

laghail [Loghal] *adj* lawful, legal.

laghairt [Lo.ɪršd'] *f* lizard.

Laideann [Lad'əN] *f* Latin (language).

Laidinneach [Lad'ɪN'əch] *adj* Latin.

làidir [Lād'ɪr'] *adj* strong; potent.

laigh [Lay] *v* lie (down); (*plane, etc*) land; subside.

laighe [Lai.ɪ] *f* recumbent position.

laighe na grèine [Lai.ɪ nə gr'ēnɪ] *f* sunset.

laigse [Lag'šɪ] *f* weakness; infirmity; faint.

làimhsich [Laišɪch'] *v* touch, handle; wield.

lainnir [LaN'ɪr'] *f* glint, sparkle; radiance.

lainnireach [LaN'ɪr'əch] *adj* sparkling; radiant.

làir [Lār'] *f* mare.

làithean-saora [Lai.ənsūrə] *mpl* holidays.

làitheil [lai.el] *adj* daily; everyday.

là-luain [La.ə LuaN'] *m* doomsday.

làmh [Lāv] *f* hand; handle.

làmhainn [LāvɪN'] *f* glove.

làmh an uachdair [Lāv ən uachgɪr'] *m* the upper hand.

làmh-lèigh [Lāvley] *m* surgeon.

làmh-sgrìobhadh [Lāvsgr'īvəgh] *m* handwriting; manuscript.

làmhthuagh [Lāvhuə] *f* hatchet, chopper.

lampa [Laumbə] *m* lamp.

làn [Lān] *adj* full. • *adv* fully. • *m* one's fill.

Là na Sàbaid [La.ə nə sābɪd'] *m* Sunday, the Sabbath.

làn beòil [Lān byōl] *m* mouthful.

làn chinnteach [Lān ch'īN'd'əch] *adj* completely certain, convinced.

làn chumhachd [Lān chu.əchg] *m* absolute power.

làn chumhachdach [Lān chu.əchgəch] *adj* all-powerful.

làn dùirn [Lān dūrN'] *m* handful, fistful.

làn fhada [Lān adə] *adj*/*adv* full-length.

langa [Langə] *f* (*fish*) ling.

langanaich [Langanɪch'] *v* (*animals*) bellow; low.

langasaid [Langəsɪd'] *f* sofa, couch.

làn-mara [Lānmarə] *m* high tide.

làn mo bhroinn de. [Lān mə bhrəiN'd'e] *m* (*fam*) my bellyful of.

lann [LauN] *f* blade; (*fish*) scale; enclosure; repository.

lanntair [LauNder'] *m* lantern.

làn spàine [Lān sbāN'ɪ] *m* spoonful.

laoch [Lūch] *m* hero; warrior.

laochan [Lūchan] *m* wee boy, wee hero.

laogh [Lūgh] *m* calf.

laoidh [Lūy] *f* poem; hymn.

laoigh-fheòil [Lūi.yōl] *f* veal.

làr [Lār] *m* ground, floor.

làrach [Lārəch] *f* trace, mark; ruin; site.

làrna-mhàireach [Lārnəvār'əch] *m* the morrow, the next day.

las [Las] *v* set alight; blaze; (*fig*) light up.

lasadair [Lasədər'] *m* match (*for striking*).

lasaich [Lasɪch'] *v* loosen; soothe.

lasair [Lasɛr'] *f* flame(s); flash.

lasgan [Lasgan] *m* outburst; (*of anger, etc*) fit.

lasrach [Lasrəch] *adj* flaming; blazing.

lastaig [Lasdɪg'] *f*/*adj* elastic.

latha [La.ə] *m* day.

latha a' bhràtha [La ə vrāhə] *m* judgement day.

latha-breith [La.ə br'e] *m* birthday.

latha-fèille [La.əfēL'ɪ] *m* holiday, feastday.

làthair [Lāhɪr'] *f* presence; sight, view.

latha no latheigin [La.ə nə La.eg'ɪn] *adv* some day or other, one fine day.

latha-trasg [La.ətrasg] *m* fast day.

latheigin [La.eg'ɪn] *m* some day.

le [le] (*before art* **leis** [leš]) *prep* with; by; belonging to.

leabaidh [L'ebɪ] *f* bed.

leabhar [L'ɔ.ər] *m* book.

leabharlann [L'ɔ.ərLəN] *f* library.

leabhar-latha [L'ɔ.ərLa.ə] *m* diary, journal.

leabhran [L'ɔ.ran] *m* booklet; brochure.

leac [L'ɛʰk] *f* (*rock*) slab, ledge.

leacag [L'ɛʰkag] *f* tile.

leac teallaich [L'ɛʰk t'ɛLɪch'] *f* hearthstone.

leac uaighe [L'ɛʰk uə.ɪ] *f* gravestone.

leac ùrlair [L'ɛʰk ūrLɪr'] *f* paving stone.

leag [L'eg] *v* fell; demolish; (*carpet, etc*) lay; (*window, etc*) lower.

leag càin air [L'eg kāN' ɛr'] *v* tax, subject to taxation.

leag gu làr [L'eg gə Lār] *v* raze (*to ground*).

leagh [L'ɔ] *v* melt, thaw; dissolve.

leam [ləm] *prep pron* with/by me.

leamhaich [L'ɛvɪch'] *v* exasperate; plague.

leamhach [L'ɛvəch] *adj* insipid.

leamhan [L'ɛvan] *m* elm.

lean [L'ɛn] *v* follow; continue; understand. • *excl* **lean ort!** [L'ɛn ōršt] keep going! ... **a leanas** [ə lɛnəs] the following ...

leanabail [L'ɛnabal] *adj* childish, silly; infantile.

leanaban [L'ɛnaban] *m* baby; small child.

leanabh [L'ɛnav] *m* baby; infant; child.

leanailteach [L'ɛnalt'ɘch] *adj* continuous, incessant.

leann [L'ūN] *m* beer, ale.

leannan [L'ɛNan] *m* lover; sweetheart, boyfriend, girlfriend.

leannanachd [L'ɛNanɘchg] *f* courting, courtship.

leannra [L'auNrɘ] *m* sauce.

leantainneach [L'ɛndıN'ɘch] *adj* continuous; persevering; lasting.

leas [Les] *m* benefit, advantage; improvement; **cha leig thu leas . . .** [cha L'eg' u les] you don't need to . . .

leasachadh [L'esɘchɘgh] *m* improvement; development.

leasaich [L'esıch'] *v* improve; develop.

leasan [L'esan] *m* lesson.

leat [laʰt] *prep pron* with/by you (*sing*).

leatha [le.ɘ] *prep pron* with/by her, with/by it (*f*).

leathad [L'ɛhɘd] *m* slope, hillside.

leathann [L'ɛhɘN] *adj* broad, wide.

leathar [L'ɛhɘr] *m* leather.

le chèile [le ch'ēlı] *adv* together; both.

le deagh dhùrachd [le d'ō ghūrɘchg] (*corres*) with compliments.

le dùrachd [le dūrɘchg] (*corres*) yours sincerely.

le foill [le foiL'] *adv* fraudulently.

leibh [leiv] *prep pron* with/by you (*pl*).

leig [L'eg'] *v* let, allow; leave to; let out, utter; (*weapon*) fire.

leig air [L'eg' ɛr'] *v* pretend; give away.

leig air dhearmad [L'eg' ɛr' dh'ɛramɘd] *v* neglect.

leig anail [L'eg' anal] *v* take a breather.

leig às [L'eg' as] *v* let off/out.

leig braidhm [L'eg' broim] *v* fart.

leig bruchd [L'eg' brūchg] *v* belch.

leig cnead [L'eg' kred] *v* groan.

leig de [L'eg' d'e] *v* give up, cease.

leig fead [L'eg' fed] *v* whistle.

leigheas [L'e.ɘs] *m* cure, remedy.

leighis [L'e.ıš] *v* cure, heal.

leig le [L'eg' le] *v* leave alone, let be.

leig leas *see* **leas**.

leig ma sgaoil [L'eg' mɘ sgūl] *v* let loose.

leig 'na theine [L'eg' nɘ henı] *v* set on fire.

leig osna [L'eg' ɔsnɘ] *v* heave/breathe a sigh.

leig seachad [L'eg' šɛchɘd] *v* give up, relinquish.

lèine [L'ēnı] *f* shirt.

leinn [leiN'] *prep pron* with/by us.

lèir [L'ēr'] *adj* visible; evident; **is lèir dhomh (gu)** [ıs L'ēr' ghɔ gu] (*ml*) it's clear to me (that).

lèirmheas [L'ēr'vɘs] *m* (*book, etc*) review.

lèirsinn [L'ēr'šıN'] *f* sight; perceptiveness.

lèirsinneach [L'ēr'šıN'ɘch] *adj* visible; perceptive.

leis[1] [L'eš] *f* thigh.

leis[2] [leš] *prep pron* with/by him, with/by it (*m*).

leis a' bhruthaich [leš ɘ vru.ıch'] *adv* with the slope.

leis an t-sruth [leš ɘn truh] *adv* downstream.

leis a sin, leis sin [leš ɘ šin] [leš šin] *adv* whereupon, at that.

leisg [L'ešg'] adj lazy; reluctant. • f laziness.

le gach deagh dhùrachd [le gach d'ō ghūrəchg] (corres) with best wishes.

leisge [L'ešg'ı] f laziness.

leisgear [L'ešgər] m lazy person, lazybones.

leisgeul [L'ešg'iaL] m excuse; pretext.

leis sin see leis a sin.

leiteis [L'eʰt'ıš] f lettuce.

leitheach [L'ehəch] adv half, semi-.

leitheach slighe [L'ehəch šli.ı] adv halfway.

leithid (de) [L'ehıd'] f the like(s) (of); **a leithid de . . .** [ə lehıd' d'e] such a . . .

leitir [L'eʰtır'] f slope, hillside.

Leòdhasach [L'ō.əsəch] m/adj Lewisman; from Lewis.

leòmhann [L'ō.əN] m lion.

leòinteach [L'ōN'd'əch] m casualty, victim; pl (with art) **na leòintich** [nə L'ōN'd'ıch] the injured; the wounded.

leòman [L'ōman] m moth.

leòn [L'ōn] v wound; hurt; injure. • m wound; hurt; injury.

leònte [L'ōnd'ı] adj wounded; hurt; injured.

leòr [L'ōr] f enough, sufficiency; **mo leòr de . . .** [mə lōr d'e] my fill of . . .

leotha [lɔ.ə] prep pron with/by them.

le sùrd [le sūrd] adv with a will.

leth [L'e]

[šia gu L'e] m half; side; **sia gu leth** six and a half; **leth-** one of a pair.

leth-asal [L'e.asaL] f mule.

lethbhreac [L'evreʰk] m (book, etc) copy, reproduction; match.

lethcheann [L'ech'auN] m cheek; side of head.

leth-cheud [L'ech'iad] m fifty.

leth-chuid [L'echud'] f half.

leth-fhuar [L'e.uər] adj lukewarm.

leth uair [L'e huər'] f half an hour.

leth-shean [L'ehɛn] adj middle-aged.

le tuiteamas [le tuʰt'əməs] adv by accident, by chance.

leud [L'iad] m breadth, width.

leudaich [L'iadıch'] v widen; extend.

leudaichte [L'iadıch't'ə] adj widened; flattened.

leug [L'iag] f jewel.

leugh [L'ēv] v read.

leum [L'ēm] v jump, leap; (nose) bleed. • m jump, leap.

leum-sròine [L'ēmsdrōN'ı] m nosebleed.

leum-uisge [L'ēmušg'ı] m waterfall.

le ur cead [ler k'ed] by your leave.

leus [L'ias] m light; ray of light; torch; blister.

Lia-Fàil [L'iə fāl] f (with art) **an Lia-Fàil** [ən L'iə fāl] the Stone of Destiny.

liagh [L'iə] f ladle, scoop.

liath [L'iə] v make or become grey. • adj grey.

liath-reòthadh [L'iərō.əgh] m frost, hoar frost.

lìbhrig [L'īvrıg'] v (goods, etc) deliver.

lide [L'id'ı] m syllable.

lighiche [L'i.ıch'ə] m doctor, physician.

lili [lili] f lily.

lìnig [L'īnɪg'] v line.

linn [L'IN'] m age, period; generation; century; (pl with art) na Linntean Dorcha [nə L'ĪN'tən dərɔchə] the Dark Ages.

linne [L'iN'ɪ] f pool; waterfall.

liomaid [L'imɪd'] f lemon.

lìomh [L'iəv] v polish, shine. • f polish, gloss.

lìomharra [L'iəvəRə] adj polished, glossy.

lìon¹ [L'iən] v fill; (tide) come in.

lìon² [L'iən] m net; web. • m flax, lint.

lìon damhain-allaidh [L'iən davɛN'aLɪ] m cobweb.

lìonmhor [L'iənvər] adj numerous; abundant.

lionn [L'ūN] m liquid.

lionn-tàthaidh [L'ūNtāhɪ] m concrete, cement.

lionsa [L'insə] f lens.

liopard [L'ipərd] m leopard.

lios [L'is] m garden; enclosure.

Liosach [L'isəch] m/adj Lismore person, from Lismore.

liosda [L'isdə] adj boring.

Lios Mòr [L'is mōr] m Lismore.

liosta [L'isdə] f list.

liotair [L'iʰtɛr'] m litre.

lip [L'iʰp] f lip.

lite [L'iʰt'ɪ] f porridge.

litir [L'iʰt'ɪr'] f letter.

litreachadh [L'iʰtr'əchəgh] m spelling.

litreachas [L'iʰtr'əchəas] m literature.

litrich [L'iʰtr'ɪch'] v spell.

liùdhag [L'ū.ag] f doll.

liut [L'uʰt] f knack.

lobh [Lo] v rot, decay.

lobhadh [Lo.əgh] m rot, putrefaction.

lobhar [Lo.ər] m leper.

lobhta [Loftə] m flat; storey; loft.

locar [Lɔʰkər] m (tool) plane.

lòcast [Lɔ̄ʰkəsd] m locust.

loch [Lɔch] m loch, lake.

lochan [Lɔchan] m small loch, pond.

lochd [Lɔchg] m fault; harm.

lochdach [Lɔchgəch] adj harmful.

Lochlann [LɔchLəN] f Scandinavia.

Lochlannach [LɔchLəNəch] m/adj Norseman; Norse; Scandinavian; Viking.

lòchran [Lōchran] m lamp, lantern.

lof [Lɔf] m loaf.

loidhne [Lɔinɪ] f line.

loingeas [Lɔing'əs] m shipping; fleet.

lòinidh [Lɔ̄N'ɪ] f (with art) an lòinidh [ən Lɔ̄N'ɪ] rheumatism.

loisg [Lɔšg'] v burn; (gun) fire.

loisgte [Lɔšg't'ɪ] adj burnt.

lòistear [Lɔ̄dtɛr] m lodger.

lòistinn [Lɔ̄šd'ɪN'] m lodging(s), digs; accommodation.

lom [Lɔum] v strip; shave; shear; mow. • adj bare; bleak; thin.

lomadair [Lɔmədər'] m shearer.

loma làn [Lɔmə Lān] adj full to the brim.

lomnochd [Lɔumnəchg] adj naked.

lòn¹ [Lɔ̄n] m food, provisions.

lòn² [Lɔ̄n] m pool; puddle; meadow.

lònaid [Lɔ̄nɪd'] f lane.

lon-dubh [Lɔndu] m blackbird.

long [Lɔung] f ship.

long-bhriseadh [Lɔungvr'išəgh] m shipwreck.

long-chogaidh [Lɔungchɔgɪ] *f* warship, battleship.

long-fhànais [lɔungānɪš] *f* spaceship.

lorg [Lɔrɔg] *v* find; track down, trace. • *f* vestige; footprint; track.

los [Lɔs] *m* purpose, intention. • *conj* **los gu**, **los gun** [Lɔs gu/gun] in order that.

lòsan [Lōsan] *m* pane.

losgadh-bràghad [Lɔsgəghbrā.əd] *m* heartburn.

losgann [LɔsgəN] *m* frog.

lot[1] [Lɔʰt] *f* croft; piece of land.

lot[2] [Lɔʰt] *v* wound. • *m* wound.

loth [Lɔ] *f* filly.

luach [Luəch] *m* worth, value.

luachachadh [Luəchəchəgh] *m* valuation.

luachaich [Luəchɪch'] *v* evaluate, value.

luachair [Luəchɛr'] *f* rushes.

luachmhor [Luəchvər] *adj* valuable, precious.

luadhadh [Luədəgh] *m* (*cloth*) waulking, fulling.

luaidh[1] [Luay] *v* praise. • *m* praise; beloved person. • *excl* **a luaidh!** [ə Luay] my love! (my) darling!

luaidh[2] [Luay] *v* (*cloth*) waulk, full.

luaisg [Luašg'] *v* rock, sway, toss.

luaithre[Luar'ɪ], **luath** [Luə] *f* ash(es).

luaths [Luəs] *m* speed; agility.

luath[1] [Luə] *adj* fast, quick.

luath[2] [Luə] *f same as* **luaithre**

luathaich [Luəhɪch'] *v* accelerate; hurry on.

luaths [Luəs] *m same as* **luas**.

luath-thrèan [Luərēnə] *f* express (train).

lùb [Lūb] *v* bend; bow. • *f* bend; loop.

lùbach [Lūbəch] *adj* bending; winding; flexible.

lùb a' ghlùin [Lūb ə ghLŪN'] *v* kneel, pray.

luch [Luch] *f* mouse.

lùchairt [Lūchɪršd'] *f* palace.

luchd[1] [Luchg] *m* cargo.

luchd[2] [Luchg] *m* people.

luchdaich [Luchgɪch'] *v* load.

luchd-càraidh [Luchkārɪ] *m* repairers.

luchd-ciùil [Luchk'ūl] *m* musicians.

luchd-eòlais [Luchg'ɔ̄Lɪš] *m* acquaintances.

luchd-frithealaidh [LuchgfrihəLɪ] *m* attendants.

luchdmhor [Luchgvər] *adj* capacious.

luchd-obrach [Luchgobrəch] *m* workers; workforce.

luchd-siubhail [Luchgšu.al] *m* (*coll*) travellers.

luchd-stiùiridh [Luchgšd'ūr'ɪ] *m* managers, management.

luchd-turais [Luchgturɪš] *m* (*coll*) tourists.

luchraban [Luchraban] *m* dwarf, midget.

lùdag [Lūdag] *f* little finger; hinge.

lugha [Lughə] *comp adj* smaller, smallest.

lùghdachadh [Lūdəchəgh] *m* reduction; abatement.

lùghdaich [Lūdɪch'] *v* lessen; shrink; abate.

Lugsamburg [Lugsəmburg] *m* Luxembourg.

Lugsamburgach [Lugsəmburgəch] *m/adj* Luxembourger, from Luxembourg.

luibh [Luiv] *f* herb; plant; weed.

luibh-eòlas [Luivyɔ̄Ləs] *m* botany.

luibhre [Luir'ɪ] *f* leprosy.

luideach [Lud'əch] *adj* shabby, scruffy.

luideag [Lud'ag] *f* rag.

luidhear [Lui.ɛr] *m* funnel, chimney.

Luinn [LuiN'] *f* Luing.

Luinneach [LuiN'əch] *m/adj* Luing person, from Luing.

luinneag [LuiN'ag] *f* song, ditty.

Lùnasdal [LūnəsdaL] *m* (*with art*) an Lùnasdal [ən LūnəsdaL] August;

Latha Lùnasdail [La.ə Lūnəsdal] Lammas Day.

lurach [Lurəch] *adj* pretty; nice; beloved.

lurgann [LurugəN] *f* shin.

lus [Lus] *m* herb; plant; weed.

lus na meala [Lus nə myaLə] *m* honeysuckle.

lùth [Lū], lùths [Lūs] *m* power of movement; energy.

lùthmhor [Lūvər] *adj* strong; agile; energetic.

lùths *m same as* lùth.

M

ma [ma] *conj* if.

màb [māb] *v* revile, vilify.

mac [maʰk] *m* son; mac bràthar [maʰk brāhar], mac piuthar [maʰk pyu.ar] *m* nephew.

mac an aba [maʰkənabə] *m* ring finger.

mac an donais! [maʰk ən dɔnɪš] *excl* damn it!

mac an duine [maʰk ən duN'ɪ] *m* humanity, humankind.

macanta [maʰkandə] *adj* meek, submissive.

machair [machɛr'] *f* machair; plain; (*with art*) a' Mhachair Ghallda [ə vachɛr' ghauLdə] the Lowlands.

machlag [machlag] *f* womb, uterus.

mac-meanmna [makmɛnamnə] *m* imagination.

mac-meanmnach [makmɛnamnəch] *adj* imaginary; imaginative.

mac na bracha [maʰk nə brachə] *m* malt whisky.

mac-samhail [maʰksau.al] *m* equal,

match; likeness.

mac-talla [maʰktaLə] *m* echo.

madadh-allaidh [madəghaLɪ] *m* wolf.

madadh ruadh [madəgh ruəgh] *m* fox.

madainn [madɪN'] *f* morning. • *adv* sa' mhadainn [sə vadɪN'] a.m.

ma dh'fhaoidte [ma ghūt'ɪ] *adv/conj* maybe, perhaps.

mag (air) [mag ɛr'] *v* mock, make fun (of).

màg [māg] *f* paw.

magadh [magəgh] *m* mockery.

magail [magal] *adj* mocking, jeering.

magairle [magɪrlə] *m* testicle.

maghar [ma.ər] *m* fly, bait.

maide [mad'ɪ] *m* wood, timber; stick; maide-droma [mad'ɪdromə] *m* ridge pole, roof-tree.

maide poite [mad'ɪ pɔʰtɪ] *m* spirtle.

maidse [mad'šɪ] *m* match (*for striking*).

màidsear [mādšɛr] *m* (*rank*) major.

maighdeann [moid'əN] *f* maiden; virgin; spinster. (*address*) **a Mhaighdeann X!** [ə void'əN] Miss X!

maighdeannas [moid'əNəs] *m* maidenhood, virginity.

maighdeann-mhara [moid'əNvarə] *f* mermaid.

maigheach [mai.əch] *m* hare.

maighstir [maišd'ɪr'] *m* master; (*address*) **a Mhaighstir X!** [ə vaišd'ɪr'] Mister X!

maighstir-sgoile [maišd'ɪr'sgɔlɪ] *m* schoolmaster.

màileid [mālɪd'] *f* suitcase; briefcase; bag.

màileid-droma [mālɪd'dromə] *f* rucksack.

màileid-làimhe [mālɪd'Laivɪ] *f* handbag.

maille [maL'ɪ] *f* slowness; delay.

maille ri [maL'ɪ r'i] *prep* with, along with.

maillich [maL'ɪch'] *v* delay; procrastinate.

mair [mar'] *v* last, continue; **mair beò** [mar' byɔ̄] live, survive.

maireann [mar'əN] *adj* living; enduring; **X nach maireann** [nach mar'əN] the late X.

maireannach [mar'əNəch] *adj* eternal; durable; long-lived.

màirnealach [mārN'aLəch] *adj* dilatory; boring.

mairtfheoil [maršd'ɔl] *f* beef.

maise [mašɪ] *f* beauty.

maiseach [mašəch] *adj* beautiful.

maisich [mašɪch'] *v* beautify; decorate; (*face*) make up.

màithreil *see* **màthaireil**

màl [māL] *m* rent.

mala [maLə] *f* brow; eyebrow.

malairt [maLɪršd'] *f* trade, business; barter.

malairtich [maLɪršdɪch'] *v* trade; barter.

màlda [māLdə] *adj* coy, bashful.

mall [mauL] *adj* slow, tardy.

mallachd [maLəchg] *f* curse.

mallaich [maLɪch'] *v* curse.

mallaichte [maLɪch'tə] *adj* cursed, damned.

mamaidh [mamɪ] *f* Mummy.

manach [manəch] *m* monk.

manachainn [manachɪN'] *f* monastery.

manadh [manəgh] *m* omen.

manaidsear [manɪd'šɛr] *m* manager.

Manainneach [manɪN'əch] *m/adj* Manxman; Manx.

mang [mang] *f* fawn.

maodal [mūdəL] *f* paunch.

maoidh [muy] *v* threaten.

maoil [mūl] *f* forehead, brow.

Maoil [mūl] *f* (*with art*) **a' Mhaoil** [ə vūl] the Minch.

maoile [mūlɪ] *f* baldness.

maoin [mūN'] *f* wealth; goods, chattels.

maol [mūL] *m* cape, promontory; rounded hill. • *adj* blunt; bald.

maorach [mūrəch] *m* shellfish.

maor-eaglais [mūregLɪš] *m* church officer.

maor-obrach [mūrobrəch] *m* foreman, gaffer.

maoth [mū] *adj* soft; tender-hearted.

maothaich [mū.ɪch'] *v* soften.

mapa [maʰpə] *m* map.

mar [mar] *prep* as; like. • *conj* **mar a** [mar ə]as, how; **mar gun** [mar gun] as if, as though.

mar a bheatha [mar ə vɛhə] *adv* for dear life.

marag [marag] *f* pudding.

maraiche [marɪch'ə] *m* sailor, seafarer.

mar an ceudna [mar ən k'iadnə] *adv* likewise, too.

marbh [marav] *v* kill. • *adj* dead.

marbhaiche [maravɪch'ə] *m* killer; murderer.

marbhan [maravan] *m* corpse.

marbhrann [maravraN] *m* elegy.

marbhtach [maravtəch] *adj* deadly, fatal.

mar bu chòir [mar bə chōr'] *adv* fittingly.

marcachadh [markəchəgh] *m* riding; horsemanship.

marcaich [markɪch'] *v* ride.

marcaiche [markɪch'ə] *m* rider, horseman.

margaid [maragɪd'] *m* market.

mar eisimpleir [mar ešɪmplɛr'] (*abbrev* **m.e.**) *adv* for example.

margadh [maragəgh] *m* market; **am Margadh Coitcheann** [əm maragəgh kɔʰt'əN] the Common Market.

margarain [maragərɛN'] *m* margarine.

màrmor [mārmər] *m* marble.

maille ri [maL'ɪ r'i] *prep* with, along with.

màrsail [mārsal] *f* march; marching.

mar sin [mar šin] *adv* so.

mar sin leat/leibh! [mar šin laʰt/ leiv] *excl* goodbye!

Màrt [māršt] *m* Mars; (*with art*) **am Màrt** [əm māršt] March.

mart [maršt] *m* beef animal.

màs [mās] *m* buttock; (*fam*) arse, bum.

mas e do thoil e [mašə də hɔlɛ] *adv* please.

mas e ur toil e [mašə ər tɔlɛ] *adv* (*polite*) please.

mas fhìor [maš iər] *adv* kidding, pretending.

maslach [masLəch] *adj* disgraceful, shameful.

masladh [masLəgh] *m* disgrace, shame.

maslaich [masLɪch'] *v* disgrace, put to shame.

ma-tà [matā], **ma-thà** [mahā] *adv* then, in that case.

matamataig [maʰtamatɪg'] *m* mathematics.

math [ma] *m* good. • *adj* good.

ma-tha *see* **ma-tà**

mathachadh [mahəchəgh] *m* manure; fertilizer.

mathaich [mahɪch'] *v* manure; enrich.

màthair [māhɪr'] *f* mother.

màthair-chèile [māhɪr'ch'ēlɪ] *f* mother-in-law.

màthaireil [māhɪr'ɛl] *adj* motherly, maternal.

màthair-uisge [māhɪr'ušg'ɪ] *m* fountainhead.

mathan [mahan] *m* (brown) bear.

mathanas [mahanəs] *m* forgiveness, pardon.

mathan bàn [mahan bān] *m* polar bear.

mathas [mahəs] *m* goodness.

math dhà-rìreadh! [ma gharīr'ə] *excl* excellent!

math do [ma dɔ] *v* forgive.

ma thogras tu [ma hogrəs du] *if you like.*

math thu-fhèin! [ma u hēn] *excl* well done! good for you!

meadhan [mi.an] *m* middle, centre; medium, mechanism; waist; average; *pl* **na meadhanan** [nə mi.anən] (*press, etc*) the media.

meadhanach [mi.anəch] *adj* middling, so-so; average.

meadhan-aois [mi.an ūš] *f* middle age.

meadhan-aoiseil [mi.an ūšēl] *adj* medieval.

meadhan-chearcail [mi.an ch'ɛrkal] *m* equator.

meadhan-latha [mi.an La.ə] *m* midday, noon.

meadhan-oidhche [mi.an oi.ch'ɪ] *m* midnight.

Meadhan-thìreach [mi.an hīr'əch] *adj* Mediterranean.

meal [mɛL] *v* enjoy. • *excl* **meal do/ ur naidheachd!** [mɛL də/ər Nɛ.əchg] congratulations!

meal-bhucan [mɛlvuʰkan] *m* melon.

meall[1] [myauL] *v* deceive; cheat; entice.

meall[2] [myauL] *m* lump; lumpy hill.

meallach [mɛLəch] *adj* beguiling, bewitching.

mealladh [mɛLəgh] *m* deceit, deception; enticement.

meall an sgòrnain [myauL ən sgōrnɛN'] *m* Adam's apple.

meallta [myauLtə] *adj* deceived; cheated.

mealltach [myauLtəch] *adj* deceitful; cheating; deceptive.

mealltair [myauLtɛr'] *m* deceiver; cheat.

meall-uisge [myauLušg'ɪ] *m* heavy shower.

mean [mɛn] *adj* little, tiny; **mean air mhean** [mɛn er' vɛn] little by little.

mèanan [mianan] *m* yawn.

mèananaich [miananɪch'] *f* yawning.

meanbh [mɛnav] *adj* tiny, minute.

meanbh-chuileag [mɛnavchulag] *f* midge.

meang [mɛng] *f* fault, flaw; abnormality.

meangach [mɛngəch] *adj* abnormal.

meangan [mɛngan], **meanglan** [mɛngLan] *m* branch, bough.

meann [mɛuN] *m* (*goat*) kid.

mearachadh [mɛrəchəgh] *m* aberration.

mearachd [mɛrəchg] *f* mistake, error.

mearachdach [mɛrəchgəch] *adj* wrong, erroneous.

mèaran [mēran] *m* yawn.

mèaranaich [mēranɪch'] *f* yawning.

mèarrsaidh [mēRsɪ] *m* march, marching.

meas[1] [mes] *m* valuation; respect, esteem; **is mise le meas** [ɪs mɪšɪ le mes] (*corres*) yours sincerely. • *v* estimate; evaluate; esteem; think.

meas[2] [mes] *m* fruit.

measach [mesəch] *adj* fruity.

measail [mesal] *adj* respected; respectable; valued.

measail (air) [mesal ɛr'] *adj* fond (of).

measarra [mesəRə] *adj* moderate; temperate.

measarrachd [mesəRəchg] *f* moderation; abstinence.

meas-chraobh [meschrūv] *f* fruit tree.

measgaich [mesgɪch'] *v* mix, mingle.

measgaichear [mesgɪch'ɛr] *m* mixer.

meata [mɛʰtə] *adj* faint-hearted; feeble.

meatailt [mɛʰtalt'] *f* metal.

meatair [mɛʰtɛr'] *m* metre.

meatrach [mɛʰtrəch] *adj* metric.

meidh [mey] *f* scales; equilibrium.

meil [mel] *v* mill, grind.

meileabhaid [meləvɪd'] *f* velvet.

meilich [melɪch'] *v* chill; numb.

mèilich [mēlɪch'] *f* bleat, bleating; baa, baaing.

mèinn[1] [mēN'] *f* temperament; appearance.

mèinn[2] [mēN'] *f* mine; ore.

mèinneach [mēN'əch] *adj* mineral.

mèinneadair [mēN'ədər'] *m* miner.

mèinnear [mēN'ɛr] *m* mineral.

mèinnearachd [mēN'ərəchg] *f* mining; mineralogy.

mèinne-ghuail *see* **mèinn-ghuail**.

mèinneil [mēN'ɛl] *adj* mineral.

mèinn-eòlas [mēN'ɔ̄Ləs] *m* mineralogy.

mèinn-ghuail [mēN'*ghuel*] *f* coalmine.

meirg [mɛr'ig'] *v* rust. • *f* rust.

meirg-dhìonach [mɛr'ig'dh'iənəch] *adj* rustproof.

meirgeach [mer'ig'əch] *adj* rusty.

meirgich [mɛr'ig'ɪch'] *v* rust.

mèirle [mērlɪ] *f* theft.

mèirleach [mērləch] *m* thief.

meomhair [myɔ.ɛr'] *f* (*faculty*) memory.

meòmhraich [myɔ̄rɪch'] *v* recollect; muse.

meud [miad] *m* size; amount; extent.

meudachd [miadəchg] *f* magnitude.

meudaich [miadɪch'] *v* increase; enlarge.

m' eudail! [mēdal] *excl* love! darling!

meur [miar] *f* finger; branch; (*piano, etc*) key.

meuran [miaran] *m* thimble.

meur-chlàr [miarchLār] *m* keyboard.

meur-lorg [miarLɔrəg] *f* fingerprint.

mi [mi] *pron* I, me.

mì- [mī] *prefix* un-, dis-, in-, mis-, un-, -less.

mial [miaL] *f* (*parasite*) tick.

miamhail [miaval] *f* mewing, miauling.

mial-chaorach [mialchūrəch] *f* sheeptick.

miann [miaN] *m* wish; longing; (sexual) desire.

miannaich [miaNɪch'] *v* wish for; lust after.

mias [miəs] *f* platter; basin.

mias-ionnlaid [miəsiūNLɪd'] *f* washbasin.

mì-bhlasta [mī vLasdə] *adj* tasteless.

mì-cheartas [mī ch'aršdəs] *m* injustice.

mì-dhìleas [mī dh'īləs] *adj* disloyal.

mì-earbsa [mī ɛrabsə] *m* mistrust.

mì-fhoighidinn [mī oid'ɪN'] *f* impatience.

mì-fhoighidneach [mī oid'ıN'əch] *adj* impatient.

mì-ghnàthach [mī ghrāhəch] *adj* abnormal; unusual.

mil [mil] *f* honey.

mìle [mīlı] *m* thousand; mile.

milis [milıš] *adj* sweet.

mill [mīL'] *v* damage; spoil; destroy.

millean [miL'an] *m* million.

millte [mīL't'ı] *adj* damaged; spoilt; destroyed.

millteach [mīL't'əch] *adj* destructive.

milseachd [mīlšəchg] *f* sweetness.

milsean [milšan] *m* dessert, pudding.

mì-mhodhail [mī voghal] *adj* rude, ill-mannered.

mìn¹ [mīn] *adj* smooth; soft.

mìn² [min] *f* (*ground*) meal; mìn-choirce [min chər'k'ı] *f* oatmeal.

mì-nàdarra [mī nādəRə] *adj* unnatural.

mìneachadh [mīnəchəgh] *m* explanation; interpretation.

mìneachail [mīnəchal] *adj* explanatory.

min-flùir [minflūr] *f* flour.

min-iarainn [miniərıN'] *f* iron filings.

mìnich¹ [mīnıch'] *v* explain, illustrate; interpret; mean.

mìnich² [mīnıch'] *v* smoothe.

minig [minıg'] *adj* frequent.

ministear [minıšdɛr] *m* (*church, govt*) minister.

ministrealachd [minıšd'r'əLəchg] *f* (*church, govt*) ministry.

min-sàibh [minsāiv] *f* sawdust.

miodal [midaL] *m* flattery, fawning.

mìog [miəg] *f* smirk.

mìogadaich [migadıch'] *f* bleat, bleating.

mìolchu [miəLchū] *m* greyhound.

mion [min] *adj* small; minute; detailed; punctilious.

mionach [minəch] *m* entrails, guts; (*fam*) belly.

mionaid [minad'] *f* minute.

mionaideach [minıd'əch] *adj* thorough; detailed.

mion-aoiseach [minūšəch] *adj* minor.

mion-bhraide [minvraid'ı] *f* pilfering.

mion-chànan [minchānan] *m* minority language.

mion-cheasnaich [minch'esnıch'] *v* question minutely, grill.

mion-chuid [minchud'] *f* (*proportion*) minority.

mion-chùiseach [minchūšəch] *adj* meticulous.

mion-eòlas [miN'ɔ̄Ləs] *m* detailed knowledge.

mion-fhacal [minaʰkəL] *m* (*gram*) particle.

mion-gheàrr [mingh'āR] *v* cut up finely.

mionnaich [miuNıch'] *v* curse, swear.

mionnan [miuNan] *m* curse, swearword.

mion-phuing [minfuing'] *f* detail.

mìorbhail [miərval] *f* marvel; miracle.

mìorbhaileach [miərvaləch] *adj* marvellous; miraculous.

mìos [miəs] *m* month; mìos nam pòg [miəs nəm pōg] honeymoon.

mìosach [miəsəch] *adj* monthly.

mìosachan [miəsəchan] *m* calendar.

miotag [miʰtag] *f* glove; mitten.

mir [mīr'] *m* bit, particle; scrap.

mire [mir'ı] *f* mirth; light-heartedness.

mì-rùn [mī rūn] *m* malice, ill-will.

misde *see* miste

mise [mišı] *pron emphatic form of* mi.

misg [mišg'] *f* drunkenness, intoxication.

misgear [mišg'ɛr] *m* drunkard, boozer.

mì-shealbhach [mī hɛLavəch] *adv* unlucky, unfortunate.

misneachadh [mišnəchəgh] *m* encouragement.

misneachail [mišnəchal] *adj* courageous; spirited; in good heart; encouraging.

misneachd [mišnəchg] *f* courage.

misnich [mišnıch'] *v* encourage; inspire courage in.

miste [mišd'ı] *adj* the worse for; cha bu mhisde mi X [cha bə višd'ı mi] I'd be none the worse for X.

mithich [mi.ıch'] *adj* timely.

mo [mə] *poss pron* my.

moch [məch] *adj* early; bho mhoch gu dubh [vo vəch gu du] from morning till night.

mòd [mōd] *m* (*with art*) am Mòd (Nàiseanta) [əm mōd Nāšəndə] the (National) Mod.

modh [məgh] *f* manner, mode; manners; (*gram*) mood.

modhail [məghal] *adj* polite, well-bred.

Moslamach [məsLəmach] *m/adj* Mohammedan, Muslim.

mòine [mōN'ı] *f* (*collective*) peat; dèan/buain mòine [d'ian/buəN' mōN'ı] *v* cut peat.

mòinteach [mōN'd'əch] *f* moor, moorland.

moit [məʰt'] *f* pride.

moiteil [məʰt'ɛl] *adj* proud.

mol[1] [məL] *v* praise; recommend.

mol[2] [məL] *m* shingle; shingly beach.

molach [məLəch] *adj* hairy; rough.

moladh [məLəgh] *m* praise; recommendation.

moll [məuL] *m* chaff.

molldair [məuLder'] *m* (*jelly, etc*) mould.

molt [məLt] *m* wether.

mòmaid [mōmıd'] *f* moment, second.

monadail [mənədal] *adj* hilly, mountainous.

monadh [mənəgh] *m* moor, moorland; common hill grazing.

mòr [mōr] *adj* big; great; mòr aig a chèile [mōr ɛg' ə ch'ēlı] great friends/pals.

mòrachd [mōrəchg] *f* greatness, grandeur.

morair [mərɛr'] *m* lord.

mòran [mōran] *m* many, a lot of; much.

mòrchuis [mōrchūš] *f* pride, conceit.

mòr-chuid [mōrchud'] *f* (*with art*) a' mhòr-chuid the majority; most people.

morghan [mərəghan] *m* gravel, shingle.

mòr-inbhe [mōr inivı] *f* eminence; high rank.

mòr iongnadh [mōr iūnəgh] *m* astonishment, stupefaction.

mòr-roinn [mōr rəiN'] *f* continent.

mòr-shluagh [mōr Luəgh] *m* multitude.

murt [muršd] *v* murder, assassinate. • *m* murder, assassination, manslaughter.

murtair [muršdɛr'] *m* murderer, assassin.

mòr-uasal [mōr uəsəL] *m* nobleman, aristocrat.

mosach [mɔsəch] *adj* nasty; scruffy; niggardly.

mosg [mɔsg] *m* mosque.

mosgail [mɔsgal] *v* (*from sleep*) wake, waken, rouse.

mo sgrios! [mə sgr'is] *excl* woe is me!

motair [mɔʰtɛr'] *m* motor.

motair-rothar [mɔʰtɛr'rɔhər] *m* motorbike.

motha [mo.ə] *adj* bigger, greater.

mothachail [mɔhəchal] *adj* aware; observant; sensitive; conscious.

mothaich [mɔhɪch'] *v* notice; feel; experience.

mo thruaighe! [mə ruəi.ɪ] *excl* woe is me!

mo thruaighe ort! [mə ruə.ɪ ɔršt] *excl* woe unto you!

mu [mə] *prep* around, about; concerning.

muc [muʰk] *f* pig; sow.

mu choinneimh [mə chəiN'əv] *prep* opposite.

mucfheoil [muʰk'ɔl] *f* pork.

mùch [mūch] *v* extinguish, quench; smother; strangle; repress.

muc-mhara [muʰkvarə] *f* whale.

mu dheas [mə gh'es] *adv* to/in the South.

mu dhèidhinn [mə dh'ē.ɪN'] *prep* about, concerning.

mu dheireadh [mə dh'er'əgh] *adj* last. • *adv* at last; **mu dheireadh thall** [mə gh'er'əgh hauL] at long last.

muga [mugə] *f* (*drinking*) mug.

mùgach [mūgəch] *adj* morose, surly.

muidhe [mui.ɪ] *m* churn.

mùig [mūg'] *f* frown, scowl.

muinichill [munɪchɪL'] *m* sleeve.

Muileach [Muləch] *m/adj* Mull person, from Mull.

muileann [muləN] *m* mill.

muileann-gaoithe [muləNgui.ɪ] *m* windmill.

muile-mhàg [mulɪvāg] *f* toad.

muilinn *see* **muileann**

muillean *see* **milleann**

muillear [muL'ɛr] *m* miller.

muilt-fheoil [mult'ɔl] *f* mutton.

muime [muimɪ] *f* stepmother.

muin [muN'] *f* (*esp of animal*) back; top.

muineal [muN'aL] *m* neck.

muing [muing'] *f* mane.

muilcheann *see* **muinichill**

muinntir [muiN'd'ɪr'] *f* people; followers.

muir [mur'] *m&f* sea.

muir-làn [mur'Lān] *m* high tide.

mulad [muLad] *f* grief, sadness.

muladach [muLadəch] *adj* sad.

m' ulaidh! [muLɪ] my darling!, my love!.

mullach [muLəch] *m* top; summit; roof.

mult *see* **molt**

mun [mən], **mus** [məs] *conj* before.

mùn [mūn] *m* urine, piss.

muncaidh [munkɪ] *m* monkey.

mun cuairt [mun kuəršd'] *adv* around, about.

mun cuairt air [mun kuəršd' ɛr'] *prep* around, about.

mùr [mūr] *m* bulwark, rampart.

mura [murə] *conj* if not.

mus [mus] *conj same as* **mun**.

mu seach [mə šach] *adv* in turn, one by one.

mùth [mū] *v* change, alter; mutate; deteriorate.

mùthadh [mū.əgh] *m* change, alteration; mutation; deterioration.

mu thimcheall [mə himichəL] *adv* around.

mu thràth [mə rā] [mər hā] *adv* already.

mu thuath [mə huə] *adv* to/in the North.

N

na[1] [nə] *imper part* do not, don't.

na[2] [nə] *conj* than.

na[3] [nə] *rel pron* what, that which, those which.

na[4] [nə] *art* (*f sing*) of the; (*pl*) the.

nàbachas [Nābəchəs] *m* neighbourliness.

nàbaidh [Nābɪ] *m* neighbour.

nàbaidheachd [Nābɪ.əchg] *f* neighbourhood.

nàbaidheil [Nābɪ.ɛl] *adj* neighbourly.

nach [nach] *neg rel pron* that not.

nach math a rinn thu! [nach ma ə rəiN' u] *excl* well done!

'na chrùbagan [nə chrūbagən] *adv* crouched down.

'na chrùban [nə chrūban] *adv* crouching, squatting.

nàdar [Nādər] *m* nature; temperament.

nàdarrach [NādəRəch] *adj* natural.

'na dhùisg [nə dhūšg'] *adv* awake.

'na dhùsgadh [nə dhūsgəgh] *adv* awake.

nàdur see **nàdar**

na h-uile [nə chulɪ] *pron* everybody, everyone.

naidheachd [nɛ.əchg] *f* piece of news; anecdote; (*pl TV, etc*) **na naidheachdan** [nə nɛ.əchgən] the news.

nàidhlean [Nailan] *m* nylon. [mə nār'ɪ ɔršt] *f* shame, ignominy; bashfulness. • *excls* **mo nàire!** [mə nār'ɪ] for shame! **mo nàire ort!** [Nār'ɪ] shame on you!

nàisean [Nāšan] *m* nation.

nàiseanta [Nāšandə] *adj* national.

nàiseantach [Nāšandəch] *m* nationalist.

nàiseantachd [Nāšandəchg] *f* nationalism; nationhood.

naisgear [Našg'ɛr] *m* (*gram*) conjunction.

nàimhdeas [Naid'əs] *m* enmity, hostility.

nàimhdeil [Naid'ɛl] *adj* inimical, hostile.

nàireach [Nār'əch] *adj* shamefaced; bashful; diffident.

'na laighe [nə Laɪ.ɪ] *adv* lying, reclining.

nam see **nan**.

'nam aonar [nəm ūnər] *adv* on my own.

'nam bheachd-sa [nəm vyachgsə] in my opinion.

'nam chomain [nəm chomɛN'] *adj* obliged to me.

nàmhaid [Nā.ɪd'] *m* enemy.

nan[1] [nən] (**nam** [nəm] *before b, f, m, p*) *conj* if.

nan[2] [nən/nəN/nəN'] (**nam** [nəm] *before b, f, m, p*) *pl art* of the.

naoi [Nuy] *m/adj* nine.

naoidhean [Nui.an] *m* baby; infant.

naoinear [NūN'ɛr] *m* nine (people).

naomh [Nūv] *m* saint. • *adj* holy, sacred; saintly.

naomhachd [Nūvəchg] *f* holiness; saintliness.

nàr [Nār] *adj* shameful; disgraceful.

nàrach *see* **nàireach**.

nàraich [Nār'ɪch'] *v* put to shame; disgrace.

'na ruith [nə ruy] *adj* running.

nas motha [nəs mo.ə] *adv* either, (*with neg v*) neither.

'na stad [nə sdad] *adj* stationary; in abeyance.

'na shuidhe [nə hui.ɪ] *adv* seated, sitting.

nathair [Nahɛr'] *f* adder; serpent, snake.

'na thràill do [nə rāL' də] addicted to.

'na thrasg [nə rasg] *adv* fasting.

neach [N'ɛch] *m* person; one, someone.

neach-ceàirde [fɛrk'ārd'ɪ] *m* craftsman.

neach-chungaidhean [N'ɛchchungɪ.ən] *m* chemist, pharmacist.

neach-faire [N'ɛchfar'ɪ] *m* guard.

neach-fòirneart [N'ɛchfŏrN'ɛršd] *m* oppressor.

neach-fuadain [N'ɛchfuadɛN'] *m* wanderer; exile.

neach-giùlain [N'ɛchg'ūLɛN'] *m* carrier, bearer.

neach-ionnsaigh [N'ɛchiuNsɪ] *m* assailant, attacker.

neach-labhairt [N'ɛchLavɪršd'] *m* speaker; spokesman.

neach-lagha [N'ɛchLoghə] *m* lawyer, solicitor.

neach-naidheachd [N'ɛchNɛ.əchg] *m* journalist.

neach-poileis [N'ɛchpɔlɪš] *m* policeman.

neach-siubhail [N'ɛchšu.al] *m* traveller.

neach-taice [N'ɛchtaiʰk'ɪ] *m* supporter; patron, backer.

neach-teagaisg [N'ɛcht'ɛgišg'] *m* teacher.

neach-tomhais [N'ɛchto.ɪš] *m* surveyor.

neachtair [N'ɛchtɛr'] *m* nectar.

nead [N'ed] *m* nest.

nèamh [N'ɛv] *m* heaven(s).

nèamhaidh [N'ɛvɪ] *adj* heavenly, celestial.

neapaigear [N'ɛʰpɪg'ɛr] *m* handkerchief.

neapaigin [N'ɛʰpəg'ɪn] *f* napkin.

nearbhach [N'ɛrvəch] *adj* nervous; nervy.

neart [N'aršd] *m* strength, might; vigour; **an trèine a neirt** [ən tr'ēnɪ ə nɛršd'] in his prime.

neartaich [N'aršdɪch'] *v* strengthen; invigorate.

neartmhor [N'aršdvər] *adj* strong; mighty.

neas [N'es] *f* weasel; ferret; **neas mhòr** [N'es võr] stoat.

neasgaid [N'esgɪd'] *f* boil; ulcer, abscess.

neimh [N'ɛv] *m* poison; malice.

Neaptùn [Nɛʰptūn] *m* Neptune.

neo [N'ɔ] *conj same as* **no**

neo- [N'ɔ] *prefix* un-, in-, non-.

neo-chrìochnach [N'ɔch'r'iəchnəch] *adj* infinite.

neo-eisimeileach [N'ɔ ešɪmɛləch] *adj* independent.

neo-eisimeileachd [N'ɔ ešɪmɛləchg] *f* independence.

neòinean [N'ɔN'an] *m* daisy.

neòinean-grèine [N'ɔN'angr'ēnɪ] *m* sunflower.

neo-làthaireachd [N'ɔ Lā.ɪr'əchg] *f* absence.

neo-mhisgeach [N'ɔ višg'əch] *adj* sober.

neònach [N'ɔnəch] *adj* strange, curious.

neo-sheachanta [N'ɔ hɛchəndə] *adj* unavoidable, inevitable.

neul [N'ial] *m* cloud; complexion; faint.

neulach [N'iaLəch] *adj* cloudy.

neulaich [N'iaLɪch] *v* cloud over; obscure.

nì[1] [N'ī]
[ən N'ī ma] *m* thing; matter; circumstance; **an Nì Math** God.

nì[2] [N'ī] *future tense of v* **dèan**.

Nic [N'iʰk'] *(in surnames)* daughter of.

nigh [N'ī] *v* wash.

nigheadair [N'i.ədər'] *m* washer, washing machine.

nigheadaireachd [N'i.ədər'əchg] *f* washing.

nigheadair-shoithichean [N'i.ədər'ho.ɪch'ən] *m* dishwasher.

nighean [N'i.an] *f* girl; young woman; daughter; **nighean bràthar** [N'i.an brāhar]/**peathar** [N'i.an pɛhar] niece.

nimh *see* **neimh**

nimheil [N'ivɛl] *adj* poisonous; malicious.

Nirribhidh [N'iRɪvɪ] *f* Norway.

nitheil [N'i.ɛl] *adj* concrete, actual.

no [nɔ], **neo** [N'ɔ] *conj* or.

nobhail [Nɔval] *f* novel.

nochd [Nɔchg] *v* show; appear; **nochd an clò** [Nɔchg ən kLɔ̄] be printed/published.

Nollaig [NɔLɛg'] *f* Christmas.

norrag [NɔRag] *f* nap, snooze; **norrag cadail** [NɔRag kadal] a wink of sleep.

nòs [Nɔ̄s] *m* way; custom; style.

nota [Nɔʰtə] *f* note; *(money)* pound.

nuadh [Nuə] *adj* new.

nuadhaich [Nuə.ɪch'] *v* renovate.

nuallaich [NuəLɪch'] *v* howl; roar; bellow.

nurs [Nɔrs] *f* nurse.

O

o [vɔ] [ɔ] *prep* from; since.

o àm gu àm [vɔ aum gə aum] *adv* from time to time.

òb [ɔ̄b] *m* bay.

obair [obɪr'] *f* work; job, employment.

obair-ghrèise [obɪr'ɣr'ēʃɪ] *f* (*the product of*) embroidery, needlework.

obair-làimhe [obɪr'Laivɪ] *f* handiwork.

obair-lannsa [obɪr'LauNsə] *f* (*med*) operation.

obair-taighe [obɪr'tɛhɪ] *f* housework.

obann [obəN] *adj* sudden.

obh! obh! [ovɔ.əv] *excl* dear oh dear! good heavens!

obraich [obrɪch'] *v* work, function; operate.

oibrich *see* **obraich**

och (nan och)! [ɔch nə Nɔch] *excl* alas! woe is me!

ochd [ɔchg] *m/adj* eight.

ochdad [ɔchgəd] *m* eighty.

ochdamh [ɔchgəv] *adj* eighth.

ochd deug [ɔchg d'iag] *m/adj* eighteen.

ochdnar [ɔchgnər] *m* eight (people).

o chionn [ɔ ch'uN] *prep* ago; since; **o chionn ghoirid** [ɔ ch'uN ɣor'ɪd'] recently; **o chionn fhada** [ɔ ch'uN adə] long ago.

odhar [o.ər] *adj* dun(-coloured); sallow.

òg [ɔ̄g] *adj* young.

ògan [ɔ̄gan] *m* shoot, tendril.

òganach [ɔ̄ganəch] *m* young man; adolescent.

ogha [o.ə] *m* grandchild.

Òg-mhìos [ɔ̄gvias] *m* (*with art*) **an t-Òg-mhìos** [ən tɔ̄gvias] June.

ogsaigin [oʰgsəg'ɪn] *m* oxygen.

obraiche [obrɪch'ə] *m* worker, workman.

oide [od'ɪ] *m* stepfather.

oideachas [od'əchəs] *m* education; learning.

oidhche [oi.ch'ɪ] *f* night; **oidhche mhath leat/leibh!** [oi.ch'ɪ va laʰt/ leiv] goodnight! **Oidhche Challainn** [oi.ch'ɪchaLɪN'] Hogmanay, New Year's Eve; **Oidhche Shamhna** [oi.ch'ɪhaunə] Halloween.

oidhirp [o.ɪrp] *f* attempt, try; effort.

oifig *see* **oifis**

oifigeach [ɔfɪgəch] *m* official.

oifigear [ɔfɪg'ɛr] *m* officer.

oifigeil [ɔfɪg'ɛl] *adj* official.

oifis [ɔfɪš] *f* office; position; **oifis a' phuist** [ɔfɪš ə fušd']post office; **Oifis na h-Alba** [ɔfɪš nə haLabə] the Scottish Office Now Scotland Office or Scottish Parliament.

òige [ɔ̄g'ɪ] *f* youth.

òigear [ɔ̄g'ɛr] *m* youngster, adolescent.

òigh [ɔ̄y] *f* virgin; young woman.

òigheil [ɔ̄i.ɛl] *adj* virginal.

oighre [oi.r'ɪ] *m* heir, inheritor.

oighreachd [oir'əchg] *f* (*land*) estate; inheritance.

òigridh [ɔ̃g'r'ı] f (collective) young people.

oilbheum [ɔlvēm] m offence.

oilbheumach [ɔlvēməch] adj offensive.

oileanach [ɔlanəch] m student.

oileanaich [ɔlanıch'] v train; instruct.

oillt [əiL't'] f terror; horror.

oillteil [əiL't'ɛl] adj frightful, dreadful; horrible.

oilltich [əiL't'ıch'] v terrify.

oilthigh [ɔlhoy] m university.

òinseach [ɔ̃N'šəch] f (female) fool, (female) idiot.

oir [ɔr'] f edge, margin; rim; **oir an rathaid** [ɔr' ən Ra.ıd']verge; **oir a' chabhsair** [ɔr' ə chausɛr'] kerb.

oir [ɔr'] conj for.

oirbh [ɔr'ıv] prep pron on you (pl).

òirdheirc [ɔr'gh'erk'] adj magnificent; illustrious.

òirleach [ɔrləch] m inch.

oirnn [ɔrN'] prep pron on us.

oirre [ɔRı] prep pron on her, on it (f).

oirthir [ɔrhir] f coast, seaboard.

oisean[ɔšan], **oisinn** [ɔšıN'] m corner.

oiteag [ɔʰt'ag] f breeze; breath of wind.

òl [ɔL] v drink.

ola [ɔLə] f oil.

olann [ɔLəN] f wool.

olc [ɔLk] m evil, wickedness. • adj evil, wicked.

olla [ɔLə] adj woollen.

ollamh [ɔLəv] m learned man; (academic) doctor.

òmar [ɔ̃mər] m amber.

on a [vɔn ə] conj since, as.

onair [ɔnɛr'] f honour; honesty; esteem. • excl **air mo onair!** [ɛr mɔnɛr'] honestly!

onorach [ɔnərəch] adj honourable; honest; honorary.

onoraich [ɔnərıch'] v honour.

on taigh [vɔn toy] adv out; away from home.

òr [ɔr] m gold.

òraid [ɔrıd'] f speech, address; lecture.

òraidiche [ɔrıd'ıch'ə] m speaker.

orains [ɔrɛnš] adj orange.

orainsear [ɔrɛnšər] m orange.

òran [ɔ̃ran] m song; **òrain luaidh** [ɔ̃ran Luay]waulking songs; **na h-òrain mhòra** [nə hɔ̃rɛN' vɔrə] the great ballads.

òr-chèard [ɔrch'erd] m goldsmith.

òrd [ɔrd] m hammer.

òrdag [ɔrdag] f thumb.

òrdag-coise [ɔrdagkɔši] f toe.

òrdaich [ɔrdıch'] v order, command; organise, tidy.

òrdaighean [ɔrdı.ən] mpl (with art) **na h-òrdaighean** [nə hɔrdı.ən] (relig) communion.

òrdail [ɔrdal] adj orderly; ordinal.

òrdugh [ɔrdu] m order, sequence; command.

òrgan [ɔrgan] m organ.

orm [ɔrɔm] prep pron on me.

orra [ɔRə] prep pron on them.

òrraiseach [ɔRıšəch] adj squeamish.

ort [ɔršd] prep pron on you (sing).

ortha [ɔRə] f spell, charm.

osan [ɔsan] m stocking, hose.

osann [ɔsəN] m same as **osna**

os cionn [ɔs k'ūN] prep above, over.

òstair [ɔ̃sdɛr'] m hotelier, landlord, licensee.

shean [ʃɛn] *adv* of old, long ago.

s ìseal [ɔs ĩʃal] *adv* quietly; secretly.

sna [ɔsnə] *m*, osann *m* sigh; breeze.

snaich [ɔsnɪch'] *v* sigh.

spadal [ɔspədaL] *m* hospital.

spag [ɔspag] *f* sigh; breath of wind.

Ostair [ɔsdɛr'] *f (with art)* an Ostair [ə Nɔsdɛr'] Austria.

Ostaireach [ɔsdɛr'əch] *m/adj* Austrian.

othail [ɔhal] *f* hubbub, uproar.

othaisg [ɔhĩʃg'] *f* hogg, ewe-lamb.

o thùs [vɔ hũs] *adv* originally.

òtrach [ɔ̃ʰtrəch] *m* dunghill, midden.

P

aca [paʰkə] *m* pack.

acaid [paʰkɪd'] *f* packet.

àganach [pāgənəch] *m/adj* pagan, heathen.

aidh [pay] *m* pie.

aidhir [pai.ɪr'] *f* pair.

aidir [pad'ɪr'] *f* Lord's Prayer.

aidirean [pad'ɪr'an] *m* rosary.

àigh [pāy] *v* pay (for); atone (for).

àigh [pāy], pàigheadh [pāi.əgh] *m* pay, remuneration.

àillean [pāLan] *m* pavilion; large tent.

ailt [palt'] *adj* plentiful.

ailteas [palt'əs] *m* plenty.

àipear [pēʰpɛr] *m* paper.

àipear-balla [pēʰpɛrbaLə] *m* wallpaper.

àipear-gainmhich [pēʰpɛrgɛnavich'] *m* sandpaper.

àipear-naidheachd [pēʰpɛrNɛ.əchg] *m* newspaper.

àirc [pār'k'] *f* field; park.

aireafain [parəfɛN'] *m* paraffin.

àirt [pārʃd'] *m* part.

àirt-càraidh [pārʃd'kārı] *m* spare, spare part.

pàirtich [pārʃd'ıch'] *v* share out; divide up.

pàiste [pāʃd'ı] *m* baby; infant; small child.

paisg [pašg'] *v* wrap (up); fold (up).

pàiteach [pāʰt'əch] *adj* thirsty.

pana [panə] *m* pan.

pannal [paNaL] *m* panel.

Pàpa [pāʰpə] *m* Pope.

pàpanach [pāʰpanəch] *m/adj* papist, popish.

pàrant [pārand] *m* parent.

pàrlamaid [pārLəmıd'] *f* parliament.

pàrlamaideach [pārLəmıd'əch] *adj* parliamentary.

parsail [parsal] *m* parcel, package.

pàrtaidh [pārʃdı] *m* party.

partan [parʃdan] *m (edible)* crab.

pasgadh [pasgəgh] *m* packing.

pasgan [pasgan] *m* bundle; package.

pastraidh [pasdrı] *f* pastry.

pathadh [pa.əgh] *m* thirst.

pàtran [pāʰtran] *m* pattern.

peacach [pɛʰkəch] *m* sinner. • *adj* sinful.

peacadh [pɛʰkəgh] *m* sin.

peacadh-bàis [pɛʰkəghbāš] *m* mortal sin.

peacadh-gine [pɛʰkəghg'ínɪ] *m* original sin.

peacaich [pɛʰkɪch'] *v* sin.

peanas [pɛnas] *m* punishment; penalty.

peanasaich [pɛnasɪch'] *v* punish.

peann [pyauN] *m* pen.

peansail [pɛnsal] *m* pencil.

peantaich [pɛntɪch'] *v* paint.

peanta [pɛntə] *m* paint.

peantair [pɛntɛr'] *m* painter.

pearraid [pɛRɪd'] *f* parrot.

pearsa [pɛrsə] *m* person; (*play, etc*) character.

pearsanta [pɛrsəntə] *adj* personal.

pearsantachd [pɛrsəntachg] *f* personality.

peasair [pɛsɛr'] *f* pea.

peata [pɛʰtə] *m* pet.

peatroil [pɛʰtrəl] *m* petrol.

peighinn [pe.ıN'] *f* penny.

peile [pelı] *m* pail.

pèileag [pēlag] *f* porpoise.

peilear [pelɛr] *m* bullet; pellet.

peile-frasaidh [pelıfrasɪ] *m* watering can.

peinnsean [peiN'šan] *m* pension.

peirceall [per'k'əL] *m* jaw, jawbone.

peitean [pɛʰt'an] *m* vest; waistcoat.

pèitseag [pēʰt'šag] *f* peach.

peur [piar] *f* pear.

pian [pian] *v* pain, distress; torture. • *f* pain.

piàna [pyānə] *m* piano.

pianail [pianal] *adj* painful.

pic [piʰk'] *m* (*tool*) pick.

picil [piʰk'ıl] *f* pickle.

pile [pilı] *f* pill.

pìleat [pīlət] *m* pilot.

pillean [piL'an] *m* cushion; pillion.

pinc [pink'] *adj* pink.

pinnt [pīN'd'] *m* pint.

pìob [pīb] *f* pipe; tube.

pìobaire [pībər'ə] *m* piper.

pìobaireachd [pībər'əchg] *f* (bag-piping; pibroch.

piobar [pibər] *m* pepper.

pìob mhòr [pīb vōr] *f* Highland bagpipes.

piobraich [pibrɪch'] *v* add pepper to; pep up.

pìob-thombaca [pībhombaʰkə] (tobacco) pipe.

pìob-uilne [pībulını] *f* uilean pipes.

pioc [piʰk] *v* peck; nibble.

pìos [pīs] *m* piece, bit; packet lunch.

piseach [pišəch] *m* progress, improvement.

piseag [pišag] *f* kitten.

pit [pīʰt'] *f* vulva.

piuthar [pyu.ər] *f* sister.

piuthar-chèile [pyu.ərch'ēlı] *f* sister-in-law.

plaide [pLad'ı] *f* blanket.

plàigh [pLāy] *f* plague; infestation nuisance.

plàigheil [pLāi.ɛl] *adj* pestilential.

plana [pLanə] *m* plan.

planaid [pLanɪd'] *f* planet.

planaig [pLanɪg'] *v* plan.

plangaid [pLangɪd'] *f* blanket.

plap [pLaʰp] *v* flutter. • *m* fluttering.

plaoisg [pLũšg'] *v* shell; peel; skin.

plaosg [pLũsg] *m* shell; peel; skin husk.

plàsd [pLāsd] *m* sticking plaster.

plastaig [pLasdɪg'] *f/adj* plastic.

plathadh [pLahəgh] *m* glance; glimpse; instant.

pleadhag [plɛ.ag] *f (canoe, etc)* paddle.

pleadhagaich [plɛ.əgɪch'] *v* paddle.

plèana [plēnə] *f* (aero)plane.

ploc [pLɔʰk] *m* clod; turf; block; lump.

ploc-prìne [pLɔʰkpr'īnɪ] *m* pinhead.

plosg [pLɔsg] *v* gasp, pant; palpitate, throb. • *m* gasp; palpitation; throb.

plub [pLub], **plubraich** [pLubrɪch'] *m* splash, plop. • *v* splash, plop, slosh.

plucan [pLuʰkan] *m* pimple; *(sink, etc)* plug.

pluic [pLuiʰk'] *f* (plump) cheek.

plumair [pLumɛr'] *m* plumber.

Plùta [pLūʰtə] *m* Pluto.

poball [pobəL] *m* people.

poballach [pobəLəch], **poblach** [pobLəch *adj* public.

poblachd [pobLəchg] *f* republic.

poca [pɔʰkə] *m* bag; sack.

pòca [pɔ̄ʰkə] *m*, **pòcaid** [pɔ̄ʰkɪd'] *f* pocket.

poca-cadail [pɔʰkəkadal] *m* sleeping-bag.

pòcaid *see* **pòca**.

pòg [pōg] *v* kiss. • *f* kiss.

poidsear [pɔd'šɛr] *m* poacher.

poileas [pɔləs] *m* police; policeman.

poileataigeach [pɔlətɪg'əch] *adj* political.

poileataigeachd [pɔlətɪg'əchg] *f* politics.

poileataigear [pɔlətɪgɛr] *m* politicians.

poit [pɔʰt'] *f* pot.

poit-dhubh [pɔʰt'dhu] *f* (whisky) still.

pòitear [pɔ̄ʰt'ɛr] *m* drinker, boozer.

pòitearachd [pɔ̄ʰtɛrəchg] *f* boozing, tippling.

poit-fhlùran [pɔʰt'lūrən] *f* flower-pot.

poit-mhùin [pɔʰt'vūN'] *f* chamber-pot.

poit-teatha [pɔʰt'ɛ.ə] *f* teapot.

pòla [pɔ̄Lə] *m* pole; **am Pòla a Tuath/a Deas** [əm pɔ̄Lə ə tuə/ə d'es] the North/South Pole.

Pòlach [pɔ̄Ləch] *m/adj* Pole; Polish.

Pòlainn [pɔ̄LɪN'] *f (with art)* **a' Phòlainn** [ə fɔ̄LɪN'] Poland.

polas *see* **poileas**

poileasman *see* **neach-poileis**

poll [pouL] *m* mud; bog.

poll-mòna [pouLmōnə], **poll-mònach** [pouLmōnəch] *m* peat bog.

pònaidh [pɔ̄nɪ] *m* pony.

pònair [pɔ̄nɛr'] *f* bean(s); **pònair leathann** [pɔ̄ner' lɛhəN] broad bean(s); **pònair Fhrangach** [pɔ̄nɛr' rangəch] French bean(s).

pong [pɔng] *m (mus)* note.

pongail [pɔngal] *adj* concise; punctual; punctilious.

pòr [pɔ̄r] *m* seed; crops; growth.

port[1] [pɔršd] [*m* port, harbour; **port-adhair** pɔršda.ɪr'] airport.

port[2] [pɔršd] *m* tune; **port-a-beul** [pɔršd a biaL] mouth music.

Portagail [pɔršdagal] *f (with art)* **a' Phortagail** [ə fɔršdagal] Portugal.

Portagaileach [pɔršdagaləch] *m/adj* Portuguese.

portair [pɔršdɛr'] *m* porter; doorman.

pòs [pɔ̄s] v marry.

pòsadh [pɔ̄səgh] m marriage.

pòsda [pɔ̄sdə] adj married; pòsda aig [pɔ̄sdə ɛg'] married to; nuadh-phòsda [Nuə fɔ̄sdə] newly married.

post [pɔsd] m post, stake; post, mail; postman; post-adhair [pɔsdə.ır'] air mail.

posta [pɔsdə] m postman.

post-dealain [pɔsd'ɛLɛN'] (abbrev post-d) m electronic mail, email.

prabar [prabər] m rabble, mob.

prab-shùileach [prabhūləch] adj bleary-eyed.

prais [praš] f cooking pot.

pràis [prāš] f brass.

pràiseach [prāšəch] adj brass.

preantas [pr'ɛndəs] m apprentice.

preas[1] [pr'es] v crease; corrugate; crush.

preas[2] [pr'es] m bush, shrub.

preas[3] [pr'es], preasa [pr'esə] m cupboard.

preasach [pr'esəch] adj wrinkly, wrinkled.

preasadh [pr'esəgh] m wrinkle.

preasag [pr'esag] f wrinkle, crease.

preas-aodaich [pr'esūdıch'] m wardrobe.

preas-leabhraichean [pr'esL'ɔrıchən] m bookcase.

prìne [pr'īnı] m pin.

prìne-banaltraim [pr'īnıbanaLtrım] m safety pin.

priob [pr'ib] v wink; blink.

priobadh [pr'ibəgh] m wink; blink; instant.

prìobhaideach [pr'īvıd'əch] adj private.

prìomh [pr'iəv] adj main, head.

prìomhaire [pr'iəvər'ə] m prime minister.

prionnsa [pr'iuNsə] m prince.

prionnsabal [pr'iuNsəbaL] m principle.

prìosan [pr'īsan] m prison.

prìosanach [pr'īsanəch] m prisoner.

prìs [pr'īš] f price, cost.

prìseil [pr'īšɛl] adj precious; valuable.

prògram [prɔ̄gram] m programme; (comput) program.

proifeasair [prɔfɛsır'] m professor.

proifeiseanta [prɔfɛšəndə] adj professional.

pròis [prɔ̄š] f pride.

pròiseact [prɔ̄šɛkt] f project.

pròiseil [prɔ̄šɛl] adj proud.

pronn [prouN] v mash, pulverise; (fam) bash, beat up. • adj mashed, pulverised.

pronnasg [prəNasg] m sulphur; brimstone.

prosbaig [prɔsbıg'] f binoculars; telescope.

Pròstanach [prɔ̄sdanəch] m/adj Protestant.

prothaid [prɔhıd'] f (fin) profit; gain, benefit.

puball [pubaL] m marquee.

pùdar [pūdər] m powder.

pùdaraich [pūdərıch'] v powder.

puing [puing'] f point (in scale, etc); (orthog) stop, mark; stadphuing [sdadfuing'] full stop; clisg-phuing [klišg'fuing'] exclamation mark; dà-phuing [dāfuing'] colon.

puinnsean [puiN'šan] m poison.

puinnseanach [puiN'šanəch] adj poisonous.

puinnseanaich [puiN'šanıch'] v poison.

pumpa [pūmpə] m pump.

punnd [pūNd] m (weight and money) pound; punnd Èireannach [pūNd ēr'əNəch] punt (now replaced by the euro); punnd Sasannach [pūNd sasəNəch] pound sterling.

purpaidh [purpı] adj purple.

purpar [purpər] m purple.

put¹ [puʰt] v push, jostle.

put² [puʰt] m buoy.

putan [puʰtan] m button.

R

rabaid [Rabıd'] f rabbit.

rabhadh [Ravəgh] m warning; alarm.

rabhd [Raud] m idle talk; obscene talk.

ràc¹ [Rāʰk] v rake.

ràc² [Rāʰk] m drake.

racaid [Raʰkıd'] f (sports) racket.

ràcan [Rāʰkan] m rake.

rach [Rach] v go.

rach à bith [Rach a bi] v cease to be.

rach a cadal [Rach a kadəL] v go to bed.

rach à cuimhne [Rach a kuiN'ı] v be forgotten.

rach a dhìth [Rach a gh'ī] v go short.

rach air dìochuimhne [Rach ɛr' d'iəchəN'ı] v be forgotten.

rach air iomrall [Rach ɛr' imrəL] v wander; go astray, err.

rach air iteig [Rach ɛr' iʰt'ɛg'] v fly.

rach air muin [Rach ɛr' muN'] v have sex with; (animals) serve.

rach air seachran [Rach ɛr' šecharan] v wander; go astray.

rach am fad [Rach əm fad] v get/grow longer.

rach am feabhas [Rach əm fyɔ.əs] v improve, get better.

rach am meud [Rach əm miad] v get bigger.

rach an geall gu [Rach ən g'auL gu] v bet that.

rach an laigse [Rach ən Lag'šı] v faint.

rach an neul [Rach ən N'iaL] v faint, pass out.

rach an sàs ann an [Rach ən sās auN ən] v get involved in.

rach an urras (air) [Rach ən uRəs ɛr'] v guarantee, vouch (for).

rach an urras gu [Rach ən uRəs gu] v guarantee that.

rach à sealladh [Rach a šɛLəgh] v disappear, go out of sight.

rach às mo chuimhne [Rach as mə chuiN'ı] v be forgotten.

rach às mo leth [Rach as mə le] v side with me.

rach bhuaithe [Rach vuəi.ı] v deteriorate.

rach car mu char [Rach kar mə char] v roll over and over.

rach fodha [Rach fo.ə] v sink; (firm, etc) fail.

rach 'na laighe [Rach nə Lai.ı] v lie down; go to bed.

rach 'na lasair [Rach nə Lasır'] v go up in flames.

rach 'na shaighdear [Rach nə said'ɛr] v become a soldier.

rach ri taobh X [Rach r'i tūv] v take after X.

rach seachad (air) [Rach šɛchəd ɛr'] v pass by, go past.

rach thar a chèile [Rach har ə ch'ēlı] v fall out, quarrel.

radan [Radan] m rat.

ràdh [Rā] m saying, proverb.

radharc [Ro.ərk] m eyesight; sight, view.

rag [Rag] adj stiff; stubborn.

ragaich [Ragıch'] v stiffen.

rag-mhuinealach [RagvuN'əLəch] adj pig-headed.

raineach [Ranəch] f bracken, fern(s).

ràinig [rānıg'] past tense of v ruig

ràith [Rāy] f season; quarter (of year); while.

ràitheachan [Rāi.əchan] m (magazine) quarterly, periodical.

ràmh [Rāv] m oar.

ràn [Rān] v roar, yell; weep. • m roar, yell; weeping.

rann [RauN] f poetry; a verse.

rannsaich [RauNsıch'] v search; rummage; research..

raon [Rūn] m field.

raon-adhair [Rūna.ır'] m airfield.

raon-cluiche [RūnkLuch'ı] m playing field.

rapach [Raʰpəch] adj slovenly, scruffy.

rathad [Ra.əd] m road; way, route.

rathad mòr [Ra.əd mōr] m main road.

Ratharsach [Ra.ərsəch] m/adj Raasay person, from Raasay.

Ratharsair [Ra.ərsɛr'] Raasay.

rè [Rē] f time, period.

rè [Rē] prep during, throughout.

reachd [Rɛchg] m rule; command law.

reamhar [Rɛu.ər] adj fat.

reamhraich [Rɛurıch'] v fatten.

reic [Reʰk'] v sell. • m sale; selling.

reiceadair [Reʰk'ədər'] m vendor salesman; auctioneer.

rèidh [Rē] adj level; smooth cleared; **rèidh ri** [Rē r'i] on good terms with.

rèidhlean [Rēlan] m (a) green.# (not colour, but level surface covered in grass, e.g. bowling green)

rèidio [Rēd'io] m radio.

rèile [Rēlı] f rail, railing.

rèilig [Rēlıg'] f kirkyard.

rèis [Rēš] f (sport, etc) race.

rèiseamaid [Rēšəmıd'] f regiment.

rèite [Rēʰt'ı] f agreement; reconciliation; betrothal; atonement.

rèiteach [Rēʰtəch], **rèiteachadh** [Rēʰtəchəgh] m betrothal.

rèitear [Rēʰtɛr] m referee.

reithe [Re.ı] m tup, ram.

rèitich [Rēʰt'ıch'] v reconcile; appease; arbitrate; settle; adjust.

reòdh see **reòth**

reòiteag [Ryōʰt'ag] f ice cream.

reòta [Ryōʰtə] adj frozen.

reòth [Ryō] v freeze.

reòthadair [Ryō.ədər'] m freezer deep freeze.

reòthadh [Ryō.əgh] m frost.

reothairt [Ryo.ıršt'] f spring-tide.

reub [Riab] v tear; lacerate; mangle.

reubadh [Riabəgh] m rip, rent.

reubalach [RēbəLəch] m rebel.

reudan [Rēdan] *m* wood-louse.

reul [RēL] *f* star.

reuladair [RēLədər'] *m* astronomer.

reul-bhad [RēLvad] *m* constellation.

reul-eòlas [RēlyōLəs] *m* astronomy.

reul-iùil [Rēlyūl] *f* pole star.

reusan [Rēsan] *m* reason; sanity.

reusanta [Rēsandə] *adj* reasonable; sensible; fair.

ri [r'i] *prep* to; against; during.

riabhach [Riəvəch] *adj* brindled; grizzled; drab; dun.

riadh [Riəgh] *(fin)* interest.

riaghail [Rī.al] *v* rule (over), govern; regulate; manage.

riaghailt [Rī.alt'] *f* rule, regulation; system, order.

riaghailteach [Rī.alt'əch] *adj* regular; systematical.

riaghailteachd [Rī.alt'əchg] *f* orderliness; regularity.

riaghailtich [Rī.alt'ɪch'] *v* regularise; regulate.

riaghaltas [Rī.aLtəs] *m* government.

riaghladair [RiəLədər'] *m* ruler, governor.

riaghladh [RiəLəgh] *m* governing; management.

rianachd [Rianəchg] *f* administration.

rian [Rian] *m* orderliness; system; reason; *(mus)* arrangement.

rianadair [Rianədər'] *m (mus)* arranger; administrator.

rianail [Rianal] *adj* methodical.

riaraich [Riərɪch'] *v* please; satisfy; distribute; *(cards)* deal.

riatanach [Riəʰtənəch] *adj* essential.

rib [Rib] *v* trap, ensnare.

ribe [Ribɪ] *f* trap, snare.

ribean-tomhais [Ribanto.ɪš] *m* tape measure.

ruibh [Rəiv] *prep pron* to you *(pl)*.

ribheid [Rivɛd'] *f (mus)* reed.

ribhinn [RīvɪN'] *f (songs)* maiden, girl.

ridhil [Ri.ɪl] *m (dance)* reel; **ridhil-ochdnar** [Ri.ɪl ɔchgnər] eightsome reel.

ridire [Rid'ɪr'ə] *m* knight.

rìgh [Rī] *m* king.

Rìgh nan Dùl [Rī nən dūL] *m* Lord of the Universe, God.

righinn [Ri.ɪN'] *adj (material, etc)* tough.

ri mo bheò [r'im vyō] *adv* all my life; in my lifetime.

rinn[1] [rəiN'] *past tense of v* **dèan**.

rinn[2] [RĪN'] *m* point, promontory.

ruinn [rəiN'] *prep pron* to us.

rioban [Riban] *m* ribbon.

riochd [Richg] *m* likeness, form; appearance.

riochdaich [Richgɪch'] *v* represent; portray; impersonate.

riochdair [Richgɛr'] *m (gram)* pronoun.

riochdaire [Richgər'ə] *m* representative.

rìoghachadh [Rī.əchəgh] *m* reign; reigning.

rìoghachd [Rī.əchg] *f* kingdom.

rìoghaich [Rī.ɪch'] *v* reign.

rìoghail [Rī.al] *adj* royal; kingly, regal.

rìomhach [Riəvəch] *adj* beautiful; splendid.

rionnach [RuNəch] *m* mackerel.

rionnag [RuNag] *f* star.

rionnag-earbaill [RuNagɛrabiL'] *f* meteor.

ris¹ [r'iš] *prep pron* to him, to it (*m*).

ris² [r'iš] *adv* showing, exposed.

ris a' bhruthaich [r'iš ə vru.ıch'] *adv* against the slope.

ris a' ghaoith [r'iš ə ghūy] *adv* against the wind.

ris an t-sruth [r'iš ən tru] *adv* against the current.

ri taobh [r'i tūv] *prep* beside, alongside.

ri taobh a chèile [r'i tūv ə ch'ēli] *adv* abreast.

ri teachd [r'i t'ɛchg] *adv* future, to come.

rithe [r'i.ı] *prep pron* to her, to it (*f*).

ri tìde [r'i t'īd'ı] *adv* in time, eventually.

ri uchd bàis [r'i uchg bāš] *adv* at the point of death.

rium [r'ium] *prep pron* to me.

riut [r'iuʰt] *prep pron* to you (*sing*).

riutha [r'iu.ə] *prep pron* to them.

ro [Rɔ] *prep* (*time and space*) before; in front of.

ro [rɔ] *adv* too; very, extremely.

ro- [Rɔ] *prefix* fore-, pre-.

robach [Rɔbəch] *adj* hairy, shaggy; slovenly.

robh [rɔu] *past tense, neg and interrog, of v* **bith**

roc [Rɔʰk] *f* wrinkle.

rocaid [Rɔʰkɪd'] *f* rocket.

ròcail [Rɔʰkal] *f* croak(ing), caw(ing).

ròcais [Rɔ̄kɪš] *f* rook.

ro-chraiceann [Rɔchraʰk'əN] *m* foreskin.

roghainn [Rɔ.ıN'] *m* choice; preference.

roghnaich [Rɔ̄nıch'] *v* choose.

roilig [Rɔlıg'] *v* roll.

roimhe [Rɔi.ı] *prep pron* before him, before it (*m*).

roimhe [Rɔi.ı] *adv* before.

roimhear [Rɔi.ɛr] *m* preposition.

ro-innleachd [RɔīN'L'əchg] *f* strategy.

roimhpe [Rɔiʰpı] *prep pron* before her, before it (*f*).

ròineag [Rɔ̄N'ag] *f* (*single*) hair.

roinn [RəiN'] *v* divide (up); distribute; (*cards*) deal; (*arith*) divide.

roinn [RəiN'] *f* division; share; department; (*govt*) region; continent.

ròsdaich [Rɔ̄sdıch'] *v* roast; fry.

ro làimh [Rɔ Laiv] *adv* beforehand.

ròlaist [Rɔ̄Lašd'] *m* romance, romantic novel.

ro-leasachan [Rɔlesəchan] *m* (*gram*) prefix.

ròmach [Rɔ̄məch] *adj* woolly, hairy, shaggy; bearded.

Romàinia [RɔmāN'a] *f* Romania.

Romàineach [RɔmāN'əch] *m/adj* Romanian.

romhad [Rɔ.əd] *prep pron* before you (*sing*).

romhaibh [Rɔ.ıv] *prep pron* before you (*pl*).

romhainn [Rɔ.ıN'] *prep pron* before us.

romham [Rɔ.əm] *prep pron* before me.

romhpa [Rɔʰpə] *prep pron* before them.

ròn [Rɔ̄n] *m* (*animal*) seal.

rong¹ [Rɔng] *f* rung; spar; hoop.

rong² [Rɔng] *m* vital spark.

ron mhithich [Rɔn vi.ɪch'] *adv* premature(ly).

ronn [RɔuN] *m* mucus, phlegm.

ro-nochd [rɔ Nɔchg] *v* overexpose.

ro-òrdachadh [Rɔ ɔ̄rdǝchǝgh] *m* predestination.

ro-òrdaich [Rɔ ɔ̄rdɪch'] *v* predestine, predetermine.

ròpa [Rɔ̄ʰpǝ] *m* rope.

ròpa-aodaich [Rɔ̄ʰpūdɪch'] *m* clothes-line.

ro-ràdh [Rɔ rā] *m* foreword, preamble.

ròs [Rɔ̄s] *m* rose.

ròsda [Rɔ̄sdǝ] *adj* roast(ed); fried.

rosg¹ [Rɔsg] *m* eyelash.

rosg² [Rɔsg] *m* prose.

rosgrann [RɔsgrǝN] *f* sentence.

roth [Rɔ] *m* wheel.

rothach [Rɔhǝch] *adj* wheeled.

rothar [Rɔhǝr] *m* bicycle.

ro-throm [rɔ rom] *adj* overweight.

ruadh [Ruǝgh] *adj* red; red-haired; ginger.

ruaig [Ruǝg'] *v* chase; put to flight, (*milit*) rout. • *f* chase, pursuit; flight; rout; hunt.

ruamhair [Ruǝ.ɪr] *v* dig; rummage.

rubair [Rubɛr'] *m* rubber.

rubha [Ru.ǝ] *m* point, promontory.

rùchd [Rūchg] *v* grunt; belch; retch. • *m* grunt; belch; retching.

rud [Rud] *m* thing; fact.

rùda [Rūdǝ] *m* ram, tup.

rudail [Rudal] *adj* concrete, actual, real.

rùdan [Rūdan] *m* knuckle, finger-joint.

rud beag [Rud beg] *adv* a bit, somewhat.

rudeigin [Rudeg'ɪn] *pron* something, anything. • *adv* somewhat.

ruadhadh [Ruǝghǝgh] *m* blush(ing), flush(ing).

rud sam bith [Rud sǝm bi] *m* anything at all.

rug [rug] *past tense of v* beir.

rugadh mi [rugǝgh mi] *v* I was born.

ruidhle [Ruilɪ] *m same as* ridhil

ruig [Ruig'] *v* arrive (at), reach.

ruig air [Ruig' ɛr'] *v* reach for; take, seize;.

ruighe [Rui.ɪ] *f* forearm; hillslope.

rùilear [Rūlɛr] *m* (*measuring*) rule, ruler.

Ruis [Ruš] *f* (*with art*) an Ruis [ǝn Ruš] Russia.

ruisean [Rušan] *m* (*with art*) an ruisean [ǝn Rušan] the midday meal.

Ruiseach [Rušǝch] *m/adj* Russian.

rùisg [Rūšg'] *v* bare, strip; shear, fleece; peel; chafe.

rùisgte [Rūšg't'ɪ] *adj* stripped; shorn; peeled.

ruiteach [Ruʰt'ǝch] *adj* ruddy; blushing, flushed.

ruith [Rui] *v* run; flow; chase. • *f* run, running; pursuit; rout; rate, pace.

rùm [Rūm] *m* room; space.

Rumach [Rumǝch] *m/adj* from Rum.

rùm-bìdh [Rūmbī] *m* dining-room.

rùm-ionnlaid [RūmiūNLɪd'] *m* bathroom.

rùn [Rūn] *m* secret; love, affection; wish, purpose; ambition.

rùnaich [Rūnɪch'] *v* wish, desire; resolve.

rùnaire [Rūnǝr'ǝ] *m* secretary;

Rùnaire na Stàite [Rūnər'ə nə sdāʰt'ı] the Secretary of State.

rùraich [Rūrıch'] *v* rummage, grope; explore.

rìs [Rīš] *m* rice.

rùsg [Rūsg] *m* fleece; peel, skin, husk; *(tree)* bark.

S

's [s] *(for* **agus, is**) *conj* and.

-sa [sə] *suffix* this.

sabaid [sabıd'] *v* fight, scrap, brawl. • *f* fight(ing), scrap(ping), brawl-(ing).

sàbaid [sābıd'] *f* sabbath.

sàbh [sāv] *v* saw. • *m* saw.

sàbhail [sāval] *v* save, rescue; economise.

sàbhailte [sāvalt'ı] *adj* safe.

sabhal [so.əL] *m* barn.

sàbhaladh [sāvaLəgh] *m* rescuing; *(relig)* salvation; savings.

sabhs [saus] *m* sauce.

sac [saʰk] *m* sack.

sad [sad] *v* throw, toss, chuck.

sagart [sagəršt] *m* priest.

saibhear [saivɛr] *m* culvert; sewer.

saideal [sad'ɛL] *m* satellite.

saidhbhir [saivır'] *adj* wealthy, affluent.

saidhbhreas [saivr'əs] *m* wealth, affluence.

saighdear [səid'ɛr] *m* soldier.

saighead [sai.əd] *f* arrow.

sail [sal] *f* beam, joist.

sàil [sāl] *f* heel.

sailead [saləd] *m* salad.

saill[1] [saiL'] *v* salt; season *(with salt)*.

saill[2] [saiL'] *f* fat, grease.

saillear [saiL'ɛr] *f* salt-cellar.

saillte [saiL't'ı] *adj* salt, salted; salty.

sal [saL] *m* filth; dross; stain.

sàl [sāL] *m* salt water, brine; *(with art)* **an sàl** [ən sāL] *(songs, etc)* the sea, the briny.

salach [saLəch] *adj* dirty, filthy; foul.

salaich [saLıch'] *v* dirty, soil; defile, sully.

salann [saLəN] *m* salt.

salachar [saLəchər] *m* dirt, filth.

salm [saLam] *m* psalm.

saltair [saLtɛr'] *v* tread, trample.

sàmhach [sāvəch] *adj* quiet, peaceful, tranquil; silent.

samhail [sau.al] *m* likeness; match; the like(s) of.

Samhain [sau.ıN'] *f* Hallowtide; All Saints'/Souls' Day; **Oidhche Shamhna** [oi.ch'ı haunə] *f* Halloween; *(with art)* **an t-Samhain** [ən tau.ıN'] November.

sàmhchair [sāvchır'] *f* quiet(ness), tranquility; silence.

samhladh [sauLəgh] *m* resemblance; sign; *(lit)* symbol, simile, comparison, allegory; parable.

samhlaich (ri) [sauLıch' r'i] *v* resemble; compare, liken (to).

samhradh [saurəgh] *m* summer.

sanas [sanəs] *m* announcement; notice; hint.

sanas-reic [sanəsReʰk'] *m* advertisement.

san fharsaingeachd [sə NarsɪN'əchg] *adv* generally, broadly speaking.

san radharc [sən Ro.ərk] *adv* in sight.

sannt [sauNd] *m* avarice, covetousness.

sanntach [sauNdəch] *adj* greedy, avaricious.

sanntaich [sauNdɪch'] *v* covet.

saobh [sūv] *adj* foolish, wrongheaded.

saobhaidh [sūvɪ] *f* den, lair.

saobh-chràbhadh [sūvchrāvəgh] *m* superstition.

saobh-shruth [sūvru] *m* eddy, counter-current.

saobh-smuain [sūvsmuəN'] *m* whim.

saoghal [sū.əL] *m* world; life; lifetime.

saoghalta [sū.əLtə] *adj* wordly; materialistic.

saoil [sūl] *v* think, believe; suppose.

saor[1] [sūr] *v* free; (*relig*) save, redeem. • *adj* free (of charge); cheap; free, at liberty.

saor[2] [sūr] *m* joiner, carpenter.

saoradh [sūrəgh] *m* liberation; absolution; salvation.

saor-àirneis [sūrārnɪš] *m* cabinet maker.

saor-làithean [sūrLai.ən] *mpl* holiday(s).

saor bho [sūr vɔ] *adv* free from, untroubled by.

saorsa [sūrsə] *f* freedom; (*relig*) redemption.

saor an asgaidh [sūr ə Nasgɪ] *adv* free of charge.

saor-thoileach [sūr hɔləch] *adj* voluntary.

saothair [sūhɪr'] *f* labour, toil.

saothraich [sūrɪch'] *v* labour, toil.

sàr [sār] *adv* very, extremely; through and through.

sàraich [sārɪch'] *v* oppress; distress; vex; weary.

sàr mhath [sār va] *adj* excellent.

sàr obair [sār obɪr'] *f* masterpiece.

sàsaich [sāsɪch'] *v* content, satisfy; satiate.

sàsaichte [sāsɪch'tɪ] *adj* contented, satisfied; sated.

Sasainn [sasɪN'] *f* England.

Sasannach [sasəNach] *m*/*adj* Englishman; English.

sàsar [sāsər] *m* saucer.

sàth [sā] *v* stab; push, shove.

seabhag [ševag] *f* hawk, falcon.

seacaid [šɛʰɪd'] *f* jacket.

seac àraidh [šɛʰk āri] *adv* especially, particularly.

seach[1] [šɛch] *prep* instead of; rather than; in comparison to.

seach[2] [šɛch] *adv*/*prep* past, by.

seachad[1] [šɛchəd] *adj* over, finished; (*space and time*) past.

seachad[2] [šɛchəd] *adv* past, by.

seachad air [šɛchəd ɛr'] *prep* past, by.

seachainn [šɛchɪN'] *v* avoid; shun; abstain from.

seachanta [šɛchəntə] *adj* avoidable.

seachd [šɛchg] *n*/*adj* seven.

seachdad [šɛchgəd] *m* seventy.

seachdainn [šɛchgɪN'] *f* week.

seachdamh [šɛchgəv] *adj* seventh.

seachdnar [šɛchgnər] *m* (*people*) seven.

seachd searbh sgìth (de) [šɛʰk šɛrav sgī d'e] sick and tired (of).

seachran [šɛcharan] *m* wandering; going astray.

seada [šedə] *m* shed.

seadag [šedag] *f* grapefruit.

seadh [šogh] *adv* (*non-affirmative*) yes, uh-uh.

seagal [šegəL] *m* rye.

seagh [šogh] *m* sense, meaning.

sealbh [šɛLav] *m* luck; fortune, providence; heaven. • *excl* sealbh ort! [šɛLav oršd] good luck! aig Sealbh tha brath [ɛg' šɛLav ha bra] Heaven knows.

sealbh [šɛLav] *f* property; possession.

sealbhach [šɛLavəch] *adj* lucky; possessive.

sealbhadair [šɛLavədər'] *m* owner, proprietor.

sealbhaich [šɛLavɪch'] *v* own, possess.

sealg [šɛLag] *v* hunt.

sealg [šɛLag] *f* hunt, hunting.

sealgair [šɛLagɛr'] *m* hunter, huntsman; an Sealgair Mòr [ən šɛLagɛr' mōr] Orion.

seall [šauL] *v* see; look; show; watch over.

seall air [šauL ɛr'] *v* look at.

sealladh [šɛLəgh] *m* sight; view, prospect; eyesight; look; an dà shealladh [ən dā hɛLəgh] second sight.

sealladh-taoibhe [šɛLəghtuivɪ] *m* sideways look/glance.

Sealtainn [šɛLtɪN'] *m* Shetland.

Sealtainneach [šɛLtɪN'əch] *m/adj* Shetlander; from Shetland.

seamrag [šɛmarag] *f* shamrock; clover.

sean [šɛn] *adj* old; former.

seana-ghille [šɛna gh'iL'ɪ] *m* old batchelor.

seanair [šɛnɪr'] *m* grandfather; ancestor, forebear.

seanalair [šɛnaLɛr'] *m* general.

seana-mhaighdeann [šɛna vəid'əN] *f* old maid.

seanchaidh [šɛnachɪ] *m* shenachie, tradition-bearer; story-teller.

seanchas [šɛnachəs] *m* traditional lore; chat, gossip; news.

seanfhacal [šɛnaʰkəL] *m* proverb, saying, adage.

sean-fhasanta [šɛnasəndə] *adj* old-fashioned.

sean-fhleasgach [šɛnlesgəch] *m* old bachelor.

seang [šɛng] *adj* thin; slim; lank, skinny.

seangan [šɛngan] *m* ant.

seanmhair [šɛnavɪr'] *m* grandmother.

seann [šauN] *adj* *same as* sean (used before d, n, t, l, s, r).

seann-phàrant [šauNfãrand] *m* grandparent.

sinn-seanair [šĩN'šɛnɪr'] *m* great grandfather.

sinn-seanmhair [šĩN'šɛnavɪr'] *f* great grandmother.

Seapan [šɛʰpan] *f* (*with art*) an t-Seapan [ən t'ɛʰpan] Japan.

Seapanach [šɛʰpanəch] *m/adj* Japanese.

sear [šɛr] *adj/adv* east, eastern.

sear air [šɛr ɛr'] *adv* east of.

searbh [šɛrav] *adj* bitter; sour, acrid; pungent; harsh; disagreeable; sharp, sarcastic.

searbhadair [šɛravədər'] *m* towel.

searbhanta [šɛravantə] *f* servant, maid.

searg [šɛrag] *v* wither, shrivel, dry up; fade away; pine away; blight.

seargach [šɛragəch] *adj* (*tree*) deciduous.

searmon [šɛramɔn] *f* sermon.

searmonaich [šɛramɔnɪch'] *v* preach.

searrach [šɛʀəch] *m* colt, foal.

searrag [šɛʀag] *f* flask; bottle.

seas [šes] *v* stand up; stand by, support; last.

seasamh [šesəv] *m* standing position; **'na sheasamh** [nə hesəv] standing.

seasamh-chas [šesəv chas] *m* footing.

seasg [šesg] *adj* barren, sterile; (*cattle, etc*) dry.

seasgad [šesgəd] *m* sixty.

seasgair [šesgɪr'] *adj* cosy, snug; comfortably off.

seasmhach [šesvəch] *adj* firm, stable; reliable; enduring; durable.

seathar [šɛ.ər] *m* chair.

seathar-tulgaidh [šɛ.ərtuLugɪ] *m* rocking-chair.

s e do bheatha! [še də vɛhə] *excl* you're welcome!

seic [šeʰk'] *f* cheque.

Seic [šeʰk'] *f* (*with art*) **an t-Seic** [ən t'eʰk'] the Czech Republic.

Seiceach [šeʰkəch] *m/adj* Czech.

seiche [šech'ı] *f* skin, pelt, hide.

seic-leabhar [šeʰk'lɔ.ər] *m* chequebook.

sèid [šēd'] *v* blow; swell; puff up.

seilbh, seilbheach, seilbheadair, seilbhich *same as* **sealbh, sealbhach, sealbhadair, sealbhaich.**

seilcheag [šelch'ag] *f* snail; slug.

seile [šelı] *m* saliva, spittle.

seileach [šeləch] *m* willow.

seillean [šeL'an] *m* bee.

seillean mòr [šeL'an mōr] *m* bumble-bee.

sèimh [šēv] *adj* calm, mild, gentle.

sèimhe [šēvı] *f* calm(ness), mildness, gentleness.

seinn [šeiN'] *v* sing; (*instrument, etc*) play, sound.

seinn [šeiN'] *m* singing; sounding.

seinneadair [šeiN'ədər'] *m* singer.

seirbheis [šer'ivɪš] *f* service; favour.

seirbheiseach [šer'ivɪšəch] *m* servant.

seirc [šer'k'] *f* love, affection; (Christian) charity.

seirm [šerim] *v* ring (out), sound.

sèisd [šēšd'] *m* siege.

seis [šeš] *m* like(s) of; equal, match.

seisean [šešan] *m* (*meeting, etc*) session; kirk session.

's e sin a'cheist! [še šin ə ch'ešd'] that's the question/point!

's e sin a' chùis! [še šin ə chūš] that's the point!

sèist [šēšd'] *m* refrain, chorus.

seo [šɔ] *adj/pron* this.

seòbhrach [šɔvrəch] *f* primrose.

seòclaid [šɔʰkLɪd'] *f* chocolate.

seòd [šɔd'] *m* hero.

seòl [šɔL] *v* sail; steer; navigate; guide, direct; manage; govern. • *m* sail; course; method; means.

seòladair [šɔLədər'] *m* sailor, seaman.

seòladh [šɔLəgh] *m* sailing; (*house, etc*) address.

seòl-beatha [šɔLbɛhə] *m* way of life.

seòl-mara [šɔLmarə] *m* (high) tide.

seòlta [šɔ̄Ltə] *adj* cunning; resourceful; shrewd.

seòmar [šɔ̄mər] *m* room.

seòmar-cadail [šɔ̄mərkadal] *m* bedroom.

seòmar-ionnlaid [šɔ̄məriũNLɪd'] *m* bathroom.

seòmar-leapa [šɔ̄mərLɛʰpə] *m* bedroom.

seòmar-mullaich [šɔ̄mərmuLɪch'] *m* attic.

seòrsa [šɔ̄rsə] *m* sort, kind; genus, species; class.

seòrsaich [šɔ̄rsɪch'] *v* classify; sort.

seud [šēd] *m* jewel, gem.

seumarlan [šēmərLan] *m* factor, land-agent; chamberlain.

seun [šian] *m* spell; charm, amulet.

seunta [šiandə] *adj* enchanted, spellbound.

's e ur beatha! [šɛr bɛhə] *excl (polite)* you're welcome!

's fheàirrde mi X [šāRd'ɪ mi] *v* I'm better for X, X is good for me.

's fheàrr leam X [šāR ləm] *v* I prefer X.

's fheudar dhomh [šiadər ghɔ] *v* I must, I have to.

sgadan [sgadan] *m* herring.

sgàil [sgāl] *v* shade, darken, eclipse; veil, mask. • *f* shade, shadow; covering; *(occas)* ghost, spectre.

sgailc [sgalk'] *v* slap, smack. • *f* slap, sharp blow; sharp sound; *(liquid)* swig; baldness.

sgàilc *n same as* **sgailc**.

sgàilean-grèine [sgālangr'ēnɪ] *m* parasol.

sgàilean-uisge [sgālanušg'ɪ] *m* umbrella.

sgàil-lampa [sgāLaumbə] *f* lampshade.

sgàil-sùla [sgālsūLə] *f* eyelid.

sgàin [sgāN'] *v* burst, crack, split.

sgàineadh [sgāN'əgh] *m* split, crack.

sgàird [sgārd'] *f (with art)* **an sgàird** [ən sgārd'] diarrhoea.

sgairt[1] [sgaršd'] *f* diaphragm.

sgairt[2] [sgaršd'] *f* yell; gusto; vigour, activity.

sgairteil [sgaršd'ɛl] *adj* brisk; active, bustling; enthusiastic; *(weather)* blustery.

sgait [sgaʰt'] *f (fish)* skate.

sgal [sgaL] *v* yell, squeal. • *m* yell; outburst; squall.

sgàl [sgāL] *m* tray.

sgàla [sgāLə] *f (mus)* scale.

sgalag [sgaLag] *f* farm servant; skivvy.

sgalanta [sgaLəndə] *adj* shrill.

sgall [sgauL] *m* baldness; bald patch.

sgallach [sgaLəch] *adj* bald-headed.

Sgalpach [sgaLbəch] *m/adj* Scalpay person, from Scalpay.

Sgalpaigh [sgaLbay] *n* Scalpay.

sgamhan [sgavan] *m* lung.

sgaoil [sgūl] *v* spread (out); stretch out; disperse; release.

sgaoth [sgū] *m* mass, multitude, swarm.

sgaothaich [sgūhɪch'] *v (crowds, etc)* flock, mass, swarm.

sgap [sgaʰp] *v* scatter.

sgar [sgar] *v* separate; sever.

sgaradh [sgarəgh] *m* separation.

sgaradh-pòsaidh [sgarəghpɔ̄sɪ] *m* separation (legal separation from partner).#

sgarbh [sgarav] *m* cormorant.

sgarbh an sgumain [sgarav ən sgūmεN'] *m* (*bird*) shag.

sgarfa [sgarfə] *m* scarf.

sgàrlaid [sgārLɪd'] *f/adj* scarlet.

sgath [sga] *v* cut off; prune.

sgàth [sgā] *m* shadow; protection; fear.

sgàthan [sgāhan] *m* mirror.

sgeadaich [sg'edɪch'] *v* adorn, embellish; dress up; (*lamp, fire, etc*) attend to, trim.

sgealb [sg'εLab] *v* split; shatter, smash; chip; carve. • *f* chip; splinter, fragment.

sgealbag [sg'εLabag] *f* index finger.

sgealp [sg'εLp] *f* slap, smack; sharp sound.

sgeap [sg'εʰp] *f* beehive.

sgeilb [sg'elib] *f* chisel.

sgeileid [sg'elɪd'] *f* skillet.

sgeilp [sg'elp] *f* shelf.

sgeir [sg'er'] *f* rock, skerry.

sgeith [sg'e] *v* vomit, throw up.

sgeul [sg'iaL] *m* story; (*of person*) news, sign.

sgeulach [sg'iaLəch] *adj* like a story; fond of stories.

sgeulachd [sg'iaLəchg] *f* story.

sgeulachd ghoirid [sg'iaLəchg ghor'ɪd] *f* short story.

sgeulaiche [sg'iaLɪch'ə] *m* storyteller.

sgeumhach [sg'ēvəch] *adj* beautiful.

sgeumhaich [sg'ēvɪch'] *v* beautify; adorn, ornament.

sgeunach [sg'ianəch] *adj* timid, shy; skittish, mettlesome.

sgith [sg'i] *f* ski.

sgiamh [sg'iəv] *v* squeal, shriek. • *m* squeal, shriek.

sgian [sg'ian] *f* knife.

sgiath [sg'ia] *f* wing; shield; shelter.

sgiathaich [sg'iahɪch'] *v* fly.

Sgitheanach [sg'i.ənəch] *m/adj* Skye person, from Skye. • *m* an t-Eilean Sgitheanach [ən t'elan sg'i.ənəch] (the Isle of) Skye.

sgil [sg'il] *m* skill.

sgileil [sg'ilεl] *adj* skilled; skilful.

sgillin [sg'iL'ɪn] *f* penny.

sgillinn ruadh [sg'iL'ɪn ruəgh] *f* brass farthing.

sgioba [sg'ibə] *m* crew; team.

sgiobair [sg'ibεr'] *m* skipper, captain.

sgiobalta [sg'ibəLtə] *adj* neat, tidy; quick, active; handy.

sgioblaich [sg'ibLɪch'] *v* tidy; put right/straight.

sgiorradh [sg'iRəgh] *m* accident; stumble, slip.

sgiort [sg'irt] *f* skirt.

sgiths [sg'īs] *f* tiredness; weariness.

sgìre [sg'ir'ɪ] *f* (*local govt*) district; area, locality; parish.

sgìreachd [sg'ɪr'əchg] *f* parish.

sgìth [sg'ī] *adj* tired; weary.

sgitheach [sg'ihəch] *m* whitethorn, hawthorn.

Sgiathanach *see* **Sgitheanach**

sgitheil [sg'īhεl] *adj* tiring; wearisome.

sgithich [sg'īhɪch'] *v* tire; weary.

sgithich [sg'i.ɪch'] *v* ski.

sgiùrs [sg'ūrs] *v* whip, scourge.

sgiùrsair [sg'ūrsεr'] *m* whip, scourge.

sglàib [sgLāib] *f* (*building, etc*) plaster.

sglàibeadair [sgLāibədər'] *m* plasterer.

sglèat [sgliaʰt] *m* slate.

sglèatair [sgliaʰtɛr'] *m* slater.

sgleog [sglɔg] *f* slap.

sgob [sgɔb] *v* snatch; sting; peck; sprain.

sgoil [sgɔl] *f* school; schooling.

sgoil-àraich [sgɔlãrɪch'] *f* nursery school.

sgoilear [sgɔlɛr] *m* pupil; scholar.

sgoilearachd [sgɔlɛr'əchg] *f* scholarship; bursary.

sgoilt [sgɔlt'] *v* split, cleave; slit.

sgoinneil [sgɔN'ɛl] *adj* (*fam*) great, smashing.

sgol [sgɔL] *v* rinse.

sgolt *see* **sgoilt**.

sgoltadh [sgɔLtəgh] *m* split, cleft; chink; slit.

sgona [sgɔnə] *f* scone.

sgonn [sgɔuN] *m* lump, hunk.

sgòr [sgɔ̄r] *m* (*games, etc*) score.

sgòrnan [sgɔ̄rnan] *m* throat; gullet, windpipe.

sgoth [sgɔ] *f* skiff, sailing boat.

sgòth [sgɔ̄h] *f* cloud.

sgòthach [sgɔ̄həch] *adj* cloudy.

sgoth-long [sgɔ Lɔung] *f* yacht.

sgraing [sgrang'] *f* frown, scowl.

sgreab [sgr'ɛb] *f* scab.

sgread [sgr'ed] *v* scream, shriek. • *m* scream, shriek.

sgreadhail [sgr'ɛ.al] *f* trowel.

sgrèamh [sgr'ēv] *m* loathing, disgust.

sgreamhail [sgr'ɛval] *adj* loathsome, disgusting.

sgreataidh [sgr'ɛʰtɪ] *adj* loathsome, nauseating.

sgreuch [sgr'iach] *v* scream, screech. • *m* scream, screech.

sgrìob [sgr'īb] *v* scratch, scrape; furrow. • *f* scratch, scrape; furrow; trip, jaunt.

sgrìobach [sgr'ībəch] *adj* abrasive.

sgrìoban [sgr'ībən] *m* hoe.

sgrìobh [sgr'īv] *v* write.

sgrìobhadair [sgr'īvədər'] *m* writer.

sgrìobhadh [sgr'īvəgh] *m* writing; handwriting.

sgrìobhaiche [sgr'īvɪchə] *m* writer.

sgriobtar [sgr'ibdər] *m* scripture.

sgrios [sgr'is] *v* destroy; ruin. • *m* destruction; ruin.

sgriosail [sgr'isal] *adj* destructive; pernicious;(*fam*)terrible,dreadful.

sgriubha [sgr'u.ə] *f* screw.

sgriubhaire [sgr'u.ər'ə] *m* screwdriver.

sgròb [sgrɔb] *v* scratch; cross out.

sgrùd [sgrūd] *v* scrutinize; investigate; research; audit.

sgrùdadh [sgrūdəgh] *m* scrutiny; investigation; research; audit.

sguab[1] [sguəb] *v* sweep, brush. • *f* brush, broom.

sguab[2] [sguəb] *f* sheaf of corn.

sguabadair [sguəbədər'] *m* hoover, vacuum-cleaner.

sguab fhliuch [sguəb luch] *f* mop.

sgud [sgud] *v* chop.

sgudal [sgudaL] *m* rubbish, refuse; nonsense.

sguir [sgur'] *v* stop, cease; desist.

sguir de [sgur' d'e] *v* give up, stop.

sgur [sgur] *m* stopping, ceasing.

sgùrr [sgūR] *m* peak, pinnacle.

shìos [hiəs] *adv* down; below (*location*).

shìos bhuam [hiəs vuəm] *adv* below me, down from me (*location*).

shuas [huəs] *adv* up; above (*location*).

shuas bhuam [huəs vuəm] *adv* above me, up from me (*location*).

sia *n*/ [šia] *adj* six.

siab [šiab] *v* wipe, rub; (*snow*) drift.

siabann [šiabəN] *m* soap.

siach [šiəch] *v* sprain, strain.

sia deug [šia d'iag] *m*/*adj* sixteen.

sian¹ [šian] *f* storm; (*wind*) blast; *pl* (*with art*). **na siantan** [nə šiantən] the elements.

sian² [šian] *m* thing; anything, (*with neg v*) nothing.

sianar [šianər] *m* (*people*) six.

siar [šiər] *adj*/*adv* west, western. • **na h-Eileanan Siar** [nə helanən šiər] *mpl* the Western Isles. **an Cuan Siar** [ən kuən šiər] *m* the Atlantic Ocean. **an taobh siar** [ən tūv šiər] *m* the west.

siar air [šiər ɛr] *prep* west of.

sibh [šiv] *pers pron pl* you.

side [šīd'ı] *f* weather. **side nan seachd sian** [šīd'ı nən šɛchg šian] appalling weather.

sil [šil] *v* (*liquids*) drip, drop, flow, rain.

silidh [šilı] *m* jam; jelly.

silteach [šilt'əch] *adj* (*liquids*) dripping, dropping, flowing.

similear [šimılɛr] *m* chimney.

simplidh [šīmplı] *adj* simple, uncomplicated; simple-minded.

sin [šin] *adj* that; those. • *pron* that.

sin [šīn] *v* stretch, extend; pass, hand.

sinc [šink'] *m* zinc.

since [sink'ı] *f* (*kitchen*) sink.

sine [šinı] *f* nipple, teat.

sineach [šinəch] *adj* mammal.

sineadh [šīnəgh] *m* stretching; recumbent position. • **'na shineadh** [nə hīnəgh] *adv* stretched out, lying down.

sineas [šīnəs] *m* dole.

singilte [šing'ılt'ə] *adj* single; (*gram*) singular.

sinn [šiN'] *pron* we.

sinnsear [šīN'šɛr] *m* ancestor, forefather.

sinn-sinn-seanair [šīN' šīN' šɛnır'] *m* great-great-grandfather.

sinn-sinn-seanmhair [šīN' šīN' šɛnavir'] *f* great-great-grandmother.

sinteag [šīnt'ag] *f* hop; stride.

sin thu! [šin u], **sin thu-fhèin!** [šin u hēn] *excl* well done! good for you!

siobhag [šifag] *f* wick.

siobhalta [šīvəLtə] *adj* civil, polite.

siobhaltair [šīvəLter'] *m* civilian.

siochail [šiəchal] *adj* peaceful.

sioda [šiədə] *m* silk.

sìol [šiaL] *m* seed; race; progeny.

sìolachan [šiəLəchan] *m* strainer, filter.

sìolaidh [šiəLı] *v* subside, settle; filter, strain.

sìol-cuir [šiəLkur'] *m* seed corn.

sìol-ghinidh [šiəLgh'inı] *m* semen.

sìoman [šiəman] *m* straw rope.

sìon *see* **sian**²

Sìn [šīn] *f* (*with art*) **an t-Sìn** [ən t'īn] China.

Sìneach [šīnəch] *m*/*adj* Chinaman; Chinese.

sionnach [šuNəch] *m* fox.

sionnsar [šūNsər] *m* (*bagpipe*) chanter.

sìor- *pre* [šiər] *fix* ever-.

sìor-mhaireannach [šiərvar'əNəch] *adj* everlasting; immortal.

siorrachd [šiRəchg] *f* sheriffdom; county, shire.

siorram [šiRəm] *m* sheriff.

sìorraidh [šiəRɪ] *adj* everlasting, eternal.

sìorraidheachd [šiəRɪ.əchg] *f* eternity.

siorramachd [šiRəməchg] *f same as* siorrachd.

sìor-uaine [šiəruəN'ɪ] *adj* evergreen.

sìos [šiəs] *adv* down (*motion*).

siosar [šisər] *f* scissors.

siosarnaich [šisərnich'] *f* hissing; whispering; rustling.

sìos 'na inntinn [šiəs nə īN'd'ɪN'] *adv* depressed.

sir [šir'] *v* seek, search for; require.

siris [širʼiš] *f* cherry.

siteag [šihtʼag] *f* dunghill, midden.

sìth[1] [šī] *f* peace; tranquility.

sìth[2] [šī] *adj* fairy.

sìthean [šihan] *m* fairy hill.

sitheann [šihəN] *f* venison; game.

sìtheil [šihɛl] *adj* peaceable; tranquil.

sìthich [šī.ich] *v* pacify.

sìthiche [šī.ichə] *m* fairy.

sitir [šihtʼɪr'] *f* braying, neighing, whinnying.

siubhail [šu.al] *v* travel; seek; die.

siubhal [šu.əL] *f* travel.

siùbhlach [šūLəch] *adj* speedy; fluent; fluid.

siùcar [šūhkər] *m* sugar; *pl* siùcairean [šūhkɪr'ən] sweets.

siud [šid] *pron* that, yonder.

siuga [šugə] *f* jug.

siuthad [šu.əd] (*sing*), siuthadaib [šu.ədɪv] (*pl*) *imper* on you go! ge on with it!

slabhraidh [sLavrɪ] *f* chain.

slac [sLahk] *v* thrash, beat, thump bruise, maul.

slàinte [sLāN'd'ɪ] *f* health. • *excl* slàinte! cheers! good health slàinte mhath/mhòr! [sLāN'd'ɪ va vōr]good health! air do dheag shlàinte! [ɛr' də gh'ō LāN'd'ɪ] you very good health!

slaman [sLaman] *m* curds, crowdie

slàn [sLān] *adj* well, healthy; complete. • *excl* slàn leat! goodbye farewell!

slànaich [sLāNich] *v* heal, cure; ge better.

slànaighear [sLāNɪ.ɛr] *m* (with art an Slànaighear [ən sLāNɪ.ɛr] the Saviour.

slàn is fallain [sLān ɪs faLɛN'] saf and sound.

slaod [sLūd] *v* drag, haul. • *m* sledge.

slaodach [sLūdəch] *adj* slow; long drawn-out, boring.

slaodair [sLūdɛr'] *m* trailer.

slaod-uisge [sLūdušg'ɪ] *m* raft.

slaoightear [sLuit'ɛr] *m* rascal rogue.

slapag [sLahpag] *f* slipper.

slat [sLaht] *f* (*length*) yard; twig rod; (*vulg*) penis, cock; spear javelin.

slat-iasgaich [sLahtiasgɪch'] *f* fishing rod.

slat-rìoghail [sLahtriə.al] *f* sceptre.

slat-thomhais [sLahto.ɪš] *f* yardstick

sleamhainn [šlɛu.ɪN'] *adj* slippy slippery.

sleamhnag [šlɛunag] f (*children's*) slide.

sleamhnaich [šlɛunɪch'] v slip, slide.

's leisg dhomh. [sL'ešg' ghɔ] v I hesitate to.

sleuchd [šliachg] v bow down; prostate oneself.

sliabh [šliav] m moor, moorland; hill.

sliasaid [šliasɪd'] f thigh.

slige [šlig'ɪ] f (*mollusc, military*) shell.

slighe [šli.ɪ] f path, road, track; way, route.

slinnean [šliN'an] m shoulder.

sliob [šliəb] v stroke.

sliochd [šlichg] m descendants, lineage.

slios [šlis] m side, flank.

slisinn [šlišiN'] f slice.

slisinn-èisg [šlišiN'ẽšg'] f fish slice.

slisnich [šlišnich'] v slice.

sloc [sLɔʰk] m hollow; pit.

sloinneadh [sLoN'əgh] m surname, family name.

sluagh [sLuəgh] m people, populace; crowd; army.

sluagh-ghairm [sLuəghor'im] m war-cry; slogan.

sluaghmhor [sLuəghvər] adj populous.

sluasaid [sLuasɪd'] f shovel.

slugadh [sLugəgh] m swallow, gulp; swallowing.

sluig [sLuig'] v swallow; devour.

smachd [smachg] m authority, discipline; control; rule.

smachdail [smachgal] adj commanding, authoritative.

smàil [smāl] v (*fire*) put out; quench.

smal [smaL] m spot, stain.

smàladair [smāLədər'] m candle snuffers.

smàladh [smāLəgh] m extinguishing.

smalan [smaLan] m gloom, melancholy.

smalanach [smaLanəch] adj gloomy, melancholy.

smaoin [smūN'] f thought, notion, idea.

smaoin(t)ich [smūN'(d')ɪch] v think, reflect; consider.

smàrag [smārag] f emerald.

's mar sin air adhart [ɪs mar šin ɛr' o.əršd] and so on.

's math leam X [sma ləm] v I find X good.

's math sin! [sma šin] excl smashing!

smèid (air) [smēd' ɛr'] v beckon (to); wave (to).

smeòrach [smyōrəch] f thrush.

smeur¹ [smiar] v smear, daub; grease.

smeur² [smiar] f blackberry, bramble.

's miann leam [smiəN ləm] v I wish.

smid [smid'] f (*with neg v*) word, syllable.

smig [smig'], **smiogaid** [smigɪd'] m chin.

smior [smir] m marrow; courage, spirit, guts; manliness, strength, vigour; best/pick of.

smiorail [smiral] adj strong; spirited; plucky; manly, vigorous.

smiùr [smyūr] v same as **smeur**¹.

smoc [smɔʰk] v (*tobacco*) smoke.

smocadh [smɔʰkəgh] m smoking; **smocadh toirmisgte** [smɔkəgh torimɪšg't'ɪ] no smoking.

's mòr am beud e! [smōr əm bēd ε] *excl* it's a great pity!

smuain [smuaN'] *f same as* **smaoin**.

smuain(t)ich [smuaN'(d')ıch'] *v same as* **smaoinich**.

smugaid [smugıd'] *f* spit.

smùid [smūd'] *v* smoke; smash. • *f* smoke, steam, vapour, fumes; drunkenness.

smùr [smūr] *m* dust; dross.

snagan-daraich [snagandarıch] *m* woodpecker.

snaidhm [snaim] *m* knot.

snàig [snāg'] *v* crawl, creep; grovel.

snàigeach [snāg'əch] *m* reptile.

snaigh [snaich'] *v* hew; carve.

snàmh [snāv] *v* swim; float. • *m* swimming, floating.

snasail [snasal], **snasmhor** [snasvər] *adj* neat, trim; elegant.

snàth [snā] *m* (*coll*) thread.

snàthad [snāhəd] *m* needle.

snàthainn [snāhıN'] *m* (*single*) thread.

sneachd [šN'εchg] *m* snow.

snèap [šNē^hp] *f* turnip, swede.

snigh [šNi] *v* drip, seep.

snìomh [šN'iəv] *v* spin; twist; wring.

snìomhaire [šN'iəvər'ə] *m* (*tool*) drill.

snodha-gàire [snɔ.əgār'ı] *m* smile.

snog [snog] *adj* pretty; nice.

snuadh [sNuəgh] *m* appearance; complexion.

so- [sɔ] *prefix* -able, -ible.

sòbhrach [sōvrəch] *f same as* **seòbhrach**.

socair [sɔ^hkır'] *adj* mild; tranquil, relaxed; at peace. • *f* comfort; ease, leisure. • *excl* **socair!** take it easy!

socais [sɔ^hkıš] *f* sock.

sochar [sɔchər] *f* bashfulness weakness, compliance; indulgence.

socharach [sɔchərəch] *adj* bashful weak; soft, over-indulgent.

socrach [sɔ^hkrəch] *adj* at ease; sedate, leisurely.

socraich [sɔ^hkrıch'] *v* abate; assuage; settle; set, fix.

sodal [sɔdəL] *m* adulation; fawning flattery.

so-dhèanta [sɔ gh'iand'ə] *adj* possible, feasible.

sòfa [sōfa] *f* sofa.

seilearaidh [šelərı] *m* celery.

soilleir [soL'εr'] *adj* bright, clear obvious.

soilleirich [soL'εr'ıch'] *v* brighten (up); clarify, explain.

soillse [soiL'šı] *m* light.

soillsich [soiL'šıch'] *v* shine; gleam.

soirbh [sor'ıv] *adj* easy.

soirbheachail [sor'ivəchal] *adj* successful; prosperous.

soirbhich le [sor'ivıch' le] *v* turn out well for.

sòisealach [sōšəLəch] *adj* socialist.

sòisealta [sōšəLtə] *adj* social. • *fp* **seirbhisean sòisealta** [šer'ivišər sōšəLtə] social services.

soisgeul [sɔšg'iaL] *m* gospel.

soisgeulach [sɔšg'iaLəch] *adj* evangelical.

soisgeulaiche [sɔšg'iaLıch'ə] *m* evangelist.

soitheach [so.əch] *m* (*sailing*) vessel; dish, container.

soitheamh [so.əv] *adj* gentle, good-natured.

sòlaimte [sōlımt'ə] *adj* solemn; ceremonious.

solair [sɔLɪr'] v supply, purvey.

solas [sɔLəs] m light.

sòlas [sɔ̄Ləs] m solace, consolation; joy.

sòlasach [sɔ̄Ləsəch] adj comforting, consoling; joyful.

solta [sɔLtə] adj meek, gentle.

so-lùbadh [sɔ Lūbəgh] adj flexible, pliable.

sona [sɔnə] adj happy, content.

sònraich [sɔ̄nrɪch'] v distinguish; specify, single out.

sònraichte [sɔ̄nrɪch'tə] adj special, particular; specific.

sop [sɔʰp] m wisp.

soraidh [sɔrɪ] f farewell; greeting. • excl **soraidh leat!** [sɔrɪ laʰt] farewell!

so-ruigsinneach [sɔ rug'sɪN'əch] adj attainable; accessible.

so-thuigsinneach [sɔ hig'šɪN'əch] adj intelligible, comprehensible.

spàid [sbād'] f spade.

spaideil [sbad'ɛl] adj (esp dress) smart.

spaidirich [sbad'ɪr'ɪch'] v strut.

spàin [sbāN'] f spoon.

spàin-mhilsein [sbāN'vīlšɛN'] f dessert spoon.

Spàinn [sbāN'] f (with art) an **Spàinn** [ən sbāN'] Spain.

Spàinn(t)each [sbāN'(d')əch] m/adj Spaniard; Spanish.

Spàinnis [sbāN'īš] f (language) Spanish.

spàirn [sbārN'] f exertion, effort; struggle.

spanair [sbanɛr'] m spanner.

spàrr[1] [sbāR] v drive, thrust.

spàrr[2] [sbāR] m joist, beam; roost.

speach [sbɛch] f wasp.

speal [sbɛL] f scythe.

spealg [sbɛLag] v smash, splinter. • f splinter, fragment.

spèil [sbēl] v skate. • f ice-skate.

spèis [sbēš] f love; affection; regard.

speuclairean [sbiaʰkLɪr'ən] mpl spectacles, glasses.

speuclairean-grèine [sbiaʰkLɪr'əngr'ēnɪ] mpl sunglasses.

speur [sbiar] m sky; space; pl **na speuran** [nə sbiarən] the heavens.

speur-sheòladh [sbiarhyɔ̄Ləgh] m space travel.

speuradair [sbiarədər'] m spaceman, astronaut.

speuradaireachd [sbiarədər'əchg] f astrology.

speurair [sbiarɛr'] m astrologer.

spìc [sbīʰk'] f spike.

spideag [sbid'ag] f nightingale.

spìocach [sbīʰkəch] adj miserly, mean.

spìocaire [sbīʰkər'ə] m miser.

spìon [spiən] v snatch, grab; pluck.

spionnadh [sbyuNəgh] m strength; energy.

spiorad [sbirəd] m spirit, ghost; **an Spiorad Naomh** [ən sbirəd Nūv] the Holy Spirit/Ghost.

spioradail [sbirədəl] adj spiritual.

spiosrach [sbisrəch] m spice.

spìosraich [sbisrɪch'] v spice; embalm.

spiris [sbir'īš] f perch, roost.

spleuchd [sbliachg] v stare, gape; squint. • m stare; squint.

spliuchan [sbliuchan] m pouch.

spòg [sbɔ̄g] f paw; (of clock or watch) hand; spoke.

spong [sbɔng] *m* sponge.

sporan [sbɔran] *m* purse; sporran.

spòrs [sbɔrs] *f* street; fun.

spot [sbɔʰt] *m* spot, stain.

spoth [sbɔ] *v* castrate.

spreadh [sbr'ɛ] *v* burst; explode.

spreadhadh [sbr'ɛ.əgh] *m* explosion.

sprèidh [sbr'ē] *f* livestock.

sprèig [sbr'ēg'] *v* incite, urge.

sprùilleach [sbrūL'əch] *m* crumbs.

sprùilleag [sbrūL'ag] *f* crumb.

spùill [sbūL'] *v* plunder, despoil.

spùinneadair [sbūN'əd'ɛr'] *m* plunderer, brigand.

spùinneadair-mara
[sbūN'ədɛr'marə] *m* pirate, buccaneer.

spur [sbur] *m* claw, talon.

spùt [sbūʰt] *v* spurt; squirt. • *m* spout; spurt, gush; waterfall.

sràbh [sdrāv] *m* drinking straw.

srac [sdraʰk] *v* rip, tear.

sradag [sdradag] *f* spark.

sràid [sdrād'] *f* street.

sràidearaich [sdrād'ərich'] *v* stroll, saunter.

srainnsear [sdraN'šɛr] *m* stranger.

srann [sdrauN] *f* snore; snoring.

srannartaich [sdraNərsdich'] *f* snoring.

sreang [sdr'ɛng] *f* string.

sreath [sdr'ɛ] *m* row, line, rank; layer; series.

sreothart [sdr'ɔhəršd] *m* sneeze.

sreothartaich [sdr'ɔhəršdich'] *f* sneezing.

srian [sdrian] *f* bridle, rein(s); streak, stripe.

sròn [sdrōn] *f* nose; ridge; point, promontory.

sròn-adharcach [sdrōno.ərkəch] *m* rhinoceros.

srùb [sdrūb] *v* spout; spurt; slurp. • *m* (*pot, etc*) spout.

srùbag [sdrūbag] *f* sip; snack, stroupach.

srùban [sdrūban] *m* cockle.

sruth [sdru] *v* flow, stream, run. • *m* stream, burn; flow; current.

stàball [sdābəL] *m* stable.

stad [sdad] *v* stop, cease; halt, pause. • *m* stop, end; halt, pause.

stad-phuing [sdadfuing'] *f* (*orthog*) full stop.

staid [sdad] *f* state, condition.

staidhre [sdair'ı] *f* stair, staircase.

stailc [sdalk] *f* (*industry, etc*) strike.

stàillinn [sdāL'ıN'] *f* steel.

staing [sdaing'] *f* difficulty, tight corner, fix.

stàirn [sdārN'] *f* crashing, clattering, rumbling.

stairsneach [sdaršNəch] *f* threshold.

stàit [sdāʰt] *f* (*nation*) state; (*pl*) **na Stàitean Aonaichte** [nə sdāʰt'ən ūnich't'ə] the United States. • *m* **Rùnaire na Stàite** [Rūnər'ə nə sdāʰt'ı] the Secretary of State.

stàiteil [sdāʰt'ɛl] *adj* stately.

stalc [sdalk] *m* starch.

stalcaire [sdalkər'ə] *m* fool, blockhead.

stalcaireachd [sdalkər'əchg] *f* stupidity; stupid action.

stamag [sdamag] *f* stomach.

stamh [sdav] *m* (*seaweed*) tangle.

stampa [sdambə] *v* stamp. • *f* (*postage*) stamp.

staoig [sdūg'] *f* steak.

staoin [sdūN'] *f* (*the metal*) tin.

steall [šd'auL] *v* spout, squirt, spurt, gush. • *f* outpouring. spout, spurt; (*fam*) swig, slug.

steallaire [šd'aLɪr'ə] *m* syringe.

stèidh [šd'ē] *f* base, foundation, basis.

stèidhich [šd'ē.ɪch'] *v* found, establish.

stèidhichte [šd'ē.ɪch't'ə] *adj* founded, established. • *f* **an Eaglais Stèidhichte** [ə N'egLɪš šd'ē.ɪch't'ə] the Established Church.

stèisean [sdēšan] *m* station.

stiall [šd'iaL] *v* stripe, streak.

stiall [šd'iaL] *f* stripe; tape; (*of clothing*) stitch, scrap.

stìoball [šd'ībaL] *m* steeple.

stiùbhard [šd'ū.ərd] *m* steward.

stiùir [šd'ūr'] *v* steer, direct; run, manage. • *f* rudder, helm.

stiùireadair [šd'ūr'ədɛr'] *m* steersman, helmsman.

stiùireadh [šd'ūr'əgh] *m* steering, directing; managing.

stiùiriche [šd'ūr'ɪch'ə] *m* director.

stob [sdɔb] *m* fence post; stake; (*tree*) stump.

stòbha [sdōvə] *f* stove.

stoc [sdɔʰk] *m* (*tree*) trunk, stump; livestock; scarf, cravat.

stocainn [sdɔʰkɪN'] *f* sock; stocking.

stoidhle [sdoilɪ] *f* style.

stòirich [sdɔrɪch'] *v* store.

stòiridh [sdɔr'ɪ] *m* story; humorous anecdote.

stoirm [sdor'im] *f* storm.

stòl [sdɔL] *m* stool.

stòlda [sdɔLdə] *adj* sedate, staid, serious; sober.

stòr[1] [sdɔr] *m* store; riches, wealth.

stòras [sdɔrəs] *m* riches, wealth.

stòr-dàta [sdɔrdāʰtə] *m* database.

stràc [sdrāʰk] *m* stroke, blow; (*orthog*) accent.

stràic [sdrāiʰk'] *m* (*school, formerly*) belt, tawse.

streap [sdr'ɛʰp] *v* climb.

streap mhonaidhean [sdr'ɛʰp vɔnɪ.ən] *f* hillwalking.

streap bheanntan [sdr'ɛʰp vyauNtən] *f* mountain climbing.

strì [sdr'ī] *v* struggle; compete. • *f* struggle, strife; contest.

strìochd [sdr'iəchg] *v* surrender, yield; cringe.

stripeach [sdrīʰpəch] *f* prostitute.

's truagh e/sin! [struəgh ɛ/šin] *excl* it's/that's a pity.

structair [sdruʰktɛr'] *m* structure.

struidheil [sdrui.ɛl] *adj* extravagant, prodigal. • *m* **am mac struidheil** [əm maʰk sdrui.ɛl] the prodigal son.

struth [sdru] *m* ostrich.

stuadh [sduəgh] *f* (*sea*) wave; (*house*) gable.

stuaim [sduaim] *f* abstemiousness, moderation, temperance; sobriety.

stuama [sduəmə] *adj* abstemious, moderate, temperate; sober.

stuamachd [sduəməchg] *f* abstinence, sobriety.

stùiceach [sdūiʰk'əch] *adj* surly, morose.

stuig [sduig'] *v* incite, urge.

stùr [sdūr] *m* dust.

stuth [sdu] *m* material, stuff.

suaicheantas [suɛch'əntəs] *m* badge, emblem.

suaimhneach [suɛvnəch] *adj* calm, quiet.

suain[1] [suɛN'] *v* wrap, entwine.

suain[2] [suɛN'] *f* sleep, slumber.

Suain [suɛN'] *f* (*with art*) **an t-Suain** [ən tuɛN'] Sweden.

Suaineach [suɛN'əch] *m/adj* Swede; Swedish.

suairc [suɛrk'] *adj* kind; courteous; affable.

suarach [suərəch] *adj* insignificant; petty; despicable.

suarachas [suərəchəs] *m* insignificance; pettiness.

suas [suəs] *adv* up.

suath [suə] *v* rub, wipe.

suath ri [suə r'i] *v* brush against.

sùbailte [sūbalt'ɪ] *adj* supple, flexible.

sùbh-làir [sū Lār'] *m* strawberry.

sugan [sugan] *m* straw rope.

sùgh [sū] *v* absorb; suck (up).

sùgh [sū] *m* juice; sap.

sùghach [sū.əch] *adj* absorbent.

sùgh-measa [sū mesə] *m* fruit juice.

sùghmhor [sūvər] *adj* juicy; sappy.

sùgradh [sūgrəgh] *m* mirth, merry-making; lovemaking.

suidh [suy] *v* sit down; **dèan suidhe** [suy šiəs] sit down.

suidhe [sui.ɪ] *m* seat; sitting position. • *adv* **'na shuidhe** [nə hui.ɪ] *adv* sitting.

suidheachadh [sui.əchəgh] *m* setting, site; situation.

suidheachan [sui.əchan] *m* seat; stool; pew.

suidhich [sui.ɪch'] *v* seat; place; decide/agree upon;.

suidhichte [sui.ɪch't'ə] *adj* settled, arranged; resolute; sedate, grave.

suidse [suid'šɪ] *f* switch.

suigeart [suig'əršd] *m* cheerfulness.

sùil [sūl] *f* eye; look, glance.

suilbhir [sulivir'] *adj* cheerful.

sùil-chritheach [sūl chr'i.əch] *f* quagmire.

sùileach [sūləch] *adj* forward-looking, far-sighted.

sùilich [sūlɪch'] *v* expect.

suim[1] [suim] *f* regard; attention.

suim[2] [suim] *f* (*money*) amount, sum; (*arith*) sum.

suipear [suiʰpɛr] *f* supper.

suirghe [sur'i.ɪ] *f* courting, courtship.

sùith [sūi] *m* soot.

sùlaire [sūLər'ə] *m* solan goose.

sult [suLt] *m* fat, fatness;.

Sultain [suLtɛN'] *f* (*with art*) **an t-Sultain** [ən tuLtɛN'] September.

sultmhor [suLtvər] *adj* fat, plump; lusty, in rude health.

sumainn [sumiN'] *f* (*sea*) surge, swell.

sùnnd [sūNd] *m* cheerfulness; mood.

sùnndach [sūNdəch] *adj* cheerful, in good spirits.

Suomach [su.əmch] *m/adj* Finn; Finnish.

Suomaidh [su.əmɪ] *f* Finland.

sùrd [sūrd] *m* cheerfulness; alacrity.

sùrdag [sūrdag] *f* jump, skip; bounce; caper.

sùrdagaich [sūrdəgɪch'] *v* jump, skip; bounce; caper.

's urrainn dhomh [suRɪN' ghə] *v* I can.

suth [su] *m* embryo.

sutha [su.ə] *f* zoo.

T

tàbhachdach [tāvəchgəch] *adj* sound, substantial.

tabhartaiche [tavɪršdɪch'ə] *m* donor, benefactor.

tabhannaich [tahəNɪch'] *v* bark. • *f* barking.

tabhartach [tavəršdəch] *adj* generous, liberal; (*gram*) dative.

tabhartas [tavəršdəs] *m* donation; presentation; grant.

taca [tahkə] *f* proximity.

tacaid [tahkɪd'] *f* tack, tacket.

tacan [tahkan] *m* little while.

tachair [tachɪr'] *v* happen.

tachair ri [tachɪr' r'i] *v* meet.

tachais [tachɪš] *v* scratch; itch, tickle.

tachartas [tachərštəs] *m* happening; incident.

tachas [tachəs] *m* scratching; itching, tickling.

tachd [tachg] *v* smother, choke, throttle.

tacsaidh [tahksɪ] *m* taxi.

tadhail (air) [to.al ɛr'] *v* visit, call (on).

tadhal [to.aL] *m* visit; (*sport*) goal.

tagair [tagɪr'] *v* claim; (*legal*) plead, argue.

tagh [to] *v* choose; elect, vote in.

taghadh [to.əgh] *m* choosing, choice; election.

taghta [toghtə] *adj* chosen; elected; (*fam*) great! perfect!

tagradh [tagrəgh] *m* claim; (*legal*) plea.

taibhse [taivšɪ] *f* ghost.

taibhsearachd [taivšɛrəchg] *f* second sight.

taic [taiʰk'] *f* contact; proximity; prop; (*moral and phys*) support; patronage

taic airgid [taiʰk' ɛr'ɛg'ɪd'] *f* (*fin*) support, backing.

taiceil [taiʰk'ɛl] *adj* supporting, supportive.

taidhir [tai.ɪr'] *f* tyre.

taifeid [tafɪd'] *m* bowstring.

taigeis [tag'ɪš] *f* haggis.

taigh [toy] *m* house. • *adv* **aig an taigh** [ɛg' ən toy]at home. • *m/f* **fear/bean an taighe** [fɛr/bɛn ən tchɪ] the landlord/lady.

taigh-beag [toibeg] *m* toilet.

taigh-bìdh [toibī] *m* café, restaurant.

taigh-cluiche [toikLuich'ɪ] *m* theatre.

taigh-comhairle [toikɔ.ɪrlə] *m* council house.

taigh-dhealbh [toigh'ɛLav] *m* cinema.

taigh-eiridinn [toier'ɪd'ɪN'] *m* hospital.

taigh-grùide [toigrūd'ɪ] *m* brewery.

taigh na galla do X! [toi nə gaLə də] *excl* damn X! sod X!

taigh-nighe [toiN'i.ɪ] *m* wash-house, laundry.

taigh-òsda [toiōsdə] *m* hotel; inn, pub.

taigh-tasgaidh [toitasgɪ] *m* museum.

tailceas [talk'əs] *m* contempt, disdain.

tailceasach [talk'əsəch] *adj* reproachful; contemptuous.

tàileasg [tāləsg] *m* chess; backgammon.

tàillear [tāL'ɛr] *m* tailor.

taing [taing'] *f* thanks, gratitude. • *excl* **mòran taing** [mōran taing'] thank you.

taingeil [taing'ɛl] *adj* thankful, grateful.

tàir[1] [tār'] *v* escape, make off.

tàir[2] [tār'] *f* contempt, disparagement.

tairbhe [tɛr'ivɪ] *f* advantage, benefit; profit.

tairbheach [tɛr'ivəch] *adj* advantageous, beneficial; profitable.

tairbhich [tɛr'ivich'] *v* benefit, profit, gain.

tàireil [tār'ɛl] *adj* contemptible.

tairg [tɛr'ig] *v* propose, offer; bid.

tairgse [tɛr'ig'ši] *f* offer, bid.

tàirneanach [tārN'anəch] *m* thunder.

tairsgeir [tar'sgɛr'] *f* peat iron.

tais [taš] *adj* damp, moist, humid.

taisbean [tašbən] *v* show, reveal; display, exhibit; demonstrate.

taisbeanach [tašbənəch] *adj* clear, distinct; (*gram*) indicative.

taisbeanadh [tašbənəgh] *m* display, exhibition; demonstration.

taisbeanlann [tašbənLəN] *f* art gallery; exhibition hall.

taise [taši], **taiseachd** [tašəchg] *f* moisture, damp, dampness, humidity.

taisg [tašg'] *v* store; hoard.

taisich [tašich'] *v* dampen, moisten.

taitinn (ri) [taʰt'ɪN' r'i] *v* please.

taitneach [taʰt'N'əch] *adj* agreeable, pleasant.

taitneas [taʰt'N'əs] *m* pleasantness; pleasure.

tàladh [tāLəgh] *m* attraction; allurement; soothing, calming; lullaby.

talaich [taLich'] *v* complain, grumble.

tàlaidh [tāLɪ] *v* attract; allure; tempt; calm; sing/rock to sleep.

tàlaidheach [tāLɪ.əch] *adj* attractive.

talamh [taLəv] *m* earth, soil; land; (*with art*) **an Talamh** [ən taLəv] the Earth.

tàlann [tāLəN] *m* talent, gift.

tàlantach [tāLantəch] *adj* talented, gifted.

talla [taLə] *m* hall; **talla a' bhaile** [taLə ə valɪ] the village/town hall.

talmhaidh [taLavɪ] *adj* earthly.

tàmailt [tāmalt'] *f* disgrace, shame; insult.

tàmailteach [tāmalt'əch] *adj* scandalous, shameful; insulting.

tàmailtich [tāmalt'ɪch'] *v* insult.

tamall [taməL] *m* while, time.

tàmh[1] [tāv] *v* dwell, live.

tàmh[2] [tāv] *m* rest, peace; inactivity; idleness; leisure.

tana [tanə] *adj* thin, runny; shallow; sparse.

tanaich [tanɪch'] *v* thin.

tancair [tankɛr'] *m* tanker.

tannasg [taNasg] *m* ghost.

taobh [tūv] *m* side; way, direction.

taobh an teine [tūv ən t'enɪ] *m* fireside.

taobh-duilleige [tūvduL'ɛgɪ] *m* page; **taobh-duilleige a dhà** [tūvduL'ɛgɪ ə ghā] page two.

taobh ri taobh [tūv r'i tūv] *adv* side by side.

taois [tūš] *f* dough.

taom [tūm] *v* pour (out), flow (out); empty; bale.

tap [taʰp] *f (water)* tap.

tapadh [taʰpəgh] *m* handiness, smartness; willingness.

tapadh leat/leibh! [taʰpə laʰt/leiv] *excl* thank you!

tapag [taʰpag] *f* slip of the tongue.

tapaidh [taʰpɪ] *adj* clever, quick; sturdy, manly; active.

tarbh [tarav] *m* bull.

tarbh-nathrach [tarav Narəch] *m* dragonfly.

tarcais [tarkɪš] *m* contempt, disdain.

tarcaiseach [tarkɪšəch] *adj* reproachful; contemptuous.

targaid [taragɪd'] *f* target; shield.

tàrmaich [tārmɪch] *v* beget; breed; propagate; produce.

tàrr [tāR] *v* escape, make off.

tarrag [taRag] *f (joinery)* nail.

tarraing [taRɪng'] *v* draw; drag, pull; attract.

tarraing à [taRɪng' a] *v* tease, kid.

tarraingeach [taRɪN'əch] *adj* attractive.

tarraing gu [taRɪng' gu] *v* approach.

tarraing srann [taRɪng' sdrauN] *v* snore.

tarrang [taRang] *f same as* **tarrag**

tarsainn [tarsɪN'] *adv* across, over.

tarsainn air [tarsɪN' ɛr'] *prep* across, over.

tasgadh [tasgəgh] *m* storehouse; museum; investment.

tasgaidh [tasgɪ] *m* store, hoard.

tastan [tasdan] *m* shilling.

tàth [tā] *v* join together; glue; cement; weld; solder.

tathaich [tāhɪch'] *v* frequent, haunt; visit.

tathaich air [tāhɪch' ɛr'] *v* call on.

tàthan [tāhan] *m* hyphen.

tè [t'ē] *f* one (f); woman.

teachdaire [t'ɛchgər'ə] *m* messenger; missionary.

teachdaireachd [t'ɛchgər'əchg] *f* message; mission, commission.

teachd-an-tìr [t'ɛchg ən t'ir'] *m* living, livelihood.

teachd-a-steach [t'ɛchg əšd'ach] *m* entry, entrance; income.

teadhair [t'ɛ.ɪr'] *f* tether.

teagaisg [t'ɛgɪšg'] *v* teach, instruct.

teagamh [t'ɛgəv] *m* doubt, uncertainty.

teagmhach [t'ɛgvəch] *adj* doubtful, doubting; sceptical.

teagasg [t'ɛgəsg] *m* teaching.

teaghlach [t'ōLəch] *m* family.

teallach [t'ɛLəch] *m* hearth, fireside; fireplace.

teallach ceàrdaich [t'ɛLəch k'ārdɪch'] *m* forge.

teampall [t'ɛumbəL] *m* temple.

teanchair [t'anachɛr'] *m* clamp, vice; pincers; tongs.

teanga [t'ɛngə] *f* tongue; *(occas)* language.

teann¹ [t'auN] *v* move, go, proceed.

teann² [t'auN] *adj* tight, tense; firm, secure; strict, severe.

teannachair *see* **teanchair**

teannaich [t'aNɪch] *v* tighten, tense; constrict, squeeze.

teann air¹ [t'auN ɛr'] *v* approach; begin.

teann air² [t'auN ɛr'] *prep* close to.

teann ri [t'auN r'i] *v* begin (to), set about.

teanta [tɛndə] *f* tent.

tèarainte [t'iarɪn'də] *adj* safe, secure.

tèarainteachd [t'iarɪnd'əchg] *f* safety, security.

tearc [t'ɛrk] *adj* scant, scarce, few.

tèarmann [t'ɛrməN] *m* protection; refuge, sanctuary.

teàrr [t'āR] *f* tar, pitch.

teas [t'es] *m* heat.

teasach [t'esəch] *f* fever.

teasaich [t'esɪch'] *v* heat (up).

teasairg [t'esɪrg'] *v* save, rescue.

teas-mheadhan [t'es vi.an] *m* dead centre.

teas-mheidh [t'es vey] *f* thermometer.

teasraig [t'esrɪg'] *v same as* **teasairg**.

teatha [te.ə] *f (drink)* tea.

tè bheag [t'ē veg] *f* nip, dram.

teich [t'ech'] *v* flee, abscond; desert.

teicheadh [t'ech'əgh] *m* running away; desertion.

teicneolach [teʰk'N'ɔLəch] *adj* technical, technological.

teicneolaiche [teʰk'N'ɔLɪchə] *m* technician; technologist.

teicneolas [teʰk'N'ɔLəs] *m* technology.

teicneolas-fiosrachaidh,   TF [teʰk'N'Ləsfisrəchɪ] *m* information technolology, IT.

teicnigeach [teʰk'N'ɪg'əch] *adj* technical.

teine [t'enɪ] *m* fire.

teinntean [t'eiN'dan] *m* hearth, fireplace.

teip [teʰp] *f* tape; cassette.

teip-clàraidh [teʰpkLārɪ] *f* recording tape.

teip-tomhais [teʰptɔ.ɪš] *f* measuring tape.

tèarainn [t'ērɪN'] *v* come down; go down; climb down; dismount; alight, descend.

teisteanas [t'ešd'anəs] *m* testimony, evidence; certificate, diploma; testimonial.

teisteanas breithe [t'ešd'anəs brehɪ] *m* birth certificate.

telebhisean [tɛləvíšan] *m* television.

teòclaid [t'ɔʰkLɪd'] *f/adj* chocolate.

teodhachd [t'ɔ.əchg] *f* temperature.

teòthaich [t'ɔ.ɪch'] *v* warm (up); warm to, take to.

teòma [t'ɔmə] *adj* expert, skilful; ingenious.

teòth ri [t'ɔ r'i] *v* take to.

teth [t'e] *adj* hot.

teud [t'ēd] *m (harp, etc)* string.

tha [hā] *present tense of v* **bith**.

tha amharas agam [ha avərəs agəm] *v* I suspect.

tha an t-eagal orm [ha ən t'egəL ɔrəm] I'm frightened.

tha dùil agam air X [ha dūl agəm ɛr'] *v* I expect X.

tha eagal orm [ha egəL ɔrəm] I'm afraid, I'm sorry to say.

tha mi a' cur fallas [ha mi ə kur faLəs] *v* I'm sweating.

tha feum agam air X [ha fēm agəm ɛr'] *v* I need X.

tha fios [ha fis] *adv* of course, naturally.

tha fios agam [ha fis agəm] *v* I know.

tha gràin agam air [ha grāN' agəm ɛr'] *v* I hate him/it.

thàinig [hānɪg] *past tense of v* **thig**.

thairis [har'ɪš] *prep pron* over him, over it (*m*). • *adv* across, over; beyond.

thairis air [har'ɪš ɛr'] *prep* across, over; beyond.

thairte [haršd'ɪ] *prep pron* over her, over it (*f*).

thall [hauL] *adv* over there, over yonder.

thalla [haLə] (*sing*), **thallaibh** [haLɪv] (*pl*) *Imper* go, off you go.

thall is a-bhos [hauL sə vɔs] *adv* here and there; hither and thither.

tha mi an dòchas [ha mi ən dɔchəs] *v* I hope.

tha mi an dùil [ha mi ən dūl] *v* I hope, I expect.

tha mi duilich! [ha mi dulɪch'] I'm sorry!

tha mi gu dòigheil! [ha mi gu dɔi.ɛl] I'm fine!

thar [har] *prep* across, over; beyond; more than.

thar a chèile [har ə ch'ēlɪ] *adv* in confusion; at loggerheads.

tharad [harəd] *prep pron* over you (*sing*).

tharaibh [harɪv] *prep pron* over you (*pl*).

tharainn [harɪN'] *prep pron* over us.

tharam [harəm] *prep pron* over me.

thar mo chomais [har mə chomɪš] *adv* beyond my ability.

tharta [haršdə] *prep pron* over them.

tha smùid orm [ha smūd' ɔrəm] I'm drunk.

tha ùidh agam ann an [ha ūy agəm auN ən] *v* I'm interested in it.

theab [hɛb] *defective v* nearly; **theab mi tuiteam** [hɛb mi tuʰt'əm] I nearly fell.

theagamh [hegəv] *conj* perhaps, maybe.

thèid [hēd'] *future tense of v* **rach**.

thig [hig'] *v* come; approach; arrive.

thig air adhart [hig' ɛr' o.əršd] *v* make progress.

thig am bàrr [hig' əm bāR] *v* surface.

thig am follais [hig' əm fɔLɪš] *v* come to light.

thig an uachdar [hig' ən uachgər] *v* surface; manifest itself.

thig a-steach air [hig' əšd'ach ɛr'] *v* occur to.

thig còmhla [hig' kōLə] *v* congregate, unite.

thig do [hig' də] *v* (*clothes, etc*) suit; please, suit.

thig gu inbhe [hig' gu inɪvɪ] *v* grow up.

thig ri [hig' r'i] *v* suit.

thoir [hɔr'] *v* give; bring; take.

thoir aoradh [hɔr' ūrəgh] *v* worship.

thoir air [hɔr' ɛr'] *v* make, force.

thoir air èiginn [hɔr' ɛr' ēg'ɪN'] *v* rape.

thoir air falbh [hɔr' ɛr' faLav] *v* abduct.

thoir air gabhail [hɔr' ɛr' gahal] *v* lease.

thoir am bith [hɔr' əm bi] *v* bring into being/existence.

thoir am follais [hɔr' əm fɔLɪš] *v* bring to light.

thoir an aire [hɔr' ə Nar'ɪ] v pay attention; take care.

thoir an car à [hɔr' ən kar a] v cheat.

thoir an t-siteag ort! [hɔr' ən t'iʰt'ag ɔršd] v get out! outside!

thoir bàrr air [hɔr' bāR ɛr'] v beat, cap, top.

thoir breith [hɔr' br'e] v pass judgement.

thoir buaidh air [hɔr' buay ɛr'] v defeat; influence, affect.

thoir creideas do [hɔr' kr'ed'əs dɔ] v trust; believe.

thoir cuireadh do [hɔr' kur'əgh dɔ] v invite.

thoir do chasan leat! [hɔr' də chasən laʰt] get the hell out of here!

thoir dùbhlan do [hɔr' dūLan dɔ] v challenge; defy.

thoir facal air [hɔr' faʰkəL ɛr'] v swear at.

thoir fianais [hɔr' fiənıš] v give evidence, testify.

thoir fios air [hɔr' fis ɛr'] v send for.

thoir gealladh [hɔr' gyaLəgh] v promise; vow.

thoir gu buil [hɔr' gu bul] v achieve; see through.

thoir gu stad [hɔr' gu sdad] v bring to an end/a stop.

thoir guth air [hɔr' gu ɛr'] v mention.

thoir ionnsaigh air [hɔr' iūNsı ɛr'] v attack, assault; have a shot/an attempt at.

thoir na buinn asam [hɔr' nə buiN' asəm] v take to my heels.

thoir oidhirp (air) [hɔr' o.ırp] v make an attempt (at).

thoir rabhadh do [hɔr' ravəgh dɔ] v warn; alert.

thoir seachad [hɔr' šechəd] v give, give away.

thoir seachad òraid [hɔr' šechəd ōrıd'] v give/deliver a speech.

thoir sùil air [hɔr' sūl ɛr'] v have a look at.

thoir tairgse (air) [hɔr' tɛrig'šı ɛr'] v make an offer/a bid (for).

thoir tarraing air [hɔr' taRıng' ɛr'] v mention, refer to.

thoir tuaiream air [hɔr' tuər'əm ɛr'] v guess at.

thoir urram do [hɔr' uRəm dɔ] v respect.

thoir uspag [hɔr' usbag] v (horse, etc) start, shy.

thoir X orm [hɔr' ɔrəm] v take myself off to X.

thu [ū] pers pron sing you.

thuca [huʰkə] prep pron to them.

thug [hug] past tense of v **thoir**.

thugad [hugəd] prep pron to you (sing).

thugaibh [hugıv] prep pron to you (pl).

thugainn [hugıN'] prep pron to us.

thugam [hugəm] prep pron to me.

thuice [huiʰk'ı] prep pron to her, to it (f).

thuige [huig'ı] prep pron to him, to it (m).

thun [chun] prep to, towards, up to.

thuirt [hūršd'] past tense of v **abair**.

tì [tī] f (drink) tea.

tiamhaidh [t'iavı] adj melancholy; plaintive.

tibhre [t'ivr'ı] m dimple.

tiocad [tikəd] f ticket.

tiodhlag [t'iəLag] f gift, present.

ide [t'īd'ɪ] *f* time; weather; (*with art*) **an tide** [ən t'īd'ɪ], **an tide-mhara** [ən t'īd'ɪvarə] the tide. • *excl* **bha a thìde aige!** [va hīd'ɪ ɛg'ɪ] he took his time!

idsear [tid'šɛr] *m* teacher.

ighearna [t'iərnə] *m* lord; laird, landowner; (*with art*) **an Tighearna** [ən t'iərnə]the Lord, God. • *excl* **a Thighearna!** [ə hiərnə] (Oh) Lord!

Tileach [t'īlɔch] *m/adj* Icelander; Icelandic.

ilg [t'ilig'] *v* throw; throw up; (*weapon*) fire.

ilg air [t'ilig' ɛr'] *v* accuse of, reproach with.

ilg smugaid [t'ilig' smugɪd'] *v* spit.

ill [t'īL'] *v* return, come/go back.

illeadh [t'iL'əgh] *m* return; returning.

im [t'īm] *f* time.

imcheall[1] [t'imich'əL] *adv* round.

imcheall[2] [t'imich'əL] *adv/prep* round, around, about.

imcheall air [t'imich'əL ɛr'] *prep* round, around, about.

imcheallan [t'imich'əLan] *m* roundabout.

inn [tīN'] *adj* ill, sick.

inneas [t'iN'əs] *m* illness, disease.

inneas cridhe [t'iN'əs kr'i.ɪ] *m* heart disease.

inneas mara [t'iN'əs marə] *m* seasickness.

inneas na dighe [t'iN'əs nə d'i.ɪ] *m* alcoholism.

iodhlag [t'iəLag] *m* gift, present.

iodhlacadh [t'iəLaʰkəgh] *m* burial, funeral.

iodhlaic [t'iəLɪʰk'] *v* give, donate; bury.

tiomnadh [t'umnəgh] *m* will, testament; bequest; **an Seann Tiomnadh** [ən sauN t'umnəgh] the Old Testament; **an Tiomnadh Nuadh** [ən t'umnəgh Nua] the New Testament.

tiomnaich [t'umnich'] *v* bequeathe, leave.

tiompan [t'umban] *m* cymbal.

tionail [t'unal] *v* assemble, congregate; (*stock*) gather.

tionndaidh [t'ūNdɪ] *v* turn.

tionnsgail [t'ūNsgal] *v* devise, invent.

tionnsgal [t'ūNsgəL] *m* inventiveness; invention.

tionnsgalach [t'ūNsgəLəch] *adj* inventive.

tionnsgalair [t'ūNsgəLɛr'] *m* inventor.

tioraidh! [t'īrɪ] *excl* cheerio!

tioram [t'irəm] *adj* dry; thirsty.

tiormachd [t'irəməchg] *f* dryness; drought.

tiormadair [t'irəmədɛr'] *m* dryer.

tiormaich [t'irəmich'] *v* dry; dry up.

tiota [t'iʰtə] *m* second, instant.

tiotag [t'iʰtag] *f* instant, tick.

tiotal [t'iʰtəL] *m* title.

tiotan [t'iʰtan] *m* second, instant.

tìr [t'ir'] *m&f* land; country; area, region; ground, landscape.

tìr-eòlas [t'ir'ɔ̄Ləs] *m* geography.

tìr-mòr [t'ir'mōr] *m* mainland; continent.

tiugainn! [t'ugɪN'] *imper* come along! let us go!

tiugh [t'u] *adj* thick, dense; slow-witted.

tighead [t'i.əd] *m* thickness; density.

tlachd [tLachg] *f* pleasure, enjoyment; affection, liking.

tlachdmhor [tLachgvər] *adj* pleasant; likeable.

tnù [trū] *m* envy; malice.

tobar [tobər] *m* spring, well.

tobhta [tɔʰtə] *m* ruin(s).

tocasaid [tɔʰkəsɪd'] *f* barrel, hogshead.

tòchd [tōchg] *m* stink.

tochradh [tochrəgh] *m* dowry.

todha [tɔ.ə] *m* hoe.

todhaig [tɔ.ɪg'] *v* hoe.

todhair [tɔ.ɪr'] *v* manure; bleach.

todhar [tɔ.ər] *m* manure, dung.

tog [tog] *v* raise, lift; pick up; build; (*family, etc*) bring up.

togair [togɪr'] *v* wish for; covet; **ma thogras tu** [ma hogrəs tu] if you like.

togalach [togəLəch] *m* building.

tog dealbhan [tog d'ɛLavən] *v* take photos.

tog ort [tog ɔršd] *excl* stir your stumps! get a move on!

togradh [togrəgh] *m* wish, desire.

toilbheum [tɔlvēm] *m* blasphemy.

toil [tɔl] *adj* pleasing; **is toil leam X** [ɪs tɔl ləm] I like X.

toil [tɔl] *f* will.

toileach [tɔləch] *adj* willing; content; glad.

toileachas [tɔləchəs] *m* contentment; gladness.

toilich [tɔlɪch'] *v* please, content.

toilichte [tɔlɪch't'ə] *adj* happy; pleased, satisfied.

toil-inntinn [tɔlīN't'ɪN'] *f* (*mental*) pleasure; peace of mind.

toill [tɔiL'] *v* deserve.

toillteanach (air) [tɔiL'tanəch] *adj* worthy (of).

tòimhseachan [tōišəchan] *m* puzzle; riddle.

tòimhseachan-tarsainn [tōišəchantarsɪN'] *m* crossword puzzle.

toinisg [tɔN'ɪšg'] *f* common sense.

toinisgeil [tɔN'ɪšg'ɛl] *adj* sensible, intelligent.

toinn [tɔiN'] *v* twist, wind, twine.

tòir [tōr'] *f* pursuit.

toirm [tor'im] *f* noise, din.

toirmeasg [tor'imisg] *m* forbidding, prohibition.

toirmeasgach [tor'imisg'əch] *adj* prohibitive.

toirmisg [tor'imišg'] *v* forbid, prohibit.

toiseach [tɔšəch] *m* start, beginning; vanguard; (*vehicle, etc*) front.

tòiseachadh [tōšəchəgh] *m* beginning.

tòiseachadh ùr [tōšəchəgh ūr] *m* fresh start.

tòisich (air) [tōšɪch' ɛr'] *v* start (to).

tòisich as ùr [tōšɪch' as ūr] *v* start afresh.

toit [tɔʰt'] *f* steam; smoke.

toitean [tōʰt'an] *m* cigarette.

toll [tɔuL] *v* bore, pierce, perforate; dig a hole. • *m* hole, pit, hollow; (*vulg*) arsehole.

tolladh-chluasan [tɔLəghchLuəsən] *m* ear-piercing.

tolltach [tɔuLtəch] *adj* full of holes.

toll-tòine [tɔuLtōN'ɪ] *m* anus.

tolman [tɔLəman] *m* knowe, knoll.

tom [tɔum] *m* hillock; thicket.

tomaltach [toməLtəch] *adj* sizeable; bulky; burly.

tombaca [tombaʰkə] *m* tobacco.

tomhais [tɔ.ɪš] *v* measure; calculate; guess; survey.

tomhas [to.əs] *m* measuring; dimension; calculation; guess, guessing; surveying.

tòn [tɔn] *f* anus, rectum; (*fam*) arse, bum, backside; (*building, etc*) back.

tonn [touN] *m* wave.

tonna [tɔNə] *m* ton, tonne.

tonn teasa [touN t'esə] *m* heat wave.

torrach [tɔRəch] *adj* fruitful, productive; fertile, fecund; pregnant; (*egg, etc*) fertilised.

torrachadh [tɔRəchəgh] *m* fertilisation.

torrachas [tɔRəchəs] *m* fertility.

toradh [tɔrəgh] *m* produce, fruit(s); result, effect.

toraich [tɔrich'] *v* fertilise.

torc [tɔrk] *m* boar.

torman [tɔrəman] *m* murmur, drone, hum; rumble.

tòrr [tɔR] *m* heap, mound; hill; (*fam*) lots, loads.

tòrradh [tɔRəgh] *m* burial, funeral.

tosd [tɔsd] *m* silence.

tosdach [tɔsdəch] *adj* silent, quiet.

tosgaire [tɔsgər'ə] *m* ambassador; envoy.

tosgaireachd [tɔsgər'əchg] *f* embassy.

trafaig [trafig'] *f* traffic.

tragtar [trahᵍgdər] *m* tractor.

ràghadh [trā.əgh] *m* draining; subsiding; (*car*) exhaust.

ràigh¹ [trāy] *v* drain, empty; subside, settle; ebb.

ràigh² [trāy] *f* shore, beach; tide.

ràill [trāiL'] *f* slave; drudge; addict.

ràilleachd [trāiL'əchg] *f* slavery; addiction.

tràillich [trāiL'ich'] *v* enslave.

traisg [trašg'] *v* fast.

tràlair [trāLɛr'] *m* trawler.

trang [trang] *adj* busy.

trannsa [trauNsə] *f* corridor, passage.

trasg [trasg] *f* fast, fasting.

tràth¹ [trā] *adv* early.

tràth² [trā] *m* time, season; while, period; (*gram*) tense.

tràth bìdh [trā bī] *m* mealtime.

tràthach [trāhəch] *m* hay.

treabh [tr'ɔ] *v* plough.

trealaich [tr'ɛLich'] *f* jumble; odds and ends, stuff, paraphernalia; trash, rubbish; (*pl*) **trealaichean** [tr'ɛLichən] luggage, baggage.

trèan [tr'ēn] *v* train.

trèana [tr'ēnə] *f* train.

treas [tr'es] *adj* third.

treas deug [tr'es d'iag] *adj* thirteenth.

trèig [tr'ēg'] *v* leave; abandon; relinquish.

treis [tr'eš] *f* while, time.

treiseag [tr'ešag] *f* short while.

treòrachadh [tr'ɔrəchəgh] *m* guiding, leading; guidance.

treòraich [tr'ɔrich'] *v* guide, lead.

treòraiche [tr'ɔrich'ə] *m* guide.

treubh [tr'iav] *f* tribe.

treud [tr'ēd] *m* flock, herd; group; (*derog*) crowd, gang.

treun [tr'ēn] *adj* strong, stout. • *f* **treun a neirt** [tr'ēn ə nɛršd'] his prime.

trì [tr'ī] *n/adj* three.

triall (do) [tr'iəL dɔ] *v* travel, journey (to).

trian [tr'ian] *m* third.
triath [tr'iə] *m* lord.
tric [tr'iʰk'] *adj/adv* frequent(ly).
triantan [tr'iandan] *f* triangle.
trid-shoilleir [tr'īd' hoL'ɛr'] *adj* transparent.
trioblaid [tr'iblid'] *f* trouble.
trithead [tr'īhəd] *m* thirty.
triubhas [tr'u.əs] *m* trews, trousers.
triùir [tr'ūr'] *f* (*people*) three, three-some.
triuthach [tr'u.əch] *f* (*with art*) **an triuthach** whooping cough.
tro [trɔ] *prep* through.
trobhad [tro.əd] (*sing*), **trobhadaibh** [tro.ədɪv] (*pl*) *imper* come here, come to me; come along.
tròcair [trɔʰkɛr'] *f* mercy.
tròcaireach [trɔʰkɛr'əch] *adj* merciful.
trod [trɔd] *m* quarrel, row; quarreling.
troich [troich'] *f* dwarf.
troid [trɔd'] *v* quarrel, squabble, fight.
troigh [troy] *f* (*measure*) foot.
troighean [troi.an] *m* pedal.
troimh *see* **tro**
tro chèile [trɔ ch'ēli] *adv* at loggerheads; in confusion; untidy.
troimhe [trɔi.ɪ] *prep pron* through him, through it (*m*).
troimhpe [trɔiʰpɪ] *prep pron* through her, through it (*f*).
trom [trɔum] *adj* heavy; serious; important; depressed; pregnant.
tromalach [trɔmaLəch] *f* preponderance, majority.
trombaid [trɔumbɪd'] *f* trumpet.
tromhad [trɔ.əd] *prep pron* through you (*sing*).

tromhaibh [trɔ.ɪv] *prep pron* through you (*pl*).
tromhainn [trɔ.ɪN'] *prep pron* through us.
tromham [trɔ.əm] *prep pron* through me.
tromhpa [trɔʰpə] *prep pron* through them.
trom-laighe [trɔumLai.ɪ] *f* nightmare
trosg [trɔsg] *m* cod.
trotan [trɔʰtan] *m* trot; trotting.
truacanta [truəʰkəndə] *adj* compassionate, humane.
truacantas [truəʰkəndəs] *m* compassion, pity.
truagh [truəgh] *adj* sad; poor, pitiable, abject.
truaghan [truəghan] *m* wretch. • *excl* **a thruaghain!** [ə ruəghɛN'] poor man/creature!
truaill [truaL'] *v* pollute; corrupt; pervert; defile, profane.
truaghas [tru.əs] *m* pity, compassion.
truileis [trulɪš] *f* rubbish, junk.
truimead [truiməd] *m* heaviness.
truinnsear [truiN'šɛr] *m* plate.
truis [truš], **trus** [trus] *v* bundle, roll up; (*skirt, etc*) tuck up; (*stock*) gather.
trusgan [trusgan] *m* clothes, clothing.
tuagh [tuəgh] *f* axe.
tuagh-chatha [tuəghchahə] *f* battleaxe, Lochaber axe.
tuainealach [tuaN'əLəch] *adj* dizzy, giddy.
tuainealaich [tuaN'əLɪch'] *f* dizziness, vertigo.
tuaiream [tuər'əm] *f* guess, conjecture.

tuaireamach [tuər'əməch] *adj* random, arbitrary.

tuairisgeul [tuar'ɪšg'iaL] *m* description.

tuar [tuər] *m* complexion, hue; appearance.

tuarasdal [tuərəsdaL] *f* salary, wage(s); stipend; fee.

tuasaid [tuasɪd'] *f* quarrel; scrap, tussle.

tuath[1] [tuə] *adj/f* northern, north.

tuath[2] [tuə] *f* peasantry; tenantry.

tuath air [tuəh ɛr'] *prep* north of.

tuathal [tuəhal] *adj* widdershins; anti-clockwise; awry, wrong.

tuathanach [tuəhanəch] *m* farmer.

tuathanachas [tuəhanəchəs] *m* farming.

tuathanas [tuəhanəs] *m* farm.

tubaiste [tubašd¹ɪ] *f* accident; mishap.

tubhailt [tu.alt'] *f* towel.

tubhailt-shoithichean [tu.alt'ho.ɪchən] *f* tea-towel.

tùch [tūch] *v* make hoarse; smother; extinguish.

tùchadh [tūchəgh] *m* hoarseness.

tùchanach [tūchanəch] *adj* hoarse.

tudan [tudan] *m* stack; turd.

tugh [tū] *v* thatch.

tughadh [tū.əgh] *m* thatch.

tuig [tig'] *v* understand.

tuigse [tig'šɪ] *f* comprehension; intelligence; sense, judgement.

tuigseach [tig'šəch] *adj* understanding; intelligent; sensible.

tuil [tul] *f* flood, deluge.

tuilleadh [tuL'əgh] *m* more, additional; **tuilleadh is a chòir** [tuL'əgh sə chōr'] more than enough.

tuinich [tunɪch'] *v* settle; dwell.

tuiniche [tuN'ɪchə] *m* settler.

Tuirc [Tur'k'] *m* (*with art*) **an Tuirc** [ən tur'k'] Turkey.

tuireadh [turəgh] *m* mourning; lament.

tùirse [tūršɪ] *f* sorrow.

tuiseal [tušaL] *m* (*gram*) case.

tuislich [tušlɪch'] *v* stumble, slip, trip.

tuit [tuʰt'] *v* fall.

tuit do [tuʰt' də] *v* happen to, befall.

tuiteamach [tuʰt'əməch] *adj* accidental, chance.

tuiteamas [tuʰt'əməs] *m* occurence, event; incident; accident.

tulach [tuLəch] *m* hillock.

tulg [tuLug] *v* rock, lurch, swing, toss.

tulgach [tuLugəch] *adj* rocking, lurching, swinging, tossing; rocky, unsteady.

tulgadh [tuLugəgh] *m* rocking, lurching, swinging, tossing.

tum [tūm] *v* dip, immerse; steep.

tunnag [tuNag] *f* duck.

tur [tur] *adj* whole, complete. • *adv* **gu tur** [gu tur] completely, altogether.

tùr[1] [tūr] *m* understanding; sense.

tùr[2] [tūr] *m* tower.

turadh [turəgh] *m* dry weather/ spell.

turraid [tuRɪd'] *f* tower; turret.

tùrail [tūral] *adj* sensible.

turas [turəs] *m* journey; trip; tour, touring; time.

turasachd [turəsəchg] *f* tourism.

turas-mara [turəsmarə] *m* voyage.

turas-tillidh [turəst'iLɪ] *m* return journey.

Turcach [turkəch] *m/adj* Turk; Turkish.

tursa [tursə] *m* standing stone.

tùrsach [tūrsəch] *adj* sorrowful.

tùs [tūs] *m* beginning, origin.

tùsanach [tūsanəch] *adj* aborigene

tùthag [tūhag] *f* patch.

U

uabhar [uavər] *m* pride, haughtiness, arrogance.

uachdar [uachgər] *m* surface; top; cream; upland.

uachdarach [uachgərəch] *adj* upper; superior; superficial.

uachdaran [uachgəran] *m* superior; landowner, laird.

uachdar-fhiaclan [uachgəriə^hkLən] *m* toothpaste.

uaibh [uaiv] *prep pron* from you (*pl*).

uaibhreach [uaivr'əch] *adj* proud; haughty, arrogant.

uaibhreas [uaivr'əs] *m* pride; haughtiness, arrogance.

uaigh [uay] *f* grave.

uaigneach [uaig'nəch] *adj* lonely, solitary; secluded; private, secret.

uaimh [uaiv] *f* cave.

uaine [uaN'ı] *adj* green.

uainn [uaN'] *prep pron* from us.

uaipe [uai^hpı] *prep pron* from her, from it (*f*).

uaipear [uai^hpɛr] *m* botcher, bungler.

uair [uər'] *f* hour; (*clock*) time; time, occasion. • *adv* once.

uaireadair [uər'ədɛr'] *m* timepiece, clock; watch.

uaireadair-gloinne [uər'ədɛr'gLɔN'ı] *m* hour-glass.

uaireadair-grèine [uər'ədɛr'gr'ēnı] *m* sundial.

uaireannan [uər'əNən] *adv* sometimes.

uaireigin [uər'eg'ın] *adv* some time.

uair is uair [uər' ıs uər'] *adv* time and time again.

uair no uaireigin [uər' nɔ uər'eg'ın] *adv* some time or other.

uair sam bith [uər' səm bi] *adv* any time.

uaisle [uašlı] *f* nobility, gentility.

uaithe [uai.ı] *prep pron* from him, from it (*m*).

uallach [uaLəch] *m* load, burden; onus, responsibility; stress, worry.

uam [uəm] *prep pron* from me.

uamhann [uəvəN] *m* dread, horror.

uamhas [uəvəs] *m* dread, horror; terror; atrocity.

uamhasach [uəvəsəch] *adj/adv* dreadful(ly), awful(ly), terrible, terribly.

uamhasach fhèin math [uəvəsəch hēn ma] *adv* (*fam*) wonderful, brilliant.

uan [uan] *m* lamb.

uapa [uə^hpə] *prep pron* from them.

uasal [uəsəL] *adj* noble, aristocratic, genteel. • *m* gentleman; (*pl with art*) **na h-uaislean** [nə huašlən] the nobility, the aristocracy.

uat [uə^ht] *prep pron* from you (*sing*).

ubhal [u.əL] *m* apple.

ubhalghort [u.əLghɔršd] *m* orchard.

uchd [uchg] *m* breast, bosom; lap.

uchd-leanabh [uchgL'ɛnav] *m* adopted child.

uchd-mhacaich [uchgvaʰkıch'] *v* adopt.

ud [əd] *adj* that, yonder.

ud ud! [ədəd] *excl* tut tut! now now!

uèir [uēr'] *f* wire.

ugan [ugan] *m* chest area.

ugh [ū] *m* egg.

ughach [u.əch] *m* oval. • *adj* oval.

ughagan [u.agan] *m* custard.

ùghdar [ūdər] *m* author.

ùghdarras [ūdəRəs] *m* authority; (*govt*) **ùghdarras ionadail** [ūdəRəs inədal] local authority.

ughlann [ūLəN] *f* ovary.

uibhir [ui.ir'] *f* number; amount, quantity; **na h-uibhir de** [nə hui.ir' d'e] a certain amount of; such a lot of; **uibhir eile** [ui.ir' elı] as much again.

uibhir ri [ui.ir' r'i] *prep* as much as.

Uibhist [u.ıšd'] *m* Uist.

Uibhisteach [u.ıšd'əch] *m/adj* from Uist.

ùidh [ūy] *f* hope; fondness; interest.

uidh [uy] *f* step; gradation; journey; **uidh air n-uidh** [uy ɛr' nuy] step by step, gradually.

uidheam [ui.əm] *f* equipment, tackle, gear; furnishings, trappings; harness; rigging.

uidheamaich [ui.əmıch'] *v* equip, fit out; get ready.

uile [ulı] *adj/adv* all, every; fully, completely; **a h-uile** [ə hulı] every. • *npl* **na h-uile** [nə hulı] everybody.

uileann [uləN] *f* angle; corner; elbow.

uilebheist [ulıvešd'] *m* monster.

uile-chumhachdach [ulıchu.əchgəch] *adj* all-powerful, omnipotent.

uile-fhiosrach [ulısrəch] *adj* all-knowing.

uile gu lèir [ulı gu L'ēr'] *adv* altogether, completely.

ùilleach [ūL'əch] *adj* oily.

uilleagan [uL'agan] *m* spoilt brat.

uillnich [uL'nıch'] *v* jostle, elbow.

uime [uimı] *prep pron* about him, about it (*m*).

uimpe [uimpı] *prep pron* about her, about it (*f*).

ùine [ūN'ı] *f* time; while; (*pl fam*) **ùineachan (is ùineachan)** [ūN'əchən ıs ūN'əchən] ages (and ages).

uinneag [uN'ag] *f* window.

uinnean [uN'an] *m* onion.

uinnsean [uiN'šan] *m* (*tree*) ash.

ùir [ūr'] *f* soil, earth.

uircean [ur'k'an] *m* piglet.

uiread [ur'əd] *f* a certain amount/ quantity; **na h-uiread** [nə hur'əd] such a lot; **uiread eile** [ur'əd elı] as much again; **uiread ri** [ur'əd r'i] as much as. • *adv* (*sums*) times, multiplied by.

uireasbhach [ur'əsach] *adj* needy; lacking. • *m* needy person.

uireasbhaidh [ur'əsı] *f* indigence; lack, need; shortage.

uirsgeul [ur'šg'iaL] *m* fable, legend, myth; fiction.

uirsgeulach [ur'šg'iaLch] *adj* legendary; fictional.

uiseag [ušag] *f* skylark.

uisge [ušg'ı] *m* water; rain; **tha an t-uisge ann** [ha ən tušg'ı auN] it's raining.

uisge-beatha [ušg'ıbɛhə] *m* whisky.

uisge-dìonach [ušg'ıd'ıənəch] *adj* waterproof, watertight.

uisge na stiùireach [ušg'ı nə št'ūr'əgh] *m* (*of boat, etc*) wake.

uisgich [ušg'ıch'] *v* water.

ulaidh [uLı] *f* treasure; precious object.

ulbhag [uLuvag] *f* large stone, boulder.

ulfhart [uLəršd] *m* howl, howling.

ullaich [uLıch'] *v* prepare; provide.

ullamh [uLəv] *adj* ready; handy; finished.

ultach [uLtəch] *m* load; armful; bundle.

umad [uməd] *prep pron* about you (*sing*).

umaibh [umıv] *prep pron* about you (*pl*).

ùmaidh [ūmı] *m* blockhead, dolt, fool.

umainn [umıN'] *prep pron* about us.

umam [uməm] *prep pron* about me.

umha [u.ə] *m* bronze.

umhail [u.al] *adj* humble; lowly; obedient; obsequious.

ùmhlachd [ūLəchg] *f* humbleness; lowliness; obedience; obsequiousness; bow.

ùmhlaich [ūLıch'] *v* humble; humiliate.

umpa [umpə] *prep pron* about them.

Ungair [ungır'] *f* (*with art*) **an Ungair** [ə Nungır'] Hungary.

Ungaireach [ungır'əch] *m/adj* Hungarian.

ùnnlagh [ūNLəgh] *m* fine.

ùnnsa [ūNsə] *m* ounce.

ùpag [ū^pag] *f* jostle, jab.

ùpraid [ūprıd'] *f* uproar; confusion; dispute.

ùpraideach [ūprıd'əch] *adj* rowdy, unruly.

ùr [ūr] *adj* new; recent; fresh.

ur [ər] *adj* your (*pl*).

ùrachadh [ūrəchəgh] *m* renewal; renovation; change.

ùraich [ūrıch'] *v* renew; renovate; refresh.

urchair [uruchır'] *f* shot.

urchair gunna [uruchır' guNə] *f* gun-shot.

urchasg [urchasg] *m* antidote.

ùrlar [ūrLər] *m* floor.

ùrnaigh [ūrnı] *f* prayer; praying; **Ùrnaigh an Tighearna** [ūrnı ən t'i.ərnə] the Lord's Prayer.

ùr nodha [ūr no.ə] *adj* brand new; up-to-date.

urra [uRə] *f* person; authority; responsibility.

urrainn [uRıN'] *f* power, ability.

urram [uRəm] *m* respect; honour.

urramach [uRəməch] *adj* honourable; honorary; (*with art*) (*minister*) **an t-Urramach X** [ən tuRəməch] the Reverend X.

urras [uRəs] *m* guarantee, surety; bond; bail; insurance; (*fund, etc*) trust.

ursainn [ursıN'] *f* prop, support; jamb.

ursainn chatha [ursıN' chahə] *f* (*warrior*) champion.

usgar [usgər] *m* jewel.

uspag [usbag] *f* (*horse, etc*) start, shy.

ùth [ū] *m* udder.

English–Gaelic Dictionary

A

abandon *v* trèig.
abate *v* lùghdaich.
abbey *n* abaid *f*.
abbot *n* aba *m*.
abbreviate *v* giorraich.
abdicate *v* leig dhe.
abdication *n* leigeil dhe *m*.
abdomen *n* balg *m*.
abduct *v* thoir air falbh.
abet *v* cuidich.
abhor *v* is lugha air.
abhorrence *n* gràin.
abide *v* fuirich.
ability *n* comas *m*.
abject *adj* truagh; dìblidh.
able *adj* comasach.
able-bodied *adj* fallain; corp-làidir.
abnormal *adj* mì-ghnàthach.
abnormality *n* mì-ghnàthas *m*.
aboard *adv* air bòrd.
abode *n* àite-còmnaidh *m*.
abolish *v* cuir às do.
abolition *n* cur às *m*
abominable *adj* gràineil.
aborigine *n* prìomh neach-àiteachaidh *m*.
abortion *n* breith an-abaich *f*.
abound *v* bi lìonmhor.
about *adv* (*around*) timcheall (air);
   (*surrounding*) mun cuairt (air).
   • *prep* (*around & concerning*) mu;
   mu dhèidhinn. • *pron* about me
   umam; about you (*sing*) umad;

about him, it uime; about her
   uimpe; about us umainn; about
   you (*pl*) umaibh; about them.
above *adv* shuas; gu h-àrd. • *prep*
   os cionn.
abrade *v* sgrìobaich.
abridge *v* giorraich.
abridged *adj* giorraichte.
abroad *adv* thall thairis.
abrupt *adj* cas; aithghearr.
abruptness *n* caise *f*.
abscess *n* niosgaid *f*.
abscond *v* teich, teich air falbh.
absence *n* neo-làthaireachd *f*.
absent *adj* nach eil an làthair.
absent oneself *v* dìochuimhneach,
   cùm air falbh.
absent-minded *adj* cian-aireachal.
absolute *adj* iomlan; làn.
absolutely *adv* gu h-iomlan.
absolution *n* saoradh, fuasgladh *m*.
absolve *v* saor; sgaoil.
absorb *v* sùgh, deoghail.
absorbent *adj* sùghach.
abstain *v* na buin (ri).
abstemious *adj* stuama.
abstinence *n* stuamachd *f*.
abstract *n* às-tharraing *f*.
abstract *v* às-tharraing, tarraing à.
abstracted *adj* beachdail.
absurd *adj* gòrach.
absurdity *n* gòraiche *f*.
abundance *n* pailteas *m*.

abundant adj pailt.

abuse[1] n mì-ghnàthachadh m; (verbal) càineadh f.

abuse[2] v mì-ghnàthaich; (verbally) càin.

abysmal adj uabhasach.

abyss n àibheis m.

academic adj sgoileireach. • n oilthigheach m.

academy n àrd-sgoil f.

accelerate v luathaich, greas.

acceleration n luathachadh, greasad m.

accelerator n inneal-luathachaidh m.

accent n blas m.

accept v gabh.

acceptable adj furasda gabhail ris.

access n inntrigeadh m.

accessible adj so-ruigsinneach.

accident n tubaist f.

accidental adj tubaisteach.

accommodate v gabh.

accommodation n rùm m.

accompaniment n com-pàirt f.

accompanist n com-pàirtiche m.

accomplice n fear-cuideachaidh m.

accomplish v coimhlion, thoir gu buil.

accomplished adj coimhlionta, deas.

accord n aonta, co-chòrdadh m.

according to adv a-rèir.

accordingly adv mar sin.

accordion n bocsa-ciùil m.

account n cùnntas, tuairisgeul m. • v thoir cùnntas air.

accountancy n cùnntasachd f.

accountant n cùnntasair m.

accounts book n leabhar-cùnntais m.

accumulate v cruinnich.

accumulation n co-chruinneachadh m.

accuracy n cruinneas m.

accurate adj cruinn, grinn.

accusation n casaid f.

accuse v dèan casaid.

accustom v gnàthaich.

accustomed adj gnàthach; àbhaist.

ace n an t-aon m.

acerbic adj geur.

acerbity n goirte f.

ache n goirteas, cràdh m.

achieve v coimhlion.

achievement n euchd m.

acid adj searbh; geur.

acidity n searbhachd f.

acknowledge v aidich.

acknowledgement n aideachadh m.

acoustic adj fuaimneach.

acoustics n fuaimearrachd f.

acquaintance n fear-eòlais m.

acquainted adj eòlach.

acquiesce v aontaich.

acquire v faigh, buannaich.

acquit v fuasgail.

acre n acaire m.

across adv tarsainn, thairis. • prep tarsainn air, thairis air, thar.

act n gnìomh m; (play) earran f; achd. • v obraich, dèan gnìomh; cluich.

action n gnìomh m.

active adj deas, èasgaidh; spreigeach.

activity n gnìomhachd f.

actor n cleasaiche, actair m.

actress n bana-chleasaiche, bana-actair f.

actual adj dearbh, fìor.

acute adj dian, geur.

adapt v fàs suas ri, dèan freagarrach.

adaptable adj so-fhreagarraichte.

add v cuir ri, meudaich, leasaich.

adder *n* nathair *f*.
addict *n* tràill *m/f*.
addicted *adj* fo bhuaidh.
addiction *n* tràilleachd *f*.
addition *n* meudachadh, leasachadh *m*.
additional *adj* a bharrachd, a thuilleadh.
address *n* seòladh *m*; (*oration*) òraid *f*. • *v* cuir seòladh air; dèan òraid ri.
adequate *adj* iomchaidh.
adhere *v* lean.
adherent *n* fear leanmhainn *m*.
adhesive *n* stuth leanmhainn *m*.
adjacent *adj* dlùth.
adjective *n* buadhair *m*.
adjudication *n* breitheamhnas *m*.
adjust *v* ceartaich, rèitich.
adjustable *adj* so-rèitichte.
administer *v* riaghlaich.
administration *n* riaghladh *m*.
administrative *adj* riaghlach.
administrator *n* fear-riaghlaidh *m*.
admirable *adj* ionmholta.
admiration *n* meas *m*.
admire *v* tha meas air.
admissible *adj* ceadaichte.
admission *n* cead *m*; (*confession*) aideachadh *m*.
admit *v* leig a steach; (*confess*) aidich.
ado *n* othail *f*.
adolescence *n* òigeachd *f*.
adolescent *n* òigear *m*.
adopt *v* uchd-mhacaich.
adoption *n* uchd-mhacachd *f*.
adore *v* trom-ghràdhaich.
adorn *v* sgeadaich.
adrift *adj* leis an t-sruth.
adult *adj* inbheach. • *n* inbheach *m*.

adulterate *v* truaill.
adulteration *n* truailleadh *m*.
adulterer *n* adhaltraiche *m*.
adultery *n* adhaltranas *m*.
advance *n* dol air adhart *m*; (*financial*) eàrlas *m*. • *v* rach air thoiseach; (*financial*) thoir eàrlas.
advanced *adj* adhartach.
advancement *n* àrdachadh *m*.
advantage *n* tairbhe, buannachd *f*.
advantageous *adj* tairbheach.
adventure *n* tachartas *m*.
adventurous *adj* dàna.
adverb *n* co-ghnìomhair *m*.
adverse *adj* an aghaidh.
adversity *n* cruaidh-chas *f*.
advertise *v* thoir sanas.
advertisement *n* sanas, sanas-reic *m*.
advice *n* comhairle *f*.
advise *v* comhairlich.
adviser *n* comhairleach *m*.
advocacy *n* tagradh *m*.
advocate *n* fear-tagraidh *m*.
advocate *v* tagair.
aerial *n* aer-ghath *m*.
aeronaut *n* speur-sheòladair *m*.
aeroplane *n* plèana *f*, itealan *m*.
affable *adj* suairce.
affair *n* gnothach *m*.
affect *v* drùidh air; (*let on*) leig air.
affection *n* gaol *m*.
affectionate *adj* gaolach.
affinity *n* dàimh *m/f*.
affirm *v* dearbh, daingnich.
affirmative *adj* aontach.
afflict *v* goirtich, sàraich.
affliction *n* doilgheas *m*.
affluence *n* beairteas *m*.
affluent *adj* beairteach.
afford *v* ruig air.

affront *v* maslaich.

afloat *adj* air fleòdradh.

afoot *adj* air chois; air bhonn.

aforementioned *adj* ro-ainmichte.

afraid *adj* fo eagal, eagalach.

afresh *adv* às ùr, a-rithist.

Africa *n* Afraga *f*.

African *adj* Afraganach.

after *adv* an dèidh làimhe. • *prep* an dèidh. • *pron* **after me** 'nam dhèidh; **after you** (*sing*) 'nad dhèidh; **after him, it** 'na dhèidh; **after her** 'na dèidh; **after us** 'nar dèidh; **after you** (*pl*) 'nur dèidh; **after them** 'nan dèidh.

afternoon *n* feasgar *m*.

afterthought *n* ath-smuain *f*.

again *adv* a-rithist.

against *prep* an aghaidh. • *prep* an dèidh. • *pron* **against me** 'nam aghaidh; **against you** (*sing*) 'nad aghaidh; **against him, it** 'na aghaidh; **against her** 'na aghaidh; **against us** 'nar n-aghaidh; **against you** (*pl*) 'nur n-aghaidh; **against them** 'nan aghaidh.

age *n* aois *f*. • *v* fàs aosda.

aged *adj* sean, aosda.

agency *n* ionadachd *f*.

agent *n* neach-ionaid *m*; dòigh *m*.

aggravate *v* antromaich.

aggression *n* (*phys*) ionnsaigh *m*; (*mental*) miann *m*.

aggressive *adj* ionnsaigheach.

agile *adj* lùthmhor.

agitate *v* gluais.

agitation *n* gluasad *m*.

ago *adv* air ais.

agog *adv* air bhiod.

agonise *v* bi an ioma-chomhairle.

agony *n* dòrainn *f*.

agree *v* aontaich; còrd.

agreeable *adj* taitneach.

agreement *n* còrdadh *m*, rèite *f*.

agricultural *adj* àiteachail.

agriculture *n* àiteachd *f*, tuathanachas *m*.

aground *adv* an sàs.

ahead *adv* air thoiseach.

aid *n* cuideachadh *m*. • *v* cuidich.

ailing *adj* tinn.

ailment *n* tinneas, galar *m*.

aim *n* (*missile*) cuimse *f*; (*intent*) amas *f*. • *v* cuimsich; amais.

air *n* àile; (*mus*) fonn; (*look*) aogas. • *v* leig an àile gu.

airborne *adj* air sgèith.

airmail *n* post-adhair *m*.

airport *n* port-adhair *m*.

airwave *n* tonn-adhair *m*.

aisle *n* trannsa *f*.

ajar *adv* leth-fhosgailte.

akin *adj* (*related*) càirdeach.

alacrity *n* sùrd *m*.

alarm *v* cuir eagal air.

alarming *adj* eagalach.

album *n* leabhar-chuimhneachan *m*.

alcohol *n* alcol *m*.

alcoholic *n* alcolach *m*.

alcoholism *n* alcolachd *f*.

alder *n* feàrna *f*.

ale *n* leann *m*.

alert *adj* furachail.

algebra *n* ailgeabra *f*.

alias *adv* fo ainm eile.

alien *adj* coigreach. • *n* coigreach *m*; Gall *m*.

alienate *v* fuadaich.

alight *v* teirinn.

alike *adj* co-ionnan.

alimony *n* airgead sgaraidh *m*.

alive *adj* beò.

all *adj* uile, na h-uile, iomlan.

allay *v* caisg.

allegation *n* cur às leth *m*.

allegiance *n* ùmhlachd *f*.

allegory *n* samhla *m*.

alleviate *v* aotromaich, lùghdaich.

alleviation *n* aotromachadh *m*.

alliance *n* càirdeas *m*.

alliteration *n* uaim *f*.

allow *v* leig le, ceadaich.

allowance *n* cuibhreann *f*.

allusion *n* iomradh *m*.

ally *n* caraid *m*; co-chòmragaiche *m*.

almighty *adj* uile-chumhachdach.

Almighty *n* An t-Uile-chumhachdach *m*.

almost *adv* gu ìre bhig.

alms *npl* dèircean.

aloft *adv* gu h-àrd, shuas.

alone *adj* aonarach.

along *adv* air fad; **along with** còmhla ri.

alongside *adv* ri taobh. • *pron* **alongside me** ri mo thaobh; **alongside you** (*sing*) ri do thaobh; **alongside him, it** ri 'thaobh; **alongside her** ri 'taobh; **alongside us** ri ar taobh; **alongside you** (*pl*) ri ur taobh; **alongside them** ri an taobh.

aloud *adv* gu h-àrd ghuthach.

alphabet *n* aibidil *f*.

alphabetical *adj* aibidileach.

already *adv* mar thà.

also *adv* cuideachd.

altar *n* altair *f*.

alter *v* atharraich.

alteration *n* atharrachadh *m*.

alternative *adj* eile. • *n* roghainn eile *m*.

although *conj* ged a.

altitude *n* àirde *f*.

altogether *adv* gu lèir, uile gu lèir.

aluminium *n* almain *m*.

always *adv* an-còmhnaidh, daonnan.

amalgamate *v* cuir le chèile.

amateur *adj* neo-dhreuchdail.

amaze *v* cuir iongnadh air.

amazement *n* iongantas *m*.

amazing *adj* iongantach.

ambassador *n* tosgaire *m*.

ambidextrous *adj* co-dheaslamhach.

ambiguity *n* dà-sheaghachas *m*.

ambiguous *adj* dà-sheaghach.

ambit *n* cuairt *f*.

ambition *n* glòir-mhiann *m*.

ambitious *adj* glòir-mhiannach.

ambulance *n* carbad-eiridinn *m*.

ambush *n* feallfhalach *m*.

ameliorate *v* dèan nas fheàrr.

amen *int* amen.

amenable *adj* fosgailte.

amend *v* leasaich.

amendment *n* leasachadh *m*.

amenity *n* goireas *m*.

America *n* Aimeireagaidh *f*.

American *adj* Aimeireaganach.

amiable *adj* càirdeil.

amid, amidst *prep* am measg.

amiss *adv* gu h-olc.

ammunition *n* connadh làmhaich *m*.

amnesty *n* mathanas na coitcheann *m*.

among, amongst *prep* am measg, air feadh.

amorous *adj* gaolach.

amount *n* suim, uimhir *f*; meud *m*.

amphibian *n* muir-thìreach *m*.

amphibious *adj* dà-bhitheach.

ample *adj* mòr, tomadach.

amplification *n* meudachadh *m*.
amplify *v* meudaich.
amputate *v* geàrr air falbh.
amputation *n* gearradh air falbh.
amuse *v* toilich.
amusement *n* greannmhorachd *f*.
amusing *adj* greanmhor.
anachronism *n* às-aimsireachd *f*.
anaemic *adj* cion-falach.
anaesthetic *n* pràmhaiche *m*.
analogy *n* co-fhreagarrachd *f*.
analyse *v* mion-sgrùdaich.
analysis *n* mion-sgrùdadh *m*.
analyst *n* mion-sgrùdaire *m*.
anarchist *n* ceannairceach *m*.
anatomical *adj* bodhaigeach.
anatomy *n* eòlas bodhaig *m*.
ancestor *n* sinnsear *m*.
ancestry *n* sinnsearachd *f*.
anchor *n* acair *f*.
ancient *adj* àrsaidh.
and *conj* agus, is, 's.
anecdote *n* naidheachd *f*.
anew *adv* às ùr.
angel *n* aingeal *m*.
angelic *adj* mar aingeal.
anger *n* fearg *f*.
angina *n* grèim chridhe *m*.
angle *n* uilinn *f*.
angler *n* iasgair *f*.
angling *n* iasgachd *m*.
angry *adj* feargach.
anguish *n* dòrainn *f*.
animal *n* ainmhidh *m*.
animate *v* beòthaich.
animated *adj* beòthail.
animation *n* beòthachadh *m*.
ankle *n* adhbrann *f*.
annex *n* ath-thaigh *m*.
annihilate *v* dìthich.
annihilation *n* lèirsgrios *m*.

anniversary *n* cuimhneachan, bliadhnail *m*.
annotate *v* notaich.
annotation *n* notachadh *m*.
announce *v* cuir an cèill.
annoy *v* cuir dragh air.
annoyance *n* dragh; buaireas *m*.
annoyed *adj* diombach.
annoying *adj* buaireil.
annual *adj* bliadhnail.
annually *adv* gach bhliadhna.
annul *v* cuir às.
anoint *v* ung.
anon *adv* a dh'aithghearr.
anonymous *adj* neo-ainmichte.
another *pron* fear eile. • *adj* eile.
answer *n* freagairt *f*.
answer *v* freagair.
ant *n* seangan *m*.
antagonist *n* nàmhaid *m*.
antediluvian *adj* ron Tuil.
anthem *n* laoidh *m*.
anthology *n* duanaire, cruinneachadh *m*.
anthropology *n* daonn-eòlas *m*.
anticipate *v* sùilich.
anticipation *n* sùileachadh *m*.
antidote *n* urchasg *m*.
antipathy *n* fuath *m*.
antiquary *n* àrsair *m*.
antique *adj* seann-saoghlach. • *n* seann-rud *m*.
antiseptic *n* loit-leigheas *m*.
antler *n* cabar fèidh *m*.
anvil *n* innean *m*.
anxiety *n* iomagain *m*.
anxious *adj* iomagaineach.
any *adj* sam bith, air bith, idir. • *pron* aon sam bith; aon; gin.
anyone *pron* neach sam bith.
anything *n* càil, dad *m*.

apartheid n sgaradh-cinnidh m.

apartment n seòmar m; taigh m.

apathy n cion ùidhe m.

ape n apa f.

aperture n toll, fosgladh m.

apex n binnean m; bàrr m.

apiece adv an-t-aon.

apologise v dèan leisgeul.

apology n leisgeul m.

apostle n abstol m.

apostrophe n ascair m.

appal v cuir uabhas air.

apparatus n uidheam m.

apparent adj soilleir, faicsinneach.

apparition n taibhse f.

appeal n tarraing f; (legal) ath-agairt m. • v tarraing; ath-agair.

appear v nochd.

appearance n taisbeanadh m; teachd an làthair m.

appease v rèitich.

append v cuir ri.

appendage n sgòdan m.

appendix n (anat) aipeandaig f; (book) ath-sgrìobadh m.

appetite n càil f.

applaud v bas-bhuail.

apple n ubhal m.

apple-tree n craobh-ubhal f.

appliance n goireas m.

applicable adj freagarrach.

applicant n tagraiche m.

application n cur an sàs m; (for a job) tagradh m.

applications npl (comput) cleachd-aidhean mpl.

apply v cuir a-steach.

appoint v suidhich.

appointment n suidheachadh m.

apportion v dèan roinn air.

appraise v meas.

appreciate v cuir luach air, luachaich; (grow) àrdaich.

appreciation n luachachadh m.

apprehend v (infer) thoir fa-near; (arrest) glac.

approach n modh-gabhail f. • v dlùthaich.

appropriate adj cubhaidh. • v gabh seilbh air.

approval n deagh-bharail f.

approve v gabh beachd math air.

approximate adj dlùthach.

apricot n apracot m.

April n An Giblean m.

apron n aparan m.

apropos adv a thaobh.

apt adj deas; freagarrach.

aptitude n sgil m; buailteachd f.

Arab n Arabach m.

Arabic adj Arabach.

arable adj so-àiteachaidh.

arbitrate v rèitich.

arbitrator n neach-rèiteachaidh m.

arch n stuagh m.

archaeologist n àrsair m.

archbishop n àrd-easbaig m.

archetype n prìomh-shamhla m.

architect n ailtire m.

architecture n ailtireachd f.

archive n tasglann f.

ardent adj dian, bras.

arduous adj deacair.

area n farsaingeachd, lann f.

argue v connsaich; dearbh.

argument n connsachadh m; argamaid f.

argumentative adj connsachail.

arid adj loisgte.

arise v èirich suas.

arithmetic n cùnntas m.

ark n àirc f.

arm *n* gàirdean *m*. • *v* armaich.
armchair *n* cathair-ghàirdeanach *f*.
armistice *n* fosadh *m*.
armour *n* armachd *f*.
armpit *n* achlais *f*.
army *n* arm, armailt *m*.
around *adv* mun cuairt. • *prep* timcheall, mu chuairt.
arouse *v* dùisg.
arrange *v* rèitich, còirich.
arrangement *n* rèiteachadh *m*; (*mus*) rian *m*.
array *v* cuir an òrdugh.
arrears *n* fiachan gun dìoladh *m*.
arrest *v* cuir an làimh.
arrival *n* teachd *m*.
arrive *v* ruig, thig.
arrogance *n* dànadas *m*.
arrogant *adj* dàna.
arrow *n* saighead *f*.
arsenal *n* arm-lann *f*.
art *n* ealain *f*; dòigh *f*; alt *m*; (*artifice*) seòltachd *f*.
artery *n* cuisle *f*.
artful *adj* innleachdach; seòlta.
arthritis *n* tinneas nan alt *m*.
article *n* alt *m*; (*clause*) bonn *m*.
articulate *adj* pongail.
artifice *n* seòltachd *f*.
artificial *adj* brèige.
artist *n* fear-ealain *m*.
as *adv* cho . . . ri, cho . . . is. • *conj* mar, ceart mar.
ascend *v* dìrich, streap.
ascent *n* dìreadh *m*.
ascertain *v* lorg; faigh fios.
ascribe *v* cuir às leth.
ash *n* uinnseann *m*.
ashamed *adj* nàraichte.
ashes *n* luaithre *f*.
ashore *adv* air tìr.

ashtray *n* soitheach-luaithre *f*.
Asia *n* An Aisia *f*.
Asiatic, Asian *adj* Aisianach.
aside *adv* a thaobh.
ask *v* (*request*) iarr; (*inquire after*) faighnich, feòraich.
askew *adv* cam; claon.
asleep *adj* an cadal.
asparagus *n* creamh na muice fiadhaich *m*.
aspect *n* snuadh *m*.
aspen *n* critheann *m*.
asperity *n* gairbhe *f*.
aspiration *n* dèidh *m*.
aspire *v* iarr, bi an dèidh air.
ass *n* asal *f*.
assail *v* thoir ionnsaigh air.
assailant *n* neach-ionnsaigh *m*.
assassin *n* mortair *m*.
assassinate *v* moirt, dèan mort.
assault *n* ionnsaigh *f*.
assemble *v* cruinnich.
assembly *n* mòrdhail *m*.
assent *n* aonta *m*.
assert *v* tagair.
assertion *n* tagradh *m*.
assertive *adj* tagrach.
assess *v* meas; (*for taxation*) meas a thaobh cìs.
assessment *n* meas *m*; meas a thaobh cìs *m*.
assessor *n* measadair *m*.
asset *n* taic *f*.
assiduity *n* dùrachd *f*.
assiduous *adj* leanmhainneach.
assign *v* cuir air leth.
assignation *n* cur air leth *m*; (*tryst*) coinneamh-leannan *f*.
assignment *n* obair shònraichte *f*.
assimilate *v* gabh a-steach.
assist *v* cuidich.

assistance *n* cuideachadh *m*.

assistant *n* cuidiche *m*.

associate *v* theirig am pàirt; cuir as leth.

association *n* comann *m*; ceangal *m*.

assonance *n* fuaimreagadh *m*.

assortment *n* measgachadh *m*.

assuage *v* caisg.

assume *v* gabh air.

assumption *n* gabhail *m*; (*supposition*) barail *f*.

assurance *n* dearbhachd *f*.

assure *v* dearbh.

assuredly *adv* gun teagamh.

asterisk *n* reul *f*.

astern *adv* an deireadh na luinge.

asthma *n* a' chuing *f*.

astonish *v* cuir iongnadh air.

astonishment *n* iongnadh *m*.

astray *adv* air seachran.

astride *adv* casa-gobhlach.

astringent *adj* ceangailteach; geur is tioram.

astrologer *n* speuradair *m*.

astrology *n* speuradaireachd *f*.

astronaut *n* speur-sheòladair *m*.

astronomer *n* reuladair *m*.

astronomical *adj* reul-eòlasach.

astronomy *n* reul-eòlas *m*.

asunder *adv* air leth.

asylum *n* àite-dìon *m*.

at *prep* aig. • *pron* **at me** agam; **at you** (*sing*) agad; **at him, it** aige; **at her** aice; **at us** againn; **at you** agaibh; **at them** aca.

atheism *n* neo-dhiadhachd *f*.

atheist *n* neo-dhiadhaire *m*.

athletic *adj* lùthmhor.

athletics *n* lùth-chleasachd *f*.

athwart *adv* trasd.

Atlantic Ocean *n* An Cuan Siar *m*.

atlas *n* atlas *m*.

atmosphere *n* àile *m*.

atom *n* dadam *m*.

atomic *adj* dadamach.

atone *v* dèan èirig.

atonement *n* rèite *f*.

atrocious *adj* uabhasach.

atrocity *n* buirbe *f*.

attach *v* ceangail.

attached *adj* ceangailte.

attachment *n* dàimh, gràdh *m*.

attack *n* ionnsaigh *m*. • *v* thoir ionnsaigh.

attain *v* ruig.

attainable *adj* so-ruigsinn.

attainment *n* ruigsinn *m*; (*ability*) sgil *m*.

attempt *n* oidhirp *f*. • *v* dèan oidhirp.

attend *v* fritheil; **attend to** thoir aire.

attendance *n* frithealadh *m*.

attendant *n* neach-frithealaidh *m*.

attentive *adj* furachail.

attenuate *v* tanaich.

attest *v* thoir fianais.

attestation *n* teisteas *m*.

attire *n* aodach, trusgan *m*. • *v* sgeadaich.

attitude *n* seasamh *m*.

attract *v* tarraing.

attraction *n* sùgadh *m*.

attractive *adj* tarraingeach.

attribute *v* cuir às leth.

attrition *n* bleith *f*.

attune *v* gleus.

attuned *adj* air ghleus.

auburn *adj* buidhe-ruadh.

auction *n* reic-tairgse *f*.

audible *adj* so-chlaistinneach.

audience *n* luchd-èisdeachd *m*.

audiovisual *adj* claistinn-léir-
sinneach.
audit *n* sgrùdadh *m*. • *v* sgrùd.
auditor *n* sgrùdaire *m*.
augment *v* meudaich.
augur *n* fiosaiche *m*.
augury *n* tuar *m*.
August *n* Lùnasdal *m*.
aunt *n* antaidh *f*.
aurora borealis *n* Na Fir Chlis.
auspicious *adj* fàbharach.
austere *adj* teann.
austerity *n* teanntachd *f*.
Australasia *n* Astrailàisia *f*.
Australia *n* Astràilia *f*.
Austria *n* An Ostair *f*.
authentic *adj* cinnteach.
author *n* ùghdar *m*.
authorise *v* thoir ùghdarras.
authority *n* ùghdarras, smachd *m*.
autobiography *n* fèin-eachdraich *f*.
automatic *adj* fèin-ghluasadach.
autumn *n* foghar *m*.

auxiliary *adj* taiceil.
avail *v* foghainn.
available *adj* ri fhaighinn.
avarice *n* sannt *m*.
avaricious *adj* sanntach.
avenge *v* dìol.
average *adj* gnàthach. • *n* meadhan
m.
aversion *n* fuath *m*.
avid *adj* gionach.
avoid *v* seachainn.
await *v* fuirich ri.
awake *v* dùisg.
award *n* duais *f*. • *v* thoir duais.
aware *adj* fiosrach.
away *adv* air falbh.
awesome *adj* fuathasach.
awful *adj* eagalach, uabhasach.
awhile *adv* tacan.
awkward *adj* cearbach.
awry *adj* cam.
ax, axe *n* tuagh *f*.
axle *n* aiseil *f*.

B

babble *n* glagais *f*.
baby *n* leanabh *m*.
bachelor *n* fleasgach *m*.
back *adv* air ais. • *n* cùl *m*; (*person*)
druim *m*. • *v* theirig air ais;
(*support*) seas.
backbone *n* cnàmh-droma *m*.
backgammon *n* tàileasg *m*.
backside *n* tòn *f*.
backsliding *n* cùl-sleamhnachadh *m*.
backwards *adv* an coinneamh a
chùil.
bacon *n* muic-fheòil *f*.
bacterial *adj* bacteridheach.

bad *adj* dona, olc.
badge *n* suaicheantas *m*.
badger *n* broc *m*.
badness *n* donas *m*.
bad-tempered *adj* greannach.
baffle *v* dèan a chùis air.
bag *n* pòca *m*.
baggage *n* treallaichean *f*.
bagpipe *n* pìob, a' phìob mhòr *f*.
bail *n* fuasgladh air urras *m*. •
thoir urras air.
bailiff *n* bàillidh *m*.
bait *n* maghar *m*. • *v* biadh.
bake *v* fuin; bruich ann an àmhainn.

baker *n* fuineadair, bèicear *m*.

bakery *n* taigh-fuine *m*.

balance *n* meidh *f*; (*mental*) cothrom *m*; (*fin*) còrr *m*. • *v* cuir air meidh; cothromaich.

balcony *n* for-uinneag *f*.

bald *adj* maol.

baldness *n* maoile *f*.

baleful *adj* millteach.

ball *n* ball *m*; (*dance*) bàl.

ballad *n* bailead *m*.

ballast *n* balaiste *f*.

balloon *n* bailiùn *m*.

ballot *n* bhòtadh *m*.

balm *n* ìocshlaint *f*.

bamboo *n* cuilc Innseanach *f*.

bamboozle *v* cuir an imcheist.

ban *n* toirmeasg *f*. • *v* toirmisg.

banana *n* banana *m*.

band *n* bann *m*; còmhlan *m*; (*mus*) còmhlan-ciùil *m*.

bandage *n* stìom-cheangail *f*.

bandy-legged *adj* camachasach.

baneful *adj* nimheil.

bang *n* cnag *f*; bualadh *m*. • *v* cnag; buail.

banish *v* fògair.

banishment *n* fògradh *m*.

basking shark *n* cearban *m*.

battery *n* bataraidh *m*.

bawdy *adj* drabasda.

bead *n* grìogag *m*.

beak *n* gob *m*.

beans *npl* pònair *m*.

beard *n* feusag *m*.

beast *n* beathach *m*, biast *m*.

beat *v* thoir buille.

beautiful *adj* bòidheach.

beauty maise, bòidhchead *m*.

beckon *v* smèid air.

bed *n* leabaidh *m*.

bedroom *n* seòmar-leapa *m*.

bee *n* seillean *m*.

beef *n* mairtfheoil.

beer *n* leann *m*.

beetle *n* daolag *m*.

before *prep* ro. • *pron* before me romham; before you (*sing*) romhad; before him, it roimhe; before her roimhpe; before us romhainn; before you (*pl*) romhaibh; before them romhpa.

beg *v* iarr; dèan faoighe.

beggar *n* dèirceach *m*.

behave *v* giùlain.

behaviour *n* giùlan *m*; modh *m*.

behind *prep* air cùlaibh. • *pron* behind me air mo chùlaibh; behind you (*sing*) air do chùlaibh; behind him, it air a chùlaibh; behind her air a cùlaibh; behind us air ar cùlaibh; behind you (*pl*) air ur cùlaibh; behind them air an cùlaibh.

bell *n* clag *m*.

bellow *v* beucaich.

bellows *n* balg-sèididh *m*.

belly *n* brù, broinn *f*.

belong *v* buin.

beloved *adj* gràdhach.

below *adv* shìos.

belt *n* crios *m*.

bench *n* being *f*.

bend *n* lùb *m*. • *v* lùb.

beneath *prep* fo.

benediction *n* beannachadh *m*.

benefaction *n* tabhartas *m*.

benefactor *n* taibheartach *m*.

beneficent *adj* deagh-ghnìomhach.

beneficial *adj* tairbheach.

benefit *n* sochair *m*.

benevolence *n* deagh-ghean *m*.

benevolent adj coibhneil.
benign adj suairc.
bent adj lùbte.
benumb v meilich.
bequeath v tiomnaich.
bequest n dìleab m.
bereaved adj rùisgte.
berry n dearc f, subh m.
beseech v dèan guidhe.
beside prep ri taobh. • pron **beside me** ri mo thaobh; **beside you** (sing) ri do thaobh; **beside him, it** ri 'thaobh; **beside her** ri 'taobh; **beside us** ri ar taobh; **beside you** (pl) ri ur taobh; **beside them** ri an taobh.
besides adv a bhàrr air.
besiege v dèan sèisd air.
best adj as fheàrr. • n rogha m. • v fairtlich air.
bestial adj brùideil.
bestow v builich.
bet v cuir geall.
betray v brath.
betrayal n brathadh m.
betrayer n brathadair m.
betroth v rèitich.
better adj nas fheàrr.
between adv eadar. • prep eadar. • pron **alongside us** eadarainn; **alongside you** (pl) eadaraibh; **alongside them** eatorra.
bewail v caoidh.
beware v thoir an aire.
bewitch v cuir fo gheasaibh.
beyond prep air taobh thall; seachad air.
bias n claonadh m.
bible n bìoball m.
biblical adj sgriobturail.
bicycle n bàidhseagal m.

bid n tairgse f. • v thoir tairgse.
bidding n (invitation) cuireadh m.
bide v fuirich.
biennial adj dà-bhliadhnach.
bier n carbad-adhlacaidh, giùlan m
big adj mòr.
bigamy n dà-chèileachas m.
bigot n dalm-bheachdaiche m.
bigotry n dalm-bheachd m.
bilateral adj dà-thaobhach.
bile n domblas m.
bilingual adj dà-chànanach.
bill n gob m; (account) bileag.
billion n billean m.
bin n biona f.
binary adj càraideach.
bind v ceangail.
binding n ceangal m.
biochemist n bith-cheimicear m.
biochemistry n bith-cheimiceachd
biography n beath-eachdraidh f.
biological adj bith-eòlasach.
biology n bith-eòlas m.
biped n dà-chasach m.
birch n beithe f.
bird n eun m.
bird-song n ceilear m/f.
birth certificate n teisteanas-breith
birth n breith f.
birthday n ceann-bliadhna m.
birthright n còir-bhreith f.
biscuit n briosgaid f.
bisect v geàrr sa mheadhan.
bishop n easbaig m.
bit n mìr, bideag m; (horse) cabstair
bitch n galla f.
bite v bìd, thoir grèim à.
biting adj bìdeach.
bitter adj geur.
black adj dubh, dorch.
blackbird n lon-dubh m.

blackboard n bòrd-dubh m.
blacken v dubh, dèan dubh.
black-humoured adj gruamach.
blackness n duibhead m.
blacksmith n gobha m.
bladder n aotroman m.
blade n (of grass) bilean; (of weapon) lann.
blame n coire f. • v coirich.
blameless adj neo-choireach.
blanch v gealaich.
bland adj mìn.
blank adj bàn.
blanket n plaide, plangaid f.
blasphemy n toibheum m.
blast n sgal m. • v sgrios.
blaze n teine lasrach m. • v las.
bleach v todhair.
bleak adj lom, fuar.
bleat v dèan mèilich.
bleed v leig fuil.
blemish n gaoid f.
blend n coimeasgadh m. • v coimeasgaich.
bless v beannaich.
blessed adj beannaichte.
blessing n beannachd f.
blight n fuar-dhealt.
blind adj dall. • n sgàil m.
blind man n dallaran m.
blindness n doille f.
blink v caog.
bliss n aoibhneas m.
blissful adj aoibhneach.
blister n leus m. • v thoir leus air; thig leus air.
blithe adj aoibhinn.
block n ploc m. • v caisg.
blockhead n bumailear m.
blonde n te bhàn f.
blood feud n folachd f.

blood group n seòrsa fala m.
blood n fuil f.
blood pressure n bruthadh-fala m.
blood transfusion n leasachadh-fala m.
bloodshed n dòrtadh-fala m.
bloody adj fuileach.
bloom n blàth m.
blot n dubhadh m.
blotting paper n pàipear-sùghaidh m.
blouse n blobhsa f.
blow v sèid.
blubber n saill (muice-mara) f.
blue adj gorm.
blueness n guirme f.
bluff v meall.
blunder n iomrall m.
blunt adj maol. • v maolaich.
blur v dèan doilleir.
blush n rudhadh m.
bluster v bagair.
boar n torc m.
board n bòrd m, dèile f. • v rach air bòrd.
boarding house n taigh-aoigheachd m.
boarding pass n cead-bòrdaidh m.
boast n bòsd. • v dèan bòsd.
boaster n bòsdair m.
boastful adj bòsdail.
boat n bàta m.
body n corp m; (person) neach, creutair m; (band) buidheann m.
bog n boglach, fèithe f.
bog-cotton n canach m.
boggle v bi an teagamh.
boil v goil; bruich.
boiled adj bruich.
boiler n goileadair m.
boisterous adj stoirmeil; iorghaileach.

bold *adj* dàna.

boldness *n* dànadas *m*.

bolster *v* misnich.

bolt *n* crann *m*. • *v* cuir crann air.

bomb *n* bom, boma *m*. • *v* leag bom air.

bond *n* ceangal *m*.

bondage *n* daorsa *m*.

bone *n* cnàmh *m*.

boneless *adj* gun chnàimh.

bonfire *n* tein-aighear *m*.

bonnet *n* bonaid *f*.

bonny *adj* maiseach.

bonus *n* còrr *m*.

bony *adj* cnàmhach.

book *n* leabhar *m*.

bookcase *n* preas-leabhraichean *m*.

bookish *adj* dèidheil air leughadh.

book-keeper *n* fear chumail leabhraichean *m*.

book-keeping *n* leabhar-chùnntas *m*.

bookseller *n* leabhar-reiceadair *m*.

bookshop *n* bùth-leabhraichean *m*.

boor *n* amhasg *m*.

boorish *n* amhasgail *m*.

boot *n* bròg *m*.

booty *n* cobhartach *m/f*.

booze *n* stuth òil *m*. • *v* òl.

border *n* crìoch *f*.

borderer *n* fear àiteach nan crìoch *m*.

bore *n* duine ràsanach *m*.

bore *v* cladaich.

boring *adj* fadalach.

borrow *v* faigh, gabh iasad.

borrower *n* fear gabhail iasaid *m*.

bosom *n* uchd *m*.

boss *n* ceann *m*.

botanise *v* cruinnich luibhean.

botanist *n* luibh-eòlaiche *m*.

botany *n* luibh-eòlas *m*.

both *adj* araon, le chèile, an dà; (*people*) an dithis.

bother *n* sàrachadh *m*. • *v* sàraich.

bottle *n* botal *m*.

bottom *n* lochdar *m*; grùnnd *m* màs *m*.

bottomless *adj* gun ghrùnnd.

bough *n* geug *f*.

bound *n* sìnteag *f*. • *v* thoir leum.

bountiful *adj* fialaidh.

bourgeois *adj* bùirdeasach.

bow *n* bogha *m*; (*ship*) toiseach *m* (*head*) ùmhlachd *m*.

bowels *n* innidh *f*.

bowl *n* cuach *f*, bobhla *m*.

bowsprit *n* crann-spreòid *m*.

bowstring *n* taifeid *m*.

box *n* bocsa, bucas *m*. • *v* (*sport*) dèan sabaid.

boxer *n* bocsair, dòrnadair *m*.

boxer shorts *n* briogais bocsair *f*.

boy *n* balach, gille *m*.

brace *n* (*pair*) dithis *m*.

braces *npl* galars.

bracken *n* raineach *f*.

bracket *n* camag *f*.

brae *n* bruthach *f*.

brag *v* dèan bòsd.

bragging *n* bòsd, spaglainn *m*.

brain *n* eanchainn *f*.

bramble *n* smeur *f*.

bramble-bush *n* dris *f*.

branch *n* meangan *m*, geug *f*. • *v* sgaoil.

brandish *v* beartaich.

brandy *n* branndaidh *f*.

brass *n* pràis *f*.

brat *n* isean *m*.

brave *adj* gaisgeil.

bravery *n* misneachd *f*.

brawl *n* stairirich *m*. • *v* dèan stairirich.

bray v dèan sitir.

breach n briseadh m. • v dèan briseadh.

bread n aran m.

breadcrumb n criomag arain f.

breadth n leud m.

break v bris; sgar.

breakfast n breacaist m.

breast n cìoch f.

breath n anail f.

breathe v (out) leig anail; (in) tarraing anail.

breathless adj plosgartach.

breed n seòrsa m. • v tarmaich.

breeding n oilean m.

breeze n tlàth-ghaoth f.

brevity n giorrad m.

brew v dèan grùdaireachd; tarraing.

brewer n grùdaire m.

bribe n brìb f. • v brìb.

bribery n brìbeireachd f.

brick n breice f.

bricklayer n breicire m.

bridal adj pòsda.

bride n bean-bainnse f.

bridegroom n fear-bainnse m.

bridesmaid n maighdean-phòsaidh f.

bridge n drochaid f.

brief adj geàrr.

brigand n spùinneadair m.

bright adj soilleir; (mind) tuigseach.

brighten v soillsich.

brightness n soilleireachd f.

brilliant adj boillsgeach; (mind) air leth geur.

brim n oir m.

brine n sàl m.

bring v thoir.

brink n oir m.

brisk adj beòthail.

briskness n beòthalachd f.

bristle n calg m. • v cuir calg air.

Britain n Breatainn f.

British adj Breatannach.

brittle adj brisg.

broach v (open) toll; (introduce) tog.

broad adj leathann.

broadcast v craoil.

broadcaster n craoladair m.

brochure n leabhran m.

brogue n bròg-èille f; (language) dualchainnt f.

broken adj briste.

broker n neach-gnothaich m.

brokerage n duais fir-ghnothaich f.

bronchial adj sgòrnanach.

bronchitis n at sgòrnain m.

bronze n umha m.

bronzed adj (tanned) donn, grian-loisgte.

brooch n bràiste f.

brood n àl m. • v àlaich.

brook n alltan m.

broom n bealaidh m; sguab m.

broth n eanraich f, brot m.

brothel n taigh-siùrsachd m.

brother n bràthair m.

brotherhood n bràithreachas m.

brotherly adj bràithreil.

brow n mala f; (of hill) maoilean m.

brown adj donn.

brownness n duinne f.

browse v criom; (book) thoir ruith air.

bruise n pronnadh m. • v pronn.

brunette n tè dhonn f.

brush n sguab f. • v sguab.

Brussels n A' Bhruiseal f.

brutal *adj* brùideil.
brutality *n* brùidealachd *f*.
brute *n* brùid *m*.
bubble *n* builgean *m*.
buck *n* boc *m*.
bucket *n* cuinneag *f*.
buckle *n* bucall *m*.
bud *n* gucag *f*.
budge *v* caraich.
budget *n* buidsead *f*.
buffet *n* beum *m*; (*food table*) clàr bìdh *m*.
bug *n* (*infection*) galar *m*.
bugle *n* dùdach *f*.
build *v* tog.
builder *n* togalaiche *m*.
building *n* togalach *m*.
building society *n* comann-togalaich *m*.
bulb *n* bolgan *m*.
bulk *n* meudachd *f*.
bulky *adj* tomadach.
bull *n* tarbh *m*.
bulldog *n* tarbh-chù *m*.
bulldozer *n* tarbh-chrann *m*.
bullet *n* peilear *m*.
bulletin *n* cùirt-iomradh *m*.
bullock *n* tarbh òg *m*.
bully *n* pulaidh *m*.
bum *n* màs *m*.
bump *n* meall; bualadh *m*.
bumper *n* bumpair *m*.
bun *n* buna *m*.
bunch *n* bagaid *f*.
bundle *n* pasgan *m*.
bung *n* tùc *m*.
bungle *v* dèan gu cearbach.
bungler *n* cearbaire *m*.
buoy *n* put *m*.
buoyancy *n* fleodradh *m*.
buoyant *adj* aotrom.

burden *n* eallach *m*. • *v* uallaich.
bureau *n* biùro *m*.
burgh *n* borgh *m*.
burglar *n* gadaiche-taighe *m*.
burglary *n* gadachd-taighe *f*.
burial *n* adhlacadh *m*.
burlesque *n* sgeigeireachd *f*.
burly *adj* tapaidh.
burn[1] *n* losgadh *m*. • *v* loisg.
burn[2] *n* (*stream*) alltan *m*.
burning *n* losgadh *m*.
burnish *v* lìomh.
burst *v* spreadh.
bury *v* adhlaic.
bus *n* bus *m*.
bush *n* preas *m*.
bushy *adj* preasach.
business *n* gnothach *m*, malairt *f*.
businessman *n* fear-gnothaich *m*.
bust *n* ceann is guaillean *m*.
bustle *n* othail *f*.
busy *adj* trang.
busybody *n* gobaire *m*.
but *conj*, *adv*, *prep* ach.
butcher *n* feòladair *m*. • *v* casgair.
Bute *n* Bòid *m*.
butler *n* buidealair *m*.
butt[1] *n* cùis-bhùirt *m*; (*cask*) baraill *m*; (*target*) targaid *f*.
butt[2] *v* sàth.
butter *n* ìm *m*.
buttercup *n* buidheag-an-t-samraidh *f*.
butterfly *n* dealan-dè *m*.
buttery *adj* ìmeach.
buttock *n* màs *m*.
button *n* putan *m*. • *v* putanaich.
buxom *adj* tiugh.
buy *v* ceannaich.
buyer *n* ceannaiche *m*.
buzz *n* srann *f*. • *v* srann.

buzzard *n* clamhan *m*.

by *adv* seachad; (*aside*) an dara taobh. • *prep* fasg air; le; **by and by** *adv* a dh' aithghearr, dh' aithghearr.

by-election *n* frith-thaghadh *m*.

bypass *n* seach-rathad *m*.

byre *n* bàthach *f*.

bystander *n* fear-amhairc *m*.

C

cab *n* tagsaidh *m*.

cabbage *n* càl *m*.

caber *n* cabar *m*.

cabin *n* seòmar-luinge, cèaban *m*.

cadaverous *adj* cairbheach.

cadence *n* dùnadh *m*.

cadger *n* neach-faoighe *m*.

café *n* cafaidh *m*.

cage *n* cèidse *f*.

cairn *n* càrn *m*.

cajole *v* breug.

cake *n* breacag *f*.

calamitous *adj* dosgainneach.

calamity *n* dosgainn *f*.

calculate *v* tomhais.

calculation *n* tomhas *m*.

calculator *n* àireamhair *m*.

calculus *n* riaghailt-àireamh *f*.

Caledonia *n* Alba *f*.

calendar *n* mìosachan *m*.

calf *n* laogh *m*; (*leg*) calpa *m*.

calibre *n* meudachd *f*.

call *v* glaodh.

call-box *n* bocsa-fòn *m*.

calligraphy *n* làmh-sgrìobhaidh *f*.

calling *n* eughachd *f*; (*vocation*) dreuchd *f*.

calliper *n* cailpear *m*.

callous *adj* cruaidh-chridheach.

calm *adj* ciùin; fèathach.

calm *v* ciùinich.

calumniate *v* cùl-chàin.

calve *v* beir laogh.

camel *n* càmhal *m*.

camera *n* camara *m*.

camouflage *n* breug-riochd *m*.

camp *n* càmpa *m*.

camp *v* càmpaich.

campaign *n* còmhrag *f*.

can[1] *n* canastair *m*.

can[2] *v* (*may*) faod; (*be able*) is urrainn do.

Canadian *adj* Canadach.

canal *n* clais-uisge *f*.

cancel *v* dubh a-mach.

cancellation *n* dubhadh a-mach *m*.

cancer *n* aillse *f*.

cancerous *adj* aillseach.

candid *adj* neo-chealgach.

candidate *n* iarradair *m*.

candle *n* coinneal *f*.

candlestick *n* coinnlear *m*.

candour *n* fosgarrachd *f*.

canine *adj* conail.

cannibal *n* canabail *m*.

canny *adj* cùramach.

canonise *v* cuir an àireamh nan naomh.

canter *n* trotan *m*.

canvas *n* canabhas *m*.

canvass *v* beachd-rannsaich.

canvasser *n* sireadair *m*.

cap *n* bonaid *m/f*, ceap *m*.

cap *v* còmhdaich; (*fig*) thoir bàrr air.

capability *n* cumhachd *m*.

capable *adj* comasach.
capacious *adj* farsaing.
capacity *n* comas *m*.
cape *n* rubha *m*; cleòc *m*.
caper *v* leum.
capital *n* ceanna-bhaile *m*.
capital letter *n* corr-litir *f*.
capitalism *n* calpachas *m*.
capitalist *n* calpaire *m*.
capitulate *v* strìochd.
capitulation *n* strìochdadh *m*.
caprice *n* neònachas *m*.
capricious *adj* neònach.
capsule *n* capsal *m*.
captain *n* caiptean *m*.
caption *n* tiotal *m*; fo-thiotal *m*.
captive *n* ciomach *m*.
captivity *n* ciomachas *m*.
capture *n* glacadh *m*.
capture *v* glac.
car *n* càr, carbad *m*.
carbohydrate *n* gualaisg *m*.
carbon *n* gualan *m*.
carcass *n* cairbh *m*.
card *n* cairt *f*.
card *v* càrd.
cardboard *n* cairt-bhòrd *m*.
cardiac *adj* cridhe.
cardiac disease *n* tinneas cridhe *m*.
cardinal *adj* prìomh. • *n* càirdineal.
card index *n* clàr-amais cairt *m*.
care *n* cùram *m*. • *v* gabh cùram.
career *n* (*rush*) rèis *f*; (*work*)
dreachd *f*.
careful *adj* cùramach.
careless *adj* mì-chùramach.
carelessness *n* mì-chùram *m*.
caress *v* cnèadaich.
caretaker *n* neach-aire *m*.
cargo *n* lùchd *m*.

caricature *n* dealbh-magaidh *m*.
carnage *n* àr *m*.
carnal *adj* feòlmhor.
carnival *n* fèill *f*.
carnivorous *adj* feòil-itheach.
carousal *n* fleadh *m*.
carpark *n* pàirc-chàraichean *f*.
carpenter *n* saor *m*
carpet *n* brat-ùrlair *m*.
carriage *n* carbad *m*; (*gait*) giùlan *m*.
carrier *n* neach-ghiùlain *m*.
carrion *n* ablach *m*.
carrot *n* curran *m*.
carry *v* giùlain, iomchair, thoir.
cart *n* cairt *f*. • *v* giùlain le cairt.
cartilage *n* maoth-chnàimh *m*.
cartoon *n* dealbh-èibhinn *m/f*.
cartridge *n* catraisde *f*.
carve *v* geàrr; snaigh.
carving *n* snaigheadh *m*.
cascade *n* eas *m*.
case *n* còmhdach *m*; ceus *m*; staid
m; cùis *m*; tuiseal *m*.
cash *n* airgead ullamh *m*.
cash-book *n* leabhar-airgid *m*.
cashier *n* glèidheadair-airgid *m*.
cash machine *n* inneal-airgid *m*.
cash register *n* inneal-cùnntaidh
airgid *m*.
cask *n* buideal *m*.
cassock *n* casag *f*.
cast *v* tilg, cuir; **cast loose** *v* sgaoil.
caste *n* dual-fhìne *f*.
castigate *v* cronaich.
castle *n* caisteal *m*.
castrate *v* spoth.
casual *adj* tuiteamach.
casualty *n* leòinteach *m*.
cat *n* cat *m*.
catalogue *n* ainm-chlàr *m*.
catalyse *v* cruth-atharraich.

catapult *n* tailm *m*.

cataract *see* cascade; (*eye*) *n* meamran sùla *m*.

catarrh *n* an galar smugaideach *m*.

catastrophe *n* droch thubaist *f*.

catch *n* glacadh *m*. • *v* glac, greimich.

catching *adj* gabhaltach.

catechism *n* leabhar-cheist *m*.

categorical *adj* làn-chinnteach.

category *n* gnè *f*.

cater *v* solair.

caterpillar *n* burras *m*.

caterpillar-tracked *adj* burrasach.

cathedral *n* cathair-eaglais *f*.

Catholic *adj* Caitligeach.

catholic *adj* coitcheann.

cattle *n* spreidh *f*.

cattle show *n* fèill a' chruidh *f*.

cauldron *n* coire mòr *m*.

cauliflower *n* colag *f*.

causal *adj* adhbharach.

causation *n* adhbharachadh *m*.

cause *n* adhbhar *m*; cùis *m*. • *v* dèan, thoir gu buil.

causeway *n* cabhsair *m*.

caustic *adj* loisgeach.

caution *n* cùram *m*. • *v* cuir air fhaicill.

cautious *adj* cùramach.

cavalry *n* marc-shluagh *m*.

cave *n* uamh *f*.

cavity *n* lag *m/f*, sloc *f*.

cease *v* stad.

cease-fire *n* stad-losgaidh *m*.

ceaseless *adj* gun stad.

cedar *n* seudar *m*.

cede *v* gèill.

ceilidh *n* cèilidh *m/f*.

ceiling *n* mullach *m*.

celebrate *v* glèidh; bi subhach.

celebrity *n* neach iomraiteach *m*.

celestial *adj* nèamhaidh.

celibacy *n* aontamhachd *f*.

celibate *adj* aontamhach.

cell *n* cealla; prìosan *f*.

cellar *n* seilear *m*.

cello *n* beus-fhidheall *f*.

cellular *adj* ceallach.

celluloid *n* ceallaloid *m*.

Celt *n* Ceilteach *m*.

Celtic *adj* Ceilteach.

cement *n* saimeant *m*. • *v* tàth.

cemetery *n* cladh *m*.

censor *n* caisgire *m*. • *v* caisg.

censorious *adj* cronachail.

censure *n* coire *f*. • *v* coirich.

census *n* cùnntas-sluaigh *m*.

centenary *n* ceud bliadhna *m*.

centennial *adj* ceud-bhliadhnach.

centimetre *n* ceudameatair *m*.

central *adj* anns a' mheadan.

central heating *n* teasachadh meadhanach *m*.

central processing unit *n* prìomh-ghnìomh-inneal *m*.

centre *n* meadhan *m*.

centrifugal *adj* meadhan-sheachnach.

centripetal *adj* meadhan-aomachail.

century *n* ceud bliadhna, linn *m*.

cereal *n* gràn *m*.

ceremony *n* deas-ghnàth *m*.

certain *adj* cinnteach.

certainly *adv* gu cinnteach.

certainty *n* cinnt *f*.

certificate *n* teisteanas *m*.

certify *v* teistich.

cesspool *n* poll-caca *m*.

chagrin *n* mìghean *m*.

chain *n* slabhraidh *f*. • *v* cuibhrich.

chain store *n* bùth-sreatha *f*.

chair *n* cathair *f*.

chairman *n* cathraiche *m*.

chalk *n* cailc *f*.

challenge *n* dùbhshlan *m*.

chamber *n* seòmar *m*.

chambered *adj* seòmrach.

champ *v* cagainn.

champion *n* gaisgeach *m*.

championship *n* urram gaisgeachd *m*.

chance *n* tuiteamas *m*.

change *n* caochladh *m*; (*money*) iomlaid *f*. • *v* mùth.

changeable *adj* caochlaideach.

channel *n* amar, caolas *m*.

chant *v* sianns.

chanter *n* feadan *m*.

chaos *n* eucruth *m*.

chapel *n* caibeal *m*.

chapter *n* caibideil *m/f*.

character *n* beus, mèinn *f*; (*story*) pearsa *m*.

characteristic *adj* coltach.

charcoal *n* gual-fiodha *m*.

charge *n* earbsa *f*; ionnsaigh *f*; prìs *f*. • *v* earb; thoir ionnsaigh; cuir.

charity *n* gràdh, coibhneas *m*.

charm *n* mealladh *m*; (*spell*) ortha *f*. • *v* meall; cuir fo dhraoidheachd.

chart *n* cairt-iùil *f*.

charter *v* fasdaidh.

chase *n* sealg. • *v* ruith.

chaste *adj* geanmnaidh.

chastity *n* geanmnachd *f*.

chat *v* dèan còmhradh.

chatter *v* dèan cabaireachd.

cheap *adj* saor; air bheag prìs.

cheapness *n* saoiread *m*.

cheat *n* mealltair *m*. • *v* dèan foill air.

check *n* casg *m*. • *v* caisg.

checkmate *n* tul-chasg *m*.

cheek *n* gruaidh *f*.

cheer *v* brosnaich.

cheese *n* càise *m*, càbag *f*.

chemical *adj* ceimiceach.

chemist *n* ceimicear *m*; neach-chungaidhean.

cheque *n* seic *f*.

cherry *n* sirist *f*.

chess *n* fidhcheall *m*.

chest *n* ciste *f*; cliabh *f*.

chew *v* cagainn.

chicken *n* isean *m*.

chief *n* ceann-feadhna *m*.

chilblain *n* cusp *f*.

child *n* leanabh *m*.

childhood *n* leanabas *m*.

childless *adj* gun sliochd.

children *n* clann *f*.

chill *v* fuaraich.

chilly *adj* fuar.

chimney *n* similear *m*.

chin *n* smig *m*.

China *n* An t-Sìn.

chocolate *n* teòclaid *f*.

choice *n* roghainn *m*.

choir *n* còisir-chiùil *f*.

choke *v* tachd.

choose *v* roghnaich.

chop *n* staoig. • *v* sgud.

chord *n* còrda *f*.

chorus *n* sèist *f*; co-sheirm *f*.

Christ *n* Crìosd *m*.

christen *v* baist.

Christmas *n* Nollaig *f*.

chronic *adj* leantalach.

chronicle *n* eachdhraidh *f*.

church *n* eaglais *f*.

churchyard *n* cladh *m*.

churlish *adj* mùgach.

cigarette *n* toitean *m*.

cinema *n* taigh-dhealbh *m*.

circle *n* cearcall; còmhlan *m*. • *v* cuairtich.

circuit *n* cuairt *f*.

circular *adj* cruinn.

circulate *v* cuir mun cuairt.

circumnavigate *v* seòl mun cuairt.

circumstance *n* cùis *f*.

circus *n* soircas *m*.

citizen *n* neach-àiteachaidh *m*.

city *n* cathair *f*.

civil *adj* sìobhalta.

civilian *n* sìobhaltair *m*.

civilisation *n* sìobhaltachd *f*.

civilise *v* sìobhail.

claim *n* tagairt *f*. • *v* tagair.

claimant *n* tagraiche *m*.

clan *n* fine *f*, cinneadh *m*.

clanship *n* cinneadas *m*.

clap *n* buille *f*. • *v* buail ri chèile.

claret *n* clàireat *f*.

clarify *v* soilleirich.

clash *v* dèan glagadaich.

clasp *n* dubhan *m*.

class *n* buidheann *f*, clas *m*. • *v* seòrsaich.

classical *adj* clasaigeach.

classify *v* seòrsaich.

claw *n* iongna *f*.

clay *n* crèadh *f*.

claymore *n* claideamh-mòr *m*.

clean *adj* glan. • *v* glan.

cleanness *n* gloinead *m*.

clear *adj* soilleir. • *v* soilleirich.

cleft *n* sgoltadh *m*.

cleg *n* crèithleag *f*.

clench *v* dùin.

clergy *n* clèir *f*.

clergyman *n* pears-eaglais *m*.

clever *adj* tapaidh.

click *v* cnag.

clientèle *n* luchd-dèilig *m*.

cliff *n* creag *f*, sgùrr *m*.

climate *n* clìomaid *f*.

climb *v* dìrich, streap.

climber *n* streapaiche *m*.

climbing *n* dìreadh *m*.

cling *v* slaod.

clinic *n* clionaic *f*.

clink *v* thoir gliong.

clip *v* geàrr.

clipper *n* gearradair *m*.

clock *n* uaireadair, cleoc *m*.

clod *n* ploc *m*.

clog *v* tromaich.

cloister *n* clabhstair *m*.

clone *n* lethbhreac ginteil *m*. • *v* mac-samhlaich.

close[1] *adj* (*near*) faisg; (*stuffy*) dùmhail. • *n* (*entry*) clobhsa *m*.

close[2] *v* dùin. • *n* dùnadh *m*.

clot *n* meall *m*.

cloth *n* aodach *m*.

clothe *v* còmhdaich.

clothes *npl* aodach, trusgan *m*.

cloud *n* neul *m*.

cloudy *adj* neulach.

clout, *n* (*cloth*) clùd *m*.

clover *n* clòbhar *m*.

clown *n* amadan *m*.

cloy *v* sàsaich.

club *n* (*stick*) cuaille, caman *m*.

cluck *v* dèan gogail.

clump *n* tom *m*.

clumsy *adj* cearbach.

cluster *n* bagaid *f*.

clutch *n* grèim *m*; (*car*) put. • *v* greimich.

coagulate *v* binndich.

coal *n* gual *m*.

coalesce *v* aonaich.

coarse adj garbh.

coast n oirthir f.

coastguard n freiceadan-oirthire m.

coastline n iomall-fairge m.

coat n còta m. • v cuir brat air.

coax v tàlaidh.

cobweb n eige f.

cockle n coilleag f.

cocksure adj coccanta, spairisteach.

cock n coileach m.

cod n trosg m.

code n riaghailt f.

co-education n co-fhoghlam m.

coerce v ceannsaich.

coeval adj co-aimsireach.

co-exist v bi beò le.

coffee n cofaidh m.

coffin n ciste-laighe f.

cog n fiacaill f.

cogent adj làidir.

cohabitation n co-fhuireachd f.

cohere v lean.

coherent adj so-leantainn.

coil n cuibhleachadh m. • v cuibhlich.

coin n bonn airgid m.

coinage n cùinneadh m.

coincide v co-thuit.

coincidence n co-thuiteamas m.

cold adj fuar. • n fuachd m; cnatan m.

coldness n fuairead m.

collaborate v co-oibrich.

collapse v tuit am broinn a chèile.

collapsible adj so-thuiteamach.

collar n coilear m.

collarbone n ugan m.

colleague n co-oibriche m.

collect v cruinnich.

collective adj co-choitcheann.

college n colaisde f.

collision n co-bhualadh m.

collusion n co-rùn m.

colonel n còirneal m.

colony n tìr-imrich f.

colour n dath m. • v dath.

column n colbh m.

coma n trom-neul m.

comb n cìr f. • v cìr.

combination n co-aontachadh m.

combine v co-aontaich.

come v thig; (imper) trobhad!

comedian n cleasaiche m.

comedy n cleas-chluich f.

comet n reul-chearbach f.

comfort n cofhurtachd f.

comfortable adj cofhurtail.

comic adj àbhachdach.

coming n teachd m.

comma n cromag f.

command n òrdugh m.

commemorate v cuimhnich.

commend v mol.

commendable adj ri a mholadh.

comment n facal m. • v thoir tarraing.

commerce n malairt f.

commercial adj malairteach.

commiserate v co-bhàidhich.

commission n ùghdarras m.

commit v earb; (crime, etc) ciontaich.

committee n comataidh f.

commodious adj luchdmhor.

commodity n badhar m.

common adj coitcheann.

Commonwealth n Co-fhlaitheas m.

communicate v com-pàirtich.

communication n com-pàirteachadh m; **communications** npl eadar-cheangal m.

community n pobal m.

commute v malairtich; triall.

compact *adj* teann.
compact disc *n* meanbh-chlàr *m*.
companion *n* companach *m*.
company *n* cuideachd *f*; companaidh *f*.
compare *v* coimeas.
compass *n* combaist *f*; meud *m*.
compassion *n* truas *m*.
compatible *adj* co-chòrdail.
compatriot *n* co-thìreach *m*.
compel *v* co-èignich.
compensate *v* diol.
compete *v* strì.
competition *n* co-fharpais *f*.
competitor *n* farpaiseach *m*.
complacent *adj* somalta.
complain *v* gearain.
complaint *n* gearan *m*; (*illness*) galar.
computer *n* coimpiutair *m*.
conjugate *v* co-naisg.
conjunction *n* naisgear *m*.
conjure *v* cuir impidh air.
connection *n* ceangal *m*.
connoisseur *n* neach-eòlach *m*.
conquer *v* ceannsaich.
conquest *n* buaidh *f*.
conscience *n* cogais *f*.
conscientious *adj* cogaisach.
conscious *adj* mothachail.
consciously *adv* le mothachadh.
consecrate *v* coisrig.
consecutive *adj* leanmhainneach.
consent *n* aonta *m*.
consent *v* aontaich.
consequence *n* toradh *m*.
consequently *adv* uime sin.
conservancy *n* glèidhteachas *m*.
conservation *n* glèidheadh *m*.
conserve *v* taisg.
consider *v* smaoinich.

considerable *adj* math, cudromach.
consideration *n* tuigse *f*.
consignment *n* lìbhrigeadh *m*.
consistency *n* seasmhachd *f*.
consolation *n* sòlas *m*.
console *v* furtaich.
consonant *n* co-fhoghar *m*.
consort *n* cèile *m*.
conspicuous *adj* faicsinneach.
conspire *v* dèan co-fheall.
constancy *n* neo-chaochlaideachd *f*.
constant *adj* daingeann.
constellation *n* reul-bhad *m*.
constipation *n* teannachadh-innidh *m*.
constituency *n* roinn-taghaidh *f*.
constitution *n* dèanamh, nàdar *m*; (*political*) bonn-stèidh *f*.
constriction *n* teannachadh *m*.
construct *v* tog.
construction *n* togail *f*.
consult *v* gabh comhairle.
consume *v* caith.
consumer *n* caitheadair *m*.
consummate *v* crìochnaich.
contact *v* (*physical*) suath ann; (*message*) cuir fios gu.
contain *v* cùm; caisg.
container *n* bocsa-stòraidh *m*.
contemplate *v* beachd-smuainich.
contemporary *adj* co-aoiseach.
contempt *n* tàir *f*.
contemptuous *adj* tarcaiseach.
content *adj* toilichte.
context *n* co-theacs *m*.
continent *n* mòr-thìr *f*.
contingent *adj* tuiteamach.
continual *adj* sìor.
continually *adv* gun sgur.
continue *v* lean air.
continuous *adj* leanailteach.

contour n (*map*) loidhne àirde f.

contraception n casg-gineamhainn m.

contract n cùnnnradh. • v teannaich; rèitich.

contraction n teannachadh m.

contradict v cuir an aghaidh.

contradiction n breugnachadh m.

contrary adj an aghaidh.

contrast v eadar-dhealaich.

contravene v bris.

contribute v cuir ri.

contribution n cuideachadh m.

contrivance n innleachd f.

control n smachd m.

control v ceannsaich; stiùir.

controversial adj connsachail.

controversy n connspaid f.

convalescence n iar-shlànachadh m.

convalescent adj iar-shlànach.

convener n fear-gairm m.

convenient adj goireasach.

convent n clochar m.

converge v co-aom.

conversation n còmhradh m.

converse v dèan còmhradh.

conversion n iompachadh m.

convert v iompaich.

convex adj os-chearclach.

conveyance n còir-sgrìobhte f.

conveyancer n sgriobhadair-chòirichean m.

convict n ciomach m. • v dearbh.

conviction n dìteadh m.

convivial adj cuideachdail.

convulsion n criothnachadh m.

cook n còcaire m. • v deasaich, bruich.

cooker n cucair m.

cookery n còcaireachd f.

cool v fuaraich.

cooperate v co-oibrich.

cope v dèan an gnothach.

copious adj pailt.

copper n copar m.

copulate v cuplaich.

copy n lethbhreac m. • v ath-sgrìobh.

copyright n dlighe-sgrìobhaidh.

coral n corail m.

cord n còrd m.

cordial adj càirdeil.

core n cridhe m.

cork n àrc f. • v cuir àrc ann.

corkscrew n sgriubha àrc m.

corn n coirce m.

corner n oisean f.

cornice n bàrr-mhaise m.

coronary adj coronach.

coronation n crùnadh m.

corpse n corp m.

corpuscle n corpag f.

correct adj ceart. • v ceartaich.

correspond v co-fhreagair.

correspondence n (*mail*) co-sgrìobhadh m.

corridor n trannsa f.

corrie n coire m.

corrode v meirgnich.

corrosion n meirg f.

corrugated adj preasach.

corrupt adj grod.

cosmetic n cungaidh maise f.

cosmopolitan n os-nàiseanta m.

cost n cosgais f. • v cosg.

costly adj cosgail.

costume n culaidh f.

cosy adj seasgair.

cottage n bothan m.

cotton n cotan m.

couch n uirigh f.

cough n casd m. • v dèan casd.

council n comhairle f.

councillor *n* comhairliche *m*.

count *v* cùnnt.

countenance *n* gnùis *f*.

counter *n* cuntair *m*.

counteract *v* cuir bacadh air.

counter-clockwise *adv* tuathal.

counterfeit *v* feall-chùinneach.

countersign *v* cuir ainm ri.

counting *n* cùnntas *m*.

countless *adj* do-àireamh.

country *n* dùthaich, tìr *m*.

countryman *n* fear-dùthcha *m*.

county *n* siorrachd *f*.

couple *n* càraid *f*.

couplet *n* rann dà-shreathach *f*.

coupon *n* cùpon *m*.

courage *n* misneach *f*.

courageaous *adj* misneachail.

courier *n* teachdaire *m*.

course *n* slighe *m*.

court *n* cùirt *f*. • *v* dèan suirghe.

courtesy *n* modh *f*.

courthouse *n* taigh-cùirte *m*.

cousin *n* co-ogha *m*.

cove *n* bàgh, camas *m*.

cover *n* còmhdach, brat *m*. • *v* còmhdaich.

cow *n* bò *f*.

coward *n* gealtaire *m*.

cowardice *n* geilt *f*.

cowherd *n* buachaille *m*.

coy *adj* nàrach.

crab *n* partan *m*, crùbag *f*.

crack *n* sgàinneadh *m*. • *v* sgàin.

cradle *n* creathail *f*.

craft *n* cèaird *m*; (*cunning*) seòltachd *f*; (*vessel*) bàta *m*.

craftsman *n* neach-ceàirde *m*.

crag *n* creag *f*.

cram *v* dìnn.

crane *n* crann *m*.

crannog *n* crannag *f*.

cranny *n* cùil *f*.

crash *v* co-bhuail.

craving *n* miann *m/f*.

crawl *v* snàig.

crazy *adj* às a chiall.

creak *v* dèan dìosgan.

cream *n* uachdar *m*.

crease *n* filleadh *m*.

create *v* cruthaich.

creation *n* cruthachadh *m*.

creature *n* creutair *m*.

credible *adj* creideasach.

crèche *n* ionad-latha leanaban *m*.

credit *n* creideas *m*. • *v* creid.

credit card *n* cairt-iasaid *f*.

creditor *n* creideasaiche *m*.

creed *n* creud *f*.

creel *n* cliabh *m*.

cremate *v* loisg.

crest *n* cìrean *m*.

crew *n* sgioba *m/f*.

crime *n* eucoir *f*.

criminal *adj* eucoireach. • *n* eucoireach *m*.

crimson *adj* crò-dhearg.

cringe *v* crùb.

cripple *n* crioplach *m*.

crisis *n* gàbhadh *m*.

crisp *adj* brisg; fionnar.

criterion *n* slat-tomhais *m*.

critic *n* sgrùdair *m*.

critical *adj* breitheach.

criticise *v* dèan sgrùdadh.

criticism *n* breithneachadh *m*.

croak *v* dèan gràgail.

crockery *npl* soitheachan-crèadha.

croft *n* croit *f*.

crofter *n* croitear *m*.

crook *n* cromag *f*; (*person*) cruc *m*.

crooked *adj* cam, crom.

croon v crònaich.
crop n bàrr m. • v beàrr, buain.
cross adj crosta. • n crois f. • v rach tarsaing.
cross-breed n tar-sìolaich m.
cross-examine v ath-cheasnaich.
cross-roads n crois a' rathaid f.
crossword puzzle n tòimhseachan-tarsainn m.
crotch n gobhal m.
crotchet n (music) dubh-nota m.
crouch v crom.
crow n feannag f.
crowd n sluagh m. • v dòmhlaich.
crowdie n gruth m.
crown n crùn m. • v crùn.
crucible n soitheach-leaghaidh m.
cruciform adj crasgach.
crude adj amh.
cruel adj an-iochdmhor.
cruelty n an-iochdmhorachd m.
cruise n cùrsa mara m.
crumb n criomag f.
crumple v rocaich.
crush v pronn.
crust n plaosg m.
crutch n crasg f.
cry v èigh; guil.
cub n cuilean m.
cube n ciùb m.

cuckoo n cuach m.
cuff n bun-dùirn m.
culprit n ciontach m.
cultivate v àitich.
culture n saothrachadh m; (art) cultur m.
cup n cupan m.
cupboard n preas m.
cupidity n sannt f.
curable adj so-leigheas.
curb v bac.
curdle v binndich.
cure n leigheas m. • v leigheis.
curious adj ceasnachail.
curl n bachlag f. • v bachlaich.
curlew n guilbneach m.
currency n sgaoileadh m; airgead n
current adj gnàthaichte. • n sruth m
curse n mallachd f. • v mallaich.
curtain n cùrtair m.
curvature n caime f.
curve v crom.
cushion n pillean m.
custody n cùram m.
custom n àbhaist m.
customary adj àbhaisteach.
cut n gearradh m. • v geàrr.
cutlery n uidheam-ithe f.
cynical adj searbhasach.
cyst n ùthan m.

D

dabble v crath uisge air.
dad n dadaidh m.
daffodil n lus a' chrom-chinn m.
dagger n biodag f.
daily adj làitheil. • adv gach latha.
dainty adj mìn.
dairy n taigh-bainne m.

daisy n neòinean m.
dale n dail f.
dam n dàm m.
damage n dochann m. • v dochainn
damnable adj damaichte.
damnation n dìteadh m.
damp adj tais.

dampen v taisich.
dance n dannsa m. • v danns.
dandelion n beàrnan-brìde m.
dandle v luaisg.
danger n cunnart m.
dangerous adj cunnartach.
dappled adj ball-bhreac.
dare v gabh air.
daring adj neo-sgàthach.
dark adj dorch.
darken v dorchaich.
darkness n dorchadas m.
darling n annsachd, eudail f, luaidh m.
darn v càirich.
dash v spealg.
database n stòr-dàta m.
date n ceann-latha m; (fruit) deit f.
daub v smeur.
daughter n nighean f.
daughter-in-law n ban-chliamhainn f.
dawn n camhanach f.
day n latha m.
daylight n solas an latha m.
daze v cuir bho mhothachadh.
dazzle v deàrrs.
dead adj marbh.
deadlock n glasadh m.
deadly adj marbhtach.
deaf adj bodhar.
deafen v bodhair.
deafness n buidhre f
deal n cùnnradh m. • v dèilig.
dealer n malairtaiche m.
dealing n dèiligeadh m.
dear adj gaolach; (cost) daor.
dearness n (cost) daoire f.
dearth n gainne f.
death n bàs m.
debar v bac.

debase v truaill.
debate n deasbad m. • v deasbair.
debit n fiach-shuim f. • v cuir fiach-shuim.
debts npl fiachan.
decade n deichead m.
decadent adj air claonadh.
decant v taom.
decanter n searrag ghlainne f.
decay n crìonadh m. • v caith.
deceit n cealg f.
deceive v meall, breug.
December n An Dùbhlachd.
decency n beusachd f.
decent adj beusach.
deception n mealladh m.
decide v co-dhùin.
deciduous adj seargach.
decimal adj deicheach.
decision n breith f.
decisive adj cinnteach.
deck n bòrd-luinge m. • v sgiamh-aich.
declaration n dearbhadh m.
declare v cuir an cèill.
decompose v lobh.
decorate v sgeadaich.
decoration n sgeadachadh m.
decorous adj cubhaidh.
decrease n lùghdachadh m. • v lùghdaich.
decrepit adj breòite.
decry v càin.
dedicate v coisrig.
deduce v tuig.
deduct v beagaich.
deduction n beagachadh m.
deed n gnìomh m; (legal) gnìomhas m.
deep adj domhainn.
deepen v doimhnich.

deer n fiadh m.
deer-forest n frìth f.
deface v mill.
defamation n tuaileas m.
defame v cùl-chàin.
default n dearmad m.
defeat n call m. • v gabh air, faigh buaidh.
defect n easbhaidh f.
defective adj easbhaidheach.
defence n dìon m; leisgeul m.
defenceless adj gun dìon.
defend v dìon.
defensive adj dìona.
defer v cuir air dàil.
deference n ùmhlachd f.
deferment n dàil f.
defiance n dùlan m.
deficiency n dìth m.
deficit n easbhaidh f.
definable adj sònrachail.
define v sònraich.
definite adj comharraichte.
definition n comharrachadh m.
deflect v aom.
deform v cuir à cumadh.
deformity n mì-dhealbh m.
defraud v feallaich.
deft adj ealamh.
defy v thoir dùlan do.
degenerate v meath. • adj meath-aichte.
degrade v ìslich.
degree n inbhe f; (academic) ceum m; (temp) puing f.
deign v deònaich.
deity n diadhachd f.
dejected adj fo bhròn.
delay n maille f. • v cuir maille air.
delegate n neach-ionaid m.
delegation n luchd-tagraidh m.

delete v dubh às.
deliberate adj mall. • v meòraich.
delicacy n mìlseachd f.
delicate adj fìnealta.
delicious adj ana-bhlasta.
delight v toilich.
delightful adj aoibhneach.
delinquency n ciontachd f.
delinquent adj ciontach.
delirium n breisleach f.
deliver v saor; (baby) asaidich.
delivery n teàrnadh m; post m (baby) asaid m.
dell n lagan m.
deluge n tuile f.
demand n tagradh m. • v tagair.
demean v ìslich.
demented adj air bhoile.
dementia n seargadh-inntinn m.
demerit n lochd m.
democracy n sluagh-fhlaitheas m.
democrat n sluagh-fhlaithear m.
demolish v sgrios.
demon n deamhan m.
demonstrable adj so-dhearbhte.
demonstration n taisbeanadh m.
demote v thoir ceum a-nuas.
demur v cuir teagamh ann.
demure adj stuama.
den n saobhaidh m.
denial n àicheadh m.
denigrate v dèan dìmeas air.
dense adj tiugh; (mind) maol.
density n dlùths m.
dent v dèan lag ann.
dentist n fiaclaire m.
denture n deudach m.
denude v rùisg.
deny v àicheidh.
depart v imich.
department n roinn f.

departure n falbh m.

depend v (on) cuir earbsa ann.

dependence n eisimealachd f.

dependent adj eisimealach.

depict v dealbh.

deplorable adj truagh.

deplore v caoidh.

deportment n giùlan m.

depose v cuir às oifig.

deposit n tasgadh m. • v tasgaich.

depravity n truailleachd f.

depreciate v cuir an dìmeas.

depress v brùth sìos.

depressant n ìocshlaint-ìsleach-aidh f.

depression n ìsleachadh m.

deprive v toirt air falbh.

depth n doimhneachd f.

depute adj leas-. • v sònraich.

derelict adj trèigte.

deride v dèan fanaid air.

derision n fanaid f.

derivation n sìolachadh m.

derive v sìolaich.

descend v teirinn.

descent n teàrnadh m.

describe v thoir tuaraisgeul air.

description n tuaraisgeul m.

desert[1] n fàsach m/f.

desert[2] v trèig.

deserve v toill.

design n rùn m; (art) dealbh m.

design v rùnaich; deilbh.

designer n dealbhadair m.

desire n miann m. • v miannaich.

desist v stad.

desk n deasg m.

despair n eu-dòchas m. • v leig thairis dòchas.

desperate adj eu-dòchasach; damainnte.

despicable adj suarach.

despise v dèan tàir air.

despite prep a dh'aindeoin.

dessert n mìlsean m.

destiny n dàn m.

destitute adj falamh.

destroy v sgrios.

destruction n milleadh m.

detach v dealaich.

detail n mion-chùnntas m; mion-phuing f.

detain v cùm air ais.

detect v lorg.

detective n lorg-phoileas m.

determination n diongbhaltas m.

determine v cuir roimh.

determinism n cinnteachas m.

detest v fuathaich.

detestation n fuath m.

detonate v toirm-spreadh.

detour n bealach m.

detract v thoir air falbh.

detriment n dolaidh f

devalue v di-luachaich.

devastate v lèirsgrios.

devastation n lèirsgrios m.

develop v leasaich; fàs.

development n leasachadh m.

deviate v claon.

device n innleachd f.

devil n diabhal m.

devious adj seachranach.

devise v innlich.

devolution n sgaoileadh-cumhachd m.

devolve v thig fo chùram; (political) sgaoil cumhachd.

devotion n cràbhadh m; teas-ghràdh m.

devour v sluig.

dew n dealt m.

dexterity n deisealachd f.

diagnose v breithnich.

diagnosis n breithneachadh m.

diagonal adj trasdanach.

dial n aodann m. • v comharraich àireamh.

diameter n meadhan-thrasdan m.

diarrhoea n a' bhuinneach f.

dice npl dìsnean.

dictate v deachd.

dictionary n faclair m.

die v bàsaich.

diesel n dìosail m.

diet n riaghailt bidhe f.

differ v eadar-dhealaich.

difference n eadar-dhealachadh m.

different adj air leth.

differentiate v diofaraich.

difficult adj duilich.

difficulty n duilgheadas m.

dig v cladhaich.

digest v cnàmh.

digestible adj so-chnàmhta.

digit n meur f; (number) meur-àireamh f.

digital adj meurach.

dignified adj urramaichte.

dilate v leudaich.

dilemma n imcheist f.

diligent adj dìcheallach.

dilute v tanaich.

dim adj doilleir; (person) mall 'na intinn.

dimension n tomhas m.

diminish v lùghdaich.

dimple n tibhre m.

din n toirm f.

dine v gabh dìnnear.

dining-room n seòmar-bidhe m.

dinner n dìnnear f.

dinner-time n tràth-dìnneireach m.

dip n tumadh m. • v tum, bog.

diplomacy n seòltachd f.

dipsomania n miann-daoraich m/f.

direct adj dìreach. • v seòl.

direction n seòladh m; àird f.

direction-finder n àird-lorgair m.

directly adv air ball; dìreach.

director n stiùiriche m.

dirk n biodag f.

dirt n salchar m.

dirty adj salach.

disability n neo-chomas m.

disadvantage n mì-leas m.

disagree v rach an aghaidh.

disagreement n eas-aonta f.

disappear v rach à sealladh.

disappoint v meall.

disapprove v coirich.

disaster n mòr-thubaist f.

disbelieve v dì-chreid.

disc n clàr m.

discard v cuir dhe.

discerning adj tuigseach.

discharge n di-luchdachadh m. • v di-luchdaich; cuir à dreuchd.

disclaim v àicheidh.

disclose v foillsich.

discomfort n anshocair f.

disconnect v sgaoil.

disconsolate adj brònach.

discontented adj mì-thoilichte.

discord n mì-chòrdadh m; (mus) dì-chòrda m.

discount n lasachadh m. • v lasaich

discourage v mì-mhisnich.

discover v nochd; leig ris.

discovery n nochdadh m.

discrepancy n diofar m.

discretion n cùram m.

discriminate v (in favour of) gabl taobh; (against) rach an aghaidh.

discuss v deasbair.

discussion n deasbaireachd f.

disease n euslaint f.

disembark v cuir air tìr.

disengage v dealaich.

disentangle v fuasgail.

disfavour n mì-fhàbhar m.

disgrace n masladh m. • v maslaich.

disgraceful adj maslach.

disguise n breug-riochd m. • v cuir breug-riochd air.

disgust n gràin f.

disgusting adj gràineil.

dish n soitheach m.

dish-cloth n tubhailt-shoithichean f.

dishearten v mì-mhisnich.

dishonest adj mì-onorach.

dishonesty n mì-onair f.

dishwasher n nigheadair-shoithichean m.

disillusion n briseadh-dùil m.

disinclined adj neo-thoileach.

disinherit v buin còir bhreith o.

disinterested adj neo-fhèinchùiseach.

disjointed adj an-altaichte.

disk drive n clàr-inneal m.

disk n clàr m.

dislike v mì-thaitneamh.

dislodge v cuir à àite.

disloyal adj neo-dhìleas.

dismal adj dubhach.

dismay n uabhas m.

dismember v spion o chèile.

dismiss v cuir air falbh.

disobedience n eas-ùmhlachd f.

disobey v bi eas-umhail do.

disorder n mì-riaghailt f.

disown v na gabh ri.

disparity n neo-ionnanachd f.

dispel v fògair.

dispensation n riarachadh m.

dispense v riaraich.

dispersal n sgàpadh m.

displace v cuir à àite.

display n foillseachadh m. • v foillsich.

displease v mì-thoilich.

dispose v suidhich.

disprove v breugnaich.

disputatious adj connsachail.

dispute v connsaich.

disqualification n neo-iomchaidheachd f.

disqualify v dèan neo-iomchaidh.

disregard v dèan dìmeas air.

disrepair n droch-chàradh m.

disrespect n eas-urram m.

disrupt v bris, reub.

disruption n briseadh m.

dissatisfaction n mì-thoileachadh m.

dissatisfied adj mì-riaraichte.

dissect v sgrùd; geàrr suas.

dissertation n tràchd f.

disservice n droch-chomain f.

dissimilar adj eu-coltach.

dissipate v sgap.

dissociate v eadar-sgar.

dissolute adj drùiseil.

dissolve v leagh; fuasgail.

dissuade v comhairlich an aghaidh.

distance n astar m, fad m.

distant adj cèin.

distaste n droch-bhlas m.

distasteful adj neo-bhlasta.

distil v tarraing.

distiller n grùdaire m.

distillery n taigh-staile m.

distinct adj soilleir.

distinction n eadar-dhealachadh m; (merit) cliù m.

distinctive adj so-aithnichte.

distinguish v eadar-dhealaich.
distort v fiaraich.
distract v buair.
distress n àmghar m. • v sàraich.
distribute v roinn, compàirtich.
district n ceàrn m.
district nurse n banaltram sgìre f.
distrust v an-earbsa.
disturb v cuir dragh air.
disturbance n aimhreit f.
disunite v eadar-sgar.
disunity n eadar-sgaradh m.
disuse n mì-cleachdeach m.
ditch n clais f.
ditto adv an nì ceudna.
ditty n luinneag f.
dive v daoibhig.
diver n daoibhear m.
diverge v iomsgair.
diverse adj eugsamhail.
diversify v sgaoil.
diversion n claonadh m; (pastime) fearas-chuideachd f.
diversity n eugsamhlachd m.
divert v claon.
divide v roinn, pàirtich.
dividend n earrann f.
divination n fàistneachd f.
divine adj diadhaidh. • v dèan a-mach.
divisible adj so-roinnte.
division n roinn f.
divorce n dealachadh pòsaidh m. • v dealaich ri.
dizzy adj tuainealach.
do v dèan.
dock[1] n port m.
dock[2], **docken** n copag f.
dockyard n doca m.
doctor n lighiche, doctair m; (academic) ollamh m.

doctrine n teagasg m.
document n sgrìobhainn f.
documentary adj aithriseach.
dodge v seachainn.
doe n maoiseach f.
dog n cù m.
dogged adj doirbh, dùr.
dogmatic adj dìorrasach.
dole n dòil m.
dollar n dolair m.
domain n tighearnas m.
domestic adj teaghlachail.
domesticate v càllaich.
domicile n fàrdach f.
dominate v ceannsaich.
domineer v sàraich.
dominion n uachdranachd f.
donate v thoir tabhartas.
donor n tabhartaiche m.
doom n binn m. • v dìt.
doomsday n là-luain m.
door n doras m.
dope n druga, drugaichean f.
dose n tomhas m.
dot n puing f.
dotage n leanabachd na h-aoise f.
double adj dùbailte. • n dùbladh m. • v dùblaich.
double-bass n prò-bheus m.
doubt n teagamh m. • v cuir an teagamh.
doubtful adj teagmhach.
doubtless adv gun teagamh.
dough n taois f.
dour adj dùr.
down prep shìos, a-nuas.
downfall n tuiteam m.
downhill adv leis a' bhruthach.
downright adv air fad.
downstairs adv shìos staidhre.
downward adj le bruthach.

downwards *adv* sìos.

dowry *n* tochradh *m*.

doze *v* rach an clò-chadal.

dozen *n* dusan *m*.

drag *v* slaod.

drain *n* drèana *f*. • *v* sìolaidh.

drake *n* dràc *m*.

dram *n* drama *m*.

dramatist *n* dràmaire *m*.

draught *n* (*drink*) tarraing *f*; (*wind*) gaoth troimh tholl. *f*

draughts *n* dàmais *f*.

draughtsman *n* neach-tarraing *m*.

draw *v* tarraing; (*liquid*) deoghail; (*art*) dèan dealbh.

drawer *n* drabhair *m*.

drawing *n* dealbh *m*/*f*.

drawing-pin *n* tacaid *f*.

dread *n* oillt *f*. • *v* oilltich.

dreadful *adj* eagalach.

dream *n* aisling *f*. • *v* bruadair, faic aisling.

dreamer *n* aislingiche *m*.

dredge *v* glan grùnnd.

dregs *npl* druaip *f*.

drench *v* dèan bog-fliuch.

dress *v* cuir aodach air.

dresser *n* dreasair *m*.

dressing *n* ìoc-chòmhdach *m*.

dribble *v* sil; (*sport*) drioblaig.

drift *v* siab.

drill *v* drilich.

drilling platform *n* clàr-tollaidh *m*.

drink *n* deoch *f*. • *v* òl, gabh.

drinker *n* neach-òil *m*.

drip *v* snigh.

drive *v* greas; (*car*) stiùir.

drivel *n* briathran gòrach *mpl*, sgudal *m*.

driver *n* dràibhear *m*.

driving licence *n* cead-dràibhidh *m*.

drizzle *n* ciùthran *m*.

droll *adj* neònach; èibhinn.

drone *n* torman *m*; (*pipes*) dos *m*.

droop *v* searg.

drop *n* boinne *f*. • *v* leig às.

drought *n* turadh *m*.

drove *n* dròbh *m*.

drover *n* dròbhair *m*.

drown *v* bàth.

drowsy *adj* cadalach.

drudgery *n* dubh-chosnadh *m*.

drug addict *n* tràill-dhrugaichean *m*.

drug *n* droga *f*.

druggist *n* drugadair *m*.

druid *n* draoidh *m*.

druidism *n* draoidheachd *f*.

drum *n* druma *f*.

drum-major *n* màidseir-druma *m*.

drummer *n* drumair *m*.

drumstick *n* bioran-druma *m*.

drunk *adj* air misg.

drunkard *n* misgear *m*.

drunkenness *n* misg *f*.

dry *adj* tioram. • *v* tiormaich.

dub *v* dùblaich.

duck[1] *n* tunnag *f*.

duck[2] *v* tum; crùb.

dud *n* rud gun fheum *m*.

due *adj* dligheach.

duel *n* còmhrag-dithis *f*.

duet *n* òran-dithis *m*.

dull *adj* trom-inntinneach; tiugh.

dullness *n* truime *m*.

dulse *n* duileasg *m*.

duly *adv* gu riaghailteach.

dumb *adj* balbh.

dummy *n* fear-brèige *m*, breagag *f*.

dump *n* òcrach *m*. • *v* caith air falbh.

dumpling *n* turraisg *f*.

dunce *n* ùmaidh *m*.

dung n innear f.

dunghill n dùnan m.

duplicate n dùblachadh m.

duplicity n dùbailteachd f.

durable adj maireannach.

duration n fad m, rè f.

during prep rè.

dusk n duibhre f.

dusky adj ciar.

dust n dust, stùr m. • v glan stùrdhe.

dustbin n biona-stùir m.

Dutch adj Duitseach.

dutiful adj umhail.

duty n dleasdanas m; (customs) cìs-chusbainn f.

duty-free adj saor o chìs-chusbainn.

dwarf n troich m.

dwell v tuinich.

dwelling n fàrdach f.

dwindle v crìon.

dye n dath m. • v dath.

dyke n gàradh m.

dynamic adj fiùghantach.

dynamite n dineamait m.

dynasty n rìgh-shliochd m.

dyspepsia n an do-chnàmh m.

E

each adj gach, gach aon. • pron gach aon; an duine.

eager adj dealasach.

eagle n iolair f.

ear n cluas f.

earl n iarla m.

early adj tràth.

earn v coisinn.

earnest adj dùrachdach.

earphone n cluasan m.

earring n cluas-fhail f.

earth n talamh f.

earthenware n soitheach criadha m.

earthly adj talmhaidh.

earthworm n daolag f.

ease n fois f.

easel n dealbh-thaic f.

east n ear, an àirde an ear f.

Easter n Càisg f.

easterly adj an ear.

easy adj furasda.

eat v ith.

eatable adj so-ithte.

ebb n tràghadh m. • v tràigh.

eccentric adj iomrallach.

eccentricity n iomrallachd f.

echo n mac-talla m.

eclipse n dubhadh-grèine m; (lunar) dubhadh-gealaich m.

ecology n eag-eòlas m.

economics n eaconomachd m.

economise v caomhain.

economist n eaconomair m.

economy n eaconomaidh f; banas-taighe m.

ecstasy n àrd-èibhneas m.

ecstatic adj àrd-èibhneach.

ecumenical adj uil-eaglaiseil.

eddy n saobh-shruth m.

edge n oir, iomall m; faobhar m. • v dèan oir.

edgewise adv air oir.

edible adj so-ithte.

edict n reachd m.

edifice n aitreabh m.

edify v teagaisg.

Edinburgh *n* Dùn Èideann.
edit *v* deasaich.
edition *n* deasachadh *m*.
editor *n* deasaichear *m*.
educate *v* foghlaim.
education *n* foghlam *m*.
educational *adj* oideachail.
effect *n* buaidh *f*. • *v* thoir gu buil.
effective *adj* buadhach.
effeminate *adj* boireannta.
effervescent *adj* bruichneach.
efficacy *n* èifeachd *f*.
efficient *adj* èifeachdach.
effigy *n* ìomhaigh *f*.
effluent *n* sruthadh *m*.
effort *n* dìcheall *m*.
egg *n* ugh *m*.
egghead *n* eanchainn mhòr *m*.
egotism *n* fèin-spèis *f*.
Egypt *n* An Eiphit *f*.
eight *n* ochd.
eighteen *n* ochd deug.
eighth *adj* ochdamh.
eightsome *n* ochdnar *m*.
eightsome reel *n* ruidhle ochdnar *m*.
eighty *n* (*old system*) ceithir fichead; (*new system*) ochdad.
either *conj* **either . . . or . . .** an dara cuid . . . no . . . . • *adv* a bharrachd, nas motha.
ejaculate *v* cuir a-mach.
eject *v* tilg a-mach.
elaborate *adj* saothraichte.
elapse *v* rach seachad.
elastic *adj* sùbailte.
elate *v* tog suas.
elbow *n* uileann *f*.
elder *n* (*church*) eildear *m*; (*tree*) droman *m*. • *adj* nas sine.
elderly *adj* sean.
elect *v* tagh.

election *n* taghadh.
electioneering *n* taghadaireachd *f*.
elector *n* taghadair *m*.
electorate *n* luchd-taghaidh *m*.
electric *adj* dealain.
electricity *n* dealan *m*.
electrification *n* dealanachadh *m*.
electrocute *v* dealan-marbh.
electronic *adj* leactronach.
elegance *n* grinneas *m*.
elegant *adj* grinn.
elegiac *adj* caointeach.
elegy *n* tuireadh *m*.
element *n* dùil *f*.
elementary *adj* bun.
elephant *n* ailbhean *m*.
elevate *v* àrdaich.
eleven *n* aon deug.
eligible *adj* ion-roghnaidh.
eliminate *v* geàrr às.
elixir *n* ìocshlaint *f*.
elm *n* leamhan *m*.
elongate *v* fadaich.
elope *v* teich.
eloquence *n* deas-bhriathrachd *f*.
else *adj/adv* eile.
elude *v* seachainn.
elusive *adj* èalaidheach.
e-mail *n* post dealain *m*.
emancipate *v* saor.
embalm *v* spìosraich.
embargo *n* bacadh *m*.
embark *v* cuir air bòrd.
embarrass *v* cuir troimhe chèile.
embarrassment *n* beag-nàrachadh *m*.
embassy *n* tosgaireachd *f*.
ember *n* èibhleag *f*.
embezzle *v* dèan maoin-èalachadh.
emboss *v* gràbhail.
embrace *v* iath an glacaibh.

embroider v cuir obair-ghrèis air.
embryo n suth m.
emerald n smàrag f.
emerge v thig an uachdar.
emergency n bàlanaich m.
emigrant n eilthireach m.
emigrate v dèan eilthireachd.
eminent adj àrd.
emit v leig a-mach.
emotion n tòcadh m.
emotional adj tòcail.
emphasis n cudrom m.
emphatic adj làidir.
empire n ìompaireachd f.
empirical adj deuchainneach.
employ v fasdaich.
employee n neach-obrach m.
employer n fastaidhear m.
empty adj falamh.
emulation n strì f.
enable v dèan comasach.
enact v òrdaich.
enamel n cruan m.
enchant v cuir fo gheasaibh.
enchantment n draoidheachd f.
enclosure n crò m.
encourage v misnich.
encroach v thig a-steach.
encumbrance n uallach m.
end n deireadh m, crìoch f. • v cuir crìoch air.
endemic adj dùthchasach.
endless adj neo-chrìochnach.
endorse v cùl-sgrìobh.
endowment n bronnadh m.
enemy n nàmhaid m.
energetic adj brìoghmhor.
energy n brìogh f.
enforce v co-èignich.
engagement n gealladh-pòsaidh m.
engine n inneal m.

engineer n innleadair m. • v innlich.
England n Sasainn f.
English n Beurla f.
Englishman n Sasannach m.
enhance v meudaich.
enigma n dubhfhacal m.
enjoy v meal.
enlarge v meudaich.
enlighten v soillsich.
enlist v liostaig.
enormous adj uabhasach.
enough adv gu lèor.
enquire v feòraich.
enrage v feargaich.
ensue v lean.
ensure v dèan cinnteach.
enter v rach/thig a-steach.
enterprise n iomairt f.
enterprising adj ionnsaigheach.
entertainer n oirfideach m.
entertainment n aoigheachd f.
enthusiasm n dìoghras m.
entice v tàlaidh.
entire adj iomlan.
entirely adv gu lèir.
entitle v thoir còir.
entrance n dol a-steach m.
entreat v guidh.
entrepreneur n neach-tionnsgain m.
envelope n cèis f.
environment n comhearsnachd f; (ecology) àrainn-eachd f.
envy n farmad m.
ephemeral adj geàrr-shaoglach.
episode n tachartas m.
epitaph n leac-sgrìobhadh m.
epoch n tùs-aimsir f.
equal adj seise.
equalise v dèan co-ionann; (game) ruig an aon àireamh.
equation n co-ionannas m.

equator *n* meadhan-chearcall na talmhainn *m*.

equidistant *adj* co-fhad air falbh.

equinox *n* co-fhreagradh nan tràth *m*.

equip *v* uidheamaich.

equipment *n* uidheam *f*.

equipped *adj* uidheamaichte.

equity *n* ceartas *m*; (*fin*) stoc-roinn *f*.

equivalent *adj* co-ionann.

erase *v* dubh às.

erect *v* tog.

erection *n* togail *m*.

erode *v* meirg.

erotic *adj* drùis-mhiannach.

err *v* rach iomrall.

errand *n* gnothach *m*.

erratic *adj* iomrallach.

error *n* mearrachd *f*.

eruption *n* brùchdadh *m*.

escalator *n* streapadan *m*.

escape *n* èaladh *m*. • *v* teich.

esoteric *adj* às an rathad.

essay *n* aiste *f*.

essence *n* gnè *f*.

essential *adj* riatanach.

establish *v* suidhich.

estate *n* oighreachd *f*.

esteem *n* meas *m*.

estimate *v* meas.

estrange *v* dèan fuathach.

estuary *n* inbhir *m*.

eternal *adj* bith-bhuan.

eternity *n* sìorraidheachd *f*.

ethical *adj* modhannach.

ethnic *adj* cinnidheach.

eunuch *n* caillteanach *m*.

Europe *n* An Roinn Eòrpa *f*.

European *adj* Eòrpach.

evaporate *v* deataich.

even *adj* rèidh. • *adv* eadhon; fhèin.

evening *n* feasgar *m*.

event *n* tuiteamas *m*.

ever *adv* aig àm sam bith, idir.

evergreen *adj* sìor-uaine.

everlasting *adj* sìorraidh.

evermore *adv* gu bràth.

every *adj* gach, na h-uile.

everyday *adj* làitheil.

everyone *pron* gach duine.

everything *pron* gach nì.

evict *v* fuadaich.

eviction *n* fuadachadh *m*.

evidence *n* fianais *f*.

evident *adj* soilleir.

evil *adj* olc. • *n* olc *m*.

ewe *n* othaisg *f*.

exact *adj* pongail.

exact *v* buin.

exactly *adv* dìreach.

exaggerate *v* cuir am meud.

examination *n* ceasnachadh *m*.

examine *v* ceasnaich.

example *n* eisimpleir *m*.

excavate *v* cladhaich.

excavation *n* cladhach *m*.

exceed *v* rach thairis air.

exceedingly *adv* glè.

excel *v* thoir bàrr.

excellence *n* feabhas *m*.

excellent *adj* barrail.

except *v* fàg a-mach. • *prep* ach a-mhàin; **except for** saor o.

exceptional *adj* sònraichte.

exchange rate *n* luach-iomlaid *m*.

exchange *v* malairtich.

exchequer *n* stàitchiste *f*.

exciseman *n* gàidsear *m*.

excite *v* gluais.

excitement *n* brosnachadh *m*.

exclaim *v* glaodh.

exclamation mark *n* clisg-phuing *f*.

exclamation *n* glaodh *m*.

exclusive *adj* dlùth.

excrement *n* cac *m*.

excrete *v* cac.

excuse *n* leisgeul *m*. • *v* gabh leisgeul, math.

executive *n* neach-gnìomha *m*.

executor *n* neach-cùraim tiomnaidh *m*.

exercise *n* eacarsaich *f*. • *v* obraich, cleachd.

exertion *n* spàirn *f*.

exhaust *v* falmhaich.

exhaustion *n* traoghadh *m*.

exile *n* fògarrach *m*.

exist *v* bi, bi beò.

existence *n* bith *f*.

exit *n* dol a-mach *m*.

exonerate *v* fìreanaich.

exorbitant *adj* ana-cuimseach.

exotic *adj* coimheach.

expand *v* sgaoil.

expatriate *adj* às-dhùthchach.

expect *v* bi dùil aig.

expedient *adj* coltach.

expedite *v* luathaich.

expedition *n* turas *m*.

expeditious *adj* cabhagach.

expend *v* caith.

expenditure *n* caiteachas *m*.

expensive *adj* cosgail.

experience *n* cleachdadh *m*. • *v* mothaich.

experiment *n* deuchainn *f*.

expert *adj* ealanta. • *n* eòlaiche *m*.

expire *v* analaich; (*die*) bàsaich.

explain *v* mìnich.

explanation *n* mìneachadh *m*.

explicit *adj* fosgailte.

explode *v* spreadh.

exploit *n* euchd *m*. • *v* dèan feum de.

explore *v* rannsaich.

export *n* eas-tharraing *f*. • *v* cuir thairis.

expose *v* nochd.

exposure *n* nochdadh *m*.

express train *n* luath-thrèana.

express[1] *v* cuir an cèill.

express[2] *adj* luath.

expression *n* fiamh *m*.

exquisite *adj* òirdheirc.

extensive *adj* leathann.

exterior *n* taobh a-muigh *m*.

extinct *adj* bàthte.

extinguish *v* smàl.

extinguisher *n* smàladair *m*.

extra *adj* fìor, ro-. • *adv* a bharrachd.

extraordinary *adj* anabarrach.

extravagant *adj* ana-caiteach.

extreme *adj* fìor.

extricate *v* saor.

extrovert *n* duine fosgarra *m*.

exuberance *n* braise.

exuberant *adj* bras.

eye *n* sùil *f*. • *v* seall.

eyesight *n* fradharc *m*.

eyesore *n* cùis mhì-thlachd *f*.

eyrie *n* nead iolaire *m*.

F

fable *n* uirsgeul *m*.

fabric *n* aodach *m*; togalach *m*.

facade *n* aghaidh *f*.

face *n* aghaidh, gnùis *f*.

facet *n* taobh *m*.

facilitate *v* soirbhich.

facilities *npl* goireasan.

fact *n* beart *m*.

factor *n* seumarlan *m*.

factory *n* factaraidh *m*.

faculty *n* comas *m*; (*university*) dàmh *m*.

fad *n* àilleas *m*.

fade *v* searg.

fail *v* dìobair.

failure *n* fàilinn *f*.

faint *adj* fann. • *v* fannaich.

fair *n* fèill *f*.

fairly *adv* an ìre mhath.

fairness *n* maisealachd *f*.

fairway *n* prìomh-raon *m*.

fairy *adj* sìdh. • *n* sìdhiche *m*.

faith *n* creideamh *m*.

faithful *adj* dìleas.

fake *n* rud brèige *m*.

fall *n* tuiteam *m*. • *v* tuit.

fallacy *n* saobh-chiall *f*.

fallow *adj* bàn.

false *adj* meallta.

falsehood *n* breug *f*.

falter *v* lagaich.

fame *n* cliù *m*.

familiar *adj* càirdeil.

familiarise *v* gnàthaich.

family *n* teaghlach *m*.

famine *n* goirt *f*.

famous *adj* ainmeil.

fanatic *n* eudmhoraiche *m*.

fancy *adj* guanach. • *v* smaoinich.

fank *n* faing *f*.

fantastic *adj* ro-iongantach.

fantasy *n* sgeul guaineis *m*.

far *adj* fada, fad às. • *adv* fada, fas às.

fare *n* faradh *m*; biadh *m*.

farewell *n* soraidh *m*.

farm *n* baile-fearainn, tuathanas *m*.

farmer *n* tuathanach *m*.

fart *n* (*audible*) braidhm *m*; (*inaudible*) tùd *m*.

farther *adv* nas fhaide.

fascinate *v* cuir fo gheasaibh.

fascination *n* geasachd *f*.

fascism *n* faisisteachas *m*.

fashion *n* fasan *m*. • *v* cum.

fashionable *adj* fasanta.

fast *adj* luath; daingeann.

fast food *n* grad-bhiadh *m*.

fasten *v* ceangail.

fastidious *adj* àilleasach.

fat *adj* reamhar. • *n* reamhrachd *m*.

fatal *adj* marbhtach.

fate *n* dàn *m*.

father *n* athair *m*. • *v* bi mar athair.

father-in-law *n* athair-cèile *m*.

fatherly *adj* athaireil.

fathom *v* ruig air.

fatigue *n* sgìos *f*. • *v* sgìthich.

fatuous *adj* baoth.

fault *n* coire *f*.

faultless *adj* neo-chiontach.

faulty *adj* easbhaidheach.

favour *v* bi fàbharach.

favourite *n* annsachd *f*.
fawn *n* mang *f*.
fax *n* facs *m*.
fear *n* eagal *m*. • *v* gabh eagal.
fearful *adj* eagalach.
fearless *adj* gun eagal.
feast *n* fèisd *f*, fleadh *m*.• *v* dèan fèist.
feat *n* euchd *m*.
feather *n* ite *f*.
February *n* An Gearran *m*.
federal *adj* feadarail.
fee *n* duais *f*.
feeble *adj* fann.
feed *v* biath.
feel *v* fairich.
feeling *n* faireachdainn *f*.
felicitous *adj* sona.
feline *adj* mar chat.
fellowship *n* companas *m*.
felon *n* slaoightear *m*.
female *adj* boireann, baineann.
feminine *adj* banail.
fence *n* lann. • *v* dùin.
fender *n* dìonadair *m*.
ferment *n* brachadh *m*. • *v* brach.
fermentation *n* brachadh *m*.
fern *n* raineach *f*.
ferret *n* feocallan *m*.
ferry *n* aiseag *m*. • *v* aisig.
ferry-boat *n* bàta-aiseig.
fertile *adj* torach.
fertilise *v* toraich.
fertility *n* torachas *m*.
fervent *adj* dian.
fervour *n* dèine *f*.
fester *v* at.
festive *adj* fleadhach.
fetch *v* faigh.
feu *n* gabhail *m*.
feud *n* falachd *f*.

fever *n* fiabhras *m*.
feverish *adj* fiabhrasach.
few *adj* beag, tearc. • *n* beagan *m*.
fibre *n* snàithleach *m*.
fibrous *adj* snàithlainneach.
fickle *adj* caochlaideach.
fiction *n* uirsgeul *m*.
fiddle *n* fidheall *f*. • *v* dèan fidhleir-eachd; foillich.
fiddler *n* fidhlear *m*.
fidelity *n* dìlseachd *f*.
field *n* achadh *m*.
field-glasses *n* prosbaig *f*.
field-mouse *n* luch-fheòir *f*.
fierce *adj* garg.
fierceness *n* gairge *f*.
fiery *adj* teinnteach.
fifteen *n* còig deug *m*.
fifth *adj* còigeamh.
fiftieth *adj* leth-cheudamh; (*old system*) an dà fhiceadamh 's a deich; (*new system*) an caogad-amh.
fifty *n* leth-cheud; (*old system*) dà fhichead 's a deich; (*new system*) caogad.
fig *n* fiogais *f*.
fight *n* còmhrag *f*. • *v* còmhraig.
figure *n* dealbh *m*; figear *m*.
file *n* eighe *f*; (*documents*) còmh-lachadh *m*. • *v* lìomh; còmhlaich.
filial *adj* macail.
fill *v* lìon.
fillet *v* colpaich.
filly *n* loth *f*.
film-star *n* reul film *m*, reultag film *f*.
filter *n* sìolachan *m*. • *v* sìolaidh.
filth *n* salchar *m*.
filthy *adj* salach.
final *adj* deireannach.
finalise *v* thoir gu crìch.

finance *n* maoineachas *m*. • *v* maoinich.

financier *n* maoiniche *m*.

find *v* faigh, lorg.

fine[1] *adj* grinn.

fine[2] *n* ùnnlagh *m*. • *v* leag ùnnlagh.

finery *n* rìomhachas *m*.

finger *n* meur, corrag *f*.

fingernail *n* ìne *f*.

finish *n* crìoch *f*. • *v* crìochnaich.

fir *n* giuthas *m*.

fire *n* teine *m*. • *v* cuir 'na theine.

fire-arm *n* airm-theine *m*.

fire-escape *n* staidhre-èalaidh *f*.

fire-proof *adj* teine-dhìonach.

fireside *n* teallach *m*.

firewood *n* fiodh connaidh *m*.

firm[1] *adj* teann.

firm[2] *n* companaidh *f*.

first *adj* a' chiad. • *adv* (*time*) an toiseach; (*sequence*) air thoiseach.

first aid *n* ciad-fhuasgladh *m*.

first-born *n* ciad-ghin *m*.

firth *n* caol *m*.

fiscal *adj* fìoscail.

fish *n* iasg *m*. • *v* iasgaich.

fisher *n* iasgair *m*.

fishing *n* iasgaireachd *f*.

fishing rod *n* slat-iasgaich *f*.

fishing-line *n* driamlach *m*.

fishy *adj* mar iasg; neònach.

fist *n* dòrn *m*.

fit[1] *adj* freagarrach.

fit[2] *n* taom *m*.

five *adj/n* còig.

fix *v* dèan teann; suidhich.

fixture *n* rud socraichte *m*.

fizz *n* copraich *f*.

flabby *adj* plamach.

flag *n* bratach *f*.

flagrant *adj* follaiseach.

flagstone *n* leac *f*.

flair *n* liut *m*.

flake *n* bleideag *f*.

flame *n* lasair *f*.

flannel *n* flannain *f*.

flap *n* cleitearnach *m*. • *v* crath.

flare *n* lasair-bhoillsg *m*.

flash *n* lasair *f*. • *v* boillsg.

flask *n* searrag *f*.

flat[1] *adj* còmhnard; (*mus*) maol, flat.

flat[2] *n* còmhnard *m*; flat *m*.

flatten *v* laigh ri; (*mus*) maolaich.

flatter *v* dèan sodal.

flattery *n* sodal *m*.

flautist *n* cuisleannach *m*.

flavour *n* blas *m*. • *v* blasaich.

flea *n* deargann *f*.

fleece *n* rùsg *m*. • *v* rùisg.

fleecy *adj* rùsgach.

fleet *n* cabhlach *m*.

fleeting *adj* siùbhlach.

flesh *n* feòil *f*.

fleshy *adj* sultmhor.

flex *n* fleisg *f*.

flexible *adj* so-lùbaidh.

flicker *v* priob.

flight *n* itealadh *m*.

flimsy *adj* tana.

flinch *v* clisich.

flint *n* ailbhinn *f*.

flippant *adj* beadaidh.

flit *v* èalaidh; (*house*) dèan imrich.

float *v* snàmh.

flock *n* treud *m*.

flood *n* tuil *f*. • *v* còmhdaich le uisge.

floodlight *n* tuil-sholas *m*.

floor *n* ùrlar *m*. • *v* cuir ùrlar ann.

floppy disk *n* clàr sùbailte *m*.

floral *adj* flùranach.

flounder *n* leòbag *f*.

flour *n* flùr *m*.

flourish *v* fàs gu math; beartaich.

flow *v* ruith.

flower *n* blàth, flùr *m*.

fluctuate *v* atharraich.

fluency *n* fileantachd *f*.

fluent *adj* fileanta.

fluid *adj* silteach. • *n* lionn *m*.

flush *v* fàs dearg; (*toilet*) sruth-laich.

fluster *v* cuir gu cabhaig.

flute *n* cuisle chiùil *f*.

fly[1] *n* cuileag *f*; (*fishing*) maghar *m*.

fly[2] *v* theirig air iteig.

fly[3] *adj* carach.

foal *n* searrach *m*.

foam *n* cop *m*. • *v* cuir cop dhe.

focus *n* cruinn-ionad *m*; fòcas *m*. • *v* faigh cruinn-shealladh.

fodder *n* fodar *m*.

foetus *n* toircheas *m*.

fog *n* ceò *m/f*.

foggy *adj* ceòthach.

foil *v* cuir casg air.

fold *n* buaile *f*. • *v* cuir an crò.

folded *adj* fillte.

foliage *n* duilleach *m*.

folk *n* muinntir *f*.

folklore *n* beul-aithris *f*.

folk-song *n* mith-òran *m*.

folk-tale *n* mith-sgeul.

follow *v* lean.

folly *n* amaideachd *m*.

fond *adj* dèidheil.

fondle *v* cniadaich.

food *n* biadh *m*.

fool *n* amadan *m*. • *v* thoir an car à.

foolish *adj* gòrach.

foolproof *adj* do-mhillte.

foot *n* cas, troigh *f*.

footpath *n* frith-rathad *m*.

footwear *n* caisbheart *f*.

for *prep* (*to*) do • *pron* **for me** dhomh; **for you** (*sing*) dhut; **for him, it** dhà; **for her** dhì; **for us** dhuinn; **for you** (*pl*) dhuibh; **for them** dhaibh; (*for the sake of*) airson • *pron* **for me** air mo shon; **for you** (*sing*) air do shon; **for him, it** air a shon; **for her** air a son; **for us** air ar son; **for you** (*pl*) air ur son; **for them** air an son; (*because*) a chionn; (*instead of*) an àite; (*on account of*) do bhrìgh.

forage *v* solair.

forbid *v* toirmisg.

forbidding *adj* gruamach.

force *n* neart *m*. • *v* co-èignich.

forceps *n* teanchair *m*.

ford *n* àth *m*.

fore *adj* toisich.

forearm *n* ruighe *f*.

forecast *n* ro-aithris *f*. • *v* ro-aithris.

forefather *n* sinnsear *m*.

forefinger *n* sgealbag *f*.

forego *v* fàg.

foreground *n* ro-ionad *m*.

forehead *n* bathais *m*.

foreign *adj* gallda, coimheach.

foreigner *n* Gall, coigreach *m*.

foreknow *v* ro-aithnich.

foreknowledge *n* ro-aithne *f*.

foremost *adj* prìomh.

forerunner *n* ro-ruithear *m*.

foresail *n* seòl-toisich *m*.

foresee *v* faic ro làimh.

foresight *n* ro-shealladh *m*.

forest *n* coille *f*.

forester *n* forsair *m*.

forestry *n* forsaireachd *f*.
foretaste *n* ro-bhlasad *m*.
foretell *v* ro-innis.
forever *adv* a chaoidh.
forewarn *v* cuir air earalas.
foreword *n* ro-ràdh *m*.
forge *v* dèan goibhneachd.
forger *n* fallsaidhear *m*.
forget *v* dìochuimhnich.
forgetful *adj* dìochuimhneach.
forgetfulness *n* dìochuimhne *f*.
forgive *v* thoir mathanas.
forgotten *adj* air dìochuimhne.
fork *n* greimire, forc *m*. • *v* fàs gòbh-lach.
forlorn *adj* aonaranach.
form *n* cumadh *m*. • *v* dealbh, cum.
formal *adj* dòigheil, foirmeil.
formality *n* deas-ghnàth *m*.
format *n* cruth *m*.
formidable *adj* cumhachdach.
formula *n* foirmle *f*.
formulate *v* riaghailich.
fornicate *v* dèan strìopachas.
fornication *n* strìopachas *f*.
forsake *v* cuir cùl ri.
forsaken *adj* trèigte.
fort *n* daingneach *f*, dùn *m*.
forth *adv* a-mach.
forthwith *adv* gun dàil.
fortitude *n* cruadal *m*.
fortnight *n* cola-deug *f*.
fortuitous *adj* tuiteamach.
fortunate *adj* fortanach.
fortune *n* sealbh *m*.
fortuneteller *n* fiosaiche *m*.
forty *adj/n* (*old system*) dà fhichead; (*new system*) ceathrad.
forward *adj* iarrtach. • *adv* air adhart.
forwards *adv* air adhart.

fossil *n* fosail *f*.
foster *v* altrum.
foster-father *n* oide *m*.
foster-mother *n* muime *f*.
foster-sibling *n* co-dhalta *m*.
foul[1] *adj* breun.
foul[2] *n* fealladh *m*.
found *v* stèidhich.
foundation *n* stèidh *f*.
founder[1] *n* stèidhichear *f*.
founder[2] *v* theirig fodha.
foundling *n* faodalach *m*.
fountain *n* fuaran *m*.
four *adj/n* ceithir; (*persons*) ceath-rar.
foursome *n* ceathrach *f*.
fourteen *adj/n* ceithir deug.
fourteenth *adj* ceathramh deug.
fourthly *adv* sa cheathramh àite.
fowl *n* eun *m*.
fox *n* sionnach *m*.
fraction *n* bloigh *f*.
fracture *n* bristeadh *m*.
fragile *adj* brisg.
fragment *n* fuigheall *m*.
fragrant *adj* cùbhraidh.
frail *adj* lag.
frailty *n* laige *f*.
frame *n* cèis *f*.
France *n* An Fhraing *f*.
frank *adj* faoilidh.
frank *v* (*stamp*) saor.
frantic *adj* air bhoile.
fraternal *adj* bràithreil.
fraud *n* foill *f*.
freak *n* tuiteamas *m*.
freckled *adj* breac-bhallach.
freckles *npl* breacadh-seunain *m*.
free *adj* saor; an-asgaidh.
free trade *n* saor-mhalairt *f*.
free will *n* saor-thoil *f*.

freedom *n* saorsa *f*.
freelance *adj* neo-cheangailte.
freemason *n* saor-chlachair *m*.
free-range *adj* saor-thogta.
freeze *v* reòth.
freezer *n* reòthadair *m*.
freight *n* luchd *m*.
French *adj* Frangach. • *n* Fraingis *f*.
frenzy *n* boile *f*.
frequency *n* tricead *m*.
frequent *adj* tric. • *v* tadhail.
fresh *adj* (*air*) fionnar; (*food*) ùr.
fret *v* luaisg.
fretful *adj* frionasach.
friar *n* bràthair-bochd *m*.
friction *n* suathadh *m*.
Friday *n* DihAoine *m*.
friend *n* caraid *m*, bana-charaid *f*.
friendliness *n* càirdeas *m*.
friendly *adj* càirdeil.
fright *n* eagal *m*.
frighten *v* cuir eagal air.
frightful *adj* oillteil.
frigid *adj* fuar.
frill *n* grinneas *m*.
frisky *adj* mireagach.
frivolity *n* faoineas *m*.
frivolous *adj* faoin.
fro *adv* air ais.
frock *n* froca *m*.
frog *n* losgann *m*.
from *prep* o • *pron* **from me** uam; **from you** (*sing*) uat; **from him, it** uaidhe; **from her** uaipe; **from us** uainn; **from you** (*pl*) uaibh; **from them** uapa; (*out of & from a place*) à • *pron* **from me** asam; **from you** (*sing*) asad; **from him, it** ás; **from her** aiste; **from us** asainn; **from you** (*pl*) asaibh; **from them** asta.

front *n* aghaidh *f*.
front-door *n* doras-mòr *m*.
frontier *n* crìoch *f*.
frost *n* reòthadh *m*.
frostbitten *adj* reo-sheargte.
frosty *adj* (*frozen*) reòta.
frown *n* gruaim *f*.
frugal *adj* glèidhteach.
frugality *n* glèidhteachd *f*.
fruit *n* meas *m*.
fruity *adj* measach.
frustrate *v* mill dùil.
fry *v* ròsd.
frying pan *n* aghann *f*.
fuck *v* rach air muin.
fuel *n* connadh *m*.
fugitive *n* fògarrach *m*.
fulfil *v* coilion.
fulfilment *n* coilionadh *m*.
full *adj* làn.
full stop *n* stad phuing *f*.
full-grown *adj* aig làn fhàs.
full-time *adj* làn-aimsireach.
fumble *v* làimhsich gu cearbach.
fun *n* spòrs *f*.
function key *n* (*comput*) iuchair gnìomha *f*.
function *n* dreuchd *f*.
fundamental *adj* bunaiteach.
funeral *n* adhlacadh *m*.
funny *adj* sùgach, èibhinn.
fur *n* bian *m*.
furnish *v* uidheamaich.
furniture *n* àirneis *f*.
furrow *n* clais *f*.
furry *adj* molach.
further, furthermore *adv* rud eile, a bhàrr air sinn.
fury *n* cuthach *m*.
fuse *n* leagadh *m*.
fusty *adj* malcaidh.

futile *adj* dìomhain.
futility *n* dìomhanas *m*.

future *adj* ri teachd. • *n* àm ri teachd *m*.

G

gable *n* stuadh *f*.
gadget *n* uidheam *f*.
Gael *n* Gàidheal *m*.
Gaelic *adj/n* Gàidhlig.
gaiety *n* cridhealas *m*.
gaily *adv* gu cridheil.
gain *v* buannaich.
gale *n* gaoth mhòr *f*.
gallant *adj* basdalach.
gallery *n* lobhta *m*.
galley *n* birlinn *f*.
gallon *n* galan *m*.
gallop *v* luath-mharcaidh.
Galloway *n* A' Ghall-Ghàidhealtachd *f*.
gallows *n* croich *f*.
galore *adv* gu lèor.
gamble *v* iomair air gheall.
gambler *n* ceàrraiche *m*.
gambling *n* ceàrrachas *m*.
game *n* cluiche *f*; (*meat*) sitheann *f*.
gamekeeper *n* geamair *m*.
gander *n* gànradh *m*.
gang *n* buidheann *f*.
gannet *n* sùlaire *m*.
gaol *n* prìosan *m*.
gap *n* beàrn *m*.
gape *v* spleuchd.
garage *n* garaids *f*.
garbage *n* fuighleach *m*.
garble *v* cuir às a riochd.
garden *n* lios *m*.
gardener *n* gàirnealair *m*.
garland *n* blàth-fhleasg *f*.
garlic *n* creamh *m*.

garment *n* bad aodaich *m*.
garron *n* gearran *m*.
garrulity *n* goileam *m*.
garrulous *adj* cabach.
garter *n* gartan *m*.
gas fire *n* teine gas *m*.
gas-cooker *n* cucair-gas *m*.
gash *n* gearradh *m*.
gasp *v* plosg.
gastronomic *adj* sòghail.
gastronomy *n* sòghalachd *f*.
gate *n* geata *m*.
gather *v* cruinnich.
gathering *n* cruinneachadh *m*.
gaudy *adj* basdalach.
gauge *n* tomhas *m*.
gaunt *adj* lom.
gawky *adj* sgleòideach.
gay *adj* sùnndach; (*sexuality*) co-sheòrsach.
gaze *v* dùr-amharc.
gear *n* (*car*) gèar *m*.
gem *n* seud *m*.
gender *n* gnè *f*.
genealogical *adj* sloinnnteachail.
genealogist *n* sloinntear *m*.
genealogy *n* sloinntearachd *f*.
general *adj* coitcheann.
generalise *v* ginearalaich.
generally *adv* am bitheantas.
generation *n* àl *m*; linn *m*.
generator *n* gineadair *m*.
generic *adj* gnèitheach.
generosity *n* fialaidheachd *m*.
generous *adj* fial.

genetic *adj* ginteil.

genial *adj* coibhneil.

genitals *npl* buill gineamhainn.

genius *n* sàr-ghin *m*.

genteel *adj* suairce.

gentle *adj* ciùin.

gentleman *n* duine uasal *m*.

gentlewoman *n* bean uasal *f*.

gentry *npl* uaislean.

genuine *adj* fìor.

geography *n* cruinn-eòlas *m*.

geological *adj* geòlach.

geologist *n* geòlaiche *m*.

geology *n* geòlas *m*.

geometry *n* geoimeatras *m*.

germ *n* bitheag *f*.

German *n* Gearmailteach *m*. • *adj* Gearmailteach.

Germany *n* A' Ghearmailt *f*.

germinate *v* ginidich.

gestation *n* torrachas *m*.

gesture *n* gluasad *m*.

get *v* faigh, coisinn.

ghastly *adj* oillteil.

ghost *n* taibhse *m/f*, bòcan *m*.

ghostly *adj* taibhseil.

giant *adj* ana-mhòr. • *n* famhair *m*.

gibber *v* dèan goileam.

gibe *n* sgeig *f*.

giddy *adj* guanach.

gift *n* tiodhlac *m*.

gifted *adj* tàlantach.

gigantic *adj* fuamhaireil.

gild *v* òraich.

gill *n* giùran *m*.

gin *n* sine *f*; (*trap*) ribe *f*.

gingerbread *n* aran-crì *m*.

gipsy *n* giofag *f*.

giraffe *n* sioraf *m*.

girdle *n* greideal *f*.

girl *n* caileag, nighean *f*.

girth *n* giort *f*.

give *v* thoir.

glaciation *n* eighreachadh *m*.

glacier *n* eighre-shruth *m*.

glad *adj* toilichte.

glance *n* grad-shealladh *m*. • *v* grad-amhairc.

gland *n* fàireag *f*.

glare *n* deàrrsadh *m*.

Glasgow *n* Glaschu *f*.

glass *n* glainne *f*.

glassy *adj* glainneach.

gleam *v* soillsich.

glean *v* dìoghlam.

glee *n* mire *f*.

glen *n* gleann *m*.

glib *adj* cabanta.

glide *v* gluais.

glimmer *n* fann-sholas *m*.

glister *v* deàrrs.

glitter *n* lainnir *f*.

gloaming *n* fionnaraigh *f*.

global *adj* domhanta.

global warming *n* blàthachadh na cruinne *m*.

globe *n* cruinne *f*.

gloom *n* duibhre *f*.

gloomy *adj* doilleir.

glory *n* glòir *f*.

glossy *adj* lìomharra.

glove *n* miotag *f*.

glow *n* luisne *f*. • *v* luisnich.

glower *v* seall fo na mùgan.

glue *n* glaodh *m*.

glum *adj* gruamach.

glutton *n* craosaire *m*.

gluttony *n* craos *m*.

gnash *v* gìosg.

gnaw *v* creim.

go *v* falbh, imich, theirich, rach, gabh.

goal *n* crìoch *f*; gòil *m*.

goalie *n* neach-bàire *m*.

goalpost *n* post-bàire *m*.

goat *n* gobhar *m*.

goblin *n* bòcan *m*.

god *n* dia *m*.

goddess *n* ban-dia *f*.

going *n* falbh *m*.

gold *n* òr *m*.

golden *adj* òir, òrach.

golf *n* goilf *m*.

good *adj* math, deagh.

goodbye *interj* mar sin leat; beannachd leat.

goodness *n* mathas *m*.

goods *npl* bathar *m*; (*possessions*) cuid *f*.

goodwill *n* gean math *m*.

goose *n* gèadh *f*.

gooseberry *n* gròiseid *f*.

gore *v* sàth.

gorge[1] *n* clais-mhòr *f*.

gorge[2] *v* lìon craos.

gorgeous *adj* greadhnach.

gorse *n* conasg *m*.

gory *adj* gaorrach.

gospel *n* soisgeul *m*.

gossip *n* goistidh *m*. • *v* bi a' gobaireachd.

govern *v* riaghail.

government *n* riaghaltas *m*.

gown *n* gùn *m*.

grab *v* gabh grèim air.

grace *n* gràs *m*; (*prayer*) altachadh *m*; (*manner*) loinn *m*. • *v* sgeadaich.

graceful *adj* maiseach.

grace-note *n* nota-altaidh *m*.

gracious *adj* gràsmhor.

grade *n* ceum *m*.

gradient *n* àrdachadh *m*.

gradual *adj* beag is beag.

gradually *adv* beag is beag.

graduate *n* ceumnaiche *m*.

graduation *n* ceumnachadh *m*.

graft *n* nòdachadh *m*. • *v* nòdaich; (*toil*) saothraich.

grain *n* gràinne *f*.

graip *n* gràpa *m*.

granary *n* sìol-lann *f*.

grand *adj* mòr, uasal.

grandchild *n* ogha *m*.

grandeur *n* mòrachd *f*.

grandfather *n* seanair *m*.

grandmother *n* seanmhair *f*.

granite *n* clach-ghràin *f*.

grant *n* tabhartas *m*.

granular *adj* cnapach.

grape *n* fìon-dearc *f*.

grapefruit *n* seadag *f*.

grapple *v* greimich.

grasp *n* grèim *m*. • *v* dèan grèim air, glac.

grass *n* feur *m*.

grassy *adj* feurach.

grate *n* cliath-theine *f*.

grate *v* sgrìob.

grateful *adj* taingeil.

grater *n* sgrìoban *m*.

gratitude *n* taingealachd *f*.

gratuity *n* tiodhlac *m*.

grave[1] *adj* stòlda.

grave[2] *n* uaigh *f*.

gravel *n* grinneal *m*.

gravestone *n* leac-uaghach *f*.

graveyard *n* cladh *m*.

gravity *n* iom-tharraing *f*.

graze[1] *v* (*browse*) feuraich.

graze[2] *v* (*scrape*) suath.

grease *n* saill *f*. • *v* crèisich.

greasy *adj* crèiseach.

great *adj* mòr; àrd.

greatness *n* mòrachd *f*.
Greece *n* A' Ghrèig *f*.
greed *n* sannt *m*.
greedy *adj* sanntach.
Greek *adj* Grèigeach. • *n* Grèigis *f*.
green *adj* uaine.
greenness *n* uainead *m*.
greet *v* fàiltich.
greeting *n* fàilte *f*.
gregarious *adj* greigheach.
grey *adj* glas, liath.
grey-haired *adj* liath.
grid *n* cliath *f*.
griddle *n* greideal *f*.
grief *n* mulad *m*.
grieve *v* cràidh.
grill *v* grìosaich.
grilse *n* bànag *f*.
grim *adj* gnù.
grimace *n* mùig *m*.
grin *n* braoisg *f*. • *v* cuir braosg air.
grind *v* meil.
gristle *n* maothan *m*.
grit *n* grian *m*.
grizzled *adj* grìsfhionn.
groan *n* cnead *m*. • *v* dèan cnead.
groceries *n* bathair grosaireach *m*.
groin *n* loch-bhlèin *f*.
groove *n* clais *f*.
grope *v* rùraich.
gross[1] *adj* dòmhail.
gross[2] *n* dà dhusan deug *m*.
grotesque *adj* mì-nàdurrach.
ground *n* grùnnd *m*. • *v* socraich.
group *n* còmhlan *m*.
grouse[1] *n* (*bird*) eun-fhraoich *m*.

grouse[2] *n* (*grumble*) gearan *m*.
grove *n* doire *m*.
grovel *v* snàig.
grow *v* fàs, meudaich.
growl *n* dranndan *m*. • *v* dèan dranndan.
growth *n* fàs *m*.
grudge *n* diomb *m*. • *v* talaich.
grumble *v* gearain.
grunt *n* gnòsail *f*. • *v* dèan gnòsail.
guarantee *n* barrantas *m*.
guard *n* faire *f*; (*individual*) freiceadan *m*. • *v* dìon.
guardian *n* (*tutor*) taoitear *m*.
guess *n* tomhas *m*. • *v* tomhais.
guest *n* aoigh *m*.
guide *n* treòraiche *m*. • *v* treòraich.
guided missile *n* urchair thrèoraichte *f*.
guillemot *n* eun dubh an sgadain *m*.
guilt *n* ciont *m*.
guilty *adj* ciontach.
gulf *n* camas *m*.
gully *n* gil *f*.
gulp *n* slugadh *m*. • *v* sluig.
gum *n* càireas.
gumption *n* ciall *f*.
gun *n* gunna *m*.
gunwale *n* beul-mòr *m*.
gurgle *n* glugan *m*.
gust *n* oiteag *f*.
gusto *n* cridhealas *m*.
gusty *adj* stoirmeil.
gut *n* caolan *m*.

H

habit *n* cleachdadh *m*; (*monk*) earradh *m*.

habitual *adj* gnàthach.

hack *v* geàrr.

haddock *n* adag *f*.

haft *n* cas *m*.

hag *n* cailleach *f*.

haggis *n* taigeis *f*.

haggle *v* dèan còmhstri mu phrìs.

hailstones *npl* clachan-meallain.

hair *n* falt *m*.

hairy *adj* molach.

half *n* leth *m*.

half-bottle *n* leth-bhotal *m*.

half-way *adj* leathach-slighe.

hall *n* talla *m/f*.

Hallowe'en *n* Oidhche Shamhna *f*.

hallucination *n* mearachadh *m*.

halo *n* fàinne-solais *f*.

halt *v* stad.

halter *n* aghastar *m*.

halve *v* roinn 'na dhà leth.

ham *n* hama *m*.

hamlet *n* clachan *m*.

hammer *n* òrd *m*. • *v* buail le òrd.

hamper[1] *n* bascaid bìdh *f*.

hamper[2] *v* bac.

hand *n* làmh, cròg *f*. • *v* sìn.

handbag *n* poca làimhe *m*.

handful *n* dòrlach *m*.

handicap *n* bacadh *m*.

handkerchief *n* neapaigear *f*.

handle *n* làmh, cas *f*. • *v* làimhsich.

handshake *n* crathadh làimhe *m*.

handsome *adj* eireachdail.

handwoven *adj* làmh-fhighte.

handy *adj* deas.

hang *v* croch.

hangover *n* ceann daoraich *m*.

happen *v* tachair.

happening *n* tachartas *m*.

happiness *n* sonas *m*.

happy *adj* sona.

harass *v* sàraich.

harbour *n* cala, acarsaid *m*. • *v* gabh ri.

hard *adj* cruaidh.

hard disk *n* clàr cruaidh *m*.

harden *v* cruadhaich.

hardihood *n* cruadal *m*.

hardly *adv* gann.

hardship *n* cruaidh-chàs *m*.

hardware *n* cruaidh-bhathar *m*; (*comput*) bathar-cruaidh *m*.

hare *n* maigheach *f*.

hare-brained *adj* gaoitheanach.

harm *n* cron *m*. • *v* dèan cron air.

harmful *adj* cronail.

harmless *adj* neo-chronail.

harmonic *adj* co-cheòlach.

harmonious *adj* co-chòrdach.

harmonise *v* ceòl-rèim.

harmony *n* co-sheirm *m*.

harp *n* clàrsach *f*.

harper *n* clàrsair *m*.

Harris *n* Na Hearadh.

Harris tweed *n* clò na Hearadh *m*.

harrow *v* cliath.

harsh *adj* garg.

harshness *n* gairge *f*.

hart *n* damh-fèidh *m*.

harvest *n* buain *f*.

haste *n* cabhag *f*.

hasten *v* greas.

hasty adj cabhagach.

hat n ad f.

hatch n gur m; (ship) saidse f.

hatchet n làmh-thuagh f.

hate n fuath m. • v fuathaich.

hateful adj fuathach.

haughty adj àrdanach.

haul v tarraing.

haunch n leis f.

haunt v tathaich.

hauteur n àrdan m.

have v bi aig; seilbhich; (eat, etc) gabh; (have to) feum.

hawk n seabhag m/f.

hawser n taod m.

hawthorn n sgitheach m.

hay n feur, feur caoin m.

haystack n goc, tudan m.

haze n ceò m.

hazy adj ceòthach.

he pron e, (emphatic) esan.

head n ceann m.

headache n cràdh-cinn m.

header n buille-cinn f.

headland n rubha m.

headlight n solas-mòr m.

headmaster n maighstir-sgoile m.

headmistress n bana-mhaighstir-sgoile f.

headquarters n prìomh-àras m.

headstrong adj ceann-làidir.

headway n adhartas m.

heady adj bras.

heal v leighis.

healer n slànaighear m.

health n slàinte f.

healthy adj slàn.

heap n tòrr m. • v cruach.

hear v cluinn, èisd.

hearer n neach-èisdeachd m.

hearing n claisneachd f.

hearing-aid n inneal-claistinn m.

hearsay n iomradh m.

hearse n carbad-mharbh m.

heart n cridhe m.

hearten v misnich.

hearth n teinntean m.

hearty adj sùnndach.

heat n teas m. • v teasaich.

heater n uidheam teasachaidh f.

heathen n pàganach m. • adj pàganach.

heather n fraoch m.

heathery adj fraochach.

heave n togail f. • v tarraing.

heaven n nèamh m.

heavenly adj nèamhaidh.

heaviness n truime f.

heavy adj trom.

Hebrides n Innse Gall.

heckle v tras-cheusnaich.

hedge n callaid f.

hedgehog n gràineag f.

heed n aire m. • v thoir aire.

heedful adj faicilleach.

heedless adj neo-aireach.

heel n sàil f.

heifer n agh f.

height n àirde f.

heighten v àrdaich.

heir n oighre m.

heiress n ban-oighre f.

helicopter n heileacoptar m.

hell n ifrinn f.

help n cuideachadh m. • v cuidich.

helpful adj cobhaireach.

hem n faitheam m.

hemisphere n leth-chruinne m.

hen n cearc f.

hence adv às a seo.

henceforth adv o seo a-mach.

her pron i, ise. • poss adj (with in-

alienables) a; (*with alieanables*)
... aice.

herald *n* teachdaire *m*.

herb *n* lus *m*.

herbal *adj* lusragach.

herd *n* treud, buar *m*. • *v*
buachaillich.

herdsman *n* buachaille *m*.

here *adv* (*with a noun*) seo;
(*location*) an-seo.

hereafter *n* an ath-shaogal *m*.

hereby *adv* le seo.

hereditary *adj* dùthchasach.

heredity *n* dùchas *m*.

heresy *n* saobh-chreideamh *m*.

heritage *n* oighreachd *f*.

hermit *n* aonaran *m*.

hero *n* curaidh, laoch *m*.

heroic *adj* gaisgeach.

heroine *n* bana-ghaisgeach *f*.

heron *n* corra-ghritheach *f*.

herring *n* sgadan *m*.

herring-gull *n* faoileag *f*.

herself *pron* ise, i fhèin.

hesitate *v* bi an imcheist.

hesitation *n* imcheist *f*.

hiccup *n* aileag *f*.

hide *v* ceil.

hideous *adj* gràineil.

hiding-place *n* àite-falaich *m*.

high *adj* àrd; mòr; urramach.

high tide *n* muir-làn *m/f*.

high-frequency *adj* àrd-tricead.

Highland *adj* Gàidhealach.

Highlander *n* Gàidheal *m*.

Highlands *n* A' Ghàidhealtachd *f*.

highlight *v* leig cudthrom air.

high-minded *adj* ard-intinneach.

high-powered *adj* mòr-chumhachd-ach.

highway *n* rathad-mòr *m*.

hike *v* gabh cas.

hill *n* cnoc *m*.

hillock *n* cnocan, sìthean *m*.

hillside *n* leathan *m*.

hilly *adj* cnocach.

hilt *n* dòrn *m*.

himself *pron* e fhèin.

hind *n* eilid *f*.

hinder *v* bac.

hinge *n* bann *m*.

hint *n* sanas *m*.

hip *n* cruachann *f*.

hire purchase *n* cìs-cheannach *m*.

hire *v* fasdaidh.

his *pron* a. • *poss adj* (*with inaliena-bles*) a; (*with alienables*) ... aige.

hiss *v* siosarnaich.

historian *n* eachdraiche *m*.

historical *adj* eachdraidheil.

history *n* eachdraidh *f*.

hit *n* buille *f*. • *v* buail.

hither *adv* an-seo.

hive *n* sgeap *f*.

hoard *n* ulaidh *f*. • *v* taisg.

hoar-frost *n* liath-reòthadh *m*.

hoarse *adj* tùchanach.

hoarseness *n* tùchadh *m*.

hobby *n* cur-seachad *m*.

hobnail *n* tacaid *f*.

hoe *n* todha *m*. • *v* todhaig.

Hogmanay *n* Callain, Oidhche
Challain *f*.

hold *v* cùm.

hole *n* toll *m*.

holiday *n* saor-latha *m*.

hollow *n* còs *m*.

hollowness *n* falamhachd *m*.

holly *n* cuileann *m*.

holy *adj* naomh.

homage *n* ùmhlachd *f*.

home *n* dachaigh *f*. • *adv* dhachaigh.

home rule *n* fèin-riaghladh *m*.
homesick *adj* cianalach.
homesickness *n* cianalas *m*.
homespun *adj* dachaigheil.
homosexual *adj* co-sheòrsach.
honest *adj* onarach.
honesty *n* onair *f*.
honey *n* mil *f*.
honeymoon *n* mìos nam pòg *f*.
honeysuckle *n* lus na meala *m*.
honour *n* onair *f*; urram *m*. • *v* onar-aich.
hood *n* cochall *m*.
hoof *n* iongna *f*.
hook *n* dubhan *m*.
hooked *adj* crom.
hooligan *n* ùpraidiche *m*.
hoot *v* goir.
hop *n* sinteag *f*. • *v* dèan sinteag.
hope *n* dòchas *m*. • *v* tha dùil aig.
hopeful *adj* dòchasach.
hopeless *adj* eu-dòchasach.
horizon *n* fàire *f*.
horizontal *adj* còmhnard.
horn *n* adharc *f*; (*musical instrument, drink*) còrn *m*.
hornet *n* connspeach *f*.
horoscope *n* reul-shealladh *m*.
horrible *adj* oillteil.
horrid *adj* dèisinnneach.
horror *n* uamhann *m*.
horse *n* each *m*.
horseman *n* marcaiche *m*.
horseshoe *n* crudha *m*.
hose *n* (*sock*) osan *m*; (*pipe*) pìob *f*.
hospitable *adj* fialaidh.
hospital *n* taigh-eiridinn *m*.
hospitality *n* aoigheachd *f*.
host *n* fear-taighe *m*; sluagh *m*.
hostage *n* bràigh *m*.
hostess *n* bean-taighe *f*.

hostile *adj* nàimhdeil.
hostility *n* nàimhdeas *m*.
hot *adj* teth.
hotel *n* taigh-òsda *m*.
hour *n* uair *f*.
hourly *adv* gach uair.
house *n* taigh *m*. • *v* thoir taigh do.
household *n* teaghlach *m*.
hover *v* fo-luaimnich.
how *adv* ciamar?; dè cho?
however *adv* co-dhiù.
howl *n* donnal *m*. • *v* dèan donnal.
huddle *v* còmhlaich.
hug *v* glac teann.
hull *n* cochall *m*.
hum *n* srann *f*. • *v* dèan torman.
human *adj* daonna.
humane *adj* caomh.
humanity *n* daonnachd *f*.
humankind *n* an cinne daonna *m*.
humble *adj* umhal. • *v* ùmhlaich.
humid *adj* tais.
humorist *n* neach-àbhachdais *m*.
humorous *adj* àbhachdach.
humour[1] *n* àbhachd *f*.
humour[2] *v* toilich.
hump *n* croit *f*.
hundred *adj/n* ceud.
hundredth *adj* ceudamh.
hunger *n* acras *m*.
hungry *adj* acrach.
hunt *n* sealg *m*. • *v* sealg.
hunter *n* sealgair *m*.
hurricane *n* doinnean *f*.
hurry *n* cabhag *f*. • *v* luathaich.
hurt *n* dochann *m*. • *v* goirtich.
hurtful *adj* cronail.
husband *n* an duine aig . . . ; fear pòsda *m*.
hush *v* sàmhaich.
hut *n* bothan *m*.

hybrid *n* cros-chineal *m*.
hydro-electric *adj* dealan-uisgeach.
hydro-electricity *n* dealan-uisge *m*.
hygiene *n* slàinteachas *m*.
hymn *n* laoidh *m*.

hypocrisy *n* breug-chràbhadh *m*.
hypocrite *n* breug-chràbaiche *m*.
hysterical *adj* lethtaobhail.
hysterics *npl* lethtaobhachd *f*.

I

I *pron* mi; (*emphatic*) mise.
ice *n* deigh *f*.
iceberg *n* cnoc-eighre *m*.
ice-cream *n* reòiteag *f*.
icicle *n* caisean-reòta *m*.
icing *n* còmhdach-siùcair *m*.
icy *adj* reòta.
idea *n* beachd-smuain *f*.
ideal *adj* sàr. • *n* sàr-beachd *m*.
identical *adj* ionann.
identification *n* aithneachadh *m*.
identify *v* dearbh-aithnich.
identity *n* dearbh-aithne *f*.
idiom *n* gnathas-cainnt *m*.
idiot *n* amadan *m*.
idle *adj* dìomhain.
idleness *n* dìomhanas *m*.
idler *n* leisgean *m*.
idol *n* iodhal *m*.
if *conj* ma (+ *present*/*future*); nan, nam (+ *past conditional*).
if not *conj* mur.
ignite *v* cuir teine ri.
ignition *n* adhnadh *m*.
ignominious *adj* nàr.
ignorance *n* aineolas *m*.
ignorant *adj* aineolach.
ignore *v* leig le.
ill *adj* tinn.
illegal *adj* neo-laghail.
illegality *n* mì-laghalachd *f*.
illegible *adj* do-leughte.

illegitimate *adj* dìolain.
ill-health *n* euslainte *f*.
illiterate *adj* neo-litireach.
illness *n* tinneas *m*.
illogical *adj* mì-reusanta.
illuminate *v* soilleirich.
illumination *n* soillseachadh *m*.
illusion *n* mealladh *m*.
illusory *adj* meallach.
illustrate *v* dealbhaich.
illustrator *n* dealbhadair *m*.
ilustrious *adj* ainmeil.
image *n* ìomhaigh *f*.
imaginable *adj* so-smuainich.
imaginary *adj* mac-meanmnach.
imagination *n* mac-meanmna *m*.
imagine *v* smaoinich.
imbecile *n* lethchiallach *m*.
imbibe *v* òl.
imbue *v* lìon.
imitate *v* dèan atharrais air.
imitation *n* atharrais *f*.
immaculate *adj* fìorghlan.
immaterial *adj* neo-chorporra; coma.
immature *adj* an-abaich.
immaturity *n* an-abaichead *m*.
immediate *adj* ciad.
immediately *adv* gun dàil.
immense *adj* an-mhòr.
immerse *v* cuir fodha.
immigrant *n* inn-imriche *m*.

immigration *n* inn-imrich *f*.

imminent *adj* gus teachd.

immodest *adj* mì-nàrach.

immoral *adj* mì-bheusach.

immorality *n* mì-bheus *f*.

immortal *adj* neo-bhàsmhor.

immortality *n* neo-bhàsmhorachd *f*.

immunise *v* dìon o ghalar.

immunity *n* saorsa *f*; dìon *m*.

imp *n* spruis.

impair *v* mill.

impalpable *adj* do-fhaireachdainn.

impart *v* com-pàirtich.

impartial *adj* ceart-bhreitheach.

impassable *adj* do-shiubhal.

impassive *adj* socair.

impatience *n* mì-fhoighidinn *f*.

impatient *adj* mì-fhoighidneach.

impede *v* bac.

impediment *n* bacadh *m*.

impel *v* greas.

impenetrable *adj* do-inntrig.

imperative *adj* òrduigheach.

imperceptible *adj* do-mhothaichte.

impersonal *adj* neo-phearsanta.

impersonate *v* pearsonaich.

impertinence *n* mì-mhodh *f*.

impertinent *adj* mì-mhodhail.

impervious *adj* do-ruighinn.

impetuous *adj* cas, bras.

impetus *n* dèine *f*.

impinge *v* buail.

implacable *adj* gamhlasach.

implement *n* inneal *m*.

implement *v* thoir gu buil.

implicate *v* cuir an sàs.

implication *n* ribeadh *m*.

implicit *adj* fillte.

implore *v* aslaich.

imply *v* ciallaich.

impolitic *adj* neo-sheòlta.

import *n* brìgh *f*; (*goods*) bathar o chèin *m*. • *v* thoir a-steach bathar.

importance *n* cudrom *m*.

important *adj* cudromach.

impose *v* cuir air.

impossibility *n* nì do-dhèanta *m*.

impossible *adj* do-dhèanta.

impostor *n* mealltair *m*.

impotence *n* eu-comas *m*.

impotent *adj* eu-comasach.

impoverish *v* dèan bochd.

impracticable *adj* do-dhèanta.

impregnable *adj* do-ionnsaighe.

impressive *adj* drùidhteach.

imprison *v* cuir am prìosan.

improbability *n* mì-choltas *m*.

improbable *adj* mì-choltach.

improper *adj* neo-iomchaidh.

improve *v* leasaich.

improvement *n* leasachadh *m*.

improvident *adj* neo-fhreasdalach.

imprudent *adj* neo-chùramach.

impudence *n* dànachd *f*.

impulsive *adj* spreigearra.

impure *adj* neoghlan.

impute *v* cuir às leth.

in *prep* an, ann an. • *pron* **in me** annam; **in you** (*sing*) annad; **in him, it** ann; **in her** innte; **in us** annainn; **in you** (*pl*) annaibh; **in them** annta. • *adv* ann; (*movement into*) a-steach (*inside location*) a-staigh.

inability *n* neo-chomas.

inaccurate *adj* neo-chruinn.

inadequate *adj* uireasach.

inadvertent *adj* neo-aireach.

inane *adj* faoin.

inarticulate *adj* gagach.

inasmuch as *conj* aig a' mheud 's a.

incarnate *adj* san fheòil.

incense¹ *n* tùis *f.*

incense² *v* feargaich.

incest *n* col *m.*

incestuous *adj* colach.

inch *n* òirleach *f.*

inclement *adj* an-iochdmhor.

inclination *n* aomadh *m.*

incline *v* aom.

include *v* cuir san àireamh.

incognito *adv* gu dìomhair.

income *n* teachd a-steach *m.*

income tax *n* cìs cosnaidh *f.*

incomparable *adj* gun choimeas.

incompatible *adj* neo-fhreagarrach.

incomplete *adj* neo-choileanta.

incomprehensible *adj* do-thuigsinn-
each.

inconvenience *n* neo-ghoireasachd
f.

inconvenient *adj* mì-ghoireasach.

incorrect *adj* mearachdach.

increase *n* meudachadh *m.* • *v*
meudaich; rach am meud.

incredible *adj* do-chreidsinneach.

incredulous *adj* às-creideach.

incriminate *v* ciontaich.

incubate *v* guir.

incur *v* bi buailteach do.

incurable *adj* do-leigheasach.

indebted *adj* an comain.

indecent *adj* mì-chuibheasach.

indeed *adv* gu dearbh.

indelible *adj* do-sgriosta.

indemnify *v* theirig an urras air.

indent *v* eagaich.

independence *n* neo-eisimeileachd
f.

independent *adj* neo-eisimeileach.

index *n* clàr-amais *m.* • *v* clàraich.

indicate *v* comharraich.

indifferent *adj* coma.

indigestion *n* cion-meirbhidh *m.*

indignant *adj* diombach.

indignation *n* diomb *m.*

indiscreet *adj* neo-chrìonna.

indiscretion *n* neo-chrìonnachd *f.*

individual *adj* air leth.

individual *n* urra *f.*

indoor *adj* (*location*) a-staigh.

indulge *v* leig le.

indulgent *adj* bàigheil.

industrial *adj* tionnsgalach.

industrious *adj* gnìomhach.

industry *n* (*abstract*) saothair *f;*
gnìomhachas *f.*

inedible *adj* do-ithe.

inept *adj* baoth.

inequality *n* neo-ionnanachd *f.*

inert *adj* marbhanta.

inexcusable *adj* neo-leisgeulach.

inexpensive *adj* saor.

inexperienced *adj* neo-eòlach.

inexplicable *adj* do-mhìneachaidh.

inextricable *adj* do-fhuasglaidh.

infallible *adj* do-mhearachdach.

infant *n* naoidhean *m.*

infantile *adj* leanabail.

infantry *n* cois-shluagh *m.*

infect *v* cuir galar air.

infection *n* galar-gabhail *m.*

inferior *adj* ìochdarach.

infertile *adj* mì-thorrach.

infest *v* claoidh.

infinitesimal *adj* beag bìodach.

infirm *adj* anfhann.

inflammable *adj* so-losgaidh.

inflate *v* sèid.

inflation *n* (*money*) at cùinnidh *m.*

inflict *v* leag peanas air.

influence *n* buaidh *f.* • *v* treòraich.

influenza *n* fliù *f.*

inform *v* innis.

informal adj neo-fhoirmeil.
information n fiosrachadh m.
information technology n teicneol-as-fiosrachaidh m.
infrequent adj ainmig.
infringe v bris.
ingenious adj innleachdach.
ingenuous adj fosgarra.
ingot n uinge f.
ingredient n tàthchuid f.
inhabit v àitich.
inhabitable adj so-àiteachaidh.
inhabitant n neach-àiteachaidh m.
inhale v tarraing anail.
inherit v faigh mar oighreachd.
inhibit v cùm air ais.
inhibition n urchall m.
inhospitable adj neo-fhialaidh.
inhuman adj mì-dhaonna.
initial adj ciad. • n ciad litir f.
inject v ann-steallaich.
injection n ann-stealladh m.
injure v ciùrr.
injurious adj cronail.
injury n ciùrradh m.
ink n dubh m.
inland adj a-staigh san tìr.
inlet n caolas m.
inn n taigh-òsda m.
innate adj dualach.
inner adj an taobh a-staigh.
innkeeper n òsdair m.
innocent adj neo-chiontach.
innovate v ùr-ghnàthaich.
innovation n ùr-ghnàthachadh m.
innovator n ùr-ghnàthadair m.
innuendo n fiar-shanas m.
inoculate v cuir a' bhreac air.
inquire v feòraich.
inquiry n ceasnachadh m.
inquisitive adj faighneachail.

insane adj air chuthach.
insanitary adj mì-shlàinteil.
insanity n cuthach m.
insect n meanbh-fhrìde f.
insecure adj neo-thèarainte.
inseparable adj do-sgairte.
insert v cuir a-steach.
in-shore adj cladaich.
inside prep am broinn. • adv air an taobh a-staigh.
insincere adj neo-onorach.
insipid adj neo-bhlasda.
insist v cùm air.
insolvency n briseadh-creidis m.
insolvent adj ann am briseadh-creidis.
insomnia n bacadh cadail m.
inspect v sgrùd.
inspection n sgrùdadh m.
instal v cuir an dreuchd.
instalment n earrann f.
instance n eisimpleir m.
instant adj grad. • n tiota m.
instead prep an àite. • adv an àite sin.
instil v teagaisg.
instinct n dùchas m.
instinctive adj dùchasach.
institute n stèidheachadh m.
institution n stèidheachadh m.
instrument n inneal m, beart f.
insular adj eileanach.
insulate v dealaich.
insult n tàmailt f. • v tàmailtich.
insurance n urras m.
insurance policy n poileasaidh àrachais m.
insure v faigh àrachas air.
intact adj slàn.
integrity n ionracas m.
intellect n inntinn f.

intellectual *adj* inntleachdail.

intelligence *n* tuigse *f*.

intelligible *adj* so-thuigsinneach.

intend *v* cuir roimhe.

intense *adj* teann.

intensify *v* teinnich.

intensity *n* dèine *f*.

intention *n* rùn *m*.

intentional *adj* a dh'aon rùn.

intercede *v* dèan eadar-ghuidhe.

intercept *v* ceap.

intercourse *n* co-chomann *m*; (*sexual*) co-ghineadh *m*.

nterest *n* ùidh *f*.

nteresting *adj* ùidheil.

nterfere *v* buin ri.

nternal *adj* san leth-a-staigh.

nternational *adj* eadar-nàiseanta.

nternet *n* eadar-lìon *m*.

nterpret *v* (*explain*) mìnich; (*translate*) eadar-theangaich còmradh.

nterpreter *n* neach-mìneachaidh ; (*translator*) eadar-theangadair còmhraidh *m*.

nterrupt *v* cuir casg air.

nterruption *n* casgadh *m*.

ntertwine *v* eadar-thoinn.

ntervene *v* thig eadar.

ntervention *n* eadar-ghabhail *m*.

nterview *n* agallamh *m*. • *v* agallaich.

ntestine *n* greallach *f*.

ntimacy *n* dlù-chaidreamh *m*.

ntimate *adj* dlù-chaidreach.

nto *adv* a-steach do; ann an.

ntonation *n* guth-cheòl *m*.

ntricate *adj* eadar-fhighte.

ntrigue *n* cluaineireachd *f*. • *v* dèan cluaineireachd.

ntrinsic *adj* gnèitheach.

ntroduce *v* cuir an aithne.

introduction *n* cur an aithne.

intrude *v* brùth a-steach.

intruder *n* bruthaiche-steach *m*.

intuition *n* imfhios *m*.

invalid[1] *adj* neo-bhrìgheach.

invalid[2] *adj* (*ill*) tinn. • *n* euslainteach *m*.

invariable *adj* neo-chaochlaideach.

invent *v* innlich.

invention *n* innleachd *f*.

inventor *n* tionnsgalair *m*.

inventory *n* cùnntas *m*.

Inverness *n* Inbhir Nis.

invert *v* cuir bun os cionn.

invest *v* èid; (*money*) cuir an seilbh.

invisible *adj* do-fhaicsinneach.

invitation *n* cuireadh *m*.

invite *v* iarr.

invoice *n* maoin-chlàr *m*.

involuntary *adj* neo-shaor-thoileach.

involve *v* gabh a-steach.

inward *adv* a-staigh.

inwards *adv* a-steach.

Ireland *n* Èirinn *f*.

Irish *adj* Èireannach.

irksome *adj* buaireasach.

iron *n* iarann *m*. • *adj* iarrain. • *v* iarnaich.

ironic *adj* ìoronta.

irony *n* ìoronas *m*.

irrational *adj* eu-cèillidh.

irregular *adj* mì-riaghailteach.

irrelevant *adj* nach buin ri.

irreverent *adj* eas-urramach.

irrigate *v* uisgich.

irrigation *n* uisgeachadh *m*.

irritable *adj* crosda.

irritation *n* frionas *m*.

island *n* eilean *m*.

islander *n* eileanach *m*.

Islay n Ìle f.

isolated adj air leth.

issue n ceist f; (descendants) sliochd m.

isthmus n aoidh f.

it pron e, (emphatic) esan; i, (emphatic) ise.

Italian adj Eadailteach.

Italy n An Eadailt f.

itch n tachas m.

itchy adj tachasach.

itinerary n cùrsa m.

its pron aige, aice.

itself pron e fhèin, i fhèin.

ivory n ìbhri f.

J

jab n briogadh m. • v briog.

jacket n seacaid f.

jacobite adj seumasach.

jagged adj eagaich.

jail n carcair m.

jam n silidh m; (traffic) dòmhlachd m.

jamb n ursainn f.

jangle v dèan gleadhraich.

janitor n dorsair m.

jar n sileagan m.

jargon n goileam m.

jaundice n a' bhuidheach f.

jaunt n cuairt f.

jaunty adj sgeilmeil.

jaw n giall f.

jawbone n peirceall m.

jealous adj eudmhor.

jealousy n eud m.

jeans npl dìnichean.

jeer v mag.

jelly n slaman-milis m.

jellyfish n muir-tiachd m.

jerkin n còta-geàrr m.

jersey n geansaidh m.

jest n abhcaid f.

jester n cleasaiche m.

jet plane n diet-itealan m.

jettison v tilg a-mach.

jetty n cidhe m.

jewel n seud m.

jib[1] n dioba f.

jib[2] v cuir stailc ann.

jig n port-cruinn m.

jilt v trèig.

job n car-oibre m.

jockey n marcach m.

jog v put; (run) dèan dabhdail.

join v ceangail.

joiner n saor m.

joinery n saorsinneachd m.

joint adj co-; co-cheangail. • n a m; (piece of meat) spòld m.

jointed adj altach.

jointly adv le chèile.

joke n fealla-dhà f.

jollity n cridhealas m.

jolly adj cridheil.

jolt n crathadh m. • v crath.

jostle v brùth.

jot n pong m.

journal n leabhar-latha; pàipea làitheil m.

journalism n naidheachdas m.

journalist n naidheachdair m.

journey n turas m, cuairt f.

jovial adj fonnmhor.

jowl n giall f.

joy n aoibhneas m.
joyful adj aoibhneach.
joyfully adv gu h-aoibhinn.
jubilant adj lùthghaireach.
jubilee n àrd-fhèill f.
judge n britheam m. • v thoir breith.
judgment n breitheanas m.
judicial adj dligheil.
judicious adj geur-chùiseach.
jug n siuga f.
juggle v dèan cleasachd.
jugular adj sgòrnanach.
juice n sùgh m.
juicy adj sùghmhor.
July n Iuchar m.
jump n leum m. • v leum.
jumper n leumadair m.

junction n ceangal m.
June n An t-Òg-mhìos m.
jungle n dlùth-fhàsach m.
junior adj às òige; (rank) iar-.
juniper n aiteann m.
junk n truilleis m.
junket, junketing n cuirm f.
juror n neach-diùraidh m/f.
just adj còir. • adv dìreach; (barely) air èiginn.
justice n còir f.
justifiable adj reusanta.
justification n fìrinneachadh m.
justify v fìrinnich.
jut v seas a-mach.
juvenile adj òganta.
juxtapose v chomhgharaich.

K

kail n càl m.
keel n druim m.
keen[1] adj geur.
keen[2] v caoin.
keenness n gèire f.
keep n daingneach f. • v cùm, glèidh.
keeping n glèidheadh m.
keepsake n cuimhneachan m.
kelp n ceilp f.
kennel n taigh-chon m.
kerb n cabhsair m.
kernel n eitean m.
kettle n coire m.
key n iuchair f; (mus) gleus f.
keyboard n meur-chlàr f.
keystone n clach-ghlasaidh f.
kick n breab m. • v breab.
kid n meann m.

kidnap v goid air falbh.
kidney n dubhag f.
kill v marbh.
killer n marbhaiche m.
kilogram n cileagram m.
kilometre n cileameatair m.
kilowatt n cileawatt m.
kilt n fèileadh, fèileadh beag m.
kin n cinneadh m.
kind[1] adj coibhneil.
kind[2] n gnè f.
kindle v las, fad.
kindly adj bàigheil.
kindred adj dàimheil.
kindred n muinntir f.
king n rìgh m.
kingdom n rìoghachd m.
kinsfolk npl luchd-dàimh.
kinsman n caraid m.

kinswoman *n* bana-charaid *f.*
kiosk *n* kiosk *f.*
kipper *n* ciopair *m.*
kiss *n* pòg *f.* • *v* pòg.
kit *n* trusgan *m.*
kitbag *n* màileid *f.*
kitchen *n* cidsin *m.*
kite *n* clamhan *m*; (*model*) iteileag *f.*
kitten *n* piseag *m.*
knack *n* liut *f.*
knapsack *n* aparsaig *f.*
knave *n* slaightear *m.*
knead *v* fuin.
knee *n* glùn *f.*
kneecap *n* failmean *m.*
kneel *v* sleuchd.
knickers *npl* drathars.

knife *n* sgian *f.*
knight *n* ridire *m.*
knighthood *n* ridireachd *m.*
knit *v* figh.
kniter *n* figheadair *m.*
knitting needle *n* bior-fighe *m.*
knob *n* cnap *m.*
knock *n* buille *f.* • *v* buail.
knoll *n* tolm *m.*
knot *n* snaidhm *m.* • *v* snaidhmich
knotted, knotty *adj* snaidhmeach.
know *v* aithnich; tuig; bi eòlach air.
knowing *adj* eòlach.
knowingly *adv* gu h-eòlach.
knowledgeable *adj* fiosrach.
knuckle *n* rùdan *m.*
kyle *n* caol *m.*

L

label *n* bileag *f.*
labial *adj* liopach.
laboratory *n* deuchainn-lann *f.*
laborious *adj* deacair.
labour *v* saothraich.
labourer *n* oibriche *m.*
labyrinth *n* ioma-shlighe *f.*
lace[1] *n* lios *f.*
lace[2] *n* barrall *f.* • *v* (*shoe, etc*) dùin.
lacerate *v* reub.
laceration *n* reubadh *m.*
lack *n* easbhaidh *f.* • *v* bi a dh'easbhaidh.
lad, laddie *n* gille *m.*
ladder *n* fàradh *m.*
ladle *n* liagh *f.*
lady *n* bean-uasal *f.*
ladybird *n* an daolag dhearg-bhreac *f.*

ladylike *adj* bainndidh.
lair *n* saobhaidh *f.*
laird *n* tighearna *m.*
lake *n* linn *f*, loch *m.*
lamb *n* uan *m*; (*roast*) uainfheòil *m*
lame *adj* bacach.
lameness *n* crùbaiche *f.*
lament *n* cumha *m.*
lament *v* caoidh.
lamentable *adj* tùrsach.
lamp *n* làmpa *m.*
lance *v* leig fuil.
lancet *n* lannsa *f.*
land *n* tìr, dùthaich *f.* • *v* rach a
tìr.
landholder *n* neach-fearainn *m.*
landing *n* ceann staidhre *m*; (*c*
aeroplane) laighe *m.*
landing strip *n* raon-laighe *m.*

landlady *n* bean an taighe *f*.

landlocked *adj* tìr-dhruidte.

landmark *n* comharradh *m*.

landscape *n* dealbh tìre *m*.

landslide *n* beum-slèibhe *m*.

landward *adv* gu tìr.

lane *n* lònaid *f*.

language *n* cànan *m*; (*speech*) cainnt *f*.

languish *v* fannaich.

lanky *adj* fada caol.

lantern *n* lanntair *m*.

lap[1] *n* uchd *m*.

lap[2] *v* sùgh.

lapel *n* liopaid *f*.

lapse *n* mearachd *f*. • *v* sleamhnaich.

lapwing *n* curracag *f*.

larceny *n* braide *f*.

larch *n* learag *f*.

lard *n* blonag *f*.

larder *n* preas-bìdh *m*.

large *adj* mòr.

lark *n* uiseag *f*.

lass, lassie *n* nighean *f*.

last[1] *adj* deireannach, mu dheireadh. • *adv* mu dheireadh.

last[2] *v* mair.

lasting *adj* maireannach.

late *adj* anmoch.

lately *adv* o chionn ghoirid.

lateness *n* fadalachd *m*.

latent *adj* dìomhair.

lather *n* cop *m*. • *v* dèan cop.

Latin *n* Laideann *f*.

latitude *n* leud *m*; (*line*) domhanleud *m*.

latter *adj* deireannach.

laugh *n* gàire *m*. • *v* dèan gàire.

laughter *n* gàireachdaich *f*.

launch *v* cuir air bhog.

laurel *n* labhras *m*.

lavatory *n* taigh-failcidh, taighbeag *m*.

lavish *adj* sgapach. • *v* sgap.

law *n* lagh, reachd *m*.

lawful *adj* laghail.

lawn *n* rèidhlean *m*.

law-suit *n* cùis lagha *f*.

lawyer *n* neach-lagha *m*.

laxative *n* purgaid *f*.

lay *v* càirich, cuir, leag sìos.

lay-by *n* far-rathad *m*.

layer *n* filleadh *m*.

layman *n* neo-chlèireach *m*.

laziness *n* leisge *f*.

lazy *adj* leisg.

lead[1] *n* luaidhe *m/f*.

lead[2] *n* (*dog*) iall *f*. • *v* treòraich.

leaden *adj* luaidhe.

leader *n* ceannard *m*.

leaf *n* duilleag *f*.

leafy *adj* duilleagach.

league *n* co-cheangal *m*; (*sport*) lìg *m*.

leak *v* leig a-steach.

leaky *adj* ao-dìonach.

lean[1] *adj* caol.

lean[2] *v* leig do thaic air.

leap *v* leum.

leap-year *n* bliadhna-leum *f*.

learn *v* ionnsaich.

learner *n* neach-ionnsachaidh *m*.

lease *n* lìos *m*.

least *adj* as lugha.

leather *n* leathar *m*.

leave *n* fòrladh *m*. • *v* fàg, trèig.

lecher *n* drùisire *m*.

lecherous *adj* drùiseil.

lecture *n* òraid *f*. • *v* teasgaig.

ledge *n* oir *m*.

ledger *n* leabhar-cùnntais *m*.

lee, lee-side n taobh an fhasgaidh m.
leech n deala f.
leek n cainneann m.
leet n (list) ciad-thaghadh m.
left hand n làmh chlì f.
left n an taobh ceàrr m.
left-handed adj ciotach.
leg n cas f.
legacy n dìleab f.
legalise v dèan laghail.
legend n fionnsgeul f.
legendary adj fionnsgeulach.
legibility n so-leughtachd f.
legible adj so-leughte.
legislate v dèan lagh.
legitimate adj dligheach.
leisure n suaimhneas m.
leisurely adj athaiseach.
lemon n liomaid f.
lend v thoir an iasad.
lender n iasadaiche m.
length n fad m.
lengthen v cuir am fad.
lengthwise adv air fhad.
lenient adj tròcaireach.
lenition n sèimheachadh m.
lens n lionsa f.
Lent n Carghas m.
leper n lobhar m.
leprechaun n luchraban m.
less adj nas lugha.
lessen v lùghdaich.
lesson n leasan m.
lest conj air eagal gu.
let[1] n bacadh m; (house) n gabhail f.
let[2] v leig; thoir air ghabhail.
lethal adj bàsmhor.
letter n litir f.
letter-box n bocsa-litrichean m.
lettuce n leiteis f.
level adj còmhnard.

level n còmhnard m. • v dèan còmh‐
  nard.
lever n luamhan m.
lewd adj draosda.
lewdness n draosdachd f.
Lewis n Leòdhas m.
liability n buailteachd f.
liable adj buailteach.
liar n breugaire m.
libel v dèan cliù-mhilleadh.
liberal adj pailt-làmhach.
Liberal n Libearaileach m.
librarian n leabharlannaiche m.
library n leabharlann f.
licence n cead m.
license v ceadaich.
lichen n crotal m.
lick v imlich.
lid n ceann m.
lie[1] n breug f. • v innis breug.
lie[2] v laigh.
life n beatha f.
lifeboat n bàta-teasairginn m.
lifeguard n freiceadan m.
lifestyle n seòl-beatha m.
lift n (elevator) àrdaichear m. • v tog
light[1] adj aotrom; suarach; guanach;
  soilleir.
light[2] n solas m. • v las.
lighten v deàlraich.
light-headed adj gog-cheannach.
lighthouse n taigh-solais m.
lightness n aotromachd f.
lightning n dealanach m.
like[1] adj coltach. • n samhail f.
like[2] v is toigh le.
liken v samhlaich.
likeness n coltas m.
likewise adv mar an ceudna.
limb n ball m.
lime n aol m; (fruit) n teile f.

lime tree n teile f.

limestone n aol-chlach f.

limit n crìoch m. • v cuir crìoch ri.

limited adj (*Ltd*) earranta (*Earr*).

limp[1] adj bog.

limp[2] n ceum m. • v bi crùbach.

limpet n bàirneach f.

linden tree n teile f.

line[1] n loidhne f; streath f.

line[2] v lìnig.

lineage n linn, sliochd m.

lineal adj dìreach.

linear adj streathach.

linen n anart m.

linger v gabh ùine.

linguist n cànanaich m.

link n tinne f. • v co-cheangail.

links npl machair goilf f.

linnet n gealbhonn-lìn m.

lion n leòmhann m.

lioness n ban-leòmhann f.

lip n bile f.

liquefy v leagh.

liquid adj lionnach. • n lionn m.

liquidate v glan air falbh.

lisp n liotachas m. • v bi liotach.

list n liosta f; (*items*) clàr-ainm f.
• v liostaig; cuir sìos.

listen v èisd.

listener n neach-èisdeachd m.

listless adj coma; gun smior.

literacy n litireachd f.

literal adj litireil.

literate adj litir-foghlaimte.

literature n litreachas m.

litre n liotair m.

litter n treamsgal m; (*young*) cuain
m. • v dèan treamsgal; beir.

little adj beag.

littoral n cladach m.

liturgy n ùrnaigh choitcheann f.

live[1] adj beò.

live[2] v bi beò.

livelihood n teachd-an-tìr m.

lively adj beòthail.

liver n adha m.

livid adj dùghorm.

lizard n laghairt m.

load n luchd m. • v luchdaich.

loaf n buileann f, lof m.

loan n iasad m.

loath adj aindeonach.

loathe v fuathaich.

loathing n gràin f.

loathsome adj gràineil.

lobster n giomach m.

lobster-pot n cliabh-ghiomach f.

local adj ionadail.

locality n àite m.

locate v (*situate*) cuir 'na àite.

loch n loch m.

lock[1] n glas f. • v glais.

lock[2] n (*hair*) dual m

locket n glasag-mhuineil f.

locksmith n gobha-ghlasan m.

lodge n taigh-gheata m. • v suidhich; gabh còmhnaidh.

lodger n lòisdear m.

loft n lobhta m.

log n sgonn m.

logic n loidig f.

logical adj loidigeach.

loiter v dèan màirneal.

loll v seas ri taic.

London n Lunnainn.

lone adj aonarach.

loneliness n aonaranachd f.

long ago adv o chionn fhada.

long[1] adj fada; buan.

long[2] v miannaich.

longevity n fad-shaoghalachd f.

longing n miann m.

longitude *n* domhan-fhad *m*.

long-suffering *adj* fad-fhulangach.

long-term *adj* fad-ùineach.

long-wave *adj* fad-thonnach.

long-winded *adj* fad-anaileach.

look *n* fiamh *m*; sùil *f*. • *v* seall, amhairc; look for sir.

looking-glass *n* sgàthan *m*.

loop *n* lùb *f*.

loophole *n* fosgladh *m*.

loose *adj* sgaoilte. • *v* fuasgail.

lop *v* sgath.

lop-sided *adj* leathoireach.

lord *n* tighearna, morair *m*.

lore *n* oilean *m*.

lorry *n* làraidh *f*.

lose *v* caill.

loser *n* neach a chaill *m*.

loss *n* call *m*.

lost *adj* air chall.

lotion *n* cungaidh *f*.

lottery *n* crannchur *m*.

loud *adj* labhar.

loudness *n* faram *m*.

loudspeaker *n* glaodhaire *m*.

lounge *n* seòmar-suidhe *m*. • *v* seàrr.

lour, lower *v* (*face*) bi an gruaim.

louse *n* mial *f*.

lousy *adj* mialach.

lout *n* burraidh *m*.

love *n* gaol, gràdh *m*.

lovely *adj* àlainn.

lover *n* leannan *m*.

lovesick *adj* tinn le gaol.

loving *adj* gràdhach.

low *adj* ìosal.

lower[1] *v* ìslich.

lower[2] *see* lour.

lowest *adj* as ìsle.

Lowland *adj* Gallda.

Lowlands *n* A' Ghalltachd *f*.

lowly *adj* iriosal.

loyal *adj* dìleas.

loyalty *n* dìlse *f*.

lubricate *v* lìomh.

lucid *adj* soilleir.

luck *n* fortan *m*.

lucky *adj* fortanach, buidhe.

lucrative *adj* buannachail.

ludicrous *adj* amaideach.

luggage *n* treallaich *f*.

lukewarm *adj* meadh-bhlàth.

lull *v* cuir a chadal.

lullaby *n* òran tàlaidh *m*.

luminous *adj* deàlrach.

lump *n* meall *m*.

lumpy *adj* meallanach.

lunacy *n* cuthach *m*.

lunar *adj* gealachail.

lunch *n* ruisean *m*.

lung *n* sgamhan *m*.

lurch[1] *n* sitheadh *m*.

lurch[2] *v* dèan sitheadh.

lure *n* mealladh *m*. • *v* meall, buair.

lurid *adj* cròn.

lurk *v* falaich.

luscious *adj* sòghmhor.

lust *n* ana-miann *m*.

lustre *n* deàlradh *m*.

lusty *adj* sultmhor.

luxuriant *adj* fàsmhor.

luxurious *adj* sòghail.

luxury *n* sògh *m*, *n* sòghalachd *f*.

lyre *n* cruit *f*.

lyric *n* liric *f*.

M

mace n cuaille-suaicheantais m.

machine n inneal m.

machinery n innealradh. m.

mackerel n rionnach m.

magazine n iris f.

magic adj draoidheil. • n draoidheachd f.

magician n draoidh m.

magistrate n bàillidh m.

magnet n clach-iùil f.

magnification n meudachadh m.

magnificence n greadhnachas m.

magnificent adj òirdheirc.

magnify v meudaich.

magnitude n meudachd m.

magpie n pioghaid f.

maid n maighdeann f.

mail n litrichean pl; post m. • v
seòl.

mail order n òrdugh-puist m.

main adj prìomh.

mainland n tìr-mòr m.

mainly adv anns a' mhòrchuid.

maintain v glèidh.

maintenance n glèidheadh m.

majestic adj flathail.

majesty n mòrachd f.

major adj as motha. • n màidsear m.

make v dèan, dealbh; **make to do**
thoir air; **make towards** dèan air.
• n dèanamh m.

maker n dealbhadair m.

make-up n rìomhadh m.

making n dèanamh m.

male adj fireannach. • n fireannach
m.

malevolence n gamhlas m.

malice n mì-rùn m.

malicious adj mì-rùnach.

malign v càin.

malignant adj millteach; (med)
ailseach.

mallet n fairche m.

malt n braich f.

maltster n brachadair m.

maltreat v droch ghrèid.

mam, mammy n mam, mamaidh f.

mammal n sineach m.

man n fear, duine m.

manage v stiùir.

manageable adj so-riaghlaidh.

management n riaghladh m.

manager n manaidsear m.

manageress n bana-mhanaidsear f.

mane n muing f.

manful adj duineil.

manger n prasach f.

mangle v reub.

manhood n fearalas m.

maniac n dearg amadan m.

manifest v taisbein.

manifestation n foillseachadh m.

manifesto n gairm-fhollaiseach f.

manipulate v oibrich.

mankind n cinne-daonna m.

manner n modh m/f.

mannerism n magaid f.

mannerly adj modhail.

manners npl modh m.

manse n mansa m.

mansion n taigh-mòr m.

mantelpiece n breus m.

manual adj làmhach. • n leabhar-
tuairisgeil m.

manufacture v saothraich.
manure n mathachadh m. • v mathaich.
manuscript n làmh-sgrìobhainn m.
many adj mòran; iomadh. • n mòran, tòrr m.
map, n map m.
mar v mill.
marble n màrmor m.
March n Am Màrt m.
march n màrsail f. • v dèan màrsail.
mare n làir f.
marijuana n a' bhang f.
marine adj mara.
mariner n maraiche m.
maritime adj fairgeach.
mark n comharradh m.
market n fèill f, margadh m/f.
marketable adj margail.
maroon v cuir air eilean uaigneach.
marquee n puball m.
marriage n pòsadh m.
marriageable adj so-phòsaidh.
married adj pòsda.
marry v pòs.
marshy adj bog, fèitheach.
marten n taghan m.
martial adj gaisgeanta.
martyr n martarach m.
marvel n iongnadh m. • v gabh iongnadh.
marvellous adj iongantach.
mascot n suaichnean m.
masculine adj fireannta.
mash v pronn.
mask n aghaidh-choimheach f.
mason n clachair m.
masonry n clachaireachd m.
mass n tomad m; meall m; (church) aifreann m.

massacre n casgradh m. • v casgair.
massage n suathadh m.
massive adj tomadach.
mast n crann m.
master n maighstir m.
masterly n ealanta m.
masterpiece n euchd m.
masturbate v brod.
mat n brat m.
match n lasadair m; seise m. • v freagair.
matchless adj gun choimeas.
mate n cèile m; (ship) meite m; (chess) clos m. • v cuir clos air.
material n stuth m.
maternal adj màithreil.
maternity n màthaireachd f.
mathematics n matamataig.
matins npl maidnean.
matrimony n dàimh-pòsaidh m/f.
matter n stuth m; brìgh f; gnothach m.
mattress n bobhstair m.
mature adj abaich.
maul v pronn.
mavis n smeòrach m.
maw n goile f.
maximum n cuid as motha f.
May n An Cèitean m.
may v faod.
May Day n Là Bealltainn.
maze n ioma-shlighe f.
me pron mi, mise.
meadow n lòn m.
meagre adv gann.
meagreness n gainne f.
meal n min f; (repast) biadh f.
mealy adj mar mhin.
mean[1] adj suarach.
mean[2] n cuibheasachd f.

mean³ *v* ciallaich.

meaning *n* ciall *f*.

means *npl* comas *m*; seilbhean *fpl*.

meantime *adv* an dràsda.

measles *n* a' ghriùthlach *f*.

measurable *adj* so-thomhaiste.

measure *v* tomhais. • *n* tomhas *m*.

measurement *n* tomhas *m*.

meat *n* feòil *f*.

mechanic *n* meacanaig *m*.

mechanism *n* meadhan *m*.

medal *n* bonn *m*.

meddle *v* buin ri.

mediate *v* rèitich.

mediation *n* eadraiginn *f*.

mediator *n* eadar-mheadhanair *m*.

medical *adj* lèigh.

medicinal *adj* ìocshlainteach.

medicine *n* (*science*) eòlas-leighis; (*medication*) ìocshlaint *m*.

medieval *adj* meadhan-aoiseil.

mediocre *adj* meadhanach.

meditate *v* beachd-smuainich.

meditation *n* beachd-smuaineach-adh *m*.

medium *n* meadhan *m*.

medium-wave *adj* meadhan-thonnach.

meek *adj* macanta.

meekness *n* macantas *m*.

meet *v* coinnich.

meeting *n* coinneachadh *m*; (*official*) coinneamh *f*.

megalith *n* tursa *m*.

melancholy *adj* dubhach.

melancholy *n* leann-dubh *m*.

mellifluous *adj* mealach.

mellow *adj* tlàth.

melodious *adj* fonnmhor.

melody *n* binneas *m*; fonn *m*.

melon *n* meal-bhucan *m*.

melt *v* leagh.

member *n* ball *m*.

member of parliament *n* ball-pàrlamaid *m*.

membership *n* ballrachd *f*.

memento *n* cuimhneachan *m*.

memoir *n* tràchdas *m*; beatha-aisneis *m*.

memorable *adj* ainmeil.

memorise *v* cùm air mheomhair.

memory *n* cuimhne *f*.

mend *v* càraich.

menstrual *adj* mìosach.

menstruation *n* fuil-mìos *f*.

mental *adj* inntinneil.

mention *v* ainmich.

menu *n* cairt-bìdh *f*.

merchant *n* ceannaiche *m*.

mercy *n* tròcair *m*.

mere *adj* a-mhain.

merely *adv* a-mhain.

merge *v* rach an aon.

merit *n* luach *m*.

mermaid *n* maighdeann-mhara *f*.

merriment *n* aighear *m*.

mess *n* truidhleis *f*.

message *n* teachdaireachd *f*.

messenger *n* teachdaire *m*.

metal *n* meatailt *f*.

metallic *adj* meatailteach.

meteor *n* dreag *f*.

meter *n* inneal-tomhais *m*.

method *n* dòigh *f*.

metre *n* meatair *m*; (*verse*) rannaigh-eachd *m*.

mettle *n* smioralachd *f*.

microbe *n* bitheag *f*.

microwave oven *n* àmhainn mheanbh-thonn *f*.

mid *adj* eadar-mheadhanach.

middle *n* meadhan *m*.

middle-aged *adj* leth-shean.
midge *n* meanbh-chuileag *f*.
midnight *n* meadhan-oidhche *m*.
midwife *n* bean-ghlùine *f*.
might *n* cumhachd *m*.
migrate *v* dèan imrich.
mild *adj* ciùin.
mile *n* mìle *f*.
military *adj* cogail.
milk *n* bainne *m*. • *v* bleoghain.
milky *adj* bainneach.
mill *n* muileann *m/f*.
millennium *n* am mìle-bliadhna *m*.
miller *n* muillear *m*.
million *n* millean *m*.
mime *n* mìm *f*.
mimicry *n* atharrais *f*.
mince *n* mions *m*.
Minch *n* An Cuan Sgìth.
mind *n* inntinn *f*.
mind *v* thoir an aire; cuimhnich.
mine[1] *n* mèinne *f*.
mine[2] *poss pron* (*with inalienables*) mo ... -sa; (*with alienables*) an ...agamsa.
mineral *adj* mèinneach. • *n* mèinn-earach *m*.
mingle *v* measgaich.
miniature *n* meanbh-dhealbh *m/f*.
minister *n* ministear *m*. • *v* fritheil.
minor *n* neach fo làn-aois *m*. • *adj* beag, as lugha.
minstrel *n* oirfideach *m*.
minus *prep* as aonais.
minute[1] *adj* meanbh.
minute[2] *n* mionaid *f*.
minx *n* aigeannach *f*.
miracle *n* mìorbhail *f*.
mirage *n* mearachadh-sùla *m*.
mirror *n* sgàthan *m*.
misapprehension *n* mì-thuigsinn *f*.

misbehaviour *n* droch-ghiùlan *m*.
miscarriage *n* asaid anabaich *f*.
mischief *n* aimhleas *m*.
mischievous *adj* aimhleasach.
misdeed *n* dò-bheart *f*.
miser *n* spìocaire *m*.
miserable *adj* truagh.
misinterpret *v* mì-bhreithnich.
misogyny *n* fuath-bhan *m*.
Miss *n* A' Maighdeann, A' Mh *f*.
miss *v* rach iomrall; ionndrainn.
missing *adj* a dhìth.
missionary *n* misionairidh *m*.
mist *n* ceò *m*.
mistake *v* mì-aithnich.
Mister *n* Maighstir, Mgr *m*.
mistletoe *n* uil-ìoc *m*.
mistress *n* bana-mhaighstir *f*; (*sexual*) coileapach *f*.
misty *adj* ceòthach.
misunderstand *v* mì-thuig.
mite *n* fineag *f*.
mix *v* measgaich.
mixture *n* measgachadh *m*.
moan *n* gearan *m*. • *v* gearain.
mob *n* gràisg *f*.
mobile phone *n* fòn-làimhe *f*.
mock *v* mag.
model *n* cumadh *m*. • *v* deilbh.
moderate *adj* stuama.
moderation *n* stuaim *m*.
modern *adj* ùr, nodha.
modernise *v* ùraich.
modest *adj* nàrach.
modesty *n* beusachd *f*.
moist *adj* tais, bog.
moisten *v* taisich.
mole[1] *n* famh *f*.
mole[2] (*spot*) ball-dòrain *m*.
molest *v* cuir dragh air.
mollify *v* maothaich.

mollusc n maorach m.

moment n tiota m.

momentary adj grad-ùineach.

momentous adj cudromach.

monarch n monarc m.

monastery n mannachain f.

Monday n DiLuain m.

money n airgead m.

monitor n foillsear m.

monk n manach m.

monkey n muncaidh m.

monopoly n lèir-shealbhachd f.

monotony n aon-ghuthachd f.

monster n uilebheist m.

month n mìos m.

monthly adj mìosach.

monument n carragh f.

mood n gleus m.

moody adj gruamach.

moon n gealach f.

moor[1] n mòinteach f.

moor[2] v tilg acair.

moral n beus f.

morale n misneach f.

morality n deagh bheusachd f.

more adv tuilleadh. • n tuilleadh m.

moreover adv a thuilleadh.

morning n madainn f.

mortal adj bàsmhor.

mosquito n còrr-mhial m.

moss n còinneach f.

most adj as motha. • n a' mhòr chuid m.

mostly adv mar as trice.

moth n leòman m.

mother n màthair f.

mother-in-law n màthair-chèile f.

motherly adj màithreil.

motion n gluasad m.

motive n adhbhar m.

motor n motair m.

motorist n motairiche m.

motto n facal-suaicheantais m.

mould n molldair m.

mouldy adv cloimh-liathach.

moult v tilg fionnadh.

mound n tom m.

mountain n beinn f, meall m.

mountaineer n streapaiche m.

mourn v caoidh.

mourning n bròn m.

mouse n luch f.

moustache n stais f.

mouth n beul m.

mouth-music n port-á-beul m.

mouthful n balgam m.

move v gluais; luaisg; imich.

mow v geàrr.

Mrs n A' Bhean, A' Bh f.

much adv mòran.

muck n salchar m.

mud n poll m.

muddle n troimhe-chèile f.

muddy adj eabarach.

mug n muga f.

Mull n Muile f.

multiple adj ioma-sheòrsach.

multiply v meudaich.

mumble v dèan brùnndail.

mumps n an tinneas-plocach m.

murder n mort m.

murderer n mortair m.

murmur n monmhor m.

muscle n fèith f.

museum n taigh-tasgaidh m.

mushroom n balgan-buachrach m.

music n ceòl m.

musical adj ceòlmhor.

musical instrument n inneal ciùil m.

mussel n feusgan m.

must v feum, 's èiginn, 's fheudar.

muster n cruinneachadh m.

mutation *n* mùthadh *m*.
mute *adj* balbh.
mutilate *v* ciorramaich.
mutiny *n* ceannairc *f*.
mutton *n* feòil caorach *f*.
mutual *adj* aontachail.
my *pron* (*with inalienables*) mo, m';
  (*with alienables*) . . . agam.

myself *pron* mi fhìn.
mysterious *adj* dìomhair.
mystery *n* dìomhaireachd *f*.
mystical *adj* fàidheanta.
myth *n* miotas *m*.
mythical *adj* miotasach.
mythology *n* miotas-eòlas *m*.

N

nag *v* dèan dranndan.
nail *n* tarrag *f*.
naive *adj* soineannta.
naked *adj* lomnochd.
name *n* ainm *m*. • *v* ainmich.
nap *n* dùsal *m*.
narrate *v* aithris.
narrative *n* aithris *m*.
narrow *adj* cumhang.
nasal *adj* srònach.
nasty *adj* truaillidh.
nation *n* nàisean *m*.
national *adj* nàiseanta.
nationalism *n* nàiseantachd *f*.
nationalist *n* nàiseantach *m*.
nationality *n* nàiseantachd *m*.
native *adj* dùthchasach. • *n* dùthchasach *m*.
natural *adj* nàdarrach.
nature *n* nàdar *m*.
naughty *adj* dona.
nausea *n* dèistinn *f*.
nauseous *adj* sgreamhail.
nautical *adj* seòlaidh.
navel *n* imleag *f*.
neap-tide *n* conntraigh *f*.
near *adj* faisg.
nearly *adv* faisg air. • *adv* (*conj*) cha mhòr (nach).

near-sighted *adj* geàrr-fhradharcach.
neat *adj* grinn.
necessary *adj* riatanach.
necessity *n* èiginn; aimbeart *f*.
neck *n* amhach *f*.
need *n* feum *m*. • *v* feum.
needle *n* snàthad *f*.
needy *adj* feumach.
negative *adj* àicheanach.
neglect *v* dèan dearmad.
negligent *adj* dearmadach.
negotiate *v* dèan gnothach ri.
neighbour *n* nàbaidh *m*.
neither *adv/conj/pron* cha mhò.
nephew *n* mac-peathar *m*.
nerve *n* fèith-mhothachaidh *f*;
  (*cheek*) aghaidh *f*.
nest *n* nead *m*.
net *n* lìon *m*.
Netherlands *n* An Òlaind *f*.
nettle *n* deanntag *f*.
neutral *adj* neo-phàirteil.
never *adv* a chaoidh, gu brath.
nevertheless *adv* gidheadh.
new *adj* ùr, nuadh.
New Year *n* A' Bhliadhna Ùr *f*.
news *n* naidheachd *f*.
next *adj* an ath . . . .

nice *adj* gasta.

niche *n* oisinn *f*.

nickname *n* farainm *m*.

niece *n* nighean-peathar *f*.

night *n* oidhche *f*.

nightingale *n* spideag *f*.

nil *n* neoni *m*.

nine *adj/n* naoi; (*persons*) naonar.

nineteen *adj* naoi deug.

ninety *adj* (*old system*) ceithir fichead 's a deich; (*new system*) naochad.

ninth *adj* naoidheamh.

nip *n* teumadh *m*; (*whisky*) tè bheag *m*.

nipple *n* sine *f*.

noble *adj* uasal, flathail.

nod *n* cromadh *m*.

noise *n* fuaim *m*.

noisy *adj* fuaimneach.

nominate *v* ainmich.

nonconformity *n* neo-aontachd *f*.

nonsense *n* amaideas *m*.

non-stop *adj* gun stad.

noon *n* meadhan-latha *m*.

nor *conj* no, nas mò.

normal *adj* gnàthach.

normally *adv* an cumantas.

north *adj* tuath. • *n* tuath *m*, an àirde tuath *f*.

northeast *n* ear-thuath *m*.

northern *adj* tuathach.

northwest *n* iar-thuath *m*.

nose *n* sròn *f*.

note *n* nota *f*. • *v* thoir fa-near.

notebook *n* leabhar-notaichean *m*.

nothing *n* neoni *m*.

notice *n* sanas, fios *m*. • *v* thoir fa-near.

notify *v* thoir fios do.

nuclear *adj* niuclasach.

nuclear waste *n* sgudal niuclasach *m*.

numb *adj* meilichte; (*cold*) air lathadh.

number *n* àireamh *f*; (*a lot*) mòran *f*. • *v* cùnnt, àireamhaich.

numeral *n* cùnntair *m*.

numerous *adj* lìonmhor.

nurse *n* banaltram *f*. • *v* altraim.

nursery *n* (*plants*) lios-àraich *m*; (*children*) sgoil-àraich *f*.

nursing home *n* taigh-altraim *m*.

nut *n* cnò *f*.

nutshell *n* plaosg-cnotha *m*.

O

oak *n* darach *m*.

oar *n* ràmh *m*.

oatcake *n* bonnach coirce *m*.

oath *n* bòid *f*.

oatmeal *n* min-choirce *f*.

obdurate *adj* rag-mhuinealach.

obedience *n* ùmhlachd *f*.

obey *v* gèill do.

object[1] *n* adhbhar *m*.

object[2] *v* cuir an aghaidh.

objection *n* gearan *m*.

oblige *v* cuir mar fhiachaibh air; (*help*) cuir fo chomain.

oblique *adj* siar.

oblivion *n* dìochuimhne *f*.

oboe *n* obo *m*.

obscene *adj* drabasda.

obscenity *n* drabasdachd *f*.

observant *adj* aireil.
observe *v* amhairc.
obsession *n* beò-ghlacadh *m*.
obsolete *adj* o fheum.
obstinacy *n* rag-mhuinealas *m*.
obstinate *adj* rag-mhuinealach.
obvious *adj* follaiseach.
occasion *n* fàth; cothrom *m*.
occasional *adj* corra.
occult *adj* dìomhair.
occupancy *n* seilbh *f*.
occupy *v* gabh sealbh.
ocean *n* cuan *m*, fairge *f*.
octagon *n* ochd-shliosach *f*.
octave *n* ochdad *m*.
October *n* An Dàmhair *m*.
octopus *n* ochd-chasach *m*.
ocular *adj* sùil, shùilean.
odd *adj* còrr.
ode *n* duanag *f*.
odour *n* boladh *m*.
of *prep* de. • *pron* **of me** dhìom; **of you** (*sing*) dhìot; **of him, it** dheth; **of her** dhith; **of us** dhinn; **of you** dhibh; **of them** dhiubh.
off *adv* dheth; (*away*) air falbh. • *prep* (*from*) o; bhàrr (+ *gen*).
offence *n* oilbheum *m*.
offend *v* dèan oilbheum do.
offer *n* tairgse *f*.
office *n* (*place*) oifis *f*; (*job*) dreuchd *f*.
officer *n* oifigeach *m*.
officious *adj* bleideil.
often *adv* tric; *adv* gu tric.
ogle *v* caog.
oil *n* ola *f*. • *v* olaich.
oil-field *n* ola-raon *m*.
oil-rig *n* crann-ola *m*.
oily *adj* uilleach.
ointment *n* ol-ungaidh *f*.

old *adj* aosda, sean.
old-fashioned *adj* sean-fhasanta.
omen *n* manadh *m*.
ominous *adj* droch-fhàistinneach.
omit *v* fàg às.
on *adv* air. • *prep* air. • *pron* **on me** orm; **on you** (*sing*) ort; **on him, it** air; **on her** oirre; **on us** oirnn; **on you** oirbh; **on them** orra.
once *adv* uair.
one *adj* aon. • *n* a h-aon *m*.
onion *n* uinnean *m*.
only *adj* aon. • *adv* a-mhàin. • *conj* ach.
onward *adv* air adhart.
ooze *v* drùidh.
open *adj* fosgailte. • *v* fosgail.
opening *n* fosgladh *m*.
operation *n* gnìomhachd *m*; (*surgical*) obair-lannsa *m*.
opinion *n* barail *f*.
opponent *n* nàmhaid *m*.
opportune *adj* tràthail.
opportunity *n* cothrom *m*.
oppose *v* cuir an aghaidh.
opposite *prep* fa chomhair.
oppress *v* claoidh.
oppressive *adj* fòirneartach.
optic *adj* fradharcach.
optimism *n* soirbh-dhùil *f*.
optimistic *adj* soirbh-dhùileach.
or *conj* no, air neo.
oral *adj* labhartha.
orange *adj* orainds.
orator *n* cainntear *m*.
orbit *n* reul-chuairt *f*.
orchard *n* ubhalghort *m*.
ordain *v* socraich.
order *n* òrdugh *m*. • *v* òrdaich.
ordinary *adj* gnàthaichte.
ore *n* mèinn *f*.

organ n ball m; orghan m.
organic adj innealach.
organise v eagraich.
organiser n eagraiche m.
orgasm n reachd f.
orgy n ruitearachd f.
oriental adj earach.
origin n tùs, bun m.
originality n bun-mhèinn f.
originate v tàrmaich.
Orkney n Arcaibh.
ornithology n eun-eòlas m.
orphan n dìlleachdan m.
osprey n iolair-uisge f.
ostensible adj a-rèir coltais.
ostrich n struth m.
other pron eile.
otherwise adv air modh eile.
otter n dòbhran m.
ought v bu chòir do.
ounce n ùnnsa m.
our pron (with inalienables) ar, (before vowel) ar n-; (with aliena-bles) . . . againn.
ours pron (with inalienables) ar . . .-ne, (before vowels) ar n-. . .-ne; (with alienables) an . . . againne.
ourselves pron sinn fhìn.
out adv (location) a-muigh.
outdo v buadhaich air.
outlaw n neach-cùirn m.
out-of-date adj às an fhasan.
outrage n sàrachadh m.
outright adv gu buileach. • adj dearg.

outside adv (location) a-muigh.
outskirts n iomall m.
outspoken adj fosgarra.
outward adj faicsinneach.
outwit v thoir an car às.
oven n àmhainn f.
over prep (location) os cionn • pron **over me** os mo chionn; **over you** (sing) os do chionn; **over him, it** os a chionn; **over her** os a cionn; **over us** os ar cionn; **over you** os ur cionn; **over them** os an cionn; (motion) thairis air. • adv (here) a-null; (there) a-nall.
overall adv thar a chèile.
overboard adv thar bòrd.
overcharge v cuir tuilleadh 's a chòir.
overflow n cur thairis m. • v tar-shruth.
overnight adj ri linn oidhche.
overrrule v cuir fo smachd.
overseas adv thall thairis.
overtake v beir air.
overtime n seach-thìm f.
overturn v cuir bun os cionn.
overweight adj ro-throm.
owe v bi fo fhiachaibh.
owl n comhachag f.
own pron fhèin, (after forms of I and we) fhìn.
owner n seilbheadair m.
oxter n achlais f.
oyster n eisir m.

P

pace n ceum m. • v ceumnaich.
pacifism n sìochantas m.
pacifist n sìochantair m.
pack v paisg.
packet n pacaid f.
pact n cùmhnant f.
pad n pada f.
paddle v pleadhagaich.
paddling n plubraich f.
padlock n glas-chrochaidh f.
page n duilleag f; (boy) pèidse m.
pageant n taisbeanadh m.
pain n pian f.
painful adj piantach.
painless adj neo-phiantach.
paint n peant m. • v peant.
painting n dealbh m.
pair n càraid f.
palace n lùchairt f.
palate n bràighe-beòil m.
pale adj bàn. • v bànaich.
pallid adj bàn.
palm n bas f.
pamper v dèan peata de.
pan n pana f.
pancake n foileag f.
pane n gloinne f.
panic n clisgeadh m.
pant v plosg.
pantry n seòmar-bìdh m.
pants npl pantaichean.
papal adj pàpanach.
paper n pàipear m.
parable n cosamhlachd f.
paradise n pàrras m.
paradox n frith-chosamhlachd f.
paragraph n earran sgrìobhaidh f.

parallel adj co-shìnteach.
paralysis n pairilis m.
parapet n uchd-bhalla m.
parcel n parsail m.
pardon n mathanas m. • v math.
parent n pàrant m.
parish n sgìre f.
park n pàirc f.
Parliament n Pàrlamaid f.
parody n sgig-athrais f.
parrot n pearraid f.
parsimonious adj spìocach.
parsley n peirsill f.
part¹ n cuid f.
part² v dealaich.
partake v com-pàirtich.
participate v com-pàirtich.
particle n gràinean m.
particular adj àraidh.
parting n dealachadh m.
partition n roinneadh m; (wall) cailbhe m.
partly adv ann an cuid; gu ìre bhig.
partner n companach m.
partridge n cearc-thomain m.
party n (company) cuideachd f (political or gathering) pàrtaidh f.
pass¹ n bealach m.
pass² v gabh seachad; (sport) pasaig.
passable adj cuibheasach.
passage n turas m; (in building) trannsa f.
passion n boile f.
passionate adj dìoghrasach.
passive resistance n aghaidheachd fhulangach f.

passivity *n* fulangachd *m*.

passport *n* cead-siubhail *m*.

past *adj* seachad. • *n* an t-àm a dh'fhalbh *m*.

pastry *n* pastra *f*.

pasture *n* feurach *m*. • *v* feuraich.

pat *v* slìob.

patch *n* tùthag *f*.

paternal *adj* athaireil.

path *n* ceum *m*, slighe *f*.

pathetic *adj* tiamhaidh.

patience *n* foighidinn *f*.

patient *n* euslainteach *m*. • *adj* foighidneach.

patrimony *n* dualchas *m*.

patronymic *n* ainm sinnsireil *m*.

pattern *n* pàtran *m*.

paunch *n* maodal *f*.

pause *n* stad *m*. • *v* fuirich.

paw *n* spòg *f*.

pawn[1] *n* pàn *m*.

pawn[2] *v* thoir an geall.

pay *n* pàigheadh *m*. • *v* pàigh.

pea *n* peasair *f*.

peace *n* sìth, fois *f*.

peaceful *adj* sìothchail.

peach *n* pèitseag *f*.

peak *n* stùc *f*, binnean *m*.

pear *n* peur *f*.

pearl *n* neamhnaid *f*.

peat *n* mòine *f*; (*single*) fad *m*.

peat-stack *n* cruach-mhònach *f*.

pebble *n* dèideag *f*.

peck *v* pioc.

pectoral *adj* uchdail.

peculiar *adj* àraid.

pedal *n* troighean *m*.

pedantry *n* rag-fhoglam *m*.

peddle *v* reic.

pedestrian *n* coisiche *m*.

pee *v* dèan mùn.

peel *n* rùsg *m*. • *v* ruisg.

peep *n* caogadh *m*. • *v* caog.

peevish *adj* dranndanach.

peewit *n* curracag *f*.

pelt *v* caith air.

pen *n* peann *m*.

penalty *n* peanas *m*.

penance *n* aithridh *f*.

pending *adj* ri thighinn.

penetrate *v* drùidh.

peninsula *n* leth-eilean *m*.

penis *n* bod *m*.

penny *n* peighinn *f*.

pension *n* peinnsean *m*.

pensioner *n* peinnseinear *m*.

people *n* sluagh, poball *m*.

pepper *n* piobair *m*.

per cent *adv* ... sa cheudad.

perceive *v* tuig, mothaich.

perch *n* spiris *f*. • *v* rach air spiris.

percolator *n* sìolachan *m*.

percussion *n* faram *m*.

perennial *adj* maireannach.

perfect *adj* foirfe. • *v* dèan foirfe.

perform *v* coimhlion.

perfume *n* cùbhrachd *f*.

perhaps *adv* is dòcha, ma dh'fhaoite.

period *n* cuairt *f*.

perish *v* faigh bàs.

perishable *adj* neo-sheasmhach.

permanence *n* maireannachd *f*.

permanent *adj* buan.

permissive *adj* ceadachail.

permit *n* bileag-cead *f*. • *v* ceadaich.

perpendicular *adj* dìreach.

perquisite *n* frith-bhuannachd *f*.

persecute *v* geur-lean.

persevere *v* lean air.

persistent *adj* leanailteach.

person n neach m.
personal adj pearsanta.
persuade v cuir ìmpidh air.
persuasion n ìmpidheachd f.
pertinent adj iomchaidh.
peruse v leugh.
perverse adj claon.
pervert n claonair m.
pessimist n neach gun dòchas m.
pest n plàigh f.
pestle n plocan m.
pet n peata m.
petition n iarrtas m. • v aslaich.
petrol n peatroil m.
petticoat n còta-bàn m.
pew n suidheachan m.
phantom n faileas m.
pheasant n easag f.
phenomenon n iongantas m.
philosopher n feallsanach m.
philosophy n feallsanachd f.
phlegmatic adj ronnach.
phone n fòn m. • v (cuir) fòn.
phosphorescence n teine-ghealan m.
photograph n dealbh m.
phrase n abairt m.
physical adj fisigeach; corporra.
pianist n cluicheadair piano m.
piano n piano m.
pibroch n ceòl-mòr f.
pick v tagh.
pickle v saill.
Pict n Cruithneach m.
picture n dealbh m.
picturesque adj àillidh.
pie n paidh m.
piece n pìos m.
pier n ceadha m.
pierce v toll.
pig n muc f.
pigeon n calman m.

pigsty n fail-mhuc f.
pile v cruach.
pilfer v dèan braide.
pilgrim n eilthireach m.
pill n pile f.
pillar n carragh f.
pillow n cluasag f.
pilot n pìleat m. • v treòraich.
pimple n plucan m.
pin n dealg f.
pinch v fàisg.
pine n giuthas m.
pink adj pinc.
pipe n pìob f.
piper n pìobaire m.
pirate n spùinneadair(-mara) m.
piss n mùn m. • v mùin.
pistol n daga m.
pitch n bìth f; (mus) àirde f; (field) raon-cluiche m.
pitiful adj truacanta.
pittance n suarachas m.
pity n truas m. • v gabh truas de.
place n àite m. • v suidhich.
placidity n ciùineachd f.
plague v plàighich.
plaice n lèabag-mhòr f.
plaid n breacan m.
plain adj còmhnard; soilleir.
plait n figheachan m.
plan n innleachd, plana f. • v innlich.
planet n planaid f.
plank n clàr m.
plant n luibh m. • v cuir.
plantation n planntachadh m.
plaster n sglàib f; plàsd m.
plastic adj plastaig; coineallach • n plastaig f.
plate n truinnsear m.
plateau n àrd-chlàr m.

plausible *adj* beulach.
play *v* cluich.
player *n* cluicheadair *m*; cleasaiche *m*.
plead *v* tagair.
pleasant *adj* taitneach.
please *v* toilich, riaraich, taitinn, còrd.
pleasure *n* tlachd *f*.
pleat *n* pleat *f*.
plenty *adv* gu leòr.
plenty *n* pailteas *m*.
plight *n* cor *m*.
plod *v* saothraich.
plot *n* goirtean *m*; (*scheme*) cuil-bheart *f*.
plough *n* crann *m*. • *v* treabh.
plug *n* plucan *m*.
plum *n* plumas *m*.
plumb *v* feuch doimhneachd.
plump *adj* sultmhor.
plunder *n* cobhartach *m*. • *v* spùinn.
plunge *v* tum.
plural *adj* iolra.
plus *prep* agus.
poach *v* poidsig.
poacher *n* poidsear *m*.
pocket *n* pòcaid *f*.
poem *n* dàn *m*.
poet *n* bàrd *m*.
poetry *n* bàrdachd *f*.
point *v* comharraich.
poison *n* puinnsean *m*.
police *n* poileas *m*.
polish *n* lìomh *f*.
polite *adj* modhail.
pollute *v* truaill.
pompous *adj* mòr-chùiseach.
pond *n* linne *f*.
pony *n* pònaidh *m*.
pool *n* linne *f*.

poor *adj* bochd.
Pope *n* Pàpa *m*.
popular *adj* coiteanta.
population *n* sluagh *m*.
porch *n* sgàil-thaigh *m*.
porridge *n* lite *f*.
port *n* port *m*.
portable *adj* so-ghiùlan.
portion *n* earrann *f*.
Portugal *n* A' Phortagail *f*.
positive *adj* cinnteach.
possess *v* sealbhaich.
possible *adj* comasach.
possibly *adv* is dòcha.
post office *n* oifis a' phuist *f*.
post *v* cuir air falbh.
postal order *n* òrdugh-puist *m*.
postcard *n* cairt-phostachd *f*.
postcode *n* còd-puist *m*.
postman *n* posta *m*.
pot *n* poit *f*.
potato *n* buntàta *m*.
pottery *n* crèadhadaireachd *f*.
pound *n* pùnnd *m*.
pour *v* dòirt; (*rain*) sil.
powder *n* fùdar *m*.
power *n* cumhachd *f*.
power station *n* stèisean dealain *m*.
practicable *adj* so-dhèanamh.
practice *n* cleachdadh *m*.
practise *v* cleachd.
praise *n* moladh *m*. • *v* mol.
prank *n* cleas *m*.
prawn *n* muasgan-caol *m*.
pray *v* guidh.
prayer *n* guidhe *f*.
preach *v* searmonaich.
precarious *adj* cugallach.
precaution *n* ro-chùram *m*.
precentor *n* neach togail fuinn *m*.
precious *adj* prìseil.

precipitous *adj* cas.
precise *adj* pongail.
precocious *adj* ro-abaich.
predatory *adj* creachach.
predict *v* ro-innis.
predominant *adj* buadhach.
preface *n* ro-ràdh *m*.
prefer *v* is fheàrr le.
pregnant *adj* trom.
prehistoric *adj* ro-eachdraidheil.
prejudice *n* claon-bhàigh *f*.
preliminary *adj* tòiseachail.
premises *n* aitreabh *m*.
premonition *n* ro-fhiosrachadh *f*.
prepare *v* ullaich.
preposterous *adj* mì-reusanta.
prescription *n* òrdugh-cungaidh *f*.
presence *n* làthaireachd *f*.
present[1] *n* an t-àm tha làthair *m*
present[2] *n* (*gift*) tiodhlac *m*. • *v* thoir do.
presently *adv* an ceart uair.
president *n* ceann-suidhe *m*.
press release *n* aithris-naidheachd *f*.
pretence *n* leigeil air *m*.
pretend *v* leig air.
pretty *adj* brèagha.
prevailing *adj* buadhach.
previously *adv* ro làimh.
prey *n* creach *f*. • *v* creach.
price *n* prìs *f*.
prick *v* stuig.
prickly *adj* biorach.
pride *n* àrdan *m*.
priest *n* sagart *m*.
prim *adj* frionasach.
primary school *n* bunsgoil *f*.
primitive *adj* tùsach.
primrose *n* sòbhrach *f*.
prince *n* prionnsa *m*.

print *v* clò-bhuail.
printer *n* clò-bhualadair *m*.
print-out *n* lethbhreac clo-bhuailte *m*.
private *adj* uaigneach.
privilege *n* sochair *f*.
prize *n* duais *f*.
probable *adj* coltach.
probably *adv* is dòcha.
probity *n* treibhdhireas *m*.
problem *n* ceist *f*.
problematic *adj* ceisteach.
process *n* cùrsa *m*.
proclaim *v* èigh.
procurator fiscal *n* fioscail *m*.
prod *v* stob.
produce *n* toradh *m*. • *v* thoir gu cinneas.
producer *n* riochdaire *m*.
profession *n* dreuchd *f*.
professor *n* ollamh *m*.
profit *n* buannachd *f*. • *v* tairbhich.
profound *adj* domhainn.
profuse *adj* pailt.
program(me) *n* prògram *m*.
programming language *n* cànan-prògramaidh *m*.
progress *n* imeachd *f*; piseach *f*.
prohibit *v* toirmisg.
prolific *adj* torrach.
prominent *adj* faicsinneach.
promise *n* gealladh *m*. • *v* geall.
promontory *n* rubha *m*.
prompt *adj* deas.
pronoun *n* riochdair *m*.
pronounce *v* fuaimnich.
proof *n* dearbhadh *m*.
prop *v* cùm suas.
proper *adj* iomchuidh.
property *n* seilbh *f*.
prophesy *v* fàisnich.

proportion *n* co-rèir *m*.
proprietor *n* sealbhadair *m*.
propulsion *n* sparradh *m*.
prose *n* rosg *m*.
prosecute *v* cùisich.
prosper *v* soirbhich.
prostitute *n* strìopach *f*.
prostrate *adj* sleuchdte.
protect *v* dìon.
protection *n* dìon *m*.
protest *v* tog casaid.
Protestant *adj* Pròsdanach.
proud *adj* uaibhreach.
prove *v* dearbh.
proverb *n* seanfhacal *m*.
provide *v* solair.
province *n* roinn *f*.
provocation *n* buaireadh *m*.
provoke *v* buair.
provost *n* pròbhaist *m*.
prow *n* toiseach *m*.
prowl *v* èalaidh.
prude *n* leòmag *f*.
prudent *adj* glic.
prune *v* sgath.
pry *v* lorgaich.
psalm *n* salm *m*.
psalter *n* salmadair *m*.
psychic *adj* anamanta.
ptarmigan *n* tàrmachan *m*.
pub *n* taigh-seinnse *m*.
public *adj* follaiseach.
public relations *n* dàimh phoblach *f*.
publicity *n* follaiseadh *m*.

publish *v* foillsich.
pudding *n* marag; mìlsean *f*.
puddle *n* lòn *m*.
puffin *n* buthaid *m*.
pull *v* tarraing.
pulpit *n* cùbaid *f*.
pulse *n* cuisle *f*.
pump *n* pumpa *m*; (*shoe*) bròg-dannsa *f*.
punctual *adj* pongail.
puncture *n* tolladh *m*.
punish *v* peanasaich.
punishment *n* peanasachadh *m*.
pupil *n* sgoilear *m*; (*eye*) dubh na sùla *m*.
puppy *n* cuilean *m*.
pure *adj* fìorghlan.
purge *v* glan.
purity *n* glaine *f*.
purple *adj* purpaidh.
purse *n* sporan *m*.
pursue *v* lean.
pursuer *n* neach-tòire *m*.
pursuit *n* tòir *f*.
push *n* bruthadh *m*. • *v* brùth.
pussy cat *n* piseag *f*.
put *v* cuir, suidhich.
putrid *adj* grod.
putt *v* amas.
puzzle *n* imcheist. • *v* cuir an imcheist, bi an imcheist.
pylon *n* paidhlean *m*.
pyramid *n* biorramaid *f*.

Q

quack n màgail f; (sound) mhàg mhàg! • v dèan màgail.

quaint adj neònach.

qualification n feart m.

qualify v ullaich.

quality n gnè f.

quantify v àirmhich.

quarrel n còmhstri m. • v connsaich.

quarrelsome adj connspaideach.

quarry n cuaraidh m; creach m. • v cladhaich.

quarter n ceathramh m; (season) n ràith f.

quartz n èiteag f.

quaver n crith f; (mus) n caman m.

queasy adj sleogach.

queen n ban-rìgh f.

quell v smachdaich.

quench v bàth.

quern n brà f.

question n ceist f. • v ceasnaich.

question-mark n comharradh ceiste m.

queue n ciudha f.

quibble v car-fhaclaich.

quick adj bras, luath.

quicksand n beò-ghainmheach f.

quiet adj sàmhach.

quiet n sàmhchair m.

quieten v sàmhaich.

quilt n cuibhrig m.

quirk n car m.

quit v fàg.

quite adv gu tur, gu lèir; gu math.

quiver[1] n balg-shaighead m.

quiver[2] v dèan ball-chrith.

quiz n ceasnachadh m.

quotation n luaidh m; (price) luach m.

quote v luaidh; thoir mar ùghdarras.

R

rabbit n coineanach m.

rabid adj cuthachail.

race n rèis f; (human) cinneadh f.

racism n cinneadachd f.

racket n gleadhraich f.

radiant adj lainnireach.

radiate v deàlraich.

radiator n rèididheatar m.

radical adj bunasach.

radio n rèidio m.

raffle n crannchur-gill m.

raft n ràth m.

rafter n taobhan m.

rag n luideag f.

rage n boile f.

raid n ruaig f.

railway n rathad-iarainn m.

rain n uisge m; frasachd f. • v sil, dòirt.

rainbow n bogha-frois m.

rainy adj frasach.

raise v àrdaich, tog.

rake v ràc.

ram n reithe m.

ram v spàrr.

rambler n neach-fàrsain m.

rampant adj sùrdagach.

rancid adj breun.

random adj tuaireamach.

range n sreath m. • v siubhail.

rank n (status) inbhe f; (line) sreath m.

rankle v feargaich.

ransom n èirig f. • v fuasgail.

rapacious adj gionach.

rape n toirt air èiginn f. • v èignich.

rapidity n braise f.

rare adj tearc.

rarity n annas m.

rash[1] n broth m.

rash[2] adj dàna.

raspberry n subh-craoibh m.

rat n radan m.

rate n ràta m.

rather adv rudeigin.

ravage v sgrios.

rave v bi air bhoile.

raven n fitheach m.

ravenous adj cìocrach.

raw adj amh.

razor n ealtainn f.

reach n ruigheachd f. • v ruig.

read v leugh.

reader n leughadair m.

readily adv gu rèidh.

readiness n ullamhachd f.

ready adj ullamh.

real adj fìor.

realise v tuig.

reality n fìrinn f.

really adv gu dearbh.

reap v buain.

rear n deireadh m.

reason n reusan m.

rebate n lùghdachadh m.

rebel n reubalach m. • v dèan ar-a-mach.

rebuff n diùltadh m.

rebuild v ath-thog.

recall v cuimhnich air.

recede v rach air ais.

receive v gabh.

recent adj ùr.

recently adv o chionn ghoirid.

reception n fàilteachadh m.

receptive adj so-ghabhail.

recession n ìsleachadh m.

recipe n modh m.

reciprocal adj malairteach.

recital n aithris; (mus) ceadal f.

reckless adj neo-chùramach.

reckon v cùnnt.

reclaim v ath-leasaich.

recline v sìn.

recognise v aithnich.

recommend v cliùthaich.

reconcile v rèitich.

reconnoitre v feuch.

record n cùnntas m; clàr m. • v sgrìobh; clàraich.

recover v (regain) faigh air ais; (improve) fàs nas fheàrr.

recovery n (regain) faighinn air ais f; (improve) fàs nas fheàrr m.

recreation n cur-seachad m.

rectify v ceartaich.

rector n ceannard m.

recur v tachair a-rithist.

red adj dearg; ruadh.

redeem v ath-cheannaich.

redirect v ath-sheòl.

redouble v dùblaich.

reduce v ìslich.

redundant adj anbharra.

reed n cuilc f; (mus) ribheid f.

reef n sgeir f.

reel n ruidhle m; (*thread*) piorna f.

refer v cuir gu.

referee n breitheamh, reaf m.

reference n iomradh m; teisteanas m.

refill v ath-lìon.

refit v ath-chàirich.

reflect v tilg air ais; (*think*) smaoinich.

reform n leasachadh m. • v ath-leasaich.

refrain n luinneag f.

refresh v ùraich.

refreshment n ùrachadh m; deoch f.

refuge n tèarmann m.

refund v ath-dhìol.

refusal n diùltadh m.

refuse v diùlt.

refute v breugnaich.

regard n suim f. • v gabh suim ann.

register n clàr m.

regret n duilchinn f. • v bi duilich.

regulate v riaghlaich.

rehearsal n ath-aithris f.

rehearse v ath-aithris.

reign v rìoghaich.

reimburse v ath-phàigh.

rein n srian f.

reinforce v ath-neartaich.

rejoice v dèan aoibhneas.

relate v innis.

related adj (*akin*) càirdeach.

relation n caraid m, bana-charaid f.

relative adj dàimheach.

relax v lasaich.

release v cuir ma sgaoil.

relent v taisich.

relentless adj neo-thruacanta.

relevant adj a' buntainn ri.

reliable adj earbsach.

relic n fuidheall m.

relief n furtachd f.

relieve v furtaich.

religion n diadhachd f.

relish n tlachd f. • v gabh tlachd de.

reluctant adj aindeonach.

rely v earb.

remain v fuirich.

remains npl fuidhleach m; (*human*) duslach m.

remark n facal m. • v thoir fa-near.

remarkable adj suaicheanta.

remedy n leigheas m.

remember v cuimhnich.

remind v cuimhnich do.

reminiscence n cuimhneachadh m.

remorse n agartas-cogais m.

remorseful adj cogaiseach.

remote adj iomallach.

renaissance n ath-bheòthachadh m.

rend v srac.

renew v nuadhaich.

rent n (*tear*) sracadh m; (*fee*) màl m. • v gabh air mhàl.

repair n càireadh m. • v càirich.

repay v ath-dhìol.

repeat v aithris.

repel v tilg air ais.

replace v cuir an àite.

replay v ath-chluich.

replete adj làn.

reply n freagairt f. • v freagair.

report v thoir iomradh.

representative n riochdaire m.

reprieve n stad-bhreith f.

reprimand n casaid f.

reprisal n èirig f.

reproach v cronaich.

reproduce v gin.

reproduction n gintinn m; (*copy*) macsamhlachadh m.

reptile n pèist f.

republic n poblachd f.
reputation n cliù m.
request n iarrtas m. • v iarr.
rescue n fuasgladh m. • v fuasgail.
research v rannsaich.
researcher n rannsaichear m.
resent v gabh tàmailt dhe.
resentment n doicheall m.
reserve n tasgadh m. • v caomhain.
reservoir n tasgadh-uisge m.
residence n ionad-còmhnaidh m.
resign v thoir suas, gèill.
resistance n strì f.
resolute adj gramail.
resonant adj glòrach.
resource n goireas m.
respect n urram m. • v thoir urram do.
respectable adj measail.
respectful adj modhail.
respective adj àraidh.
respite n anail f.
responsibility n cùram m.
responsive adj freagairteach.
rest n fois f; (mus) clos m. • v gabh fois.
restaurant n taigh-bìdh m.
restful adj sàmhach.
restless adj mì-fhoisneach.
restore v thoir air ais.
restrict v grab.
result n buil f.
retain v cùm.
reticent adj tosdach.
retire v rach air chluainidh, leig dreuchd dhe.
retirement n cluaineas m.
retreat v teich.
retribution n ath-dhìoladh m.
return n tilleadh m. • v till.
reveal v nochd.

revelation n taisbeanadh m.
revenge n dìoghaltas m.
reverend adj urramach.
reverent adj iriosal.
review v ath-bheachdaich.
revise v ath-sgrùd.
revival n dùsgadh m.
revive v dùisg.
revolve v iom-chuartaich.
reward n duais f. • v dìol.
rheumatic adj lòinidheach.
rheumatism n an rumatas m.
rhubarb n rua-bhàrr m.
rhyme n comhardadh m. • v dèan rann.
rib n aisean f.
ribbon n rioban m.
rice n rìs m.
rich adj beairteach.
riddle n tòimhseachan m.
ride v marcaich.
rider n marcaiche m.
ridge n druim m.
ridiculous adj amaideach.
right adj ceart; (hand) deas. • n ceartas m; dlighe f. • v cuir ceart.
rigid adj rag.
rigour n cruas m.
rim n oir m.
rind n rùsg m.
ring n fàinne f; cearcall m. • v seirm.
rinse v sgol.
ripe adj abaich.
ripen v abaich.
ripple n luasgan m.
rise v èirich.
risk n cunnart m. • v feuch.
rival n co-dheuchainniche m. • adj còmhstritheach.
rivalry n còmhstri f.
river n abhainn f.

rivulet *n* sruthan *m*.
road *n* rathad *m*, slighe *f*.
roam *v* rach air fàrsan.
roar *n* beuc *m*. • *v* beuc.
roast *v* ròist.
rob *v* spùinn, spùill.
robber *n* spùilleadair *m*.
robbery *n* goid *f*.
robe *n* fallaing *f*.
robin *n* brù-dhearg *m*.
rock[1] *n* carraig *f*.
rock[2] *v* luaisg.
rod *n* slat *f*.
roe *n* earba, ruadhag *f*; (*fish*) glasag *f*.
rogue *n* slaoightear *m*.
roll *n* rolla *f*. • *v* fill.
romance *n* romansachd *f*; (*tale*) ròlaist *m*.
romantic *adj* romansach.
roof *n* mullach *m*.
rook *n* ròcas *m*.
room *n* seòmar, rùm *m*.
roomy *adj* farsaing.
root *n* freumh *m*.
rope *n* ròpa, ball *m*.
rosary *n* paidirean *m*.
rose *n* ròs *m*.
rosy *adj* ruiteach.
rot *n* grodadh *m*.
rotten *adj* grod.

rough *adj* garbh, molach.
round *adj* cruinn. • *adv* mun cuairt.
rouse *v* dùisg.
rout *n* ruaig *f*.
routine *n* gnàth-chùrsa *m*.
row *n* (*rank*) sreath *m*; (*fight*) sabaid *f*.
rowan *n* caorann *f*.
rower *n* ràmhaiche *m*.
rub *v* suath.
rubbish *n* salchar, brusgar *m*.
rudder *n* stiùir *f*.
rude *adj* borb.
rue *v* crean.
rueful *adj* dubhach.
ruffian *n* brùid *f*.
rug *n* bràt-urlair *m*.
ruin *n* sgrios *m*; (*house*) làrach *m*.
rule *n* riaghailt *f*. • *v* riaghail.
rumble *v* dèan rùcail.
rummage *v* rannsaich.
rumour *n* fathann *m*.
run *v* ruith.
runnel *n* srùlag *f*.
rural *adj* dùthchail.
rush *v* brùchd.
rushes *npl* luachair *f*.
rust *n* meirg *f*.
rut *n* clais *f*; (*animal*) dàmhair *f*.
ruthless *adj* neo-thruacanta.

S

sabbath *n* sàbaid *f*.
sack[1] *n* poca *m*.
sack[2] *v* sgrios; cuir à obair.
sacrcastic *adj* searbh.
sacred *adj* naomh.
sacrifice *n* ìobairt *f*. • *v* ìobair.

sad *adj* brònach.
sadden *v* dèan brònach.
saddle *n* dìollaid *f*.
sadness *n* bròn, mulad *m*.
safe *adj* sàbhailte.
safety *n* tèarainteachd *f*.

saffron n cròch m.

sag v tuit.

sagacious adj geur-chùiseach.

sail n seòl m. • v seòl.

sailor n seòladair m.

saint n naomh m.

sake n sgàth m.

salad n sailead m.

sale n reic m.

saleable adj reiceach.

saliva n seile m.

sallow adj lachdann.

salmon n bradan m.

salmon trout n bànag f.

salt n salann m.

salt-cellar n saillear m.

salutary adj slàinteil.

salute v fàiltich.

salvage n tàrrsainn m.

same adj ionann, ceudna.

sameness n co-ionannachd.

sample n samhla m.

sanctify v naomhaich.

sanctuary n comraich f.

sand n gainmheach f.

sandstone n clach-ghainmhich f.

sandy adj gainmheil.

sane adj ciallach.

sapling n faillean m.

sapphire n gorm-leug f.

sarcasm n searbhas m.

satanic adj diabhlaidh.

satchel n màileid f.

satellite n saideal m.

satiate v sàsaich.

satin n sròl m.

satire n aoir f.

satirical adj aoireil.

satirist n èisg f.

satisfaction n sàsachadh m.

satisfied adj sàsaichte.

satisfy v sàsaich.

Saturday n DiSathairne m.

sauce n sabhs m.

saucepan n sgeileid f.

saucer n sàsar m.

sausage n isbean m.

save v sàbhail.

saved adj saorte.

savour v feuch blas.

savoury adj blasda.

saw n sàbh m. • v sàbh.

say v abair.

saying n ràdh, facal m.

scald v sgàld.

scale n cothrom m; (fish) lann m;
(mus) sgàla m.

scalp n craiceann a' chinn m.

scaly adj lannach.

scan v sgrùd.

scandal n sgainneal m.

scandalise v sgainnealaich.

scandalous adj maslach.

scanty adj gann.

scar n leòn m.

scarce adj tearc.

scare v cuir eagal air.

scarecrow n bodach-ròcais m.

scarf n stoc m.

scatter v sgap.

scattering n sgapadh m.

scene n sealladh m.

scent n fàileadh m.

scented adj cùbhraidh.

sceptical adj às-creideach.

scheme n innleachd f.

school n sgoil f.

schoolmaster n maighstir-sgoile m.

schoolmistress n bana-mhaighstir-
sgoile f.

science n saidheans m.

scientific adj saidheansail.

scissors n siosar f.

scold v troid.

scone n bonnach m, sgona f.

scorch v dadh.

score v cuir; sgrìob.

scorn n tàir f.

scornful adj tàireil.

Scotland n Alba f.

Scottish adj Albannach.

scour v nigh.

scourge v sgiùrs.

scout n beachdair m.

scowl v bi fo ghruaim.

scrape n sgrìob f.

scratch n sgròbadh m. • v sgròb.

scream n sgreuch m. • v sgreuch.

scree n sgàirneach f.

script n sgrìobhadh m.

scroll n rolla f.

scrotum n clach-bhalg m.

scrub v nigh.

scruple n teagamh m.

scrupulous adj teagmhach.

scuffle n tuasaid f.

sculptor n deilbhear m.

sculpture n deilbheadh m.

scythe n speal f. • v speal.

sea level n àirde-mhara f.

sea n muir m&f.

seagull n faoileag f.

seal n ròn m; (official) seula m. • v seulaich.

seaport n longphort m.

sear v crannaich.

search n lorg m. • v lorg, rannsaich.

seashore n cladach m.

season n ràith f.

seasonable adj tràthail.

seaweed n feamainn f.

second adj dara.

secondary adj dàrnach.

secondary school n àrdsgoil f.

second-hand adj ath-dhìolta.

secondly adv anns an dara h-àite.

secrecy n cleith f.

secret adj dìomhair. • n rùn.

secretary n rùnaire m.

secretive adj ceilteach.

secretly adv gun fhiosda.

sect n dream m.

secular adj saoghalta.

secure adj seasgair. • v glais, glac.

security n dìon m.

seduce v truaill.

seduction n truailleadh m.

see v faic, seall, amhairc.

seed n sìol m. • v sìolaich.

seeing n lèirsinn f.

seek v iarr.

seer n fiosaiche m.

seize v glac, cuir làmh ann.

seldom adv gu tearc.

select v tagh.

self pron fhèin, (after forms of I and we) fhìn.

self-interest n fèin-bhuannachd f.

selfish adj fèineil.

sell v reic.

semiquaver n leth-chaman m.

semitone n leth-phong m.

senate n seanadh m.

send v cuir.

senile adj seantaidh.

senior adj as sine.

sensation n mothachadh m.

sense n ciall f.

senseless adj gun chiall.

sensible adj ciallach.

sensitive adj mothachail.

sensual adj feòlmhor.

sensuous adj ceudfaidheach.

sentence n rosgrann m; (law) binn f.

sentimental *adj* maoth-inntinneach.

separate *v* dealaich.

separation *n* dealachadh.

September *n* An t-Sultain *f.*

septic *adj* seaptaig.

sepulchral *adj* tuamach.

sequence *n* leanmhainn *m.*

serene *adj* soinneanta.

sergeant *n* sàirdeant *m.*

series *n* sreath *m.*

serious *adj* suidhichte.

serpent *n* nathair *f.*

serrated *adj* eagach.

servant *n* seirbheiseach *m.*

serve *v* fritheil.

service *n* seirbheis *f;* dleasnas *m.*

serviceable *adj* feumail.

session *n* seisean *m.*

set *v* suidhich, cuir.

setter *n* cù-luirg *m.*

settle *v* socraich.

settlement *n* suidheachadh; tuineachadh *m.*

seven *adj* seachd. • *n (people)* seachdnar.

seventeen *n* seachd deug.

seventh *adj* seachdamh.

seventy *n (old system)* trì fichead 's a deich; *(new system)* seachdad.

sever *v* sgar.

severe *adj* cruaidh.

severity *n* cruas *m.*

sew *v* fuaigh.

sewage *n* giodar *m.*

sewing *n* fuaigheal *m.*

sex *n (gender)* gnè *f; (act)* obair-chraicinn *f,* feis *f.*

sextet *n* ceòl-sianar *m.*

sexual intercourse *n* cleamhnas *m.*

shade *n* sgàil *f.* • *v* sgàil.

shadow *n* faileas *m.*

shady *adj* dubharach.

shaggy *adj* molach.

shallow *adj* tana; faoin.

sham *adj* mealltach.

shame *n* nàire *f.* • *v* nàraich.

shameful *adj* nàr.

shape *n* cumadh *m.* • *v* cum, dealbh.

shapely *adj* cuimir.

share *n* roinn *f.* • *v* roinn, pàirtich.

shark *n* siorc *m.*

sharp *adj* geur.

sharpen *v* geuraich.

sharpness *n* gèire *f.*

shave *v* beàrr.

shawl *n* seàla *f.*

she *pron* i, *(emphatic)* ise.

shear *v* rùsg.

shearing *n* rùsgadh *m.*

sheath *n* truaill *f.*

shed[1] *n* bothan *m.*

shed[2] *v* dòirt.

sheep *n* caora *f.*

sheep-dog *n* cù-chaorach.

sheet *n* duilleag *f.*

sheiling *n* àirigh *f.*

shelf *n* sgeilp *f; (rock)* sgeir *f.*

shellfish *n* maorach *m.*

shelter *n* dìon *m.*

shepherd *n* cìobair *m.*

sheriff *n* siorraidh *m.*

Shetland *n* Sealtainn *m.*

shield *n* sgiath *f.* • *v* dìon.

shine *v* deàlraich.

shinty *n* iomain *f.*

shinty stick *n* caman *m.*

ship *n* long *f.*

shipwreck *n* long-bhriseadh *m.*

shire *n* siorrachd *f.*

shirt *n* lèine *f.*

shiver *v* crith.

shoal *n* bogha; sgaoth *m*.

shock *n* sgannradh *m*. • *v* criothnaich.

shoe *n* bròg *f*.

shoelace *n* barrall *f*.

shoemaker *n* greusaiche *m*.

shoot *v* tilg, loisg; (*grow*) fàs.

shop *n* bùth *f*.

shore *n* tràigh *f*.

short *adj* goirid.

shortage *n* dìth *m*.

shorten *v* giorraich.

shortly *adv* a dh'aithghearr.

shorts *npl* briogais ghoirid *f*.

short-sighted *adj* geàrr-sheallach.

short-wave *n* geàrr-thonnach *m*.

shot *n* urchair *f*.

shoulder *n* gualainn *f*.

shout *n* glaodh *m*.

shove *n* putadh *m*. • *v* put.

show *v* seall.

shower *n* fras *f*.

shred *n* mìr *m*.

shriek *n* sgread *m*.

shrimp *n* carran *m*.

shrink *v* seac.

shrub *n* preas *m*.

shudder *v* criothnaich.

shuffle *v* tarraing; (*cards*) measgaich.

shut *v* druid, dùin. • *adj* dùinte.

shy *adj* sochaireach.

sick *adj* tinn.

sickness *n* tinneas *m*.

side *n* taobh *m*.

sidelong *adv* air fhiaradh.

sideways *adv* an comhar a thaoibh.

siege *n* sèisd *f*.

sieve *n* criathar *m*.

sigh *v* leig osna.

sight *n* sealladh *m*; lèirsinn *f*.

sign *n* comharradh *m*.

signature *n* ainm *m*.

significant *adj* brìgheil.

signpost *n* post-seòlaidh *m*.

silence *n* sàmhchair *f*, tosd *m*.

silent *adj* tosdach.

silk *n* sìoda *m*.

sill *n* sòlla *f*.

silly *adj* gòrach.

silver *n* airgead *m*.

similar *adj* coltach.

simple *adj* sìmplidh.

simplify *v* simplich.

simultaneous *adj* còmhla.

sin *n* peacadh *m*. • *v* peacaich.

since *conj* a chionn 's gu. • *prep* o, o chionn.

sincere *adj* onorach.

sing *v* seinn, gabh òran.

singer *n* seinneadair *m*.

single *adj* singilte.

singular *adj* sònraichte.

sinister *adj* droch thuarach.

sink *n* since *f*. • *v* cuir fodha; rach fodha.

sip *v* gabh balgam.

sister *n* piuthar *f*.

sister-in-law *n* piuthar-chèile *f*.

sit *v* suidh.

sitting room *n* seòmar-suidhe *m*.

six *adj* sia. • *n* (*people*) sianar.

sixteen *adj/n* sia deug *m*.

sixty *adj/n* (*old system*) trì fichead; (*new system*) seasgad.

size *n* meud *m*.

skate[1] *n* bròg-spèilidh *f*. • *v* spèil.

skate[2] *n* (*fish*) sgait *f*.

skeleton *n* cnàimhneach *m*.

skerry *n* sgeir *f*.

sketch *n* tarraing *f*.

ski v sgithich.

skid v sleamhnaich.

ski-lift n àrdaichear-ski m.

skill n sgil m.

skim v thoir uachdar dhe.

skin n craiceann m. • v feann.

skinny adj caol.

skip v leum.

skirmish n arrabhaig f.

skirt n sgiort f.

skull n claigeann m.

sky n adhar m.

Skye n An t-Eilean Sgitheanach m.

skylark n uiseag f.

slam v thoir slàr do.

slander n sgainneal m.

slant n claonadh m. • v claon.

slap n sgailc f.

slash v geàrr.

slate n sglèat m.

slaughter n marbhadh m.

slave n tràill f.

sledge n càrn-slaoid m.

sleek adj slìom.

sleep n cadal m.

sleepy adj cadalach.

sleet n flin m.

sleeve n muinchill m.

slice n sliseag f.

slide v sleamhnaich.

slip n tuisleadh m. • v tuislich.

slipper n slapag f.

slippery adj sleamhainn.

slit n sgoltadh m.

slogan n sluagh-ghairm f.

slope n leathad m.

sloven n luid f.

slovenly adj luideach.

slow adj slaodach.

slowness n slaodachd f.

slur n tàir f; (speech) slugadh m.

sly adj carach.

smack n sglais f.

small adj beag.

smart adj tapaidh.

smattering n bloigh eòlais m.

smear v smiùr.

smell n fàileadh m. • v feuch fàileadh.

smile n snodha-gàire m. • v dèan snodha-gàire.

smith n gobha m.

smoke n ceò m. • v smocaig.

smoky adj ceòthach.

smooth adj mìn.

smoothe v mìnich.

smother v mùch.

smoulder v cnàmh-loisg.

smuggle v dèan cùl-mhùtaireachd.

smuggler n cùl-mhùtaire m.

snack n blasad bìdh m.

snake n nathair f.

snatch v glac.

sneak v snàig.

sneer v dèan fanaid.

sneeze v dèan sreothart.

sniff n boladh m. • v gabh boladh.

snipe n naosg m.

snivel v smùch.

snob n sodalan m.

snooze n norrag f.

snore v dèan srann.

snout n soc m.

snow n sneachd m. • v cuir sneachd.

snowdrift n cith m.

snug adj còsach.

snuggle v laigh dlùth ri.

so adv cho; mar seo; mar sin.

soak v drùidh.

soap n siabann m.

soapy adj làn siabainn.

sober adj stuama; sòbair.

sociable *adj* cuideachdail.
socialism *n* sòisealachas *f*.
society *n* comann *m*.
sock *n* socais *f*.
sod *n* fòid *f*.
soft *adj* bog.
soften *v* bogaich.
softness *n* buige *f*.
software *n* bathar bog *m*.
soil *n* ùir *f*. • *v* salaich.
solar *adj* na grèine.
soldier *n* saighdear *m*.
sole *n* bonn na coise *m*; (*fish*) lèabag *m*.
solemn *adj* sòlaimte.
solicit *v* aslaich.
solicitor *n* neach-lagha *m*.
solid *adj* teann.
solidarity *n* dlùthachd *f*.
solitude *n* uaigneas *m*.
solo *n* òran aon-neach *m*.
soloist *n* òranaiche *m*.
soluble *adj* so-sgaoilte.
solve *v* fuasgail.
solvent *adj* comasach air pàigheadh.
some *pron* cuid, feadhainn; pàirt.
somebody *n* cuideigin *m*.
somehow *adv* air dòigh air choreigin.
something *n* rudeigin *m*.
sometime *adv* uaireigin.
sometimes *adv* air uairibh.
somewhere *adv* an àiteigin.
son *n* mac *m*.
son-in-law *n* cliamhainn *m*.
soon *adv* a dh'aithghearr.
sophisticated *adj* ionnsaichte.
sordid *adj* suarach.
sore *n* creuchd *m*. • *adj* goirt.
sorrow *n* bròn *m*.

sorry *adj* duilich.
sort *n* seòrsa *m*. • *v* seòrsaich.
soul *n* anam *m*.
sound *n* fuaim *m*. • *v* seirm, seinn.
soup *n* eanraich *f*, *n* brot *m*.
sour *adj* geur.
south *adj/n* deas *f*.
southerly *adj/adv* deas, à deas.
sow *n* cràin *f*.
space *n* rùm *m*.
space probe *n* taisgealadh fànais *m*
spacious *adj* farsaing.
Spain *n* An Spàinn *f*.
spaniel *n* cù-eunaich *m*.
Spanish *n* Spàinnis *f*.
spare *v* caomhainn.
spark *n* sradag *f*.
sparkle *v* lainnrich.
spawn *v* sìolaich.
speak *v* bruidhinn.
spear *n* sleagh *f*.
special *adj* àraidh.
species *n* seòrsa *m*.
spectacles *npl* speuclairean.
spectre *n* tannasg *m*.
speech *n* (*language*) cainnt *f*; òraid *f*
speed *n* luas *m*.
speed *v* luathaich.
spell *v* litrich.
spend *v* caith.
spider *n* damhan-allaidh *m*.
spill *v* dòirt.
spin *v* snìomh.
spine *n* cnàimh-droma *f*.
spinning wheel *n* cuibhle-shnìomh *f*.
spirit *n* spiorad *m*.
spirited *adj* misneachail.
spit *v* tilg smugaid.
spite *n* gamhlas *m*.
splendid *adj* greadhnach.
split *v* sgoilt.

spoil *v* mill.

spoon *n* spàin *f.*

sporran *n* sporan *m.*

sport *n* spòrs *f.*

spot *n* ball *m.*

spouse *n* cèile *m.*

spreadsheet *n* duilleag-cleithe *f.*

spree *n* daorach *f.*

Spring *n* earrach *m.*

spring *n* fuaran *m*; leum *m.*

spume *n* cathadh-mara *m.*

spur *v* spor.

spy *n* beachdair *m.*

squalid *adj* sgreamhail.

squall *n* sgal *m.*

square *adj* ceithir-cheàrnach. • *n* ceàrnag *f.*

squash *v* brùth.

squat *adj* cutach.

squeak *n* bìog *m.*

squirrel *n* feòrag *f.*

squirt *v* steall.

stable¹ *adj* bunailteach.

stable² *n* stàball *m.*

stag *n* damh *m.*

stair *n* staidhre *f.*

stale *adj* cruaidh; goirt.

stalk *n* gas *f.*

stallion *n* àigeach *m.*

stammer *v* bruidhinn gagach.

stamp *n* stampa *f*; (*embossing*) stàmpa *f.*

stand *v* seas, stad.

standstill *n* stad *m.*

star *n* rionnag, reul *f.*

starboard *n* bòrd-beulaibh *m.*

stare *v* spleuchd.

starfish *n* crosgan *m.*

starry *adj* rionnagach.

start *v* clisg; (*motor*) cuir a dhol.

starvation *n* goirt *f.*

state¹ *n* staid *f*; (*country*) stàit *f.*

state² *v* cuir an cèill.

station *n* stèisean *m.*

statue *n* ìomhaigh *f.*

stature *n* àirde *f.*

stave *n* earran *f*; cliath *f.*

stay *n* stad *m.* • *v* fuirich.

steak *n* staoig *f.*

steal *v* goid.

steam *n* toit *f.*

steel *n* stàilinn *f.*

steep *adj* cas.

steer *v* stiùir.

step *n* ceum *m.*

sterile *adj* seasg.

stern¹ *adj* cruaidh.

stern² *n* deireadh *m.*

stick¹ *n* maide *m.*

stick² *v* sàth; (*adhere*) lean.

stiffen *v* ragaich.

still¹ *adv* fhathast; an dèidh sin.

still² *n* poit-dhubh *f.*

sting *n* gath *m.* • *v* guin.

stink *n* tòchd *m.*

stir *v* gluais.

stitch *n* grèim *m.*

stocking *n* stocainn *f.*

stomach *n* stamag *f.*

stone *n* clach *f.*

stool *n* stòl *m.*

stop *v* stad.

store *v* stòir.

storehouse *n* taigh-stòir *m.*

stork *n* corra bhàn *f.*

storm *n* doineann, stoirm *f.*

stormy *adj* stoirmeil.

story *n* sgeul *m.*

stove *n* stòbha *f.*

straight *adj* dìreach.

strain¹ *n* teannachadh *m*; (*mental*) uallach.

strain² v teannaich; (*filter*) sìolaidh.

strange adj iongantach.

stranger n coigreach m.

strath n srath m.

straw n connnlach f.

strawberry n subh-làir m.

streaky adj stiallach.

stream n sruth m.

street n sràid f.

strength n neart m.

stretch v sìn.

strict adj teann.

stride n sìnteag f.

strike v buail; (*work*) rach air stailc.

string n sreang f; teud f.

stringed adj teudaichte.

stroke v slìog.

stroll v siubhail.

strong adj làidir.

struggle n gleac m. • v gleac.

stubble n asbhuain f.

stubborn adj rag.

stuff n stuth m.

stupid adj baoghalta.

sturdy adj bunanta.

sty n fail-mhuc f.

stye n leamhnagan m.

style n modh m.

stylish adj baganta.

subject adj umhal, fo smachd. • v ceannsaich.

sublime adj òirdheirc.

submit v gèill.

subside v traogh.

subsidy n còmhnadh m.

substance n stuth m; brìgh f.

substitute v cuir an ionad.

subtle adj seòlta.

subtract v thoir o.

succeed v soirbhich; lean.

successful adj soirbheachail.

such adj/pron a leithid de, dhe t-seòrsa.

suck v deoghail.

suckle v thoir cìoch.

sudden adj grad.

suddenly adv gu h-obann.

sue v tagair.

suffer v fuiling.

sufferer n fulangaiche m.

sufficient adj lèor.

sugar n siùcar m.

suggest v mol, comhairlich.

suicide n fèin-mhort m.

suit n deise f. • v freagair.

suitable adj freagarrach.

sum n àireamh, suim f.

summer n samhradh m.

summit n mullach m.

summon v gairm.

sun n grian f.

sunbathe v blian.

Sunday n DiDòmhnaich m, Là n Sàbaid m.

sunny adj grianach.

sunrise n èirigh na grèine f.

sunset n laighe na grèine m.

supernatural adj os-nàdarrach.

superstition n saobh-chràbadh m.

supper n suipear f.

supple adj sùbailte.

supply v sòlaire ù.

support v cùm taic ri.

suppose v saoil.

suppress v cùm fodha.

supreme adj sàr.

sure adj cinnteach.

surely adv gun teagamh.

surface n uachdar m.

surge v brùchd.

surgeon n làmh-leigh m.

surgery n (*doctor's*) lèigh-lann m.

surly adj iargalta.
surname n sloinneadh m.
surplus n còrr m.
surprise n iongnadh m. • v cuir iongnadh air.
surprising adj neònach.
surrender n gèilleadh m.
surround v cuartaich.
survive v mair beò.
suspect v cuir an amharas.
suspend v croch.
suspense n teagamh m.
suspension bridge n drochaid crochaidh f.
suspicious adj amharasach.
swallow[1] v sluig.
swallow[2] n gòbhlan-gaoithe m.
swamp n fèith f.
swan n eala f.
swarm v sgaothaich.

swear v mionnaich.
sweat n fallas m. • v cuir fallas de.
swede n (neep) snèip f.
Sweden n An t-Suain f.
sweep v sguab.
sweet adj milis.
sweetheart n eudail f; leannan f.
sweeties npl siùcairean.
swim v snàmh.
swimming pool n amar-snàimh m.
swing n dreallag f.
switch n suidse f.
sword n claidheamh m.
symbol n samhla m.
symbolic adj samhlachail.
sympathetic adj co-mhothachail.
sympathise v co-mhothaich.
syringe n steallaire m.
syrup n siorap f.
system n siostam m.

T

table n bòrd; clàr m.
tablet n pile f; clàr m.
tacit adj gun bhruidhinn.
taciturn adj dùinte.
tack n tacaid f.
tacket n tacaid f.
tacksman n neach-baile m.
tadpole n ceann-pholan m.
tail n earball m.
taint v truaill.
take v gabh, thoir.
tale n sgeulachd f.
talent n tàlann m.
talk v bruidhinn.
tall adj àrd.
tame adj calla. • v callaich.
tangle n sàs m; (seaweed) stamh m.

tanker n tancair m.
tantalise v tog dòchas.
tap n goc m.
taper v dèan caol.
tapestry n grèis-bhrat m.
target n targaid f.
tart[1] adj searbh.
tart[2] n pithean m.
task n obair f.
taste v blais.
tasty adj blasta.
tawny adj lachdann.
tawse n stràic m.
tax v leag cìs.
tea n teatha, tì f.
teach v teasgaig.
teacher n teagasgar, tìdsear m.

teach-in *n* seisean connsachaidh *m*.

teacup *n* cupan teatha *m*.

team *n* sgioba *m*.

tear *n* deur *m*; (*rip*) sracadh *m*.

tease *v* farranaich.

tedious *adj* liosda.

teenager *n* deugaire *m*.

telephone *n* fòn *m*.

television *n* teilebhisean *m*.

tell *v* innis.

temper *n* nàdar *m*.

temperament *n* càil *f*.

temperature *n* teodhachd *f*.

tempest *n* doineann *f*.

temple *n* teampall *m*.

temporary *adj* sealach.

tempt *v* buair.

ten *adj/n* deich; (*persons*) deichnear.

tenacious *adj* leanailteach.

tenant *n* gabhaltach *m*.

tender *adj* maoth.

tennis *n* cluich-cneutaig *f*.

tent *n* teanta *f*.

tenth *n* an deicheamh earrann *f*.

term *n* (*time*) teirm *f*; (*word*) briathar *m*.

tern *n* steàrnan *m*.

terrier *n* abhag *f*.

terrorism *n* oillteachas *m*.

test *n* deuchainn *f*.

testament *n* tiomnadh *m*.

testicle *n* magairle *m*, clach *f*.

than *conj* na.

thank *v* thoir taing.

thankful *adj* taingeil.

thanks *npl* tapadh leat, tapadh leibh; taing *f*.

that *adj/pron* sin; (*distant*) siud, (*after noun*) ud. • *conj* gu(n). • *rel part* a. • *adv* a chionn, do brìgh.

thatch *n* tughadh *m*.

thaw *v* dèan aiteamh.

the *art* (*sing*) an, am, a', na (h- (*plural*) nan, nam.

theft *n* meirle *m*.

their *pron* (*with inalienables*) a am; (*with alienables*) ... aca.

them *pron* iad, (*emphatic*) iadsan.

themselves *pron* iad fhèin.

then *adv* an-sin; an dèidh sin; a uairsin.

thence *adv* às a sin.

theory *n* beachd *m*.

therapy *n* leigheas *m*.

there *adv* an-sin; (*distant*) an-siud.

thereby *adv* le sin.

therefore *adv* uime sin.

these *pron* iad seo.

they *pron* iad, (*emphatic*) iadsan.

thick *adj* tiugh.

thief *n* meirleach *m*.

thigh *n* sliasaid *f*.

thin *adj* tana.

thing *n* nì, rud *m*.

think *adj* smaoinich.

third *adj* treas.

thirst *n* pathadh *m*. • *v* bi pàiteach

thirteen *adj/n* trì deug.

thirty *adj/n* (*old system*) deich a fhichead; (*new system*) trithead.

this *pron* seo.

thistle *n* cluaran *m*.

thorny *adj* driseach.

those *pron* iad sin.

though *conj* ge, ged.

thought *n* smaoin *f*.

thousand *adj/n* mìle.

thrash *v* slaic; (*corn*) buail.

threat *n* bagairt *f*.

threaten *v* bagair.

three *adj/n* trì; (*persons*) triùir.

thrilling *adj* gaoireil.

throat *n* amhach *f*.

through *prep* tro. • *pron* **through me** tromham; **through you** (*sing*) tromhad; **through him, it** troimhe; **through her** troimhpe; **through us** tromhainn; **through you** tromhaibh; **through them** tromhpa.

throw *v* tilg.

thrush *n* smeòrach *m*.

thumb *n* òrdag *f*.

thunder *n* tàirneanach *m*.

thunderous *adj* torranach.

Thursday *n* DiarDaoin *m*.

thus *adv* mar seo.

ticket *n* bileag *f*.

ticking *n* diogadaich *f*.

tide *n* seòl-mara *m*.

tidy *v* sgioblaich.

tiger *n* tìgeir *m*.

till *prep* gu; (*up until*) gu ruig.

tiller *n* ailm *f*.

time *n* àm *m*.

timely *adj* an deagh àm.

timeous *adj* an deagh àm.

tinker *n* ceàrd *m*.

tiny *adj* crìon.

tipsy *adj* froganach.

tired *adj* sgìth.

tiresome *adj* sgìtheachail.

title *n* tiotal *m*.

to *prep* (*to, for*) do • *pron* **to me** dhomh; **to you** (*sing*) dhut; **to him, it** dhà; **to her** dhi; **to us** dhuinn; **to you** dhuibh; **to them** dhaibh; (*towards*) gu • *pron* **to me** thugam; **to you** (*sing*) thugad; **to him, it** thuige; **to her** thuice; **to us** thugainn; **to you** thugaibh; **to them** thuca; (*with verbs of speaking and looking*) ri • *pron* **to me** rium; **to you** (*sing*) riut; **to him, it** ris; **to her** rithe; **to us** ruinn; **to you** ruibh; **to them** riutha.

toad *n* muile-mhàg *f*.

toast *v* òl deoch-slàinte; tostaig.

tobacco *n* tombaca *m*.

today *adv* an-diugh.

together *adv* le chèile, còmhla.

toilet *n* taigh-beag *m*; (*preparation*) sgeadachadh *m*.

tomb *n* tuam *m*.

tomorrow *adv* a-màireach.

tone *n* fonn *m*; tòna *f*.

tongue *n* teanga *m*.

tonight *adv* a-nochd.

too *adv* cuideachd.

tool *n* inneal *m*.

tooth *n* fiacail *f*.

top *n* mullach, uachdar *m*.

torch *n* leus *m*.

torrent *n* bras-shruth *m*.

tortoise *n* sligeanach *m*.

Tory *n* Tòraidh *m*.

toss *v* luaisg.

total *adj* iomlan.

touch *v* bean do, suath ann.

tough *adj* righinn.

tour *n* turas *m*.

tourists *npl* luchd-turais.

towards *prep* a dh'ionnsaigh • *pron* **towards me** 'gam ionnsaigh; **towards you** (*sing*) 'gad ionnsaigh; **towards him, it** 'ga ionnsaigh; **towards her** 'ga h-ionnsaigh; **towards us** 'gar n-ionnsaigh; **towards you** 'gur n-ionnsaigh; **towards them** 'gan ionnsaigh.

tower *n* tùr *m*.

town *n* baile *m*.

toy *n* dèideag *f*.

trace *v* lorg.

track *v* lorg.

trade *n* malairt *f*.

tradition *n* tradisean *m*.

train *n* trèana *f*; (*retinue*) muinntir *f*.
• *v* àraich.

traitor *n* brathadair *m*.

trance *n* neul *m*.

transfer *v* thoir thairis.

transient *adj* diombuan.

translate *v* eadar-theangaich.

transmitter *n* crann-sgaoilidh *m*.

transparent *adj* trìd-shoilleir.

trap *n* ribe *f*. • *v* rib.

travel *n* siubhal *m*. • *v* siubhail.

tray *n* sgàl *m*.

treasure *n* ionmhas *m*. • *v* taisg.

treat *n* cuirm *f*. • *v* riaraich.

tree *n* craobh *f*.

tremor *n* crith *f*.

trespass *n* (*misdeed*) peacadh *m*.
• *v* inntrig gun chead.

trews *npl* triubhas *m*.

trial *n* deuchainn *f*.

tribe *n* treubh *f*, sliochd *m*.

tributary *n* leas-abhainn *f*.

trick *n* car *m*.

trim *adj* cuimir.

trip *v* tuislich.

triumph *n* gàirdeachas *m*.

triumph *v* thoir buaidh.

trivial *adj* suarach.

trot *v* dèan trotan.

trouble *n* dragh *f*. • *v* cuir dragh
air.

trousers *n* briogais *f*.

trout *n* breac *m*.

true *adj* fìor.

trump card *n* buadh-chairt *f*.

trust *n* earbsa *f*. • *v* earb à.

truth *n* fìrinn *f*.

try *v* feuch; cuir gu deuchainn.

tub *n* balan *m*.

Tuesday *n* DiMàirt *m*.

tumble *v* tuit, leag.

tumult *n* iorghail *f*.

tune *n* fonn, port *m*. • *v* gleus.

tuneful *adj* fonnmhor.

tup *n* reithe *m*.

turf *n* sgrath, fòd *f*.

turn *v* tionndaidh; cuir air falbh.

turtle *n* turtur *f*.

tutor *n* (*guardian*) taoitear *m*.

tweak *v* teannaich.

tweed *n* clò *m*.

twelfth *adj* dara deug.

twelve *adj*/*n* dà dheug.

twentieth *adj* ficheadamh.

twenty *adj*/*m* fichead.

twice *adv* dà uair.

twilight *n* eadar-sholas *m*.

twin *n* leth-aon *m*.

twist *v* toinn.

two *adj*/*n* dà; (*persons*) dithis.

two-faced *adj* beulach.

typical *adj* dualach.

typography *n* clò-bhualadh *m*.

tyrant *n* aintighearna *m*.

tyro *n* foghlamaiche *m*.

U

udder *n* ùth *m*.

ugliness *n* grànndachd *f*.

ugly *adj* grànnda.

ulcer *n* neasgaid *f*.

ultimate *adj* deiridh.

umbrella *n* sgàilean *m*.

unable *adj* neo-chomasach.

unaccustomed *adj* neo-chleachdte.

unanimous *adj* aon-inntinneach.

unarmed *adj* neo-armaichte.

unavoidable *adj* do-sheachanta.

unaware *adj* gun fhios.

unbolt *v* thoir an crann de.

uncle *n* (*paternal*) bràthair-athar; (*maternal*) bràthair-màthar *m*.

uncomfortable *adj* anshocrach.

uncommon *adj* neo-gnàthach.

unconditional *adj* gun chùmhnantan.

uncork *v* às-àrcaich.

unction *n* ungadh *m*.

undecided *adj* neo-chinnteach.

under *prep* fo • *pron* **under me** fodham; **under you** (*sing*) fodhad; **under him, it** fodha; **under her** foidhpe; **under us** fodhainn; **under you** fodhaibh; **under them** fodhpa.

undergo *v* fuiling.

underground *adj* fo thalamh.

underneath *adv* fodha. • *prep* fo.

understand *v* tuig.

underwear *n* fo-aodach *m*.

undeserved *adj* neo-thoillteanach.

undistinguished *adj* neo-chomharraichte.

undisturbed *adj* neo-bhuairte.

undo *v* fuasgail.

unemployed *adj* gun chosnadh.

unequal *adj* neo-ionnan.

uneven *adj* corrach.

unexpected *adj* gun dùil.

unfair *adj* mì-cheart.

unfinished *adj* neo-chrìochnaichte.

unfold *v* fosgail.

unfriendly *adj* neo-chàirdeil.

unfurl *v* sgaoil.

ungrateful *adj* mì-thaingeil.

uniform *n* culaidh *f*.

unimportant *adj* neo-chudromach.

uninhabited *adj* neo-àitichte.

union *n* aonadh *m*.

unique *adj* air leth.

unit *n* aonad *m*.

unity *n* aonachd *f*.

universal *adj* coitcheann.

universe *n* domhan *m*.

university *n* oilthigh *m*.

unless *conj* mur, mura.

unlike *adj* neo-choltach.

unload *v* thoir an luchd de.

unmask *v* leig ris.

unmusical *adj* neo-cheòlmhor.

unnecessary *adj* neo-fheumail.

unoccupied *adj* bàn.

unpack *v* fosgail.

unpardonable *adj* gun leisgeul.

unpleasant *adj* mì-thaitneach.

unpopular *adj* neo-ionmhainn.

unpremeditated *adj* gun ro-smuain.

unproductive *adj* neo-thorrach.

unreal *adj* neo-fhìor.

unreasonable *adj* mì-reusanta.

unrest *n* aimhreit *f*.

unripe adj an-abaich.
unsafe adj mì-shàbhailte.
unsatisfactory adj mì-shàsail.
unsightly adj duaichnidh.
unsuccessful adj mì-shealbhar.
unsuitable adj neo-iomchaidh.
untidy adj luideach.
untie v fuasgail.
until adv gu; (*up until*) gu ruig.
unto prep do, gu.
unused adj neo-chleachdte.
unusual adj neo-àbhaisteach.
unwanted adj gun iarraidh.
unwieldy adj trom.
unwise adj neo-ghlic.
unworthy adj neo-airidh.
unwrap v fuasgail.
up prep suas. • adv suas; a-nìos; shuas.
upbringing n togail f.
uphill adv ri bruthach.
uphold v cùm suas.
upland n aonach f.
upon prep air, air muin.
upper adj uachdrach.
upright adj dìreach; onorach.

uproar n gleadhar m.
upset n cur tro-chèile m.
upshot n co-dhùnadh m.
upside-down adj/adv bun os cionn.
upstairs adv (*loction*) shuas staidhre; (*motion*) suas staidhre.
upward adv suas.
urban adj cathaireil.
urge v spàrr.
urgency n (cùis-)èiginn f.
urgent adj dian.
urinal n ionad-mùin m.
us pron sinn, (*emphatic*) sinne.
usage n àbhaist f.
use n feum m. • v gnàthaich, dèan feum de.
useful adj feumail.
usefulness n feumalachd f.
useless adj gun fheum.
usual adj gnàthach.
usurp v glèidh gun chòir.
uterus n machlag f.
utmost adj as motha
utter[1] v abair, labhair.
utter[2] adj coilionta; dearg.
utterly adv gu tur.

V

vacancy n beàrn m.
vacant adj falamh.
vaccinate v cuir breac a' chruidh air.
vagabond n neach-fuadain m.
vagina n faighean f.
vague adj neo-dheimhinn.
vain adj dìomhain.
vale n srath m.
valid adj tàbhachdach.
valley n gleann, srath m.

valour n gaisge f.
valuable adj prìseil.
value n luach m.
value-added tax n cìs luach-leasaichte f.
valve n pìob-chòmhla f.
van n vana f.
vandal n creachadair, milltear m.
vanish v rach às an t-sealladh.
vapour n deatach f.
varied adj iomadh.

variegated *adj* breac.

variety *n* atharrachadh *m*.

various *adj* iomadh.

vary *v* caochail.

vase *n* vàsa *f*.

veal *n* laoigh-fheòil *f*.

vegetable *n* glasraich *f*.

vegetarian *n* feòil-sheachnair *m*.

vegetation *n* fàs *m*.

vehement *adj* dealasach.

vehicle *n* carbad *m*.

veil *n* sgàile *f*. • *v* còmhdaich.

vein *n* cuisle *f*.

velvet *n* meileabhaid *f*.

vengeance *n* dìoghaltas *m*.

venison *n* sitheann *m*.

venom *n* nimh *m*.

venture *n* tuaiream *m*.

venue *n* làthair *m*.

verdict *n* breith *f*.

verge *n* oir *f*.

verify *v* dearbh.

vermin *npl* mìolan.

vernacular *n* cainnt na dùthcha *f*.

verse *n* dànachd *f*; (*stanza*) rann *m*.

version *n* innse *f*.

vertical *adj* dìreach.

vertigo *n* tuaineal *m*.

very *adv* glè; (*truly*) fìor.

vest *n* peitean *m*.

vestige *n* lorg *f*.

vet *n* veat *m*.

vex *v* buair.

viable *adj* so-obrachadh.

vibrate *v* crith, cuir air chrith.

vicarious *adj* ionadach.

vice *n* dubhailc *f*; (*tool*) teanchair *m*.

victim *n* ìobairteach *m*.

victor *n* buadhair *m*.

victory *n* buaidh *f*.

video recorder *n* chlàraichear bhidio *m*.

view *n* sealladh *m*; (*opinion*) beachd *m*. • *v* gabh sealladh; beachdaich.

viewpoint *n* àite-seallaidh *m*; ionad-beachd *m*.

vigil *n* faire *f*.

vigour *n* spionnadh *m*.

vile *adj* gràineil.

village *n* clachan *m*.

villain *n* slaoightear *m*.

vindicate *v* fìreanaich.

vine *n* crann-fìona *m*.

vintage *n* fìon-fhoghar *m*.

violence *n* fòirneart *m*.

violent *adj* fòirneartach.

violin *n* fidheall *f*.

violinist *n* fidhleir *m*.

viper *n* nathair-nimhe *f*.

virgin *n* maighdeann, òigh *f*.

virginity *n* maighdeannas *m*.

virile *adj* fearail.

virility *n* fearachas *m*.

virtual *adj* da-rìribh.

virtue *n* subhailc *f*.

virtuous *adj* beusach.

virus *n* bioras *m*.

visibility *n* lèireas *m*.

visible *adj* faicsinneach.

vision *n* fradharc *m*; (*mental*) bruadar *m*, taibhs *f*.

visit *v* tadhail.

visitor *n* aoigh *m*.

visual *adj* fradharcach.

vital *adj* riatanach; beò.

vitality *n* beathalachd *f*.

vivacious *adj* aigeannach.

vocal *adj* guthach.

vocalist *n* òranaiche, seinneadair *m*.

vocation *n* gairm *f*.

voice n guth m.
void adj fàs. • n fàsalachd f.
voluble adj deas-chainnteach.
voluntary adj toileach.
vomit n sgeith m. • v sgeith.
vote n bhòta f. • v thoir bhòta.

voucher n fianais f.
vow n bòid f. • v bòidich.
voyage n turas-mara m.
voyager n taisdealaich m.
vulgar adj gràisgeil.
vulnerable adj so-leònte.

W

wade v siubhail tro.
wafer n abhlan m.
wag v crath.
wager n geall m.
wagon n cairt f.
wagtail n breacan-buidhe m.
wail v dèan caoineadh.
waist n meadhan m.
wait v feith; fritheil.
waitress n caileag-fhrithealaidh f.
wake n taigh-fhaire m. • v dùisg.
waken v dùisg.
Wales n A' Chuimrigh f.
walk n cuairt f. • v coisich.
walking stick n bata m.
wall n balla m.
walrus n each-mara m.
wan adj glas-neulach.
wander v rach air seachran.
wanderer n seachranaiche m.
want n dìth m; bochdainn f. • v iarr;
thig geàrr.
war n cogadh m.
warble v ceileirich.
wardrobe n preas-aodaich m.
warehouse n tasglann m.
warlike adj coganta.
warm adj blàth.
warmth n blàths m.
warn v thoir rabhadh.
warren n broclach f.

warship n long-chogaidh f.
wart n foinne f.
wary adj faicilleach.
wash v nigh.
washing n nigheadaireachd f.
wasp n speach f.
waste n ana-caitheamh m. • v cosg,
caith.
watch n uaireadair; faire m. • v
dèan faire.
watchdog n cù-faire m.
water n uisge m. • v uisgich.
waterfall n eas m.
water-power n neart-uisge m.
waterproof adj uisge-dhìonach.
watershed n uisge-dhruim m.
watertight adj dìonach.
waulk v luaidh.
waulking n luadhadh m.
wave n tonn m. • v smèid; crath.
wax n cèir f.
way n slighe f.
waylay v dèan feall-fhalach.
we pron sinn, (emphatic) sinne.
weak adj lag.
weaken v lagaich.
weave v figh.
weaver n breabadair m.
web n eige, lìon f.
webbed adj eigeil.
wed v pòs.

wedding n banais f.
Wednesday n DiCiadain m.
weed n luibh m. • v priog.
week n seachdain f.
weep v guil.
weigh v cothromaich.
weight n cudthrom m.
weir n cairidh f.
welcome n fàilte f. • v fàiltich.
well[1] adj math; faillain. • adv gu math.
well[2] n tobar m.
west adj siar. • n an iar f. • adv an iar.
westerly adj on iar.
westward adv chun na h-àirde an iar.
wet adj fliuch.
whale n muc-mhara f.
what interr pron dè? (emphatic) gu dè? • rel pron na.
wheat n cruithneachd m.
wheel n cuibhle f.
wheeze v dèan pìochan.
whelk n faochag f.
when conj nuair. • interr pron cuine?
whence adv co às.
whenever adv gach uair.
where conj far. • interr pron càite?
whereas adv do bhrìgh gu.
whereby adv leis, leis a bheil.
whereupon adv leis sin.
wherever adv ge be ar bith càite.
whether adv co-dhiù. • pron cò aca.
which rel pron a, (neg) nach. • interr pron dè?, cò?
while conj fhad 's a. • n tacan m, greis f.
whin n conasg m.
whip n cuip f. • v sgiùrs.

whirlpool n cuairt-shlugan m.
whiskers npl feusag f.
whisky n uisge-beatha m.
whisper n cagar m. • v cagair.
whistle n feadag f. • v dèan fead.
white adj geal.
who rel pron a, (neg) nach. • interr pron cò?
whoever pron cò air bith.
whole adj slàn, iomlan.
wholefood adj slàn-bhiadh.
wholesale n mòr-reic m.
whoop n glaodh m.
whose interr pron cò leis?
why adv carson?
wick n siobhag f.
wicked adj olc.
wide adj leathann.
widow n banntrach f.
widower n banntrach m.
width n leud m.
wife n bean f.
wild adj fiadhaich.
wildcat n cat fiadhaich m.
wilderness n fàsach m.
will n toil f; (last) tiomnadh m.
willing adj toileach.
willow n seileach m.
willpower n neart toile m.
wily adj seòlta.
win v coisinn.
wind n gaoth f.
window n uinneag f.
windward n fuaradh m.
windy adj gaothach.
wine n fìon m.
wing n sgiath f.
wink v caog.
winter n geamhradh m. • v geamh-raich.
wintry adj geamhrachail.

wipe *v* suath.

wire *n* uèir *m*.

wiry *adj* seang.

wisdom *n* gliocas *m*.

wise *adj* glic.

wish *n* miann *m*. • *v* miannaich.

wit *n* toinisg *f*; eirmse *f*.

witch *n* bana-bhuidseach *f*.

with *prep* le fo • *pron* **with me** leam; **with you** (*sing*) leat; **with him, it** leis; **with her** leatha; **with us** leinn; **with you** leibh; **with them** leotha; (*together with*) còmhla ri.

wither *v* searg.

withered *adj* crìon.

within *adv* (*location*) a-staigh.

without *adv* (*location*) a-muigh. • *prep* (*with noun*) gun; (*with pronoun*) as aonais • *pron* **without me** as m' aonais; **without you** (*sing*) as d' aonais; **without him, it** as 'aonais; **without her** as a h-aonais; **without us** as ar n-aonais; **without you** (*pl*) as ur n-aonais; **without them** as an aonais;.

witness *n* fianais each*m*.

witty *adj* eirmseach.

wizard *n* draoidh *m*.

wolf *n* madadh-allaidh *m*.

woman *n* boireannach *f*.

womanly *adj* banail.

womb *n* machlag *f*.

wonder *n* iongnadh *m*; iongantas *m*. • *v* gabh iongantas.

woo *v* dèan suirghe.

wood *n* coille *f*; (*timber*) fiodh *f*.

woodland *n* fearann coillteach *m*.

woodlouse *n* reudan *m*.

woodwork *n* saoirsneachd *f*.

wool *n* clòimh *f*.

woollen *adj* de chlòimh.

word *n* facal *m*; (*bond*) gealladh *m*.

word processor *n* facladair *m*.

wordy *adj* briathrach.

work *n* obair *f*. • *v* oibrich.

worker *n* oibriche *m*.

workmanship *n* ealain *f*.

world *n* saoghal *m*.

worldly *adj* saoghalta.

world-wide web *n* lìonra domhanta *m*.

worm *n* cnuimh, durrag *f*.

worn *adj* caithte.

worry *n* dragh *m*. • *v* buair, dèan dragh do.

worse *adj* nas miosa.

worsen *v* fàs nas miosa.

worship *n* adhradh *m*.

worst *adj* as miosa.

worth *n* luach *m*. • *adj* fiù.

worthless *adj* gun fhiù.

worthy *adj* airidh.

wound *n* leòn *m*. • *v* leòn, lot.

wrangle *n* connsachadh *m*. • *v* connsaich.

wrap *v* paisg, fill.

wrapper *n* filleag *f*.

wrath *n* corraich *f*.

wrathful *adj* feargach.

wreath *n* blàth-fhleasg *f*.

wreck *n* long-bhriseadh *m*. • *v* sgrios.

wren *n* dreadhan-donn *m*.

wrench *v* spìon.

wrest *v* spìon.

wrestle *v* gleac.

wrestling *n* gleac *m*.

wring *v* fàisg.

wrinkle *n* preas *m*. • *v* preas.

wrist *n* caol an dùirn *m*.

wristwatch *n* uaireadair làimhe *m*.

write *v* sgrìobh.

writer *n* sgrìobhadair *m*.
writhe *v* snìomh.
writing *n* sgrìobhadh *m*.

wrong *adj* ceàrr; coireach. • *n* eucoir *f*.
wry *adj* cam.

XYZ

xenophobe *n* gall-gamhlasaiche *m*.
xenophobia *n* gall-gamhlas *m*.
X-ray *n* gath-x *m*.
yacht *n* iacht *f*.
yard *n* gàrradh *m*; (*length*) slat *f*.
yarn *n* sgeulachd *f*; (*thread*) snàth *f*.
yarrow *n* eàrr-thalmhainn *f*.
yawl *n* geòla *f*.
yawn *n* mèanan *m*. • *v* dèan mèananaich.
year *n* bliadhna *f*.
yearly *adj* gach bliadhna.
yearn *v* iarr gu làidir.
yearning *n* iarraidh *m/f*.
yeast *n* beirm *f*.
yellow *adj/n* buidhe *m*.
yelp *v* dèan tathann.
yes *adv* (*non-affirmative*) seadh (*affirmative replies repeat verb used in question*).
yesterday *adv* an-dè.
yet *adv* fhathast. • *conj* gidheadh, an dèidh sin, ach.
yew *n* iubhar *m*.
yield *v* gèill.
yoke *n* cuing *f*. • *v* beartaich.
yolk *n* buidheagan *m*.

yon *adv* thall, ud.
you *pron* (*sing*) thu, (*emphatic*) thusa; (*pl*) sibh, (*emphatic*) sibhse.
young *adj* òg.
youngster *n* òganach *m*.
your *pron* (*sing*) (*with inalienables*) do, (*before vowels*) d'; (*with alienables*) ... agad; (*pl*) (*with inalienables*) ur, (*before vowels*) ur n-; (*with alienables*) ... agaibh.
yourself *pron* thu fhèin.
yourselves *pron* sibh fhèin.
youth *n* òigear *m*; (*state*) òige *m*.
youthful *adj* ògail.
zeal *n* eud *m*.
zealous *adj* eudmhor.
zebra *n* asal-stiallach *f*.
zenith *n* bàrr *m*.
zero *n* neoni *f*.
zest *n* smior *m*.
zigzag *adj* lùbach.
zip *n* sip *f*.
zodiac *n* grian-chrios *m*.
zoo *n* sutha *f*.
zoology *n* ainmh-eòlas *m*.